D1609469

MORALITY,
MORAL BEHAVIOR,
AND MORAL DEVELOPMENT

MORALITY, MORAL BEHAVIOR, AND MORAL DEVELOPMENT

WILLIAM M. KURTINES
JACOB L. GEWIRTZ
Florida International University

A WILEY-INTERSCIENCE PUBLICATION

JOHN WILEY & SONS

New York · Chichester · Brisbane · Toronto · Singapore

Library of Congress Cataloging in Publication Data:

Main entry under title:

Morality, moral behavior, and moral development.

"A Wiley-Interscience publication."
Includes indexes.
1. Moral development. 2. Ethics. I. Kurtines,
William M. II. Gewirtz, Jacob L., 1924–

BF723.M54M69 1984   155.2   83-16703
ISBN 0-471-88740-4

Printed in the United States of America

10 9 8 7 6 5 4 3 2 1

Preface

The basic themes that define current theory and research on morality, moral behavior, and moral development can perhaps be captured best by the terms *growth* and *evolution*. Growth is evident in the size and scope of the literature on moral issues, which has increased enormously in size over the last three decades and has now become a substantive area of scholarly and research interest in its own right. The second theme, evolution, is discernible in the alterations and transformations that have taken place in the field. Theoretical orientations have undergone dramatic change, and new perspectives have begun to emerge. Theory and research on morality and moral development is thus in the midst of a period of growth and evolution that promises to extend well into the coming decades. In this frame, the goal underlying the present book is to expedite developments in the literature on morality, moral behavior, and moral development by bringing together in one place a representative and comprehensive collection of writings by scholars and researchers in the area that (1) reflects the basic issues in current theory and research, and (2) defines new trends and directions for theory and research in the coming decades.

The chapters that follow deal with a wide range of issues. Still, three broadly defined central themes emerge in the book and point to the directions in which work in the field is moving. The first theme is the clear need for theoretical models that are more comprehensive and integrative than those developed to date. Compared with past work, theoretical accounts are becoming increasingly complex as they attempt to integrate a greater range of phenomena. These phenomena include behavior, conditioning, context, affect, and cognition. This book thus contains a number of chapters that describe work both on the expansion of existing models and on the development of new, more integrated approaches. A second basic theme is the need for more methodological rigor than has characterized past empirical work on moral development. The need for more empirical rigor, however, is accompanied by a recognition of the limitation of traditional methodologies, the unique methodological problems presented in work on morality, and the need to explore and develop alternative research strategies and tactics. A third basic theme of the book is the need further to clarify and refine the boundaries between philosophical and psychological issues and to render more explicit the variety of moral, ethical, or value positions that currently exist in the literature.

This book is a product of the collective efforts of a group of scholars and researchers with differing as well as broad backgrounds. As a collective effort, it represents a substantive contribution to the theoretical and research literatures and can extend the frontiers of the field in many directions. The background and overview part presents an analysis of central philosophical and theoretical issues and provides an overview of the current research literature. The part on the Kohlberg cognitive-developmental approach contains state-of-the-art reviews of developments and advances that have occurred within that orientation. It includes separate chapters on theory, application, and research methodology that pull together several recent significant developments in that approach. In addition, the part dealing with recent work on stage-structural and constructivist models expands the scope of concepts that are included within the stage-structural frame. Also included is a comprehensive part on learning and behavioral development approaches that ranges from a straightforward non-cognitive social-learning perspective through a modern cognitive-behavioral perspective to a recently developed integrated cognitive-social-learning model. The part on social and personality theory includes chapters advancing innovative approaches that attempt to integrate a variety of social, personality, affective, and motivational variables at both a conceptual and a methodological level. Finally, the last part of the book addresses basic issues in the literature from historical and philosophical perspectives.

This book would not have been possible without the cooperation and assistance of a number of people and institutions. Invaluable support was received at various stages in the preparation of this work from the College of Arts and Sciences, the Department of Psychology, the School of Education, and the Department of Conferences at Florida International University and from the editors and staff at John Wiley & Sons. We also wish to thank those persons whose individual contributions at various stages of the project were instrumental in its successful completion. The list of persons to whom we are indebted is too long to enumerate here. We would like simply to dedicate this book to *all* the people who helped make it possible and to Florida International University as it enters its second decade of existence.

WILLIAM M. KURTINES
JACOB L. GEWIRTZ

Miami, Florida
January 1984

Contents

Contributors

AUGUSTO BLASI is Professor of Psychology at the University of Massachusetts, Boston. He received his doctorate in Clinical Psychology from Washington University in 1971. Doctor Blasi has done extensive work in the area of moral judgment and moral action.

DWIGHT R. BOYD is Associate Professor of the History and Philosophy of Education at the Ontario Institute for Studies in Education. In 1976 he received his doctorate in the Philosophy of Education from the Harvard Graduate School of Education. Doctor Boyd's interests span a broad range of topics in the history and philosophy of education.

ROGER V. BURTON is Professor of Psychology and Director of the Developmental Psychology Program at the State University of New York at Buffalo. He received his doctorate in Psychology from Harvard University in 1959. Doctor Burton is author of studies on resistance to temptation and guilt, the socialization of self-control, and sex-identity development.

CATHERINE BUSCH is Staff Fellow at the Gerontological Research Center, National Institute of Aging, Baltimore. She received her doctorate in Personality from the Johns Hopkins University in 1983. Her research interests include personality and life-span development.

DANIEL CANDEE is Assistant Professor in the Department of Research in Health Education at the University of Connecticut Health Center, Farmington, and Associate, Graduate School of Education, Harvard University. In 1972 he received his doctorate in Psychology from the University of Chicago. Doctor Candee has conducted extensive research in the area of moral reasoning.

ANN COLBY is Lecturer in Education and Research Associate at Harvard University and Director of the Henry A. Murray Research Center at Radcliffe College. She received her doctorate in Experimental Psychology from Columbia University in 1972. Doctor Colby's current interests include cognitive, social, moral, and ego development.

WILLIAM DAMON is Professor of Psychology at Clark University. He received his doctorate in Developmental Psychology in 1973 from the University of California, Berkeley. Doctor Damon has published in the area of social and cognitive development.

JACOB L. GEWIRTZ is Professor of Psychology at Florida International University and Professor of Pediatrics at the University of Miami Medical School. He received his doctorate in Developmental and Experimental Psychology from the University of Iowa. Doctor Gewirtz's theoretical and research contributions have been on topics of social learning and development including attachment acquisition and loss, imitation/identification, parent-child interaction and directions of influence, and the behavioral effects of shifts in maintaining environments.

ANN HIGGINS is Lecturer in Education and Research Associate at Harvard University. She received her doctorate in Developmental Psychology from the Pennsylvania State University in 1979. Doctor Higgins' interests are in the area of moral assessment and the educational implications of moral development theory and research.

MARTIN L. HOFFMAN is Professor of Psychology at the University of Michigan. He received his doctorate in Personality Psychology in 1951 from the University of Michigan. Doctor Hoffman has published extensively on moral development, empathy, conscience, guilt and prosocial behavior in childhood, as well as on social cognition and parent-child relations.

ROBERT HOGAN is Professor of Psychology and Department Chairman at the University of Tulsa. He received his doctorate in Personality Psychology from the University of California, Berkeley in 1967. Doctor Hogan has conducted research and published in the area of moral conduct, moral development, and personality.

HENRY C. JOHNSON, JR. is Professor of Educational Policy Studies at the Pennsylvania State University. He received his doctorate from the University of Illinois in 1970 in the History and Philosophy of Education. Doctor Johnson's research interests center on the impact of scientific thought on American education.

HOWARD KAMINSKY is Professor of Medieval History at Florida International University. He received his doctorate from the University of Chicago in 1952, specializing in the area of Medieval European History and in particular on the Great Schism of the Western Church and on the Hussite Movement in 15th Century Bohemia. Doctor Kaminsky's current interests are in developing a general philosophy of culture and society that would include all the topics of the humanities and social sciences.

Monika Keller is Research Associate at the Max Planck Institute of Human Development and Education, Berlin. She received her doctorate in Developmental Psychology from the University of Heidelberg in 1974. Doctor Keller's research interests include moral and personality development.

Lawrence Kohlberg is Professor of Education and Social Psychology and Director of the Center for Moral Education and Development at Harvard University. He obtained his doctorate in Psychology from the University of Chicago in 1958, where he embarked upon his longitudinal study of the moral reasoning of then pre-adolescent and adolescent boys. The center, directed by Doctor Kohlberg, currently sponsors moral development research and intervention projects in schools and prisons.

William M. Kurtines is Associate Professor of Psychology at Florida International University. He received his doctorate from the Johns Hopkins University in 1973. Doctor Kurtines' current areas of interest include social, personality, and moral development.

Robert M. Liebert is Professor of Psychology and Psychiatry at the State University of New York at Stony Brook and founding director of the Media Action Research Center there. He received his doctorate in Personality from Stanford University in 1966. Doctor Liebert has written on a wide range of basic and applied topics in personality and developmental psychology, including moral development and experimental designs and methods in psychology.

Fritz Oser is Professor of Education and Director of the Pedagogical Institute at the University of Fribourg. He received his doctorate in 1975 from the University of Zürich. Doctor Oser's research interests have been in moral development and education.

Mordecai Nisan is Senior Lecturer in Educational Psychology and Head, Department of Education, at the Hebrew University of Jerusalem. He received his doctorate in Human Development from the University of Chicago in 1968. Doctor Nisan's research interests are in the area of moral judgment, self control, and content learning in moral development.

Gertrude Nunner-Winkler is Research Associate at the Max Plank Institute for Psychological Research, Munich. She received her doctorate in 1969 from the Free University of Berlin. Doctor Nunner-Winkler's research interests include moral judgment, moral action, and moral development.

Clark Power is Assistant Professor in the Program in General Studies at the University of Notre Dame. Doctor Power received his doctorate in 1979 from the Harvard University School of Education. He has been concentrating on moral education and the moral atmosphere of the school and on the relation between religious thinking and moral judgment.

JAMES R. REST is Professor of Social, Psychological and Philosophical Foundations at the University of Minnesota. He received his doctorate in Clinical Psychology from the University of Chicago in 1969. Doctor Rest has published on the assessment of moral stages and on research using his objective measure of moral reasoning.

JUDITH G. SMETANA is Assistant Professor of Education, Psychology and Pediatrics at the University of Rochester. She received her doctorate from the University of California, Santa Cruz in 1978, specializing in social and developmental psychology. Doctor Smetana has conducted research on the development of social cognition and social behavior.

ERVIN STAUB is Professor of Psychology at the University of Massachusetts, Amherst. He received his doctorate from Stanford University in 1965, specializing in the area of Personality. Doctor Staub is the author of several volumes on prosocial behavior and papers in the area of personality theory.

ELLIOT TURIEL is Professor of Education at the University of California, Berkeley. He received his doctorate in Developmental Psychology from Yale University in 1965. Doctor Turiel has conducted research on processes of development and social cognition.

HELEN WEINREICH-HASTE is Lecturer in Social Science at the University of Bath. She studied at the Universities of London and Sussex from 1964 to 1970. Her research interests are on the development of sex roles, and of social, moral, and political reasoning.

PART ONE
Background and Overview

CHAPTER 1

Certainty and Morality:
Objectivistic versus Relativistic Approaches

WILLIAM M. KURTINES AND JACOB L. GEWIRTZ

This chapter examines the issue of objectivistic versus relativistic morality using a history-of-ideas approach. A systematic reconsideration of the historical roots of this issue offers a broad perspective from which to view one of the central issues of our age. Such a perspective, we suggest, has significant implications for a critical analysis of the role of an objectivistic versus relativistic orientation in modern epistemological and moral thinking. More specifically, we attempt to show that the objectivistic orientation that characterized epistemological and moral thought for most of Western intellectual history has become increasingly overshadowed by a relativistic orientation that is now one of the main themes in the history of ideas in the West.

In our analysis of this issue we illustrate first how the largest part of Western intellectual history was dominated by an objectivistic or absolutist moral and epistemological orientation. We illustrate next how a number of intellectual developments in the modern world, and the rise of modern science in particular, were the basis for a gradual but radical relativistic transformation in the foundations of Western epistemological thought. Finally, we show that the relativistic orientation that characterizes many modern conceptions of morality differ significantly from the orientations of previous historical periods in that for the first time relativistic moral thinking is consistent with the mainstream of epistemological developments in the Western world. The present analysis leads to several significant conclusions with respect to theory and research in the area of morality, moral behavior, and moral development.

At the time of Socrates's death, near the end of the fifth century B.C., the world was on the verge of a revolution that was to alter dramatically the course of intellectual history in the West. Socrates's drinking of the hemlock

The authors thank Howard Kaminsky, Lawrence Kohlberg, and Robert Liebert for their constructive comments on an earlier version of this chapter.

set the stage for a radical transformation of the very foundations of Western morality. Based on his conviction that an objective knowledge of the good was possible, his decision to comply with the sentence of the Athenian court was one of the most influential moral judgments in the history of the Western world. The effects of the events that took place in Socrates's prison did not end with his death; on the contrary, they are still very much with us today (MacIntyre, 1966). Whether the good is objectively real and invariant or dependent on context (historical, cultural, situational, or individual), that is, the issue of objectivistic versus relativistic morality, is perhaps the most basic theme running through this book and the field (see Lickona, 1976).

In this chapter we will examine the issue of objectivistic versus relativistic morality from the perspective of the history of ideas (Lovejoy, 1961). A systematic reconsideration of the historical roots of this question, we hope to show, can offer a fresh perspective on one of the central issues of our age. Although we employ a history-of-ideas approach, this chapter is not a historical document in the formal sense, that is, a detailed chronicle of a sequence of events. Nor is our argument a historical argument in the sense of being dependent on a particular sequence of events. We will, however, draw on the ideas of writers and thinkers who we feel are representative of the various historical periods that have been instrumental in defining the issue of objectivistic versus relativistic morality. The basic "data" for our argument will thus consist of ideas as they are reflected in the major works of historical figures representative of the main periods in Western thought. Section 1 of the chapter presents a brief overview of the basic lines of our analysis; Section 2 provides several detailed examples from representative historical periods; and Section 3 presents the conclusions of the analysis. Although this chapter cannot present all views on morality, it does attempt to put the issue of objectivistic versus relativistic morality into a broader perspective. Much of moral knowledge, perhaps even its essence, derives from the great themes of literature and myth, art, drama, law, and religion—themes that would carry us far beyond the scope of this chapter. The chapter is not intended to be an exhaustive review; rather, its goal is to use a history-of-ideas approach to survey the ideas of representative thinkers from each major historical period used in our analysis. Such a perspective we feel will help to deepen our insights into the intellectual and historical forces that have shaped the moral consciousness of our age.

1. BACKGROUND AND OVERVIEW

The basic thesis of this chapter can be stated simply: We hope to show that the relativistic orientation that characterizes many modern conceptions of morality is rooted in the mainstream of intellectual developments in the modern world. We argue that from its very beginnings in classical antiquity through the Middle Ages, Western intellectual history was dominated by an objectivistic orientation (i.e., a belief in the possibility of obtaining "absolute," "objective," or "certain" knowledge), in both an epistemological and a moral sense. We further argue that during the modern age this objectivistic orientation has been overshadowed increasingly by a relativistic orientation that has now become one of the main themes in the history of ideas in the West. Although our conclusions are not based on purely a historical argument (i.e., that events in the modern age are a necessary consequence of antecedent historical events), we will use historical examples to illustrate fundamental differences between the epistemological and moral orientations of the modern world and those of previous historical periods. Central to our analysis is the view that the intellectual history of the West has been defined by three more or less identifiable periods, each characterized by a distinctive attitude toward the natural world. Each of these characteristic epistemological orientations, we argue, was instrumental in shaping the moral consciousness of that age. During the first major period of Western intellectual history, the classical age, the world was viewed as a product of natural forces, and reason served as the cornerstone for the belief in the possibility of obtaining absolute, objective, or certain knowledge. Consistent with this objectivistic epistemological orientation, the mainstream of classical moral thinking assumed the existence of objective moral standards. Thus, to the classical mind conceptions of morality were naturalistic, objectivistic, and rational.

During the Middle Ages, the mainstream of Western thought was distinctly otherworldly in its orientation, and the Western world's chief source of knowledge was the truth as imparted by divine revelation (Aiken, 1956). Divine knowledge is absolute or certain knowledge, and, consistent with this objectivistic epistemological orientation, conceptions of morality assumed the existence of objective moral standards. Medieval moral thought, however, tended to be spiritualistic rather than naturalistic and was based more on faith than on reason. Medieval moral thinking was primarily concerned with the hereafter and spiritual life—with one's relation to God and with personal salvation. For the medieval mind, conceptions of morality were otherworldly as well as objectivistic.

The mainstream of Western thought in the modern age, we argue, differs significantly from both the classical and medieval periods. In keeping with its classical heritage, Western epistemological thought is again naturalistic, but with a peculiarly modern flavor. Science has replaced both faith and reason as the Western mind's chief source of knowledge about the world, and the mainstream of modern epistemological thought is probabilistic as well as naturalistic (Burtt, 1924). Consistent with this trend, modern conceptions of morality have moved away from the supernatural, otherworldly orientation of the Middle Ages and now tend to be naturalistic. Like the classical philosopher, the contemporary moral thinker tends to view ethics and morality as part of the natural world, but with an important difference. With the rise of modern science, which has been called the most significant intellectual revolution in the entire history of the West (ibid.), conceptions of morality have tended to become relativistic as well as naturalistic. With its emphasis on probabilistic, relativistic, and contingent truth, scientific knowledge explicitly rejects the possibility of obtaining absolute, objective, or certain knowledge. In the face of the increasing pervasiveness of this naturalistic and probabilistic mode of epistemological thought, contemporary moral thinking tends no longer to be so much concerned with the justification of a particular set of universal or objective moral standards as with the question of whether such standards can be justified at all, and, for the first time in history, relativistic moral thinking has become part of the mainstream of Western thought.

2.   OBJECTIVE VERSUS RELATIVISTIC ETHICS IN HISTORICAL PERSPECTIVE

A.   The Ancient Greeks: Classical Conceptions of Morality

The history of ideas in the Western world had its beginnings in ancient Greece during the fourth and fifth centuries B.C. In this section we briefly outline the main themes of classical epistemological and moral thought as epitomized by the ideas of the three greatest thinkers of that period: Socrates, Plato, and Aristotle. The ideas of these men illustrate not only the objectivistic orientation of the period but also the naturalistic and rationalistic orientation of the age. For the classical mind, moral standards were objective, but they existed also as part of the natural world and were knowable through the process of reason. We can begin our brief survey of classical moral thought with Socrates.

The Athenian philosopher and teacher Socrates (470?–399 B.C.) was the first great thinker of the golden age of philosophy. Socrates wrote nothing and is chiefly known through the works of his student, Plato. A dramatic and literary as well as philosophic genius, Plato chose to present his philosophy in the form of dialogues, in which Socrates was immortalized as the chief spokesman for Plato's point of view. Indeed, the dialogues were so developed that it is impossible to separate the ideas of the two thinkers.

What most distinguishes Socratic from pre-Socratic philosophy is Socrates's conviction that objective knowledge of the Good is possible. Although Socrates wrote nothing, his conviction concerning the absolute (and determinable) nature of the Good served as the cornerstone on which Plato built his world view. But perhaps even more important than Socrates's belief in the objective reality of the Good, at least with respect to influencing the course of Plato's philosophizing, was the strength of his conviction concerning the truth of his belief. Socrates not only believed that there could be an absolute standard by which our thoughts and actions might be evaluated (and that the human mind could come to know it) but also was willing to die for his conviction. Although Socrates was anything but the Sophist that many of his fellow citizens thought him to be, he was eventually charged with being an atheist and of corrupting the youth of Athens. He was condemned to die for his crime by the Athenian court and willingly drank the hemlock to end his life. In the *Crito* (c. 375 B.C./1955) the young Plato describes the events surrounding Socrates's death in some of the most moving passages in all Western literature.

Plato (427?–347 B.C.) was the second great philosopher of the golden age of philosophy. As Fremantle (1954) has noted, it was Plato who invented *ideas*. He introduced the art of thinking in concepts, and ideas took on, in Plato's scheme of things, a separate metaphysical existence.

Much of Plato's thinking that seems remote to the modern mind can be viewed as his attempt to impose order on the social, political, and intellectual chaos of fourth-century Greece. For example, Plato's realism (i.e., the metaphysical doctrine that ideas have a real, objective existence) provided an answer to the Sophists' argument that in principle there can be no objective knowledge, moral or otherwise. If, as the Sophists argued (and sense perception appeared to confirm), the world is in a constant state of flux, how can there be absolute, objective knowledge? Plato's answer was that there can be objective knowledge, but not of the physical world. There exist two realms or worlds: the physical world and the world of ideas. Although it is true that the physical world is everchanging, the world of Ideal Forms is eternally enduring and unchanging. There can be objective knowledge of the Good because an objective form of the Good exists, not in the physical world but in a world of its own—the Platonic world of ideas. Furthermore, the world of ideas is a superior world in the sense that it is not subject to change and transformation as the physical world is.

Granting that an objective, never-changing form of the Good exists, does it follow that we can obtain knowledge of the Good? Plato's answer to this crucial question was unequivocal: Yes, we can obtain knowledge of the Good, but only through the use of reason. Plato's objectivistic epistemology thus provided an antidote to the Sophists' skepticism in the sense that for Plato, an objective form of the Good exists and through reason humans can obtain knowledge of the Good. Because the world of Ideas or Forms is more real for Plato than is the sensory world, it constitutes the ultimate true reality, and true knowledge of the Good (or any other aspect of reality) can never be obtained through sense experience, limited as it is to particulars. It is thus reason, the unique faculty of the human mind to apprehend Ideal Forms, that provides humanity with the possibility of obtaining objective moral knowledge.

One of the clearest statements of Plato's conception of morality can be found in his *Republic* (c. 375 B.C./1955), where he developed most fully his famous "tripartite" division of the Psyche or Soul (i.e., "appetite," "spirit," and "reason"). Like the Psyche, the State is also made up of three components (i.e., "producers," "defenders," and "governors"), and the good state is one in which all three elements are in balance. The ideal state is one ruled by reason, that is, based on the notion of justice. By justice Plato meant the application of the principle of "to each his due," and much of the dialogue in the *Republic* is devoted to clarifying the meaning of this notion. When applied to the state, the principle of justice means that each element of the state (producers, defenders, and governors) performs its appropriate function, and no element is excluded from the total organization of the state. In a similar manner, the good life is one in which all of the elements of the psyche (appetite, spirit, and reason) are organized into an integrated harmony. It is a life ruled by reason and based on the principle of justice. The just person, like the just state, ensures that the separate elements of the psyche operate in an integrated fashion. Reason rules, but it rules justly and recognizes the needs of both the spirit and the appetites. The good life for Plato was thus a life of reason, but not in the narrow sense of the term, as a life of speculative contemplation. On the contrary, the life of reason requires a considered attention to the entire organism. A life devoted to thought is no more to be desired than a life that is a slave to passions or appetites. The good person thus exhibits a full range of virtues, including temperance, courage and, most important, wisdom.

Plato's conception of morality was idealistic. He sought the true form of the Good in an ideal world, the Platonic world of ideas, a world separate and remote from the everyday world of human experience. Consequently, although Plato affirmed the reality of the Good, its actual existence was confined to a world that forever transcends the crudely materialistic world of ordinary experience. Indeed, as Plato made clear with his simile of the cave, the ultimate Good exists in a world that few if any persons will ever know. Thus, Plato's version of realism provided an answer to the Sophists' skepticism and relativism, but it also removed morality from the realm of everyday experience. Such a conception of morality lacks appeal for the type of person who is concerned with the practicalities of everyday life. Aristotle was such a man.

Aristotle (384–322 B.C.) was the third great thinker of the Greek golden age. He wrote on virtually every science known in his day, and his influence on the history of Western thought has been without parallel. All of Aristotle's most important works were unavailable in the early Middle Ages, when the mainstream of intellectual history was Platonic in its orientation. When Aristotle's works became generally available during the twelfth and thirteenth centuries, however, his influence quickly came to overshadow that of his teacher, Plato. From that time to this he has come to be recognized as one of the greatest thinkers the world has ever known. By the middle of the thirteenth century, Thomas Aquinas, one of the most influential theological thinkers of the Middle Ages, could refer to Aristotle simply as "the Philosopher."

Like Plato, Aristotle was a metaphysical realist, but with an important difference. He consistently emphasized the primacy of matter over form. This difference showed itself most clearly in their respective metaphysics and is important for the present analysis because it carried over into Aristotle's conception of the specialized sciences, which included ethics and politics as well as physics, biology, and psychology.

The Nicomachean Ethics (c. 325 B.C./1953) was Aristotle's definitive work on the science of ethics. In it Aristotle argued that Good is the goal or aim for which we strive in all of our activities and that there are many forms of Good, some more important than others. If some forms of the Good are better than others, does this mean the Sophists were right that Good is ultimately relative? Or is there some kind of Good that is to be desired above all else? Is there some end that we desire for its own sake, the others being desired for the sake of it? If there is, then this must be the Good, the absolutely Good. More importantly, would not a knowledge of such a Good be of great advantage in the conduct of our lives?

Aristotle considers first what other people felt is Good. It is generally agreed, he pointed out, that happiness in the sense of living well and doing well is considered to be such an absolute Good. But some men identify happiness with the plain and obvious—health when we are ill, wealth when we are poor, and so forth. The vulgar identify happiness with pleasure, whereas the respectable identify it with honor. But all of these views are superficial. Although it is true that we seek pleasure or honor for the happiness that it brings, we do not seek happiness for the pleasure or honor that it brings. Thus, Aristotle argued, happiness is an absolute Good. We seek it in and for itself. It is not a means to an end, it is an end. It is the end to which we all aspire. It is something final and sufficient, and the end of all action. Aristotle's conception of morality is, like Plato's, naturalistic, rationalistic, and objectivistic—and for basically the same reasons. Thus, for Aristotle, humans are natural organisms, and morality is concerned with achieving the good life in the here and now. It is rationalistic and objectivistic in that he believes there is an objective form of the Good, and that reason is the means for determining that Good.

Aristotle's conception of morality, however, was more down to earth than Plato's. To Aristotle, the good life is the actualization of those functions that are unique to humanity. In the moral sphere (i.e., the everyday world of practical affairs), it is the exercise of reason over appetitive and sensory desires. It is the life of right conduct—right conduct in relation to other persons and in relation to one's self. In the intellectual sphere, it is the search for truth. Moreover, if happiness is activity in accordance with virtue, Aristotle argues, it is reasonable that it should be in accordance with the highest virtues. Because in Aristotle's scheme the intellectual virtues are higher than the moral virtues, and because philosophic wisdom is the highest of the intellectual virtues, it follows that the good life, in addition to being one of correct conduct, is also a life devoted to the search for truth, the highest of human virtues.

Socrates's, Plato's, and Aristotle's conceptions of morality were naturalistic in that ethics and morality were viewed as part of the natural world and human beings were viewed as being concerned with achieving the good life in the present rather than in the hereafter. Those conceptions were rationalistic and objectivistic in their belief in the objective reality of the Good and in their consideration of reason as the only source of true knowledge of the Good.

The Greco-Roman Age

Although more than 700 years elapsed between Aristotle's death (322 B.C.) and the Fall of Rome (A.D. 410), which marked the end of the classical period, intellectual developments in the classical world reasonably can be said to have reached their high point with the works of Plato and Aristotle. Intellectual and cultural developments in the classical world did not cease with the death of Aristotle; on the contrary, the Greco-Roman age produced some of the finest literature, art, and architecture the world has ever known. Classical thought never again achieved the scope, coherence, and integration found in the works of Plato and Aristotle, however. The schools of thought that emerged during the remainder of the middle and late classical period were occupied either with interpreting the works of the masters or in coping with the tremendous social, political, and cultural changes that were taking place in the classical world, changes that eventually helped pave the way for the collapse of the Greco-Roman culture (Grant, 1970).

One noteworthy political and theological change occurred during the late classical period, some three centuries following Aristotle's death, that was to influence the course of Western moral thinking for the next two millennia. A small Jewish sect, which to its contemporaries may have seemed indistinguishable from other contemporary Jewish groups, managed to achieve popularity among the Jews of Palestine, then a minor eastern province of the Roman Empire. The leader and ultimately the focal figure of the sect, Jesus, a Jew of unusual charismatic appeal, was virtually single-handedly responsible for founding the religious movement that would ultimately come to dominate Western theology and thought for the next 2000 years. Born for the most part unnoticed in Palestine in about 5 B.C., Jesus was devoted to reforming Judaism. During a brief life, Jesus attracted a small band of dedicated disciples who believed that he was Judaism's long-awaited Messiah. Following Jesus's death, those disciples became convinced that Jesus rose from the dead, an event that confirmed their belief that he was the Son of God. From that point on, Jesus (in contrast to the traditional Jewish God, Yahweh) became the center of the growing religious movement. The movement spread slowly at first, appealing mainly to the lower classes, but gradually, mainly through the proselytizing skill of the early converts and the organizational ability of the founding fathers, Christianity began to spread throughout the Empire. By the fourth century A.D. it had become widespread enough to be adopted as the state religion of the empire.

With a highly organized institutional structure, the militant Christians were there to fill the social and political vacuum left by the collapse of the western province of the Roman Empire. As they gradually converted their barbarian conquerors, political power in what remained of the empire came to be shared by the Church and kings, with the Church oftentimes wielding more secular power than did the kings (Grant, 1970). The breakup of the Roman Empire brought an end to the classical period of Western thought.

B. The Middle Ages: The Thousand Years Synthesis

The thousand-year period from the Fall of Rome in the fifth century A.D. to the Renaissance in the fifteenth century was an era of spiritual harmony frequently termed the "age of belief" (Fremantle, 1954). For 10 centuries, the intellectual history of the Western world evolved within a framework unified by a single great belief: the nearly universal acceptance of the truth of the Christian revelation. Although questions arose concerning the exact nature of the truth imparted by the Scriptures (the medium of revelation), there was never any serious doubt that the "truth" had been divinely revealed or that, if one had faith, all would become understandable. This faith in the truth of the Christian revelation served as the cornerstone of Western thought for the millennium between the end of the classical age and the medieval period, and stands in the intellectual history of the West as a bridge between the ancient and modern worlds (Jones, 1969a).

The unity of medieval thought was so complete that it is sometimes difficult for the modern mind to grasp the inclusiveness of the Christian synthesis. After centuries of skepticism, the modern mind has come to take uncertainty for granted. For the medieval mind, however, there was no place for serious doubt or disbelief. The entire range of medieval thought took place within a framework whose extreme limits were defined by a body of divinely revealed truths as interpreted by the Church. For a thousand years, questions of ethics and morality (indeed, even the ultimate nature of reality) were raised within a framework that was thought capable of providing absolute or objective answers. These answers were derived from faith more than reason, but they were considered absolute and objective nonetheless. With the assimilation of the rational and secular doctrines of the ancient philosophers into the corpus of Christian thought, faith and reason were united in a synthesis powerful enough to endure for 10 centuries, and the Roman Catholic church, the institutional backbone of the synthesis, assumed a position of unquestioned preeminence in Western thought.

The main outlines of the body of thought that made up the core beliefs and doctrines of the medieval Christian thinker developed gradually following the death of Christ during the long years of the decline of Rome. Interestingly, Jesus himself had little to do with the development of the complex and elaborate corpus of thought that has come to constitute orthodox Christian doctrine. Jesus's role in the emergence of Christianity as a world religion was more inspirational than conceptual, for he was basically a simple man who preached in parables, wrote nothing, taught by example, and left no systematic body of thought. Convinced of the imminence of judgment day ("Repent: for the kingdom of heaven is at hand."), Jesus stressed forsaking things of this world ("Do not store up your riches on earth . . . , but store up your riches in Heaven.") and getting right with God the Father ("Not every one that saith unto me, Lord, Lord, shall enter into the kingdom of heaven; but he that doeth the will of my Father which is in heaven."). Like Socrates who had inspired the preceding secular age, Jesus provided the inspiration for the emerging age of faith.

The classical synthesis played an important though indirect role in the intellectual developments that took place during the Middle Ages; it provided the underlying structure for medieval thought and a foundation for the Christian synthesis. In fact, the Christian assimilation of the available works of the classical philosophers helped to preserve the intellectual heritage of the ancient world during the "dark" years that followed the collapse of the classical culture. Indeed, one of the major accomplishments of Augustine and Aquinas, the two most significant thinkers of the Middle Ages, was their respective "Christianization" of Plato and Aristotle. The works of both men epitomize the spiritualistic and objectivistic orientation of medieval moral thinking.

The most renowned of the early Western church fathers was Aurelius Augustine (345–430). Augustine's works were regarded with nearly scriptural authority throughout most of the Middle Ages and continue to exert a powerful influence in the modern world (e.g., existentialism). Augustinianism, as the complex of ideas associated with his name came to be called, emphasized the role of the direct mystical experience and divine illumination (Augustine, A.D. 400/1963). For Augustine, absolute or objective knowledge of the good was obtainable through the direct mystical experience of the divinely revealed truth of God. The Augustinian synthesis of Platonic thought and Christian doctrine provided a paradigm for Christian thinking up until the High Middle Ages, when Thomism emerged as a significant school of thought.

Thomas Aquinas (1225–1274) was the second great church thinker of the Middle Ages. The Thomastic synthesis, which has no rival in the modern world for scope and integration, brought together the diverse elements of 13 centuries of Christian tradition and fused them into a coherent whole. Thomism is the most influential and enduring school of thought to emerge from the entire medieval millenium. Thomas's *Summa Theologiae* (Aquinas, 1265–1273/1945) is one of the most integrated statements of Roman Catholicism ever produced, and Thomism is to this day the official philosophy of the Roman Catholic church.

Thomism is a grand synthesis of Aristotelian and Christian concepts that reproduces in thought, with nearly flawless fidelity, the medieval ideal that Dante (c. 1300/1976) captures in his poetry: a conception of the cosmos as a perfect harmonious whole, created and sustained by a kind and benevolent God who provides meaning and purpose to the entire universe. In Thomas's universe, no object or event, from the most insignificant to the most momentous, lacks meaning or purpose, for each object or event is a part of God's divine plan for all things. Humans and nature, morality and salvation, faith and reason—all exist in divine unity. Within the context of the Thomastic synthesis, doubt and uncertainty are eliminated, and each person is at one with the universe and with God.

With Thomas's thinking we come to another pinnacle in Western intellectual history, one without equal since Aristotle. And indeed, there are many similarities between the two thinkers. Like Aristotle, Thomas summed up an entire historical epoch. Aristotle brought a secular age to a close; Aquinas, a spiritual one. In addition, the intellectual relationship between Thomas and Augustine roughly parallels that of Aristotle and Plato. Both pairs of men were products of their ages. Plato and Aristotle shared the secular and naturalistic orientation of the Hellenistic age; Augustine and Thomas shared the spiritual and otherworldly orientation of the Middle Ages. By the thirteenth century and the time of Thomas, enthusiasm for Christianity had reached its peak in Europe and knew no serious rivals in the West. There were no longer any fundamental questions about the basic tenets of Christianity. Thomas's contribution to Western moral thought was one of synthesizing 1300 years of Christian thinking into a coherent framework capable of providing absolute answers to moral issues and questions.

Medieval conceptions of morality thus differed from classical conceptions in that they tended to be spiritual and otherworldly rather than secular and this-worldly. The ancient and medieval world did, however, share one important belief—a belief in the existence of objective moral standards. The ancient Greeks sought the knowledge of objective standards through the use of reason, the faculty of the human mind capable of the apprehension of universals; the medieval mind sought the knowledge of objective moral standards through faith in the truth of the divine revelation. Thus, although ancient and medieval thought were at odds concerning the source of objective knowledge (viz., faith or reason), they were as one concerning the possibility of achieving it. It is this sense that objective or certain knowledge was possible that, perhaps more than anything else, distinguishes the ancient and medieval world from the modern world, for the Middle Ages were the last great "age of certainty" the West was to know. Between the ancient world with its emphasis on the certainty of rational knowledge and the modern world with its emphasis on probabilistic scientific knowledge, there stood a thousand-year historical epoch that has been aptly called the age of belief.

The Renaissance

Thomas's synthesis of Aristotelian and Christian thought provided the framework for the flowering of Scholastic philosophy, which reached its apex in the thirteenth century, and for 3 centuries the anthropocentric Aristotelian view of the universe provided by the Scholastic philosophers dominated Western thought. The end of the Middle Ages came in the fifteenth century, concurrent with a spectacular revival of secular learning, art, and culture that came to be called the Renaissance. The Renaissance was the period of transition from the medieval to the modern world. The fifteenth and sixteenth centuries were an era of revolutionary economic, political, religious, and intellectual change that paved the way for the beginning of the modern age.

The Renaissance saw the breakdown of the Church's spiritual and intellectual leadership of the West. It is easy to underestimate just how important this event was. The Roman Catholic church had been the single common denominator capable of unifying the Western world from the time of Christ. For 1500 years the Church served as a symbol of the unity of the West. The Church alone had survived the fall of the empire, and it was the Church that gave the West its sense of direction during the "darkness" of early medieval times. For 1000 years the Church was the *only* institution that could make a serious claim to speak for all of the West. With the coming of the Renaissance, however, all this began to change. The Church's spiritual as well as intellectual leadership was soon being challenged from many directions. After more than a millennium of nearly universal acceptance, within a few centuries the Church lost its position of preeminence in the Christian world and the West.

C. The Modern Age: Enlightenment and Despair

We noted that the Renaissance of the fifteenth and sixteenth centuries served as a period of transition from the medieval to the modern world. The modern period of Western intellectual history began in the seventeenth century. As the sixteenth century drew to a close, the secular spirit that was one of he chief hallmarks of the Renaissance prevailed—reason triumphed over faith, and the modern age began with a period of "enlightenment." Reason's triumph, however, was more apparent than real, and the "age of enlightenment" that followed the end of the Middle Ages was relatively short-lived. What appeared to the seventeenth- and eighteenth-century thinker to be the beginning of the final phase in the enlightenment of the whole of humankind was actually the end of an era. Reason had indeed replaced faith as the cornerstone of Western knowledge, thus finalizing the break with the medieval past. But reason itself soon failed in the face of the new forces that emerged during the modern age. The West had entered a revolutionary new period. The old synthesis rapidly broke down, and because there was nothing to take its place, Western intellectual history soon found itself in the midst of a crisis. As Aiken (1956) noted, "From one point of view, the whole history of ideas in the modern age may be regarded as a history of the progressive breakdown of the medieval Christian synthesis which has been most powerfully articulated in the *Summa* of Thomas Aquinas and most movingly and persuasively expressed in Dante's *Divine Comedy*." Western thought is undergoing a "prolonged crisis of reason more profound than any that [has] occurred in Western culture since the original collision of paganism with primitive Christianity" (p. 26).

The effect that this "crisis of reason" had on Western conceptions of morality was profound. Since the fifth century A.D., the intellectual history of the West had been unified by an unshakable faith in the truth of the Christian revelation and an equally deep and abiding belief that reason (guided by faith) would ultimately provide objective or certain knowledge about the world. Consequently, for very long in the intellectual history of the Western world, questions of morality did not seem truly problematic. Issues were raised; differences encountered; fine points debated. But never did it appear that the issues could not be settled, that differences could not be resolved within a larger, commonly accepted framework. The Western world experienced a unity of thought like never before and perhaps never again. This unity of thought provided an ethic or morality. More than that, it provided a coherent world view capable of giving meaning and purpose to the universe. As Jung (1933) observed:

> How totally different did the world appear to medieval man! For him the earth was eternally fixed and at rest in the centre of the universe, encircled by the course of a sun that solicitously bestowed its warmth. Men were all children of God under the loving care of the Most High, who prepared them for eternal blessedness; and all knew exactly what they should do and how they should conduct themselves in order to rise from a corruptible and joyous existence. Such a life no longer seems real to us, even in our dreams. Natural science has long ago torn this lovely veil to shreds. That age lies far behind as childhood. (p. 204)

That age does indeed seem to lie far behind. From the time of the Renaissance, the history of Western thought has been a history of the disintegration of this unified world view. Faith and reason, the twin pillars of Western thought, collapsed in the face of an emerging secular and scientific world view, along with the ideal of objective or certain knowledge, the cherished goal of Western thinkers from the time of Socrates. The breakdown of the medieval synthesis and the ascendancy of a naturalistic world view with no place for either faith or reason gradually but radically relativized the Western person's conception of himself or herself and his or her relation to the universe. Consistent with this trend, modern conceptions of morality have also become increasingly relativistic.

The revolutionary changes that have occurred in Western conceptions of morality did not happen overnight. Consequently, we will briefly describe some of the more significant intellectual changes that have occurred in the modern world, beginning with the Enlightenment and concluding with the most significant intellectual revolutions to take place in the modern age—the emergence of modern science.

The Enlightenment

The Enlightenment is the historical period in Western society that began in the late seventeenth century and lasted to the end of the eighteenth century. By the end of the Renaissance, reason had triumphed over faith, and for a few centuries the Western world basked in a warm glow of optimism that accompanied the rediscovery of the power of the human mind. The age of belief had given way to an "age of enlightenment." During the seventeenth and eighteenth centuries optimism concerning the power of human reason eventually to solve humankind's problems was more widespread and pervasive than at any other time in the intellectual history of the West, including the Greek golden age.

The Enlightenment was also an era that was filled with a sense of progress and accomplishment. All of the revolutionary changes that took place during this period seemed to hold out the promise of a better life for the whole of humanity. For example, the Enlightenment was the period that saw the rise of modern science. The renewed interest in the natural world displayed during the Renaissance began to pay off. Startling scientific discoveries followed one after another, culminating in the work of Isaac Newton. It was during this period that modern science firmly established for itself a central role in the mainstream of Western thought, and it appeared to the Enlightenment thinker that man was on the verge of unlocking all of the secrets of the physical universe. Like modern science, modern philosophy also had its beginnings during this period. On the Continent, René Descartes proclaimed the independence of philosophy from theology (Descartes, 1628–1701/1931). Freed from the limitations and constraints of text-bound Scholastic thought, the power of human reason appeared virtually unlimited, at least to the philosophers of the Enlightenment. The British empiricists, who were the other major school of thought of this period, appeared to be more skeptical about the possibility of absolutely certain knowledge (Hume, 1748/1946). However, even they shared the rationalist's faith in the eventual triumph of human reason.

A similar conception, namely, one of the human being as a creature who is by nature rational, basically good, and capable of perfection, colored the political thought of the age. The writings of men like Voltaire, Locke, and especially Rousseau captured the social and political imagination of the period and helped to lay the foundations for the French Revolution. Finally, the numerous technological advances that fueled the fires of the Industrial Revolution seemed to hold out the promise of a coming age of plenty with material security and comfort for all. As we have seen, however, the age of enlightenment with its optimistic faith in the triumph of reason was short-lived. The secularism and naturalism of the age also laid the groundwork for the rise of the modern scientific world view, a development that was to have profound epistemological and moral implications.

Modern Science

In 1609 Galileo Galilei (1564–1642), the great scientific genius of the Renaissance, built a telescope modeled after one that had recently been invented in Holland. He then spent several years studying various celestial phenomena. What he found by looking through his telescope called into question the most basic assumptions of orthodox Aristotelian astronomy (Jones, 1969b). He discovered the mountainous nature of the surface of the moon, a finding that directly refuted the postulate of the perfect sphericity of celestial bodies. He described the appearance of sunspots, a finding that directly contradicted the assumption of celestial immutability and perfection. He also detected the existence of many previously unobserved stars, described the phases of the planet Venus, and discovered four of the moons of Jupiter, all of which in one way or another challenged the Aristotelian astronomy of medieval Scholasticism.

Galileo's physics was no less revolutionary (Galileo, 1638/1950). His work on the laws of motion of falling bodies, which he verified experimentally, similarly challenged some of the most basic assumptions of the Aristotelian physics of the Scholastic philosophers. Galileo's discoveries, however, did much more than simply present a challenge to orthodox astronomy and physics. By demonstrating systematically that the Scholastic philosophers' most basic assumptions about the natural world were false, Galileo's findings threatened to undermine the very foundations of the intellectual hegemony of Catholic Christendom. If the orthodox view of the natural world was false, then what about the Church's claim to superior knowledge in other areas? What about its claim to superior divine knowledge? Needless to say, Galileo's findings were greeted with neither universal acclaim nor immediate acceptance. Many of his more orthodox contemporaries refused to look through his telescope. They also refused to take seriously his demonstration of the uniform acceleration of falling bodies, even when a 100-pound and a 1-pound cannon ball dropped concurrently from the Tower of Pisa struck the ground at their feet at the same time. But Galileo's empirical proofs that many of the Aristotelian doctrines held by the Church to be orthodox and accepted knowledge were wrong were public and observable, at least for those who would look. Moreover, not everyone refused to look, nor was everyone unimpressed by Galileo's empirical demonstrations. The Church was forced to take action.

Unfortunately, at least for the reputation of the Church, its response to the challenge presented by Galileo's findings was both ignominious and futile— an attempt was made to crush Galileo and his work. His books were banned, and Galileo himself was summoned to Rome to face the Inquisition. At 70, after a long and protracted trial, he was forced to denounce on his knees the truth of his findings and then was sentenced to life imprisonment.

Early spokesmen for the emerging scientific world view such as Copernicus, Kepler, and Galileo were instrumental in setting the stage for the scientific revolution. It remained for Isaac Newton (1642–1727), the English mathematician and physicist, however, to establish once and for all the superiority of science in the realm of natural knowledge (Jones, 1969b). Newton made significant contributions to diverse fields of scientific inquiry, including mathematics, mechanics, astronomy, and optics. The discovery for which he is best known is his law of universal attraction. Elegant in its simplicity (every particle of matter in the universe attracts every other particle with a force varying inversely as the square of the distance between them and directly proportional to the product of their masses), yet powerful in its precision, with this one simple law Newton appeared to have solved the secret of the entire physical universe. The law of gravity was so powerful that it was capable of accounting for every type of motion the mind could conceive. In Newton's hands, the power of science to unlock the secrets of nature appeared unlimited.

Newton and his discoveries revolutionized the Western view of the natural universe. The comfortable, anthropocentric, Aristotelian world of the medieval Scholastic philosophers faltered and failed in the face of the power and precision of Newton's mechanical and mathematical model of the universe. After the publication of his *Principia* (1687/1934) (*Mathematical Principles of Natural Knowledge*), Newton was widely acclaimed to be a scientific genius of the first magnitude and became one of the first scientists ever to achieve public recognition in his own lifetime. For Newton there was no Inquisition, no degradation, no humiliation. On the contrary, Newton's *Principia* was held to be a model of scientific knowledge, and Newton himself was idealized as the perfect scientist. By the time of Newton's death, modern science had clearly come to occupy a position of preeminence in the mainstream of Western thought, a position it still holds today. Indeed, despite certain misgivings about its ultimate utility, modern science has become nearly universally recognized as our chief source of dependable knowledge about the natural world.

The beginning of the modern age was thus marked by a radical change in the Western world's view of the natural world, a change that, once begun, took place with incredible speed. The medieval Christian synthesis that had begun to break down in the fifteenth century collapsed rapidly, and the otherworldliness of the Middle Ages was replaced just as quickly by the secularism and naturalism of the modern age. Galileo may have been forced to abjure his discoveries on bended knee, but just a few short years later Newton's discoveries (Newton was born the year that Galileo died) gained for him international fame and recognition. It was not to be long before Charles Darwin's theory of natural evolution (as opposed to supernatural creation) was to extend further the range of scientific explanation. Copernican and Galilean astronomy had displaced the earth as the center of the universe, and Newtonian physics provided a mechanical explanation for the workings of the physical universe. The very origin of life itself was soon to yield to a natural explanation in the form of Darwin's evolutionary theory. Perhaps more important for our purposes, the influence of modern science has clearly extended well beyond the relatively specialized areas of inquiry that have come to make up each of the separate branches of scientific investigation. Indeed, "scientific knowledge" in the broadest sense can be justly said to provide the modern world with its paradigm of dependable knowledge. In view of the power and prestige accorded science and scientific knowledge by the modern mind, it is appropriate to ask just what it is that distinguishes scientific knowledge from other types of knowledge. How, for example, does modern science differ from ancient or medieval science? What is it that is unique about the modern scientific world view?

The answers to these questions, unfortunately, no longer appear as simple and straightforward as they once did. The question of what it is that is unique about modern science and what distinguishes scientific knowledge from other types of knowledge is a matter of debate among contemporary historians and philosophers of science. Some of the basic issues in this debate include such questions as, What are scientific laws and theories, and how do they differ from other laws and theories? What is the nature of a scientific explanation, and how does it differ from other types of explanation? What is the scientific method, and is there a single method that can be applied to all of the specialized sciences? It would, of course, be impossible to resolve these questions here. We can, however, briefly consider several of the most basic characteristics of the modern scientific world view and reach some tentative conclusions about what it is that is unique about modern science and scientific knowledge.

One of the most basic characteristics of modern science is that its metaphysical foundations are explicitly naturalistic (Burtt, 1924). Modern scientists, regardless of their areas of specialization, view the phenomena they are investigating as products of natural processes and forces and attribute to them no spiritual or supernatural significance. Scientific knowledge is knowledge about the natural world. This naturalistic attitude clearly distinguishes modern science from medieval science, but naturalism is not unique to modern science. A similar naturalistic attitude, we saw, was one of the chief characteristics of the classical mind from the pre-Socratic materialists through Plato and Aristotle. A second basic feature of modern science is that it is empirical. The scientist's laws and theories are rooted in the data of sense experience. Scientific knowledge is empirical knowledge. The empiricism of modern science, like its naturalism, clearly distinguishes modern science from medieval science, which subordinated the data of sense experience to revealed truth. Empiricism, however, is also not unique to modern science. There was, we saw, a strong empiricist tendency in the classical mind. Thus, Aristotle clearly considered it essential that knowledge of the world be firmly rooted in the particulars of sense experience.

If it is not its naturalism and empiricism that distinguishes the modern scientific world view from other ways of thinking about the world, what is it that is unique about modern science? The chief difference between *both* classical and medieval science, on the one hand, and modern science, on the other, is their respective views of the role of reason and the ideal of absolute, objective, or certain knowledge. For the classical mind, reason, the power of the human mind to obtain knowledge about the world independent of sense experience, provided humanity with its most dependable source of knowledge. Rational knowledge in this sense differs from scientific knowledge in two important respects. First, because the faculty of reason is not limited to the particulars of sense experience, it is capable of grasping universal truths. Rational knowledge is absolute, objective, or certain knowledge. Second, because the faculty of reason operates independent of sense data, the final criterion for rational truth is logical consistency rather than fidelity to empirical evidence. Even Aristotle, with his pronounced empirical tendencies, considered sense data to provide only a foundation or beginning for human knowledge. For Aristotle, as for the classical mind in general, the final goal of human reason was objective or certain knowledge.

The medieval mind similarly considered objective or certain knowledge to be available to the human mind; the principal difference was that the Christian thinker viewed the source of objective or certain knowledge to be a combination of faith and reason. Even Augustine, the chief spokesman for the mystical tradition in Christian thought, eventually found the peace of rational certainty he sought.

What is unique about modern science and distinguishes it from other ways of thinking about the world is its *explicit* rejection of the possibility of obtaining absolute, objective, or certain knowledge and its subordination of rational truth to empirical truth. The relative "truth" status of any scientific hypothesis is always contingent on available empirical data. All scientific laws and theories are, as a matter of principle, tentative and subject to revision in the light of further empirical evidence, and empirical "truths," derived as they are from limited sense data, are probabilistic and relativistic truths, contingent on empirical confirmation or refutation. Modern science thus assigns "reason" a more limited and circumscribed role in the acquisition of knowledge about the natural world. The scientist may (and does) frequently use logic and reason (particularly mathematical reasoning) in order to arrive at a hypothesis about the world, but the final criterion for the relative truth status of a particular hypothesis is always its fidelity to empirical data. Scientific knowledge, which provides the paradigm of dependable knowledge for the modern world, is thus naturalistic, empirical, and inherently relativistic.

The rise of modern science has been described as the greatest intellectual revolution in the entire history of Western thought (Burtt, 1924). Whether such an extreme view of the importance of the scientific revolution is justified cannot be settled here. That the rise of modern scientific world view did involve a dramatic reorientation of Western thought is, nevertheless, beyond question. Moreover, the profound implications that this change had for the Western thinker's view of himself or herself and his or her relation to the universe is similarly undeniable. Although there is nothing inherently anti-Christian or even antireligious about science and scientific knowledge (e.g., no self-respecting scientist would, for example, claim to be able to prove or disprove the existence of God or even claim that such a question is answerable by science), the scientist does pursue the acquisition of knowledge in a specialized field without making any supernatural assumptions. More importantly, as new specialized sciences emerged and gradually took over large areas of knowledge that were once thought to be the province of philosophy and theology, it soon became clear that scientific progress was not at all dependent on a belief in the existence of God (or the belief in absolutes of any type, religious or secular). In the case of the modern psychological sciences, for example, it is possible for the scientist to study, depending on his or her hypotheses and assumptions, any relevant dependent outcome variable (moral behavior, moral reasoning, moral affect, etc.), without making assumptions concerning the existence of objective moral standards. The scientist's quest is for determinants (present, past, context, etc.) of those outcomes connoting moral phenomena. Thus, the many advances that science has contributed to our knowledge of the world over the last several centuries have been truly impressive, but they have also been costly. The world revealed by the scientist turned out to be vastly different from that of either the classical philosopher or of the Christian revelation.

The emergence of modern science was thus clearly a significant factor in the occurrence of a profound transformation of the Western thinker's view of the possibility or necessity of obtaining absolute, objective, or certain knowledge, a transformation that has resulted in a gradual but radical relativization of the foundations of Western morality. This is not to say that skepticism and relativism are new or uniquely modern phenomena. On the contrary, there have always been skeptics, cynics, and relativists. Nor do we wish to suggest that self-conscious relativism has emerged as the principal moral orientation of the modern thinker. Quite the opposite. The current literature on morality, moral behavior, and moral development has been significantly influenced by a strong nonrelativist tradition (Kohlberg, 1981; Rawls, 1971). The question of the existence of an objective foundation for ethics or morality is thus one of the central issues in the history of ideas in the modern age and is in fact one of the basic, pervasive themes that runs through the present book. We do suggest, however, that the question of objectivistic versus relativistic morality is a vastly more difficult one in the modern world than it has ever been before and that the relativism of our age is, for the first time ever, rooted in the mainstream of Western intellectual history. As Jean Paul Sartre (1956) observed, "Dostoevsky once wrote, 'If God did not exist, everything would be permitted;' and that . . . is the starting point. Everything is indeed permitted if God does not exist" (pp. 294–295).

3. CONCLUSIONS

We can now bring our argument to a close. We have argued that the issue of objectivistic versus relativistic morality not only is basic to our field but also is a central issue in the modern world. We have further argued that although the issue is not unique to our age, a fundamental change has occurred in the way the question of objectivistic versus relativistic morality tends to be framed. Thus, although there have always been skeptics and relativists, we have argued that the greater part of Western history has been dominated by objectivist epistemological and moral thinking and that objectivistic (indeed, absolutist) conceptions of morality have been historically consistent with the mainstream of Western thought. We have further attempted to show that a number of intellectual developments in the modern world, and the rise of modern science in particular, have been the basis for a gradual but radical transformation in the very foundations of Western moral thought. For the first time, we suggest, relativistic moral thinking is consistent with the mainstream of the Western intellectual history. Finally, we suggest that these developments lead to several significant conclusions with respect to theory and research in the field of morality, moral behavior, and moral development: First, the diversity of moral views and positions (both implicit and explicit) represented in this book, which range from objectivistic, quasi-objectivistic, and semirelativistic to radically relativistic, are themselves symptomatic of the sense of moral uncertainty that characterizes our age. Second, in the absence of a broader intellectual synthesis or consensus, the field will continue to be characterized by a plurality of ethical and moral views. Third, the direction of a new synthesis, if such a synthesis is possible, will of necessity require a reconciliation of conceptions of moral standards with relativistic and probabilistic epistemology.

REFERENCES

Aiken, H. *The age of ideology*. New York: New American Library, 1956.

Aquinas, T. Summa theologica. In. A. C. Pegis (Ed.), *Basic writings of Saint Thomas Aquinas*. New York: Random House, 1945. (Originally published, 1265–1273.)

Aristotle, E. *The Nicomachean ethics* (J. A. K. Thomson, Ed. and trans.). New York: Penguin Books, 1953. (Originally published, c. 325 B.C.)

Augustine. *The confessions of St. Augustine* (R. Warner, Ed. and trans.). New York: New American Library, 1963. (Originally published, c. A.D. 400.)

Burtt, E. A. *The metaphysical foundations of modern science*. New York: Doubleday, 1924.

Dante, A. *The inferno* (F. Cary, trans.). New York: Paddington Press, 1976. (Originally published, 1300.)

Descartes, R. *The philosophic works of Descartes* (E. S. Holdane & G. R. T. Ross, trans.). New York: Cambridge University Press, 1931. (Originally published, 1628–1701.)

Fremantle, A. *The age of belief*. New York: New American Library, 1954.

Galileo, G. *Dialogues concerning two new sciences* (H. Crew & A. de Salvio, trans.). Chicago: Northwestern University Press, 1950. (Originally published, 1638.)

Grant, M. *The civilizations of Europe*. New York: New American Library, 1970.

Hume, D. *An enquiry concerning the principles of knowledge*. Lasalle, Ill.: Open Court, 1946. (Originally published, 1748.)

Jones, W. T. *Hobbes to Hume* (2nd ed.). New York: Harcourt Brace Jovanovich, 1969.(a)

Jones, W. T. *The medieval mind* (2nd ed.), New York: Harcourt Brace Jovanovich, 1969.(b)

Jung, C. *Modern man in search of a soul.* New York: Harcourt Brace, 1933.

Kohlberg, L. *The philosophy of moral development: Moral stages and the idea of justice* (Vol. 1)´: *Essays on moral development.* San Francisco: Harper & Row, 1981.

Lickona, T. Critical issues in the study of moral development and behavior. In T. Lickona (Ed.), *Moral development and behavior: Theory, research, and social issues.* New York: Holt, Rinehart and Winston, 1976.

Lovejoy, A. O. *The reason, the understanding, and time.* Baltimore: The Johns Hopkins University Press, 1961.

MacIntyre, A. *A short history of ethics: A history of moral philosophy from the Homeric age to the twentieth century.* New York: Macmillan, 1966.

Newton, I. *Mathematical principles of natural philosophy* (A Motte, trans., rev. trans. by F. Cajori). Berkeley, Calif.: University of California Press, 1934. (Originally published, 1687.)

Plato. *The republic* (D. Lee, Ed. and trans.). New York: Penguin Books, 1955. (Originally published, c. 375 B.C.)

Plato. *The crito* (D. Lee, Ed. and trans.). New York: Penguin Books, 1955. (Originally published, c. 375 B.C.)

Rawls, J. *A theory of justice.* Cambridge, Mass.: Harvard University Press, 1971.

Sartre, J. P. *Existentialism is a humanism.* In W. Kaufman (Ed. and trans.), *Existentialism from Dostoevsky to Sartre.* New York: World Publishing, 1956.

CHAPTER 2

The Major Components of Morality

JAMES R. REST

Reviews of morality research typically divide the field into moral thought, moral emotion, and moral behavior. This three-part division has perhaps been useful for demarcating different lines of research, but these divisions do not represent theoretically clear units of analysis—empirical clusters—nor do they suggest profitable ways of interrelating the various elements or for representing the various constituent processes involved in morality. Instead of this three-part division, the constituent processes involved in producing moral behavior can be construed as involving four major components: (1) interpreting the situation and identifying a moral problem (involving empathy, role-talking, and figuring out how the participants in a situation are each affected by various actions); (2) figuring out what one ought to do, formulating a plan of action that applies the relevant moral standard or ideal (involving concepts of fairness and justice, moral judgment, application of social-moral norms); (3) evaluating the various courses of action for how they would serve moral or nonmoral values and deciding what one will actually try to do (involving decision-making processes, value integration models, defensive operations); and (4) executing and implementing the moral plan of action (involving "ego strength" and self-regulation processes). Existing morality research can be organized according to this framework as involving one or more of these components (examples are given in the chapter). Adequate functioning in all four components is regarded as necessary for moral behavior. Although there is a logical sequentiality to the four components, they are interactive, not proposed as a linear decision-making model.

None of the major theoretical approaches offers an adequately comprehensive view of the psychology of morality: not the cognitive-developmental, the social learning, the psychoanalytic, or social psychology's "social norm" ap-

Portions of this chapter are adapted from J. R. Rest, "Morality," in P. Mussen, gen. ed., *Manual of Child Psychology,* volume *Cognitive Development,* ed. J. Flavell and E. Markman, 4th ed. New York: John Wiley & Sons, 1983.

proach, or the empathy-altruism approach, or the new post-Piagetian information-processing approaches, or human decision-making approaches, and
certainly not the sociobiological approach. One purpose of this chapter is to
indicate why no current theory is adequately comprehensive by pointing out
how the different theories focus on just some aspects of morality and neglect
other aspects. In order to do this, the chapter will present a list of major
questions that any complete theory of morality must answer—in effect this is
a model of the major component processes involved in the production of
moral behavior. The chapter will fit the contributions of the various theoretical approaches into various parts of this model as providing answers to some
questions. The chapter claims that *no* current theory has useful things to say
about *all* components of the model but that *most* approaches have *something*
useful to say about *some* of the components. In short, it claims that to a large
extent, the major theoretical approaches have bypassed one another in attending to different aspects of the phenomenon of morality. Secondly, the
chapter proposes to examine some of the vexing theoretical issues in the field
of morality from the perspective of the four-component model. Although the
chapter does not claim that this model "solves" the controversies, it will
claim that the model provides a useful way to construe the issues and suggests some promising lines of research.

BEHAVIOR, AFFECT, AND COGNITION

It has become somewhat customary for reviews of morality to divide the field
into behavior, affect, and cognition. According to this scheme, behaviorists
study behavior, cognitive-developmentalists study cognition, and psychoanalysts study affect. It is often presumed that different psychological mechanisms govern these three facets of morality: For instance, conditioning and
modeling govern behavior; cognitive conflict and equilibration govern thinking; and the vicissitudes of libido and the superego govern feelings. It is also
customary for such reviews to leave us dangling about how behavior, affect,
and cognition are related. Typically, some research that correlated some
measure of moral affect with some measure of moral cognition (or moral behavior) is cited, and finding low correlations, it is concluded that affect is
largely independent of cognition (or behavior)—thus suggesting that the
three elements have separate lives of their own.

This three-part scheme is deficient for many reasons, which this chapter
will not go into here (Rest, in press). Instead, this chapter proposes a different scheme for dividing morality research, starting off by asking, What do
we have to suppose went on in the head of a person who acts morally in some
situation? Starting here entails that we are primarily interested in behavior
and what produces it. This chapter agrees with the behaviorists that psychology should be interested primarily in actual behavior in the real world, that
is, observable events that have an impact on the flow of events in the world.
Subjective processes that have *no* observable effects and are not overtly ex-

pressed are of some interest, for they may tell us something about the inner, hidden life of a person, but if they do not influence behavior, they are of secondary interest. At the same time, however, this chapter does not equate this interest in moral behavior with studying the frequency counts of little bits and pieces of behavior in highly controlled and contrived situations. The psychologist's interest in "moral behavior" should be understood to be an interest in the pattern of behavior in real-life contexts with attention to the inner processes that produced the behavior. Without knowing the inner processes that gave rise to the behavior, we cannot call it "moral," nor can we know how it is likely to generalize to other situations. This concern with situational context and the inner processes that produce the behavior is not just an academic nicety, but is essential to understanding, predicting, and influencing moral behavior.

As an illustration, consider the information that the legal system is concerned with. Certainly the legal system is one of the more practical institutions that deals with people's behavior; the legal system cannot afford to be too involuted or too theoretical just for theory's sake. Let us say that an individual comes to the attention of the legal system because the person has fatally shot someone else. What does the legal system want to know about this person and his or her behavior? The law wants to know the context of the killing and the inner processes that gave rise to the killing. For instance, did the shooting occur during a hunting trip or during a bank robbery? Was the killer a policeman in a gun battle with terrorists? Was the killer drunk, hypnotized, or insane? Was the victim burglarizing the actor's home, or were the two engaged in a lover's quarrel? Was the killing premeditated, or did it occur in a fit of passion? All these factors are important to the legal system in understanding the behavior and in deciding whether the defendant ought to be punished or not, in predicting whether the defendant is a future danger to society or is a hero. If we only look at the frequency of killings by a person, we will not distinguish a Mafia hit man from a war hero, or from a heart surgeon trying to perfect a new transplant procedure. In short, the legal system is concerned about context and the inner processes that gave rise to the behavior. So also psychology should be concerned about inner processes and context.

And so what are these inner processes? What must we suppose went on in the head of someone who acts morally? This chapter proposes that there are at least four major processes, as indicated in Table 2.1: (1) interpreting the situation in terms of recognizing what actions are possible for the actor and how each course of action affects all the parties involved; (2) figuring out what one ought to do, applying moral ideals to the situation to determine the moral course of action; (3) choosing among moral and nonmoral values to decide what one actually intends to do; and (4) executing and implementing what one intends to do. Before going on to describe these four components in some detail, we will call attention to the kind of model proposed here. First, this chapter denies that moral behavior is produced by a single, unitary

TABLE 2.1.   Inner Processes Producing Behavior

Component 1

Major functions of the process: To interpret the situation in terms of how one's actions affect the welfare of others.

Exemplary research: Response to emergencies, Staub (1978, 1979) and Schwartz (1977); social cognition development, Shantz (in press) and Selman (1980); Empathy, Hoffman (1977, in press).

Cognitive-affective interactions: Drawing inferences about how the other will be affected and feeling empathy, disgust, and so on, for the other.

Component 2

Major functions: To formulate what a moral course of action would be; to identify the moral ideal in a specific situation.

Exemplary research: Cognitive-developmental, Piaget (1932/1965) and Kohlberg (1969, 1976); DIT research, Rest (1979) and Damon (1977); social psychology "norms," Berkowitz & Daniels (1963) and Schwartz (1977); post-Piagetian, Keasey (1978).

Cognitive-affective interaction: Both abstract-logical and attitudinal-valuing aspects are involved in the construction of systems of moral meaning; moral ideals are composed of both cognitive and affective elements.

Component 3

Major functions: To select among competing value outcomes of ideals, the one to act on; deciding whether or not to try to fulfill one's moral ideal.

Exemplary research: Decision-making models and factors that affect decision making, Pomazal & Jaccard (1976), Lerner (1971), Schwartz (1977), and Isen (1978); theories of moral motivation, E. Wilson (1975), Aronfreed (1968), Bandura (1977), Kohlberg (1969), Hoffman (in press), Durkheim (1925/1961), and Rawls (1971).

Cognitive-affective interactions: Calculation of relative utilities of various goals; mood influencing outlook; defensive distortion of perception; empathy impelling decisions; social understanding motivating the choice of goals.

Component 4

Major functions: To execute and implement what one intends to do.

Exemplary research: Ego strength and self-regulation, Mischel & Mischel (1976), Krebs (Note 1), and Staub (1979).

Cognitive-affective interaction: Task persistence as affected by cognitive transformation of the goal.

process. One-variable theories of morality are as untenable as one-variable theories of personality. Two people who are similar on one process need not be similar on other processes. A person who performs one process with great facility need not have great facility on other processes. Deficiency in any process can result in moral failure. Although one process might interact and influence another process, the processes ought to be distinguished from each other as performing different functions, all of which are necessary for the production of moral behavior. (Incidentally, this chapter is not firmly committed to the number 4—*four* components. Down the road it may seem useful to distinguish five processes, or seven, or whatever. We do expect, however, that the kinds of functional distinctions among the processes drawn here would be incorporated in future reformulations. Furthermore, any set of components—whatever the number—should represent the ensemble of inner processes that we regard as the necessary constituents of what it takes to behave morally.)

Second, the components represent the *processes* involved in the production of a moral act, not general *traits* of people. Assessing how a subject interprets a particular situation (Component 1) does not commit us to the view that the subject generally interprets situations in certain ways. The four components are not presented as four virtues that make up an ideal person; rather, they are the major units of analysis in tracing out how a particular course of action was produced in the context of a particular situation. This emphasis on process differs, for example, from Hogan's (1975) five-component model, which construes the components in terms of personality traits (moral knowledge, moral judgment, socialization, empathy, and autonomy). In my view, one important program of research is to account for the situational variations that cause changes in a person's processing of each component.

Third, the component model is related to existing research in providing a framework for grouping and relating existing studies. The model is not completely a priori or pure philosophical speculation, as, for instance, John Wilson's (1973) model. (Wilson's components are "phil," "emp," "gig," "dik," and "krat.") Wilson's components have been related to hardly any psychological research, as far as the author is aware. In contrast, existing psychological research is related to the components in my model, and research can be classified as providing information on one or more components, as Table 2.1 indicates under the heading "Exemplary research." Each component can be seen as raising questions to which existing research and theory provide some answers. And so the four questions corresponding to the four components are (1) How does the subject interpret the situation? (2) How does the subject define the *moral* course of action? (3) How does the subject go about choosing which valued outcome he or she will go after? and (4) How does the subject implement and follow through on his or her intention? Note that more than one theoretical approach can address the same question—for instance, both the cognitive-developmental approach and social psychology's "social norm" approach provide different answers to Component 2's question. The framework allows us to see where different approaches are addressing the same aspect of morality and where they are addressing different aspects. Note that no theoretical approach provides answers to all these questions.

Fourth, this chapter assumes that there are different affect and cognition interactions in every component. It is true, for purposes of analysis, that the cognitive or affective side of a process may be emphasized, but they are different sides of the same reality. This chapter assumes that there are no pure cognitions without affects, nor pure affects without cognitions. Furthermore, just as each component involves different cognitive processes, so also each component involves different cognitive-affective interactions—there is not just one kind of relation between cognition and affect. In fact, as a matter of personal history, I was pushed into the four-component model as I tried to make sense out of the variety of studies on cognitive-affective relations. Although each of these studies do indeed present a view of cognitive-affective relationships, the studies are not addressing the same relationship (or the same cognitions and the same affects). For instance, Hoffman (1977, in press) describes the interaction of cognition and affect in terms of how different "conceptions of the other" influence the emotion of empathy. A different kind of cognition-affect interaction is described by Kohlberg (1969) in writing about the feelings and motives that parallel cognitive structures, as both cognitions and affects are involved in a person's system of meaning. Isen and colleagues (1978) refer to yet another interaction, in describing how mood can influence memory process. Mischel and Mischel (1976) describe how cognitive reconstructions of reward objects can influence a person's willingness to persevere at tedious tasks. As Table 2.1 suggests, these different interfaces of cognitions and affects point to the necessity of positing different processes, each with distinctive cognitive and affective interfaces.

In summary, my view of the relation of behavior, cognition, and affect is that moral behavior is the manifestation and result of four inner cognitive-affective processes. Distinctive cognitions and affects are involved in each of the four processes. If we had information about all four inner processes for a given subject in a given situation, we would be able to predict behavior. Currently no study exists that simultaneously assesses all four processes and that could confirm or disconfirm my position. Indeed, anyone who can design a good study to do this deserves the Nobel Prize. A few studies do exist, however, that have assessed two components at a time (e.g., Barrett & Yarrow, 1977; Krebs, 1967), and these studies report greater predictability of behavior by taking two components simultaneously into account than by looking at only one component's predictability to behavior, one at a time.

THE FOUR COMPONENTS

Now let us consider in more detail each of the components.

Component 1

Component 1, interpreting the situation, involves imagining the possible courses of action in a situation and tracing out the consequences of action in terms of how they affect the welfare of all the parties involved.

Four findings from psychological research stand out in regard to Component 1. The first finding is that many people have great difficulty in interpreting even relatively simple situations. Research on bystander reactions to emergencies shows this. For instance, research by Staub (1978) shows that helping behavior is related to the ambiguity of the situation—if subjects are not clear about what is happening, they do not volunteer to help as much. A second finding is that striking individual differences exist among people in their sensitivity to the needs and welfare of others. For instance, this is shown in social psychological research by Schwartz (1977) on a variable he describes as "Awareness of Consequences." A third finding is that the ability to make inferences about the needs and wants of others, and about how one's actions would affect others, is a developmental phenomenon—people get better with age in being able to make inferences about others. The vast emerging field of "social cognition" is relevant here and documents this point (Shantz, in press). A fourth finding is that social situations can arouse strong feelings even before extensive cognitive encoding. Feelings can be activated before one fully understands a situation (Zajonc, 1980). For instance, Hoffman (1977) has emphasized the role of empathy in morality and views the arousal of empathy as a primary response that need not be mediated by complex cognitive operations. Hoffman's account is particularly interesting in suggesting how this primary affective response comes to interact and be modified with cognitive development to produce more complex forms of empathy. The general point here, however, is that aroused affects are part of what needs to be interpreted in a situation, and therefore part of Component 1 processing.

Component 2

Component 2 involves determining what course of action would best fulfill a moral ideal, what *ought* to be done in the situation. Two major research traditions offer descriptions of mechanisms involved in Component 2: One from social psychology postulates that *social norms* govern how a moral course of action is to be defined. Social norms are of the form "In a situation with X circumstances, a person ought to do Y." A variety of social norms have been postulated: social responsibility, equity, reciprocity, and the norm of giving. For instance, the norm of social responsibility (Berkowitz & Daniels, 1963) prescribes that if you perceive a need in another person and the other person is dependent on you, then you should help the other person. For illustration, let us apply the norm of social responsibility to Kohlberg's well-known Heinz-and-the-drug situation: Heinz should steal the drug because his wife needs the drug and cannot get it herself. According to the social norm explanation, when a person is confronted with a moral problem, he or she interprets the situation and notices a particular configuration of circumstances relevant to a particular social norm (in the example, the circumstance that someone dependent on Heinz is in need). Noticing this circumstance "activates" a social norm. So the "social norm" approach is one explanation of how people define the moral course of action in a situation. According to the social norm approach, moral *development* is a matter of acquiring a number of social norms and being set to have those norms activated by specific situations, as they arise.

The second major research tradition dealing with Component 2 is cognitive-developmental research, notably that influenced by Jean Piaget and Kohlberg. In contrast to the "social norm" approach, which focuses on the acquisition of a number of norms, the cognitive-development approach focuses on the progressive understanding of the purpose, function, and nature of social arrangements. The focus is on the rationale for establishing cooperative arrangements, particularly on how each of the participants in cooperation are reciprocating and mutually benefiting. In cooperative arrangements, the participants each benefit and incur obligations; justice is the core concept that deals with reciprocating the benefits and obligations in some balanced way. Development consists in the subject's increased awareness of the kinds of cooperative arrangements that are possible. And so, according to this view, children become first aware of fairly simple schemes of cooperation, involving only a few people who know one another through face-to-face encounters and who reciprocate in concrete, short-term exchanges. Gradually they become aware of more complicated schemes of cooperation, involving long-term, society-wide networks, institutionalized role systems, divisions of labor, and law-making and law-enforcement systems. The various schemes of cooperation (or "justice structures") are called "stages" of moral reasoning, each characterized in terms of its distinctive notion of justice, that is, progressive awareness of the possibilities and requirements for arranging cooperation among successively wider circles of participants. Each stage is viewed as an underlying *general* framework of assumptions about how people ought to act toward one another. In a specific situation, a person defines what ought to be done by assimilating the elements of the particular situation to one or another general scheme of cooperation. And so the duties of a specific actor are defined by invoking the requirements of fulfilling the cooperative arrangements of the general scheme.

For illustration, consider the Heinz dilemma again and how Kohlberg's Stage 4 might formulate a moral course of action. Stage 4, the "Law and Order Orientation," views all human interaction as taking place within an organized social system, governed by formal law, with rights and duties assigned to each role position. The general Stage 4 scheme entails that each person should do his or her job and stay within the law, expecting that other people will do the same. In this specific situation, Heinz might believe that the druggist is a scoundrel and feel desperation about helping his wife. Heinz's moral duty, however, is to stay within the law because what is involved is more than a personal transaction between Heinz and the druggist; maintenance of law and order of the entire social network is at stake. Note that in such a formulation the specific moral dilemma is assimilated into a general way of looking at social cooperation. The derivation of what is moral follows from a generalized structure that defines obligations and rights.

Although some writers regard cognitive-developmental theory in the

Piaget and Kohlberg tradition as providing a total theory of moral development, in this chapter it is regarded as an answer to the Component 2 question: How do people define what is moral in a particular situation? Reasoning about justice is no more the whole of morality than is empathy. A score from a moral judgment test does not tell us how sensitive the person is even to noticing moral problems. It does not tell us what other values may preempt or compromise one's moral ideals, nor does it tell us how well a person is able to carry through on one's moral convictions. Blasi's (1980) impressive review of the literature indicates that there is a significant link of moral judgment with behavior, nevertheless many factors besides moral judgment have to be taken into account.

Component 3

Component 3 involves deciding what one actually intends to do by selecting among competing values. Typically, a person is aware of a number of possible outcomes of different courses of action, each representing different values and activating different motives. And, it is not unusual for nonmoral values to be so strong and attractive that a person chooses a course of action that preempts or compromises the moral ideal. For instance, Damon (1977) asked young children how 10 candy bars *ought* to be distributed as rewards for making bracelets. In interviews, the children described various schemes for a fair distribution of rewards, explaining why they thought a particular distribution *ought* to be followed. When these same children *actually* were given the 10 candy bars to distribute, however, they deviated form their espoused schemes of fair distribution and instead gave *themselves* a disproportionate number of candy bars. Thus, the children's espoused moral ideals were compromised by other motives, in this case, by desire for those tasty candy bars (see Chap. 6).

Given that a person is aware of various possible courses of action in a situation, each leading to a different kind of outcome or goal, why then would a person ever choose the moral alternative, especially if it involves sacrificing some personal interest or enduring some hardship? What motivates moral behavior? A large number of answers to this question have been proposed. Some of the theories of moral motivation are briefly listed here (see Rest, in press, for more complete discussion):

1. People behave morally because evolution has bred altruism into our genetic inheritance (e.g., E. Wilson, 1975).
2. "Conscience makes cowards of us all"—that is, shame, guilt, conditioned negative affect, fear of God motivates morality (e.g., Aronfreed, 1968; Eysenck, 1976).
3. There is no special motivation to be moral; people just respond to reinforcement or modeling opportunities and "learn" social behavior (Bandura, 1977; Goldiamond, 1968).

4.   Social understanding of how cooperation functions and one's own
     stake in making it work leads to moral motivation (e.g., Dewey, 1959;
     Piaget, 1932/1965; "liberal enlightenment").
5.   Moral motivation is derived from a sense of awe and self-subjugation
     to something greater than the self—identification with a crusade, dedi-
     cation to one's country or collective, reverence for the sacred (e.g.,
     Durkheim, 1925/1961; Erikson, 1958).
6.   Empathy is the basis for altruistic motivation (e.g., Hoffman, 1977).
7.   The experience of living in just and caring communities can lead to
     understanding how cooperative communities are possible and can lead
     to moral commitment (e.g., Rawls, 1971).
8.   Concern for self-integrity and one's identity as a moral agent is what
     motivates moral action (Chaps. 6 and 7 in this book).

These eight theories about moral motivation indicate the diversity of views
on the issue. None of these views is supported by very complete or compelling research evidence at this point, and an enormous amount of work needs
to be done on this component of morality.

Component 4

Executing and implementing a plan of action involves figuring out the sequence of concrete actions, working around impediments and unexpected
difficulties, overcoming fatigue and frustration, resisting distractions and other
allurements, and not losing sight of the eventual goal. Psychologists sometimes refer to these processes as involving "ego strength" or "self-regulation
skills." Research includes that of Mischel and Mischel (1976), who have
demonstrated individual differences in "ego strength" and delay of gratification as well as self-regulation skills. Krebs (Note 1) reported that Stage 4
"Law and Order" subjects on Kohlberg's measure who were high on a measure of "ego strength" showed less cheating than Stage 4 subjects who were
low on ego strength—presumably those subjects with high ego strength had
"the strength of their convictions," whereas the Stage 4 subjects with low ego
strength had such convictions but did not act on them.

   Various other lines of research also suggest that a certain inner strength,
an ability to mobilize oneself to action, is a factor in the production of moral
behavior. In short, perseverence, resoluteness, and "strong character" characterize Component 4 processes.

FURTHER IMPLICATIONS

The four-component model is not presented as a linear decision-making
model. That is, this chapter does *not* suppose that subjects go through each
component one at a time in a certain order. Although the four components

suggest a logical sequence, each component influences the other components through feedback and feed-forward loops. A number of studies suggest the interactive nature of the components (see Table 2.2). For instance, Dienstbier and associates (1975) manipulated the interpretation of the emotion aroused in a situation (Component 1) and found differences in behavior related to that manipulation (probably due to influences in decision making, Component 3). Dienstbier further suggests that the particular ways that a person thinks of moral ideals (Component 2) influences the interpretation of aroused affect (Component 1). As another instance, Darley and Batson (1973) manipulated the ease with which a task could be carried out (time pressure in preparing and delivering a talk) and found that subjects under great time pressure were less likely to notice someone in need. In other words, subjects who were so engrossed in faithfully completing one task (highly invested in Component 4) were less attentive to detecting the needs of another person in another situation (Component 1). Overload in attending to one component decreased efficiency in another component. Also, subjects sometimes defensively reappraise the situation as the personal costs of moral action become clear (Component 3 influencing Component 1), as studies by Schwartz (1977) and Lerner (1971) indicate.

The issue of the specificity or generality of moral behavior has been much debated for some time. Considerable research has demonstrated that even seemingly trivial changes in a situation can influence behavior—for instance, changes in number of people in the vicinity, sex of the experimenter, relationships of participants, immediate prior experience, dress and attractiveness of the other participant, details of instructions to subjects, and so on. Indeed, the number of situational permutations that influence behavior has become bewilderingly large and intractable. Furthermore, some factors influence some subjects in some ways but other subjects in other ways, creating all sorts of interactions and difficulties in prediction. One possible approach to sorting out this confusion may be to classify the situational factors according to the component processes they influence. For instance, all the aspects of a situation that affect its interpretability under Component 1, interpreting the situation (see Table 2.3). The general strategy here is to attempt to catalogue situational factors in terms of how they influence each component pro-

TABLE 2.2. Exemplary Studies of Interactions among Components

1 → 2: Selman (1971, 1980)	2 + 4 → B: Krebs (Note 1)
1 → (3) → B: Dienstbier et al. (1975)	3 → 1: Lerner (1971); Schwartz (1977)
1 + 3 → B: Barrett & Yarrow (1977)	4 → 1: Darley & Bateson (1973)
2 → 1: Dienstbier et al. (1975)	1 + 2 + 3 + 4 → B: (Nobel Prize winner)

Note: Numbers represent the components. An arrow represents influence in that direction. A plus sign indicates that information from more than one component is used to predict effects on behavior.

TABLE 2.3   Situational Factors that Influence Each Component Process

Influences on Component 1

Ambiguity of people's needs, intentions, and actions

Familiarity with the situation or the people in it

Time allowed for interpretation

Degree of personal danger and susceptibility to pressure

Preoccupation with other component processes

Sheer number of elements in the situation and the embeddedness of crucial cues

Complexity in tracing out cause-effect chains

Presuppositions and prior expectations that blind a person to notice or think about certain aspects

Influences on Component 2

Factors affecting the application of particular social norms or moral ideals, or their "activation"

Delegation of responsibility to someone else

Prior conditions, promises, contracts, or expectancies that affect role responsibilities, reciprocity, or deservingness

The particular combination of moral issues involved

Preempting of one's sense of fairness by prior commitments to some ideology or code

Influences on Component 3

Factors that activate different motives other than moral motives

Mood states that influence decision making

Factors that influence estimates of costs and benefits

Factors that influence subjective estimates of the probability of certain occurrences

Factors that affect one's self-esteem and willingness to risk oneself, defensively reinterpreting the situation by blaming the victim, denying need or deservingness

Influences on Component 4

Factors that physically prevent one from carrying out a moral plan of action

Factors that distract, fatigue, or disgust a person

Cognitive transformations of the goal

Timing difficulties in managing more than one plan at a time

---

cess. By cataloguing them we begin to introduce some theoretical coherence to their seemingly limitless variety and number; then, it is hoped, we may begin to sort out how some situational variations affect certain processes of some people but not others. We might also hope to learn more about the precise nature of the constituent processes involved in the production of morality by systematically studying which situational variations affect moral processes.

The point of view advanced in this chapter has been that the production of moral behavior involves all four component processes and that deficiencies in any component can result in failure to behave morally. If a person is insensitive to the needs of others, or if a situation is too ambiguous to interpret, the person may fail to act morally (deficient in Component 1). Or a person may be deficient in formulating a moral course of action or may have simplistic and inadequate moral reasoning (Component 2). Or moral values can be compromised or preempted by other values (Component 3). Or it may be that a person has decided on a moral course of action but loses sight of the goal, is distracted, or just wears out (Component 4). Moral development entails gaining proficiency in all these component processes. It follows, then, that the goal of moral education is to promote development in functioning in all four components.

REFERENCES

Aronfreed, J. *Conduct and conscience.* New York: Academic Press, 1968.

Bandura, A. *Social learning theory.* Englewood Cliffs, N.J.: Prentice-Hall, 1977.

Barrett, D. E., & Yarrow, M. R. Prosocial behavior, social inferential ability, and assertiveness in children. *Child Development,* 1977, *48,* 475–481.

Berkowitz, L., & Daniels, L. R. Responsibility and dependency. *Journal of Abnormal and Social Psychology,* 1963, *66,* 429–436.

Blasi, A. Bridging moral cognition and moral action: A critical review of the literature. *Psychological Bulletin,* 1980, *88,* 1–45.

Damon, W. *The social world of the child.* San Francisco: Jossey-Bass, 1977.

Darley, J., & Batson, C. From Jerusalem to Jericho: A study of situational and dispositional variables in helping behavior. *Journal of Personality and Social Psychology,* 1973, *27,* 100–108.

Dewey, J. *Moral principle in education.* New York: Philosophical Library, 1959.

Dienstbier, R. A., Hillman, D., Hillman, J., Lehnhoff, J., & Valkenaar, M. C. An emotion-attribution approach to moral behavior: Interfacing cognitive and avoidance theories of moral development. *Psychological Review,* 1975, *82,* 299–315.

Durkheim, E. *Moral education: A study in the theory and application in the sociology of education.* New York: Free Press, 1961. (Originally published, 1925.)

Erikson, E. *Young man Luther.* New York: Norton, 1958.

Eysenck, H. J. The biology of morality. In T. Lickona (Ed.), *Moral development and behavior.* New York: Holt, Rinehart and Winston, 1976.

Goldiamond, I. Moral development: A functional analysis. *Psychology Today, 2*(4), Sept. 1968, pp. 31ff.

Hoffman, M. L. Empathy, its development and prosocial implications. In C. B. Keasey (Ed.), *Nebraska Symposium on Motivation* (Vol. 25). Lincoln: University of Nebraska Press, 1977.

Hoffman, M. L. Affective and cognitive processes in moral internalization. In E. T. Higgins, D. Ruble, & W. Hartup (Eds.), *Social cognition and social behavior.* New York: Cambridge University Press, in press.

Hogan, R. Moral development and the structure of personality. In D. J. DePalma & J. M. Foley (Eds.), *Moral development: Current theory and research.* Hillsdale, N.J.: Lawrence Erlbaum Associates, 1975.

Isen, A. M., Clark, M., Karp, L., & Shalker, T. E. Affect, accessibility of material in memory, and behavior: A cognitive loop? *Journal of Personality and Social Psychology,* 1978, *36,* 1–13.

Keasey, C. B. Children's developing awareness and usage of intentionality and motives. In C. B. Keasey (Ed.), *Nebraska Symposium on Motivation* (Vol. 25). Lincoln: University of Nebraska Press, 1978.

Kohlberg, L. Stage and sequence: The cognitive-developmental approach to socialization. In D. Goslin (Ed.), *Handbook of socialization theory and research.* Skokie, Ill.: Rand McNally, 1969.

Kohlberg, L. Moral stages and moralization: The cognitive-developmental approach. In T. Lickona (Ed.), *Moral development and behavior.* New York: Holt, Rinehart and Winston, 1976.

Krebs, R. L. *Some relations between moral judgment, attention, and resistance to temptation.* Unpublished doctoral dissertation, University of Chicago, 1967.

Lerner, M. J. Observer's evaluation of a victim: Justice, guilt and veridical perception. *Journal of Personality and Social Psychology,* 1971, *20,* 127–135.

Mischel, W., & Mischel, H. A cognitive social-learning approach to morality and self regulation. In T. Lickona (Ed.), *Moral development and behavior.* New York: Holt, Rinehart and Winston, 1976.

Piaget, J. *The moral judgment of the child.* (M. Gabain, trans.). New York: Free Press, 1965. (Originally published, 1932.)

Pomazal, R. J., & Jaccard, J. J. An informational approach to altruistic behavior. *Journal of Personality and Social Psychology,* 1976, *33,* 317–327.

Rawls, J. *A theory of justice.* Cambridge, Mass.: Harvard University Press, 1971.

Rest, J. R. *Development in judging moral issues.* Minneapolis: University of Minnesota Press, 1979.

Rest, J. R. Morality. In J. H. Flavell & E. M. Markman (Eds.), *Cognitive development,* volume in P. H. Mussen (Ed.), *Manual of child psychology* (4th ed.). New York: Wiley, in press.

Schwartz, S. H. Normative influences on altruism. In L. Berkowitz (Ed.), *Advances in experimental social psychology* (Vol. 10). New York: Academic Press, 1977.

Selman, R. L. The relation of role-taking to the development of moral judgment in children. *Child Development,* 1971, *42,* 79–92.

Selman, R. L. *The growth of interpersonal understanding.* New York: Academic Press, 1980.

Selman, R. L., & Jaquette, D. Stability and oscillation in interpersonal awareness: A clinical-developmental analysis. In C. B. Keasey (Ed.), *Nebraska Symposium on Motivation* (Vol. 25). Lincoln: University of Nebraska Press, 1978.

Shantz, C. U. Social cognition. In J. H. Flavell & E. M. Markman (Eds.), *Cognitive development,* volume in P. H. Mussen (Ed.), *Manual of child psychology* (4th ed.). New York: Wiley, in press.

Staub, E. *Positive social behavior and morality* (Vols. 1 and 2). New York: Academic Press, 1978, 1979.

Wilson, E. O. *Sociobiology: The new synthesis.* Cambridge, Mass.: Belknap Press of Harvard University Press, 1975.

Wilson, J. *The assessment of morality.* Rochester, Kent, England: Stanhope Press, 1973.

Zajonc, R. B. Feeling and thinking: Preferences need no inferences. *American Psychologist,* 1980, *35,* 151–175.

The Cognitive-Developmental Structural Approach

Foreword to Part Two

LAWRENCE KOHLBERG

The progression from one chapter to the next in this part represents the major themes of the book outlined in the Preface. The Colby and Kohlberg chapter, which should be read first, operates within the central traditional model and methods of structural-developmental or Piagetian psychology. The Piagetian criteria of stage—(1) progressive development; (2) invariance sequence; and (3) structured wholeness of stage—are posited for hypothetical dilemma moral reasoning, and longitudinal data are shown to fill these stage criteria. Basic to the structural-developmental model is the distinction between structural competence and actual performance in specific situations. In the Piagetian tradition, the gap between structural competence of scientific reasoning and performance in various concrete content-loaded areas or situations is treated as an issue of *décalage* or "friction," as a matter of minor theoretical importance. In the area of scientific reasoning studied by Jean Piaget, such a distinction between competence and performance and a consequent limitation of focus on the development of competence is reasonable. The Colby and Kohlberg chapter shows that it is reasonable to treat hypothetical-dilemmas reasoning in this way also. In the end, however, a cognitive-developmental theory must describe, predict, and explain moral action, not just hypothetical reasoning.

The chapter by Candee and Kohlberg relating judgment to action is more theoretically complex in its efforts to broaden the theory to include behavior as well as cognition. In order to deal more effectively with studies relating hypothetical reasoning to choice in action, the Kohlberg and Candee chapter introduces three concepts not discussed in the Colby and Kohlberg chapter.

The first is the concept of a linkage between the form or structure of a moral judgment stage and the deontic or rightness choice on dilemmas made at that stage. Stage 5 subjects using principles in judgment are found to achieve consensus of content choice on a number of dilemmas or situations, for only two principles, utility and justice, are commonly used at this stage. The second concept is that of a judgment of responsibility, a judgment correlated with stage choice but involving a further judgment of commitment to action needed to carry out a deontic judgment of rightness. This responsibility concept is used to explain the monotonic increase in consistency between deontic judgment of rightness and actual action found in the studies reported in the chapter as well as in studies reviewed by Augusto Blasi. Third is the concept of a B substage that relates to action for those below Stage 5.

Chapter 4 not only seeks to address the need for greater comprehensiveness stressed in the volume but also addresses the boundaries and connections between psychological and philosophic issues. Ultimately the definition of moral action is philosophical as well as psychological. In a spirit that attempts to be compatible with Dwight Boyd's philosophic work on moral principles (see Chap. 20), the chapter relates some moral philosophic assumptions to empirical data.

Chapter 5, by Higgins, Power, and Kohlberg, introduces a further set of concepts and a revision of methodology in order to explain theoretically phenomena of moral action or "performance." This expansion of concepts involves the effort to account for social-situational or sociological factors in moral action. To get closer to the action judgments, the authors developed a methodology of asking "real-life" school dilemmas and asking for judgments of responsibility as to what the subject would do in these situations. Marked differences between schools were found in their responsibility judgments, differences presumably due to differences in the moral atmosphere of each school as a group or community rather than simply to individual psychological attributes of the students. Schools are compared in terms of stage and phase of shared or collective norms and not simply in terms of the average behavior and judgments of individuals in each school. Taking Chapters 3, 4, and 5 together, there is a movement from an emphasis on stage as individual internal structure to a view of moral action as an interaction between features of the individual and features of the social situations.

CHAPTER 3

Invariant Sequence and Internal Consistency in Moral Judgment Stages

ANNE COLBY AND LAWRENCE KOHLBERG

This chapter presents the results of a 20-year longitudinal study of moral judgment development. The study represents an attempt to document the basic assumptions of Kohlberg's cognitive-developmental theory of moral judgment. The results of this study were interpreted as being consistent with a cognitive-developmental stage model. Subjects seemed to use a coherent structural orientation in thinking about a variety of moral dilemmas. Their thinking developed in a regular sequence of stages, neither skipping a stage nor reverting to use of a prior stage. The Standard Issue Moral Judgment Scoring System was found to be reliable and appears to be a valid measure of Kohlberg's moral judgment stages.

In this chapter we will present the results of a 20-year longitudinal study of moral development. The study represents an attempt to document the basic assumptions of Kohlberg's account of moral judgment development.

This approach to moral judgment focuses on the qualitative form of the child's moral reasoning and on developmental changes in that reasoning. Kohlberg has attempted to describe general organizational or structural features of moral judgment that can be shown to develop in a regular sequence of stages. The concept of structure implies that a consistent logic or form of reasoning can be abstracted from the content of an individual's responses to a variety of situations. It implies that moral development may be defined in terms of the qualitative reorganization of the individual's pattern of thought rather than in the learning of new content. Each new reorganization integrates within a broader perspective the insights that were achieved at lower stages. The developing child becomes better able to understand and integrate diverse points of view on a moral-conflict situation and to take more of the relevant situational factors into account. In this sense, each stage presupposes the understanding gained at previous stages. As a result, each stage provides a more adequate way of making and justifying moral judgments. The order in which the stages develop is said to be the same in each individual not because the stages are innate but because of the underlying logic of the sequence.

Kohlberg has hypothesized that the developmental levels that he has described constitute stages in a strict Piagetian sense. First, the stage concept implies that under normal environmental conditions developmental change will always be upward in direction. Second, it implies that there will be no stage skipping. The individual must pass through each stage in order to reach the next stage in the sequence. Third, the stage concept implies that individual's thinking will be at a single dominant stage across varying content, although use of the stage adjacent to the dominant stage may also be expected. The results of previous studies of moral judgment have not completely supported the strong stage claim, as critics like Kurtines and Greif (1974) have pointed out. In part, the ambiguity in some of these findings has been due to the limited reliability of Kohlberg's 1958 method of interviewing and scoring moral stage. The longitudinal data published by Holstein (1976), Kuhn (1976), and White, Bushnell, and Regnemer (1978) have shown anomalies in stage sequence. An earlier analysis of the first 10 years of Kohlberg's data also showed a substantial number of sequence anomalies (Kohlberg & Kramer, 1969; Kramer, 1968). It has not been clear whether these anomalies repesent a failure of fit of the strict stage model to moral judgment development, whether they have represented confusions in the conceptual definitions of the stages, or problems in the reliability or validity of the measure. The study described here is an attempt to address the validity of the stage model as it applies to longitudinal data and the associated problems of stage definition and measurement.

The study includes a reanalysis of Kohlberg's 1956–1968 data along with analysis of the subsequent data collected from the same subjects from 1968 through 1976. The current analysis involved the application of a new scoring method, Standard Issue Scoring, based on a substantially revised account of the stages. One especially noteworthy change in moral judgment stage scoring is the omission of Stage 6 from the current manual. Stage 6 was omitted partly because none of the interviews in the longitudinal sample seemed intuitively to be Stage 6 and partly because the standard dilemmas are not ideal for differentiating between Stages 5 and 6. The question of whether Stage 6 should be included as a natural psychological stage in the moral development sequence will remain unresolved until research using more appropriate moral dilemmas and interviewing techniques is conducted with a special sample of people likely to have developed beyond Stage 5.

Before turning to the study, let us consider briefly the development of the coding scheme. In the early 1970s Kohlberg and his colleagues began to redefine the central features of the moral judgment stages and to construct a more adequate assessment instrument. Seven of the longitudinal cases were used as the data base for this redefinition. It was expected that this process would yield a more precise and accurate picture of moral judgment development than did the earlier stage descriptions. For example, it was expected that when Kohlberg's remaining longitudinal cases were analyzed using the revised stage criteria, the data would more closely fit the core assumptions of cognitive-development theory than they did in Kramer's (1968) original analysis. Because the longitudinal interviews used to validate the reformulations were kept entirely separate from those used to generate them, the revision process avoided circularity by allowing a test of prediction to data other than those used to generate the scoring system.

The early scoring systems, Sentence Rating and Global Story Rating, were based on what was essentially a content analysis. That is, both systems focused on what concerns a subject brought to bear in resolving a dilemma (for example, a concern for love between a husband and wife, the importance of obeying the law, a fear of punishment) and treated those concerns as indicators of developmental stage. These scoring systems yielded enough sequence anomalies in the 1968 analysis of Kohlberg's longitudinal data to warrant substantial revision of the stage definitions. This revision process resulted in a clearer differentiation of moral judgment structure from content; that is, more formal or abstract features of moral judgment were identified and formed the core of the new stage conceptions.

The basic developmental concept underlying the revised stage sequence is level of sociomoral perspective, the characteristic point of view from which the individual formulates moral judgments. In regard to level of sociomoral perspective, we interpret the perspective-taking underlying the moral stages as intrinsically moral in nature rather than as a logical or social-cognitive structure applied to the moral domain. In this interpretation we follow Turiel (Note 1) and Damon (1983) in their contention that there are many types of perspective-taking, each of which develops somewhat separately as a result of experience in a particular domain. In this view, spatial, social, and moral prespective-taking are fundamentally different porcesses rather than applications of a single general structure to different content areas. That is, the form of spatial perspective-taking is intrinsically spatial, not moral or social. The form of moral perspective-taking, on the other hand, is intrinsically moral.

According to this formulation, the most basic and general defining feature of moral judgment development is development through the levels of sociomoral perspective. These levels provide a general organization of moral judgment and serve to inform and unite other more specific moral concepts, such as the nature of the morally right or good, moral reciprocity, rules, rights, obligation or duty, fairness, and welfare consequences, and moral values such as obedience to authority, preservation of human life, and maintenance of contracts and affectional relations. Within each of these specific moral concepts, the form of developmental change is to some extent specific to the nature of the particular concept in question. The general moral perspective can be seen to underlie its more specific manifestations, however. The current scoring system, Standard Issue Scoring, is based on the stage redefinitions that center on the idea of sociomoral perspective. Its aims were to achieve greater validity through the redefinition of structure and content, to achieve greater objectivity and reliability in scoring by specifying clear and concrete stage criteria, and to define the developmental sequences of the specific "moral concepts" within each stage as well as the sequence of the global or general stage structures.

The design of the original cross-sectional study, which was later followed up longitudinally, included three variables: age, social class, and sociometric status. Unfortunately, gender was not a variable. All the subjects were boys. These originally cross-sectional subjects, stratified by three levels of age (10, 13, and 16) and two levels of social class and sociometric status, were followed longitudinally at regular 3–4-year intervals for 20 years. There were 53 boys in the longitudinal study.

At each testing time subjects were interviewed on the nine hypothetical moral dilemmas making up the three forms of Kohlberg's moral judgment interview: Forms A, B, and C. Interviews were scored according to the Standard Issue Scoring Manual. Because the number of interviews to be scored was so large, a different rater scored each of the three forms, A, B, and C. Scoring of all dilemmas was done blind; that is, raters coded the responses to (or scores on) other dilemmas at the same testing time or responses to (or scores on) any of the dilemmas at other testing times.

RELIABILITY

Reliability data of several types were compiled for Standard Issue Scoring. The results indicate that the instrument is highly reliable.

Correlation coefficients for test-retest reliability are in the high 90s. Because the correlations could be very high without much absolute agreement between scores at Time 1 and Time 2, we have also calculated percentage agreement figures.

On test-retest interviews conducted about a month apart almost all subjects received scores within one-third stage of each other. About three quarters received identical scores on the two interviews when a 9-point scale is used, and between one-half and two-thirds receive identical scores with a more finely differentiated 13-point scale. When scores do change from Time 1 to Time 2, the change is as likely to be negative as positive and therefore cannot be attributed to a practice effect. There were no age or sex differences in test-retest stability.

In regard to interrater reliability, percentage agreement figures were very similar to the percentage agreement figures for test-retest reliability. The correlation coefficients for interrater reliability were in the high 90s.

Percentage agreement between forms was comparable to test-retest and interrater reliability: 100% of the interviews were given scores with one-third stage of each other for the two forms; three-quarters received identical scores for the different forms using a 9-category system; and two-thirds received identical scores for the different forms using a 13-category system. The correlations between moral maturity scores (MMS) for alternate form reliability were in the mid-to-high 90s.

VALIDITY

As we have argued elsewhere (Colby, 1978; Kohlberg, 1980), the appropriate validity concept for a developmental measure such as Standard Issue Scoring is construct validity, not prediction to an external criterion. For a measure of moral judgment stage, the two most critical empirical criteria of construct validity correspond to the two most central theoretical assumptions of the stage construct. They are invariance of stage sequence and "structural wholeness" or internal consistency (generality of stage usage across moral issues or dilemmas). The results to be presented here confirm both invariant sequence and internal consistency. Among other things, we interpret "construct validity" to mean the fit of the data obtained by means of the test to primary components of its theoretical definition. The primary theoretical definition of structural moral development is that of an organization passing through invariant sequential stages. In other words, positive results of the longitudinal analysis support not only the theoretical assumptions but also the validity of the measure. Of course, negative results could arise from either a faulty theory, a faulty test, or both.

RESULTS

Invariant Stage Sequence

According to our theoretical assumptions, the developmental sequence should be identical in every individual studied. Except under extreme circumstances, there should be no deviations from perfect sequentiality. Because we have not constructed an error-free measure, however, some discrepant scores must be expected to result from measurement error. A reasonable estimate of the number of such deviations attributable to measurement error can be derived from analysis of test-retest reliability data. We can assume that virtually none of our subjects will have changed in stage of moral judgment within the short test-retest interval. Any differences between scores at Times 1 and 2 can be attributed to measurement error. Therefore, our analysis of longitudinal sequence involved a comparison of the frequency of sequence deviations (or downward stage movement) in the longitudinal data with the frequency of negative Time 1–Time 2 changes in our test-retest data. (Of course, this comparison depends on a psychometrically adequate level of test-retest reliability.) If sequence deviations exceed test-retest instability, we cannot consider our data to support the invariant sequence assumption. A comparison with downward stage change in test-retest data for Forms A and B indicates that in every case the test-retest reversals are well over twice as great as the longitudinal reversals. Thus, it seems reasonable to attribute the violations of longitudinal sequence to measurement error. The frequency of sequence violations was 4% in the longitudinal data.

In addition to predicting that at no time will a subject move downward in the developmental sequence, cognitive-developmental theory holds that each stage is a prerequisite for those that follow it. The concept of invariant stage sequence implies that no stage will be omitted as development proceeds. Because within a four-year interval a subject might enter and leave a stage, we could not necessarily expect our data to corroborate this aspect of sequentiality. Fortunately, however, the interval seems to have been short enough in relation to our subjects' rates of development to capture each stage in the sequence for each subject. In fact, in no case on any form of the interview did a subject reach a stage in the sequence without having gone through each preceding stage. For the most part, changes across the four-year intervals were less than a full stage.

Internal Consistency

According to cognitive-developmental theory, the logic of each stage forms "a structured whole." In line with this assumption, one would expect to find a high degree of internal consistency in stage scores assigned, at least within those units that are conceptually and psychologically coherent. The data support this assumption as clearly as they do that of invariant sequence.

One indication of degree of internal consistency in moral judgment is provided by distributions for each subject of proportion of reasoning scored at each of the five stages. Our analysis of these distributions showed that most interviews received all of their scores at either a single stage or at two adjacent stages. The mean percentage of reasoning at the individual's modal stage was 68% for Form A, 72% for Form B, 69% for Form C, and 67% for Forms A, B, and C combined. The mean percentage of reasoning at the subject's two most frequently used stages (always adjacent) was 98% for Form A, 97% for Form B, 99% for Form C, and 99% for Forms A, B, and C combined. (It should be noted that there are three dilemmas per form and that each dilemma was scored without knowledge of responses to the other dilemmas, so these figures cannot be an artifact of scorer bias.)

FACTOR ANALYSES

Theoretical expectations lead us to believe that moral judgment development is a single general domain cutting across verbal dilemmas and issues. To examine this hypothesis further, a factor analysis of scores on the 18 issues across the nine dilemmas was performed. In summary, for individual age groups and for the sample as a whole, no more than one interpretable factor emerged. In all cases, the proportion of variance accounted for by the first factor far exceeded those of succeeding factors. This implies that moral judgment as measured by Standard Interview Forms A, B, and C and scored using Standard Issue Scoring is a single, general domain.

RELATION OF MORAL JUDGMENT STAGE TO AGE

As one would expect of a developmental variable, our data show a clear relationship between age and moral judgment stage. The correlation between age and MMS was .78. With regard to age norms in our sample, the interviews of most 10-year-olds were scored at Stage 1/2 or 2; a few were scored at 2/3. Most early adolescents (13–14) were 2/3, although some were Stage 2 or 3. Almost half of the late adolescents were scored as Stage 3, about one-quarter had begun the transition to Stage 4, and a little less than one-fifth were still in transition from Stage 2 to Stage 3. Youths in their early 20s were most likely to be in transition between Stages 3 and 4 or to be still solidly at Stage 3. About one-fifth of these subjects had completed the transition to Stage 4. Most subjects from the mid-20s through the mid-30s were scored as Stage 3/4 mixtures (or transitionals), with decreasing numbers at Stage 3 and increasing numbers at consolidated Stage 4. Subjects scored as postconventional (4/5 or 5) represent about one-eighth to one-sixth of the sample from the mid-20s on.

One important issue raised by the difference between this analysis and Kramer's (1968) earlier analysis is the question of adulthood stages. In light of the emergence of Stages 5 and 6 in adolescence in their analysis, Kohlberg and Kramer (1969) concluded that "there was no new way of thinking about the moral situations that was found in adulthood and not found in adolescence" (p. 105). Our interpretation of their finding is that the early scoring systems could not discriminate properly among superficially similar moral judgments at Stages 3, 4, and 5. This meant that when "true Stage 5" began to emerge in early adulthood, it was not recognized as a qualitatively new form of reasoning. We can now differentiate principled reasoning from superficially similar conventional reasoning, and we no longer see Stage 5 being used in junior high or high school. This means that there *is* a new stage in adulthood and that many of our subjects continued to develop in their 20s and 30s, rather than reaching a ceiling in mid-adolescence. This result is intuitively appealing, for 30-year-olds often do seem to be more sophisticated in their moral judgment than do 16-year-olds. It does, however, raise the question of whether Stage 5 is a "naturally developing" stage in the strict Piagetian sense (cf. Gibbs, 1979).

THE STAGE MODEL

Our data seem to provide strong support for the strict Piagetian stage model of development. With regard to the criterion of "structured wholeness" or internal consistency, we found that the great majority of our interviews were scored at only one moral judgment stage or at most at two adjacent stages. The "structured wholeness" assumption was also supported by the high degree of alternate form and test-retest reliability, the high Cronbach's alpha, and the results of factor analyses of issue scores.

As noted earlier, the factor analyses indicate that there was a single factor of general moral level across the domain of dilemmas and issues. The absence of issue or dilemma factors along with the absence of scatter across more than two adjacent stages seems to indicate that we have succeeded in defining a coherent moral domain united by a single underlying organizational structure. This position contrasts with that taken by Damon (1977), who argues that, at least in young children, the moral domain is broken down into a number of issues or dimensions, each with its own unique structure. The two moral issues on which Damon has focused are authority and distributive justice. Although his research does not use Kohlberg's hypothetical dilemmas, it is clear that Kohlberg's dilemmas do involve both authority and distributive justice. If Damon's interpretation of the moral issues as independently organized were true at the age level addressed by our study, the factor analysis would have resulted in multiple factors rather than in a single general factor of moral stage that cuts across the content of the dilemmas.

This high degree of structural coherence within each interview leads to a relatively saltatory picture of development if we compare interviews across time for any single individual. Developmental change in any given three-year period seems to involve predominantly an increase in the next higher stage of reasoning along with a simultaneous decrease in the lower stage. This means that the subject is most often in transition between two adjacent stages, has given up using all earlier stages, and uses no reasoning more than one stage above his or her modal stage. It contrasts with a model in which the distribution of a subject's reasoning extends across all five stages and in which development involves the gradual increase in usage of the higher stages along with decreases (but not decrease to zero) in use of lower stages. Kohlberg's early results based on the Sentence Rating method may have appeared to support this latter model, but we now interpret those results as artifactual, that is, due to inappropriate definition of the scoring unit and a confusion between moral judgment content and structure.

Our results also support the Piagetian stage model's assumption of invariant developmental sequence. With a few exceptions that can be attributed to scoring error, each of our subjects proceeded through the stages in the prescribed order, neither skipping stages nor regressing to an earlier level once a later stage had been attained.

This stage model of development has recently been criticized—in the cognitive domain by Flavell (1971) and, more directly, in the moral judgment domain by Rest (1979). Rest agrees with Kohlberg that qualitatively different forms of moral judgment can be identified and that development involves the increasing use of more advanced or sophisticated types and the decreasing use of less sophisticated types. He disagrees, however, wtih our claim that development proceeds through a stepwise sequence of internally consistent stages. He holds instead that individuals simultaneously use reasoning of many types and that an adequate description of an individual's moral judgment must include a quantitative account of the proportion of each type rather than a global stage designation for the individual. He interprets our finding of internal consistency as a methodological artifact and points to his own results with the Defining Issues Test (DIT) as consistent with a more complex model of development.

One interpretation of the discrepancy between Rest's results and our own derives from the fact that the DIT is measuring comprehension and preference of moral judgments made by others, whereas the Standard Issue System is measuring an individual's spontaneous production of moral judgments in response to very open-ended questions. What we are suggesting is that the development of moral judgment as a whole (including comprehension and preference as well as spontaneous production) may be too broad a scope for what Rest calls the "simple stage model." It may be the case that development of moral judgment comprehension and preference does not follow a stagelike pattern but that spontaneous production does so when assessment conditions pull for the subject's competence.

This circumstance would mean that the developing individual has one basic framework for resolving moral dilemmas and justifying those resolutions. This framework has some coherence for the individual, and it undergoes developmental transformation, hierarchically integrates the insights from lower levels, and so on. On the other hand, other aspects of moral development such as the comprehension of judgments made by others may not be stagelike in this sense. In fact, given our assumptions, there is little reason to expect that subjects will comprehend statements at only one stage (or at two adjacent stages). Rather, they can be expected to comprehend all stages below their own as well as possibly a stage or two above their own. Thus, we would not characterize the development of moral judgment comprehension as following a stagelike sequence. Preference for moral judgments made by others is somewhat more problematic. According to a simple stage model, how would one explain the endorsement of judgments that represent stages below one's own level of spontaneous production? One possible explanation derives from the assumption of hierarchical integration. That is, whereas the stage as a whole may undergo transformation as the individual develops, many of the insights achieved at the lower stages remain valid from the higher stage perspective, although they are now imbedded in a more complex and sophisticated position. For example, the Stage 3 judgment that "you ought to keep a promise because the person you promised trusts you" would be endorsed or agreed to by individuals who reason predominantly at Stages 4 and 5 as well as at Stage 3. The difference is that at the higher stages one's conception of trust and reasons for its importance have developed beyond what is available at Stage 3.

Another consideration with regard to Rest's preference data is methodological. When subjects endorse an item on the DIT, it is not clear how they understand the item. The Standard Issue Moral Judgment Interview involves probing for elaboration and clarification and pooling all responses to the dilemmas that refer to a single idea (as defined by norm and element). This system will naturally lead to greater internal consistency than will assigning a score for each unelaborated statement the subject judges to have some validity. We do not interpret our finding as an artifact. It is true that according to Standard Issue Scoring rules, an interview cannot receive more than one stage (or stage transition) score for a single dilemma issue norm element intersection. Scores at all five stages, however, may be assigned to a single issue, dilemma, or interview if interview-manual matches at those stages occur. In fact, such variance does not occur in our data even though the nine dilemmas were scored independently and by three different raters. We agree with Rest that moral judgment comprehension and preference are important aspects of moral development that are separable from spontaneous moral judgment production and that a full developmental account of an individual's moral judgment requires scores on all those aspects as well as many others. We feel, however, that a careful look at our methods and data should convince the reader of the validity of the Piagetian stage model for describing the development of spontaneous moral judgment at least within the limits of our instrument and sample.

In general, then, we interpret the results of this study as consistent with cognitive-developmental theory, in particular as consistent with a stage model of development. The results in relation to moral judgment compare favorably with longitudinal studies of the stage model in purely cognitive development (Kohn, 1969). Our subjects did seem to use a coherent structural orientation in thinking about a variety of moral dilemmas. Their thinking developed in a regular way up the stage sequence, neither skipping stages nor reverting to use of a prior stage. Our results also serve to validate the moral judgment stages as operationally defined in Standard Issue Scoring and to indicate that the Standard Issue System is a reliable and valid measure of moral judgment.

REFERENCES

Colby, A. Evolution of a moral-developmental theory. In W. Damon (Ed.), *New directions for child development: Moral development* (Vol. 2). San Francisco: Jossey-Bass, 1978.

Damon, W. *The social world of the child.* San Francisco: Jossey-Bass, 1977.

Damon, W. *Social development from childhood through adolescence.* New York: Norton, 1983.

Flavell, J. J. Stage-related properties of cognitive development. *Cognitive Psychology,* 1971, *2,* 521–543.

Gibbs, J. Kohlberg's moral stage theory: A Piagetian revision. *Human Development,* 1979, *22,* 89–112.

Holstein, C. Irreversible, stepwise sequence in the development of moral judgement: A longitudinal study of males and females. *Child Development,* 1976, *47,* 51–61.

Kohlberg, L. *The meaning and measurement of moral development.* Worcester, Mass.: Clark University Press, 1980.

Kohlberg, L., & Kramer, R. Continuities and discontinuities in childhood and adult moral development. *Human Development,* 1969, *12,* 93–120.

Kohn, N. *Performance of Negro children of varying social class background on Piagetian tasks.* Unpublished doctoral dissertation, University of Chicago, 1969.

Kramer, R. *Moral development in young adulthood.* Unpublished doctoral dissertation, University of Chicago, 1968.

Kuhn, D. Short-term longitudinal evidence for the sequentiality of Kohlberg's early stages of moral judgment. *Developmental Psychology,* 1976, *12*(2), 162–166.

Kurtines, W., & Greif, E. The development of moral thought: Review and evaluation of Kohlberg's approach. *Psychological Bulletin,* 1974, *81*(8), 453–470.

Rest, J. *Development in judging moral issues.* Minneapolis: University of Minnesota Press, 1979.

White, C. B., Bushnell, N., & Regnemer, J. L. Moral development in Bahamian school children: A three-year examination of Kohlberg's stages of moral development. *Developmental Psychology,* 1978, *14,* 58–65.

REFERENCE NOTE

1. Turiel, E. *Social-cognitive development: Domains and categories.* Paper presented at the plenary session of the Ninth Annual Symposium of the Jean Piaget Society, Philadelphia, 1979.

CHAPTER 4

The Relationship of Moral Judgment to Moral Action

LAWRENCE KOHLBERG AND DANIEL CANDEE

A model of the relationship between moral judgment and moral action that emphasizes the mediating judgments of deontic choice and responsibility is proposed. A deontic judgment refers to a judgment of what is morally right. A judgment of responsibility is a commitment to act on one's deontic judgment. Three studies that indicate a monotonic relationship between stage of moral reasoning and the performance of moral action are reviewed. Analysis of these situations supports the proposition that the relationship is due in some cases to an increase in judgments of responsibility at higher stages and in other cases to both this phenomenon and to the increased likelihood that subjects at each higher stage will make the Stage 5 deontic choice. Moral action among lower-stage subjects is explained by the construct of substage. Reasoning at the B substage of any structural moral stage approximates formal principles that are fully articulated only at Stage 5. For this reason, the behavior of subjects at Stages 3B and 4B often resembles the behavior of subjects at Stage 5.

A comprehensive review of studies relating moral judgment to moral action (Blasi, 1980) reveals that in the clear majority of studies using Kohlberg's measure of moral reasoning there is a correlation between relatively high moral judgment and what is commonly considered to be moral behavior, including honesty, resistance to temptation, and altruism. Yet despite the correlations, we have had, until recently, little theoretical understanding of why or how moral judgment and moral action are related. In this chapter we will discuss three of these studies in order to outline some theoretical relationships between moral judgment and moral action.

A longer version of this chapter appears in Kohlberg, *Essays in Moral Development*, vol. 2, *The Psychology of Moral Development* (New York: Harper & Row, 1983).

ONE-TRACK VERSUS TWO-TRACK PROCESS

Before presenting data, we will clarify what we consider to be the most important conceptual issues. One central question is engaged in Brown and Herrnstein's 1975 psychology text. These authors contrast the findings of Kohlberg-type studies of moral reasoning with the findings of social psychology studies done by Stanley Milgram, Philip Zimbardo, and Bibb Latané. When viewed together, these studies suggest that under suitable institutional and situational pressures undergraduates and adults act immorally despite their demonstrated capacity for at least conventional moral thought. Brown and Herrnstein are therefore led to call the relation of moral judgment to moral action a paradox. They express the paradox as follows:

> This is a chapter about a paradox. Students of the development of moral reasoning in children and young people have found that a great majority attains a conventional "law and order" morality, which involves obeying the laws and trying to treat people decently. In the same research period, students of social psychology have outdone one another in discovering that in certain circumstances respectable young people are capable of deceitful conformity, vandalism, and indifference to life-and-death problems of strangers who ask for help, are capable even of endangering the lives of others. For the most part, the subjects in the developmental studies and in the social psychological studies were drawn from the same population—American young people, especially college students. Therein lies the paradox.
>
> The two kinds of psychologists—developmental and social—seldom read each other's work, and since their studies are described in different courses, the paradox has largely gone unnoticed. But if a young person believes in being lawful and decent, how can he sometimes lie, destroy property, ignore a threatened stranger, and be willing to endanger another's life?
>
> Actually, there is no paradox unless you make a certain assumption. You must assume that the way people think about moral issues determines the way they act. You must believe act and thought are normally in harmony. If you do not, then there is neither paradox nor even surprise in someone talking on the high road and acting on the low road. (p. 289)

Brown and Herrnstein resolve the paradox by assuming a two-track theory of moral learning and development. In their view, moral judgment develops according to Piagetian principles of cognitive-moral conflict and sequential stage reorganizations. In contrast, moral action develops (or is learned) through some other process, possibly the laws of situational social learning and reinforcement discussed by a variety of social learning theories.

In contrast, following Jean Piaget, we see the development of moral judgment as a single-track process. In this view, moral judgment arises out of moral action itself, although there is no single causal direction. A new stage of moral judgment may guide new behavior, whereas a new action involving conflict and choice may lead one to construct a new stage of moral judgment.

The important "one-track" assumption made by Piaget does not imply that the moral judgment a child gives in a theoretical, hypothetical, or verbal dilemma is always the same in content or in stage structure as that which the child would give making a practical moral judgment. "Verbal morality appears whenever the child is called upon to judge other people's action that do not interest him directly or force him to give voice to general principles independent of his actual deeds" (Piaget, 1932, p. 171). In contrast, practical morality is "effective moral thought which leads the child to form such moral judgments as will guide him in each particular case." Such judgment represents "the child's true thought, much deeper than his verbal beliefs and somewhere below the level of formulation." "A theoretical moral problem is further removed from the child's moral practice than is an intellectual problem from his logical practice" (ibid., p. 108).

In making this distinction, Piaget is not opting for a two-track process of moral development; rather, he is arguing that a child's theoretical morality may require a reflective *"prise de conscience"* of a moral structure existing at the action level but not yet made self-conscious. If this *"prise de conscience"* has not yet occurred, the child's theoretical judgment may be only verbal and inconsistent with his or her actual practical decisions. The Piagetian one-track model does not assert the simple hypothesis that reflective moral reasoning in a hypothetical dilemma is invariably reflected in, or is a cause of, real-life moral action. It only implies that the process of moral development is a single process whether looked at from the side of development of reasoning on hypothetical dilemmas or from the side of the development of moral action. In this chapter we will elaborate the unidirectional version of the one-track model. In this model a general stage of moral judgment is applied to a particular dilemma facing the subject. The stage generates a judgment of what action is right in a particular situation, a choice that we will show is increasingly likely to be acted on at higher moral stages.

THE DEFINITION OF MORAL ACTION

The next conceptual question we ask concerns the definition of moral action. Can an act be considered moral independently of the actor's thoughts about that action? For most moral philosophers or those who analyze moral language, moral judgment competence is necessary if not sufficient for moral action. Before an act may be considered moral, the actor's reasons or motives must be examined. Socrates asks, "When is diving in a well an act of moral courage and when of foolhardiness?" If someone jumps into the Charles River to rescue a drowning person but the reason is to get a reward, is the action morally commendable or not?

Kleinberger (1982), a philosopher, identifies three types of ethical theory in relation to this question. The first type is the rationalist type, an ethic of pure intention, of which he takes Immanuel Kant and Kohlberg as representatives. This type holds moral reason as necessary and sufficient for moral action. The second is the naturalistic type, a responsibility ethic, of which he takes Aristotle and John Dewey as representatives. It holds moral reasoning as necessary but not sufficient for action. The third type is social behavioristic. Of this type, Kleinberger (1982) says:

> Since philosophers have an occupational bias in favor of reflective morality there are hardly any philosophic theories of ethics which hold overt behavior in accordance with accepted moral norms to be a sufficient condition for the morality of an act or agent. But common sense tends to make moral judgments according to such an implicit conception. Not only the man in the street seems to adopt that position but so do many social and behavioral scientists including Aronfreed, Bandura, Eysenck, and Havighurst and Taba. (p. 149)

In this view, morality can be determined without reference to the actor's thought.

In our opinion, the inability of Hartshorne's and May's (1928–1930) monumental studies to establish the proposition that such virtues as honesty and service are empirically demonstrable habits lay in their socially behavioristic approach to defining moral action. Although Hartshorne and May believed in the commonsense assumption that there are internal determinants of moral behavior, their definition of moral acts ignored judgments that might have been made by the participants in their experiments. Moral conduct was defined only by the frequency and amount of such behavior as cheating, not by the subject's own judgment of whether that particular act was wrong in a given situation.

Hartshorne and May expected to demonstrate the existence of moral character by the following hypotheses: (1) adolescents could be divided into honest and dishonest types; (2) adolescents who cheated in some situations were likely to cheat in others; and (3) an individual's moral behavior could be predicted from his or her verbal report of valuing a high standard of honesty and his or her knowledge of conventional norms of honesty.

Despite an elaborate series of studies, Hartshorne's and May's hypotheses were not borne out. Their results showed that adolescents could not be divided into honest and dishonest types. Cheating behavior was not distributed in a bimodal fashion but rather was distributed in a normal bell curve around a mean of moderate cheating. Further, they found that cheating on one test situation did not predict well to cheating in other situations. The correlations between different tests of honesty were low. Insofar as there was any order among tasks it was in terms of riskiness. Tasks where the degree of detection was perceived as high elicited less cheating. Thirdly, there was only a low correlation between having high standards of honesty as reported verbally and honest behavior in the experimental tasks. In our opinion, the Hartshorne and May studies indicated that one cannot define and study moral action by a purely behavioral approach. Moral actions involve an internal moral cognition or moral judgment component that must be directly assessed as part of the definition of an action as moral.

RELATIVISM VERSUS UNIVERSALITY

Another philosophic issue in the study of moral action is that of relativism versus universality in the standard used to judge an action as moral. A modern definition of the social or culturally relativistic position is given by Berkowitz (1964): "Moral values are evaluations of actions generally believed by members of a given society to be either 'right' or 'wrong'" (p. 44).

Hartshorne and May, like Berkowitz, started with an assumption of social relativism. They could as easily have started with an individually relativistic definition of moral action. In fact, the behavior of Hartshorne and May themselves was consistent with the assumption of individual relativism. They cheated or lied to children about their tests and its purpose, just as children cheated them. They made the judgment, however, that such dishonesty was worthwhile to further scientific knowledge about character.

This raises the whole philosophic issue as to what is a morally right action. Was sitting in at the University of California at Berkeley during the 1964 free speech controversy right or wrong? As we shall see, free speech proponents thought it morally right, a courageous protection of basic rights, and the university chancellor, the governor, and many others thought it was wrong. Another study we shall discuss, the Milgram (1974) experiment, does not seem to require an assumption of individualistic relativism. Almost everyone polled in a hypothetical form of the situation said that it was wrong to administer severe electric shocks to the victim. Can we establish standards by which to determine the morality of actions?

MORAL CONSISTENCY OR RESPONSIBILITY APPROACH

There seem to be two approaches that address the issue of what is a morally right action. The first is consistent with individual relativism. It says that not we the psychologists but the subject himself or herself should decide whether the act is right or wrong. Moral action is action consistent with the content of moral judgment, whatever that be. We shall call this consistency idea of moral action the idea of "moral responsibility." As a personality attribute, responsibility denotes first a concern for, and acceptance of, the consequences of one's actions. Second, it denotes a consistency between what one says one should or would do and what one actually does. It is dependability or follow-through in action of one's verbal moral commitments and judgments. We shall claim that persons at each higher stage of moral reasoning are more likely to act responsibility, that is, to act in accord with choices about situations that they judged to be right when they were somewhat removed from the situation itself.

In regard to responsibility, we hypothesize that there are two distinguishable but related modes or kinds of moral judgment central to moral action. The first kind or mode of moral thought is deontic. According to Frankena's

(1963) textbook, a deontic judgment is a judgment that an act is right or obligatory. Deontic judgments typically derive from a rule or a principle. Application of Kant's justice principle, the categorical imperative, or J. S. Mill's utilitarian principle of the greatest good would be examples of deontic judgments. In contrast, judgments of responsibility include an element that Frankena calls "aretaic," "a judgment of the morally good, bad, responsible or blameworthy" (p. 3). Following Galon (1980), a deontic judgment may be seen as a first-order judgment of rightness, and responsibility as a second-order affirmation of the will to act in terms of that judgment. Deontic judgments are propositional deductions from a stage or principle, whereas responsibility judgments are affirmations of a choosing will for Galon. Responsibility judgments answer not only the question, Why is X right? but answer, Why me? Why must I do X?. Following Blasi (1983, in press), "Moral judgments, before leading to action, are at times processed through a second set of rules or criteria, the criteria of responsibility. The function of a responsibility judgment is to determine to what extent that which is morally good or right is also strictly necessary for the self." According to Blasi, "The criteria used to arrive at responsibility judgments are related to one's self definition or the organization of the self. The transition from a judgment of responsibility to action is supported by the tendency toward self-consistency." "Following an action inconsistent with one's judgment of responsibility, guilt is experienced as an emotional response to the inconsistency within the self." To clarify the suggestions we take from Galon and Blasi, we might say that moral judgments of real situations go through two phases. The first phase is a judgment of rightness. The second phase is a judgment of responsibility, of the self's accountability to perform the right action, to "follow through."

Judgments of responsibility, however, may not always be preceded by a deontic judgment of rightness. This is made apparent by the research and theorizing of Gilligan (1982), who studied women's reasoning and judgments about a real decision of abortion. Often women made a judgment of responsibility without making a deontic judgment of rightness. Gilligan contrasts two orientations to moral judgment, one "an ethic of care and responsibility" and the other "an ethic of justice." Although we do not agree with Gilligan's proposition that there are two independent moralities, one of responsibility and care and one of rules and justice, we do agree that judgments of moral responsibility may be made without making judgments of principles or of justice. This circumstance may be true when acts of moral sacrifice are made for children, family, and friends, that is, in "judgments of special obligation." It may also be true of altruism toward strangers going beyond the demands of rights and justice and of moral actions that benefit a group, community, or institution, acts of social responsibility that go beyond the requirements of rights, or principles.

The action situations we will consider in this chapter, however, are actions engaging a deontic judgment of rightness or justice. A basic theoretical hypothesis we make in relation to such studies is that there is a monotonic increase in making a judgment of responsibility consistent with the deontic judgment of rightness as we move from stage to stage. This in turn means that there is a monotonic increase in the proportion of subjects acting "morally" or consistently with their deontic judgment made outside the situation. We shall cite two studies showing this monotonic trend toward moral consistency. The first, a study by Helkema (Note 1), shows that there is a monotonic increase in consistency between a deontic judgment of "should" and a verbal judgment of responsibility in a hypothetical dilemma, the Heinz dilemma. The second study, by McNamee (1978), shows that there is a monotonic increase, stage by stage, in actions consistent with what subjects at most stages said they should do, their deontic judgment.

Table 4.1, taken from Helkema, shows that although there is some increase by stage in the first-column deontic judgment (i.e., Heinz should steal), there is a much more dramatic increase by stage in the third-column judgment, "Heinz is responsible if his wife should die." The fourth column also shows an increase in the proportion of subjects making a responsibility judgment consistent with their deontic judgment.

Why is there this increase in consistency in the Helkema study? Formally, following Hare (1963), we may say that each higher stage is more prescriptive and universalizable, as stated in the paper *"From Is to Ought"* (Kohlberg, 1971). Empirically, Helkema found lower-stage subjects making excuses for failure to judge Heinz as being responsible. These excuses seem like obligations to lower-stage subjects but are merely quasi-obligations from the perspective of higher stages or from the perspective of deontic judgment at the stage itself. For example, at Stages 3 and 4 obedience to law or disapproval by authorities may be used as a reason why Heinz is not responsible for stealing even though he should do it. These quasi-obligations or excuses are motivating a judgment of responsibility even though they do not generate a deontic judgment of right or wrong.

To illustrate a stage-wise increase in the consistency of actual moral behavior and a stage-wise decrease in quasi-obligations in responsibility judgments, we will review a study by McNamee (1978). McNamee describes the situation as follows:

TABLE 4.1.   Percentage Responses to the Heinz Dilemma Responsibility Question in the Helkema Study

Stage	Should Steal	Should Not Steal	Is Responsible	Percentage of Should Steal Thinking Heinz Responsible
3 (and 3/4)	42	25	17	27
4 (and 4/3)	56	19	28	29
5 (and 4/5)	67	7	53	50

Undergraduates who agreed to be interviewed on the standard moral dilemmas were led to a testing room. As they were entering the room they were
intercepted by a student presenting himself as the next subject for the experiment. The student stated that he had just taken drugs and was having a bad
time. He had come to the experiment because he thought that the experimenter, being a psychologist, could help him. The response of the experimenter was that she was a research psychologist, not a therapist. The drug-
user persisted in soliciting aid, hoping that the experimenter could refer him
to help. The experimenter replied that she had no experience with drugs and
did not know what facility could help him. She told him to call to reschedule
his testing session. The drug-user slowly left the room. The subject was faced
with the choice of whether to remain an uninvolved bystander or whether to
intervene. [p. 27]

Subjects' moral behavior was assessed first by whether they helped or not
and second by the degree to which they intervened: offering information
about other sources of assistance to the drug user or offering personal assistance, such as taking him home or to a source of help. Subjects were 102
college students, ages 18–25, containing an equal number of males and
females.

The results of this study are displayed in Table 4.2. The first column indicates the percentage of subjects at each moral stage who verbally decided
it was right to help the drugged student. Column 2 presents the percentage of
subjects who actually did help by referring the student to some other agency.
Column 3 describes those subjects who intervened to counsel or personally
escort the victim to a helpful source. The last column contains a measure of
consistency, that is, the percentage of subjects at each stage who advocated
helping and who actually did so.

TABLE 4.2.   Percentage Helping Drugged Student, by Stage of Moral Reasoning

Stage	Thought They Should Help	Helped by Referring Victim	Helped by Personal Intervention	Consistency[a]	Stage N
2	36	9	0	25	(11)
3	77	27	0	38	(29)
4	69	38	0	55	(17)
5	83	73	20	88	(29)[b]

Source: Adapted from McNamee, 1978.
Note: Columns are percentage of subjects at that stage making the response. Mean MMS of
subjects who helped by referring was 430, of subjects who did no help, 350 ($F = 19.4$, d.f. =
1, 88, $p < .01$). Method of scoring is 1972 issue method.
[a] Consistency is percentage of subjects who thought they should help who actually did so by
referring victim.
[b] Five of these subjects were originally scored at Stage 6. Results for them would have been
100%, 100%, 60%, and 0% across the columns.

The overwhelming effect that is revealed by Table 4.2 is the monotonic nature of the act of helping. In virtually all cases the decision to help and the action of helping are evidenced increasingly more often at each higher moral stage. Similarly, the consistency between the decision that it was right to help and the act of doing so increases with moral development.

The highest stage at which failure to help the drugged student can be explained by the concept of quasi-obligations is at Stage 4. Here the most frequent reason for not helping the drugged student involved a quasi-obligation to the experimenter in his role as an authority. Of nonintervening Stage 4 subjects, 55% gave the following reason for not helping: "My role was that of a subject. I'm not qualified as a psychologist. I had to trust the experimenter's judgment. It's dangerous to be a Peanuts psychiatrist." At Stage 3, it was personal disapproval or the personal relationship with the experimenter that most frequently determined nonintervention. Typical of the reasons for not helping at Stage 3 was the following. "I was concerned about what the experimenter would think of me—her disapproval" (24%). At Stage 2 the most frequent reason for not helping was not a quasi-obligation to the experimenter but the absence of any instrumental necessity of the helping act itself. Typical of Stage 2 reasons for not intervening was the following: "It's not necessary. It's none of my business. It's his responsibility. He should have thought of the consequences before taking drugs" (44%).

The Helkema and McNamee studies support the moral responsibility or moral consistency approach to defining moral action. At each higher stage subjects are more likely to make a judgment of responsibility consistent with their deontic choice and to act on this judgment of responsibility. Lower-stage subjects often left responsibility in the hands of the experimenter because of a quasi-obligation to the experimenter and accordingly did not help. As we shall see in our discussion of the Milgram situation, the same thing occurred.

UNIVERSAL MORALITY APPROACH

Let us now turn to a much more philosophically disputable theory or hypothesis about moral judgment and action. This theory is the claim that some actions may be judged right or wrong "universally" or "objectively." For example, Kohlberg (1981) argues that it is universally right or just for Heinz to steal the drug under the circumstances of that classic dilemma. Similarly, he argues that capital punishment is wrong or unjust. The empirical springboard for this claim is the fact that almost all Stage 5 subjects (and subjects whom our theory might label Stage 6, although this stage is not well defined empirically) agreed or have consensus in such judgments. The philosophic claim involved is not that moral rightness is solved by an opinion poll. It is rather that the function of judgments of fairness is to resolve conflicting claims in a way that all could agree with, that principles of justice have the function of leading to agreement in deontic judgment given agreement on the facts. Thus, both Kant's principle of justice or respect for personality and Mill's principle of utility or the greatest welfare of the greatest number would agree in judging Heinz right to steal.

Our stages of moral judgment are defined by the form of moral judgment, not its content. Higher stages we claim are more moral in their form. Many moral philosophers agree that there is a "moral method" for arriving at moral judgment, which can lead to considerable substantive agreement about what is right and just in moral problem situations. Even if following the moral method does not lead to substantive agreement, it is the critical moral component of value judgment. An example of a critical element of "the moral method" is impartiality, the effort to consider the interests and points of view of all parties involved in moral problems, not only to consider the situation from the point of view of oneself and one's own group. "Methodological non-relativism" has been particularly stressed by formalist moral philosophers from Kant to contemporaries like Hare (1973), Frankena (1963), Baier (1965), Peters (1968), and Rawls (1971). All stress that a "moral point of view" or a moral method implies certain formal features of moral judgment, features like universalizability, prescriptivity, reversibility, and generality.

This formalist conception of moral judgment has been the basic philosophic assumption made by our stage approach to moral judgment. Kohlberg (1981) articulates the stages of moral judgment as defined formally and argues that higher stages more closely approximate the formal features of a truly moral judgment as defined by philosophers.

From our point of view, then, we can define morality in moral judgments formally without commitment to a particular code, as in the following Stage 5 response to the Heinz dilemma given by one of our research subjects:

Should Heinz steal the drug?

Yes, he should. His obligation to save his wife's life must take precedence over his obligation to respect the druggist's property rights.

Which is worse, letting someone die or stealing?

Letting someone die. Because the value of human life is logically prior to the value of property. That is, property can have no value unless human life is protected.

This subject makes a judgment that is *prescriptive,* that is *overriding* (life is overriding of other nonmoral considerations), and that is *universalizable* to any life and to anyone's point of view, for example, the druggist's. It is in this formal sense that we call the judgment fully moral.

We have clarified the sense in which judgments about the Heinz dilemma or others of our standard dilemmas can be said to be "moral" or "morally principled" in formal terms. The problem of defining moral action, however, is not yet answered. To define moral action, we need to be able to define the content of an action, the choice made, as being moral, and not just the form of the judgment accompanying the action. The Heinz dilemma asks a subject to judge whether it is right to obey the law. The dilemma is preframed so that only one of the two opposed actions can be judgments as right, either serving the moral norm of human life or serving the moral norm of law (or property). Such dilemmas tend to call for a solution by reliance on a moral principle. Philosophers distinguish between a moral *rule* or a moral norm and a moral *principle*. Do not steal, respect property, and be honest are various statements of a moral rule or a moral norm of property. In the Heinz dilemma the norm is opposed by another moral norm or rule, the norm of preserving human life. The deontic question asks, Following which rule is right? When rules or norms conflict, a principle seems required. A moral principle, as distinct from a rule, implies two things. First, it is not a "thou shalt" or "thou shalt not" engage in a kind of action; it is a way of seeing, a way of choosing, when two rules are in conflict. It is a method of moral choice. Second, it is something underneath a rule, the spirit underneath the law rather than the rule itself; it is an attitude or idea that generates rules. It is more general and universal than a rule. Among ethical principles put forward by philosophers we may note particularly Kant's principle of justice and Mill's principle of utility. Kant's principle of justice is the principle of respect for human personality or dignity—treat each person as an end in himself or herself, not as a means. Mill's principle is the principle of maximizing human happiness or welfare and minimizing human suffering—"the greatest good for the greatest number." In the Heinz situation, both moral principles lead to the same judgment, that is, that it is right to steal. It is in this sense that we consider the action of stealing the drug to be morally right.

Empirically, we have found that subjects who reason at Stage 5 do in fact agree that Heinz is right to steal the drug. More than 90% of Stage 5 subjects in the United States, Finland, and Israel make this choice, compared with about 60% of subjects at lower stages. Thus, we have found that in certain cases there is both philosophic and empirical support for an "objective right" in defining moral action.

We suggest that moral stage influences moral action in two ways: (1) through differences in deontic choice, and (2) through judgments of responsibility. Where situations are controversial, we may expect to find differences in deontic choice, with each higher stage more likely to agree on the choice determined by moral principles. In situations where there is general agreement on the deontic choice (e.g., McNamee, 1978), we still expect to find a monotonic relationship between stage and action due to increases in the judgment of responsibility.

Our philosophic considerations left us with the view that a moral action was an action (1) that was "objectively right" in the sense that philosophic principles as used by Stage 5 reasoning agreed that the action was right, and (2) that was "subjectively right" if it was both guided by a moral judgment or reason that was "right" in form and consistent in content with the objectively right choice.

This controversial philosophic view leads us to say that in at least some situations principled or Stage 5 subjects perform actions that are right in both form and content. This claim does not apply only to the highest or principled stages. Lower-stage subjects sometimes choose the "right," "just," or "principled" content on our hypothetical dilemmas. Furthermore, they choose it in a way that is formally close to what both Kant and Piaget would call autonomous. In terms of content they choose the alternative of preserving justice or human rights as against obeying laws or authorities in situations where these are arbitrary or in conflict with rights and justice. How can we identify and characterize such lower-stage subjects? In the Colby, Kohlberg, Gibbs, and Lieberman (1984) book reporting our longitudinal data (partially reported in Chap. 3 in this book), we have discussed two different orientations to the standard hypothetical dilemmas and used them to define a B type oriented to fairness rather than to rules or pragmatics. We characterized the B type as more prescriptive, more reversible, and more universalistic than the A type. In this way, judgments of responsibility made at type B are more like judgments of responsibility made at higher stages than are the judgments of type A. Judgments of responsibility made at type B contain fewer excusing complications, fewer "quasi-obligations," than do substage A judgments, just as higher-stage judgments of responsibility contain fewer excusing complications than do lower-stage judgments of responsibility. Type B responses reflect the Stage 5 "right answers" to our dilemmas and an intuitive understanding of the core reasons for these choices. A type B person is someone who intuitively or in his or her "heart" or "conscience" perceives the central values and obligations in the dilemma articulated rationally by Stage 5 and uses these intuitions to generate a judgment of responsibility or necessity in the dilemma. In the Heinz dilemma, this intuition is that of the intrinsic value or worth of all human life, its priority over property, and a resulting judgment of universal obligation to preserve such life. In the III III dilemma, it is the intuition that an act of moral conscience or rightness, such as that of Heinz, should not be legally punished regardless of legality and utilitarian deterrence or social order considerations. In the Joe and his father dilemma (I), it is the intuition of the sacredness or intrinsic worth of keeping promises (most especially) to children and the universal and prescriptive responsibility for keeping promises. These type B judgments on the three Form A dilemmas receive their full rational and principled justification only at Stage 5. But at lower stages they can still govern, or predict, responsible choices and action. We predict, then, that the minority of subjects below Stage 5 who act morally in experimental moral situations are type B. In this way we give credibility to the notion that moral action is responsible choice guided by intuitions of moral values not dependent on stage sophistication. Implied, then, is the "Platonic," "Kantian," or "intuitionist" view that conscience can dimly intuit rationally principled justice and act accordingly. Kant hypothesized that the categorical imperative was intuited by ordinary unreflective moral judgment. Therefore, if we are going to look for a relationship between moral thought and moral action, we should look to those persons who judge that it is right to perform the more moral behavior either by virtue of their Stage 5 reasoning or the type B intuitions.

There is one caveat or limit to our identification of type B on our dilemmas with moral judgments of responsibility in general and resulting moral action. Our Form A dilemmas are dilemmas of civil disobedience, of life and promises, as against legal authority. Our predictions, too, are to situations of civil disobedience. At present the free speech movement at Berkeley and the Milgram experiments are the only situations on which we have type data. Thus one could ask, if type B hinges only on content choice, then could not the consistency between "B" judgments and actions of civil disobedience be due to content consistency only. In fact, however, many subjects who chose the "civilly disobedient" alternative on our dilemmas are not scored by type B, nor do they consistently perform the moral action in the real-life situations. Our evaluation of a response as type B rests on two formal features in addition to a hierarchical preference for the chosen norm (life in III, promise in I). The first feature is that it is prescriptive (a judgment of duty governing what one says one would do). The second is that the duty is universal or universalizable. For example, in the Heinz dilemma type B subjects recognize a categorical duty or responsibility to the life of the dying person, regardless of emotions of love or lack of love. They see this responsibility as universalizable, as that which anyone should do in Heinz's place, and as universal, as an obligation to a dying person regardless of whether the person is wife, close friend, or acquaintance. On the Joe dilemma, the responsibility judgment toward keeping a promise at type B is also prescriptively preemptive or necessary and universal for all promise keeping, regardless of relationships. In Kant's or Hare's (1963) terms, at type B the maxim of moral decision is formally consistent with the categorical imperative of prescriptive universality. In that sense, it meets Kant's demand that a necessary condition for an action to be moral is that it is based on or willed by a maxim or reason consistent with and generated by the categorical imperative.

In addition to these Kantian or formal conditions type B judgment also rests on a more content-related and teleological intuition of a natural hierarchy among our nine universal moral norms. It includes the intuition of the primacy of life over law, of conscience over punishment, and of promise keeping or contract over parental authority. This hierarchy is dimly perceived at the type B perspective from Stage 2 onward, but it is only at Stage 5 that the hierarchies become consensual, because only at that stage are they directly derivable from principles, the principles of justice and benevolence, which agree in providing a similar hierarchy. Without principles, however, type B sees that there are certain "intrinsically moral" norms or values, including the values of life, conscience, and promise keeping, and other norms that are "extrinsic" or derivative from these norms, the norms of law, authority, punishment, and property. These latter norms are secondary to, and instrumental to, the preservation of the more intrinsic moral norms.

We have chosen two studies of moral judgment and moral action in which to test some of the constructs and hypotheses mentioned earlier. The two studies are Haan's, Smith's, and Block's (1968) study of the 1964 Berkeley free speak movement and Milgram's study of obedience to authority (described in Milgram, 1974). The free speech study was chosen because it is the largest and most widely cited study of moral judgment and moral action. The Milgram study was chosen because of the substantial impact that those series of experiments have had in the field of research psychology and also because the study reported here was carried out, in part, by the senior author. Both studies were rescored using the current rating system.

FREE SPEECH MOVEMENT STUDY

The free speech movement study examined the relationship between moral stage and the act of illegally occupying the administration building at the University of California at Berkeley. The sit-in was the culmination of a series of disputes between the Board of Regents of the university and groups of students advocating civil rights and radical causes. The disputes arose over the regents' enforcement of a rule banning the use of university grounds for the distribution of political literature and recruitment to political causes. The researchers gave written forms of the moral judgment interview and a special free speech dilemma to 339 students: 129 of whom had been arrested for sitting in and 210 who had been chosen randomly from a cross section of the Berkeley campus.

To begin our discussion, we must first determine whether the case is, in fact, a moral situation. From our perspective it is. A moral situation can be defined as one involving issues of justice, that is, a conflict of rights or claims. In the free speech movement, this conflict emerged between the right to free speech and one's general duty to respect the social contract "signed" with the university administration. Stated as such, we may not expect this situation to be one in which moral principles necessarily yield a single right answer. From all accounts, however, the Board of Regents seemed to be particularly intransigent and supported their position by appeals to their authority. Thus, in this case the lines between free speech and the authority of the Board of Regents were especially well drawn. In terms of social contract theories like that of Rawls (1971), the first principle of the social contract is liberty, which would justify civil disobedience.

The first hypothesis to be tested was whether a monotonic relationship exists between moral judgment and action in this situation. These results are presented in Table 4.3. As this table shows, the pattern is strongly monotonic. At each higher stage of moral reasoning a greater proportion of subjects sat

TABLE 4.3.   Percentage of Students Arrested in Free Speech Movement Sit-in, by Moral Stage

Students Arrested	Moral Stage[a]			
	3	3/4	4	4/5
Percentage sat in	10	31	44	73
N at stage	(39)	(138)	(125)	(37)

[a]$\chi^2 = 36.58$, d.f. $= 3$, $p < .001$, Kendall's tau $= .37$, $p < .001$.

in. Stage scores were assigned on the basis of standard dilemmas, not on responses to the free speech situation itself.

The pattern is consistent with the results of the McNamee (1978) study discussed earlier and with most of the studies cited by Blasi (1980) in his review. It conflicts in some important ways, however, with the results originally reported by Haan, Smith, and Block (1968). In their analysis of the data using the 1958 scoring system, they found sitting in to be bimodal. Half of the Stage 2 subjects, about 12% of the Stages 3 and 4 subjects, and more than half of the Stages 5 and 6 subjects sat in. In rescoring, we scored no individuals at Stages 2, 5, or 6. The absence of Stage 2 subjects represents revision in scoring that distinguishes "sophomoritis" relativism from Stage 2 and is consistent with other recent studies of college populations. The absence of Stage 6 subjects can be explained by the elimination of that stage from the standard scoring system (although it exists as a theoretical stage). Stage 4/5 and Stage 5 subjects could not be distinguished in the written form of the interview. Among those stages that were represented in the reanalysis, however, the pattern is clearly monotonic, not bimodal.

The second hypothesis to be tested in the current data is that there is greater consistency between deontic judgment and action at higher stages of moral reasoning. In order to test this proposition we must control the effect of deontic choice. We measured deontic choice by response to the question, Do you think it was actually right or wrong for the students to sit in? Responses were grouped into those that clearly stated it was right, those that clearly stated it was wrong, and those that mixed statements of right and wrong. Interestingly, the relationship between deontic choice and moral stage was itself monotonic. 36% of Stage 3 subjects, 50% of Stage 3/4 subjects, 62% of Stage 4 subjects, and 83% of Stage 4/5 subjects thought the students were clearly right to have a sit-in. The clear approval given to sitting in at Stage 4/5 (83%) indicates that, in fact, principled subjects did agree on a single deontic choice. This result supports the position of universality in defining moral action.

In considering these results, we must caution the reader that the data were collected two months after the sit-in took place. Thus, subjects' deontic choices as well as their supporting justifications may have been influenced by the realization that they either did or did not sit-in. Nonetheless, we consider these retrospective measures to be a useful test of our hypotheses, although not as definitive as a prospective study would have been. There is little reason to expect that the standard moral judgment responses were distorted by the free speech movement events.

The hypothesis of consistency is tested in Table 4.4. This table presents the relationship of moral stage to sitting in among subjects grouped by deontic choice. As Table 4.4 shows, the judgment that it was wrong to sit in seems sufficient in this case to lead to moral consistency to explain why no subject who judged it deontically wrong sat in. What is most interesting for our hypothesis can be found in the left-hand third of the table. As can be seen, among subjects who thought it was right to sit in a greater proportion at each higher stage of moral reasoning actually did so. In other words, the consistency between judgment and action increased monotonically with moral stage. As discussed earlier, we expect such consistency to be mediated by a judgment of responsibility. We were unable to measure that variable directly, however, in the free speech study.

We have seen that the vast majority of higher-stage subjects judged it was right to sit in and actually did so. How can we account for the act of sitting in when it occurred among lower-stage subjects? It is here that we examined the effect of substage. As previously discussed, lower-stage subjects who are of the B type intuitively make moral judgments that have many of the same formal and content characteristics as do judgments made by Stage 5 subjects. Thus, if Stage 5 subjects (represented here by Stage 4/5 subjects) commonly sat in, we would expect type B subjects at every stage also to sit in more often than would their type A counterparts. The test of this hypothesis is shown in Table 4.5. The first entry in the upper left-hand section of the table can be read as follows: Thirty subjects were scored as reasoning at Stage 3A. Among them no subjects sat in. The overall effect seen in Table 4.5 is clear.

TABLE 4.4.   Percentage of Subjects Sitting in, by Moral Stage and Free Speech Movement Deontic Choice

	Free Speech Movement Choice											
	Right[a]				Mixed[b]				Wrong			
Stage	3	3/4	4	4/5	3	3/4	4	4/5	3	3/4	4	4/5
Percentage sat in	23	54	63	75	11	17	12	60	0	0	0	0
N at stage	(13)	(66)	(71)	(29)	(9)	(30)	(24)	(5)	(14)	(37)	(20)	(1)

[a] Kendall's tau within right $= .24, p < .01$.
[b] Kendall's tau within mixed $= .11$, n.s.

At each higher stage and at each type closer to B, a greater proportion of subjects sat in.

MILGRAM SITUATION

The second study in which we were able to measure types involved the Milgram situation. Moral judgment interviews were given to 26 undergraduates who participated in an early version of Milgram's well-known series of experiments. We recently rescored these data according to our current stage and type scoring system. The results appear in Table 4.6.

The features of Table 4.6 that we will focus on here are found in the marginals. The relationship of quitting the Milgram experiment by moral stage appears in the lower margin. Most important, we find that nearly all subjects at the highest stage (in this study, Stage 4) quit (87%). This result compares with only 6% at Stage 3/4. Quitting was also high at Stage 3 (50%), although there were only four subjects at that stage. Perhaps what is most striking is found in the right-hand marginal, which summarizes the results for each type. Here, as in the free speech study, we find a monotonic increase in performing the more moral action at type B. No type A subject quit, 18% of the ambiguous subjects quit, and a full 86% of pure type B subjects quit. Thus, as expected, principled moral judgment and type B judgment both lead to quitting the Milgram experiment.

To explain the patterns, we again appeal to the hypothesized mediating judgments of deontic choice and responsibility. Deontic choice was measured by the questions of whether subjects wanted to quit, regardless of whether they actually did so. Such judgments were made by all Stage 4 subjects and all type B subjects. Although responsibility judgments in the situation were not measured directly in our version of the Milgram study, there is evidence

TABLE 4.5. Percentage of Subjects Sitting in, by Stage and Type of Moral Reasoning

	Stage			
	3	3/4	4	4/5
Type A				
Percentage sitting in	0	21	21	60
N at stage	(30)	(85)	(57)	(5)
Ambiguous B				
Percentage sitting in	44	44	53	58
N at stage	(9)	(41)	(40)	(12)
Type B				
Percentage sitting in	—	57	67	83
N at stage	(0)	(7)	(18)	(18)

TABLE 4.6. Percentage of Subjects Quitting Milgram Situation, by Stage and Type of Moral Reasoning

	Stage			Type Totals
	3	3/4	4	
Type A				
Percentage quit	0	0	0	0
N at stage	(2)	(6)	(1)	(9)
Ambiguous				
Percentage quit	100	0	100	18
N at stage	(1)	(9)	(1)	(11)
Type B				
Percentage quit	100	50	100	86
N at stage	(1)	(2)	(4)	(7)
Stage totals				
Percentage quit	50	6	87	
N at stage	(4)	(17)	(6)	(27)

from other versions conducted by Milgram that such judgments strongly influenced behavior. According to Milgram (1974), there is pressure for all subjects in the obedience experiments to enter what he called the "agentic mode." Once in this mode, an individual no longer evaluates the morality of actions for himself or herself but rather sees himself or herself as an agent carrying out the commands of superiors. Milgram reports, however, that persons who quit the experiment seem to relinquish their sense of responsibility considerably less often than do subjects who are obedient. For example, one subject in Milgram's experiment who quit reasoned as follows:

IT IS ABSOLUTELY ESSENTIAL THAT YOU CONTINUE.
Well, I won't—not with the man screaming to get out.
YOU HAVE NO OTHER CHOICE.
I do have a choice (Incredulous and indignant): Why don't I have a choice. I came here on my own free will. . . . I think I've probably gone too far already, probably.
WHO WAS RESPONSIBLE FOR SHOCKING THE LEARNER AGAINST HIS WILL?
I would put it on myself entirely. [p. 51]

In contrast, subjects who did not quit the experiment typically reasoned as follows:

WHETHER HE LIKES IT OR NOT WE MUST GO ON THROUGH ALL THE WORD PAIRS.
I refuse to take the responsibility. He's in there hollering!
IT'S ABSOLUTELY ESSENTIAL THAT YOU CONTINUE, TEACHER.

(Indicating the unused questions) : There's too many left here . . . I mean who's going to take the responsibility if something happens to that gentleman? I'M RESPONSIBLE FOR ANYTHING THAT HAPPENS TO HIM. CONTINUE, PLEASE.
All right. [p. 74]

Although we do not have standard moral judgment interviews on the two preceding subjects, it seems clear that the responsibility judgment made in the first case is consistent with type B and with Stage 4/5, whereas the lack of personal responsibility in the second quotation is consistent with type A and with Stage 3/4.

We have now reviewed three empirical studies, McNamee (1978), Milgram (1974), and the Berkeley free speech movement, and have found support for our theory of the relation of moral judgment to moral action in each of them. This theory can be summarized as follows:

1. The relation of moral judgment to moral action supports a one-track process theory.
2. Moral stage structures interpret morally relevant features of a situation. Structures influence behavior through two judgments, one deontic (a judgment of should or "right") and one responsibility (a judgment of commitment to follow through).
3. Moral action may be considered "right" in two senses. In the weaker sense right action is any action consistent with the actor's own deontic decision of what is right. We have also called this type of right action "responsible action." In the stronger sense morally right action is that which would be chosen by Stage 5 moral principles and which is, in fact, carried out with at least an intuitive sense of those principles in mind.
4. In moral situations where there is deontic agreement by persons at the conventional stages and above, we expect to find a monotonic relationship between moral stage and moral action due to increasing judgment of responsibility at each higher stage. This relationship was demonstrated in the McNamee experiment.
5. In moral situations that are controversial at conventional stages but on which Stage 5 subjects agree, we expect to find a monotonic relationship between moral stage and action because of both the increasing likelihood of subjects at each higher stage making the Stage 5 deontic choice and the increasing judgment of responsibility at each higher stage.
6. Where lower-stage subjects perform the moral action (defined in the stronger sense), we expect those subjects to be the B type. Reasoning at type B is more universal, generalizable, and internally consistent than is reasoning at type A. Persons who reason at the B type

of any moral stage can be considered to intuit the same principles that are clearly articulated only at Stage 5. This phenomenon was demonstrated in both the free speech and the Milgram studies.

These ideas can be formalized into a model of the relationship of moral judgment to moral action. That model is presented in Figure 4.1. There are four psychological functions, as indicated at the top of the figure. Each function is served by a cognition or set of cognitions. The first function, interpretation of the situation and the selection of moral principles, is served by the cognitive structures of moral stage and moral type. These structures interpret the moral situation, determine relevant claims, rights, and duties of each character, and formulate the "operative principles" on which an action should be based. Moral stage and moral substage, in turn, determine two more specific judgments that are tied directly to moral action. These are the judgments of deontic choice (which serves Function II, decision making) and judgments of responsibility or obligation (which serve Function III, follow-through).

As we have seen, deontic choice is tied to stage and type in the sense that where all universalizable moral principles lead to a single alternative as being "more moral," that choice will be made almost invariably by persons at Stage 5 and at type B. The choice will be made less often at lower stages and at type A. Judgments of responsibility or obligation are tied to both moral stage and type as well as to moral action in that subjects at each higher stage and at type B should more often hold themselves responsible for carrying their deontic choices into practice.

A fourth function, not discussed in this chapter, involves nonmoral skills needed for follow-through. Known collectively as ego controls, they include such cognitive skills as intelligence (i.e., figuring out a plan to achieve the intended moral result), attention (i.e., avoiding distractions), and delay of gratification (i.e., persevering in one's chosen plan). Studies such as that by Grim, Kohlberg, and White (1968) have shown that these nonmoral skills act in a manner that parallels what we have recently found is the effect of the

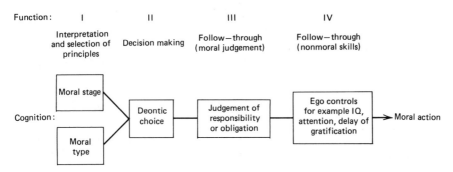

Figure 4.1.   Model of the relationship of moral judgment to moral action.

judgment of responsibility. Both sets of cognitions increase the likelihood of one acting on his or her deontic choice. Together, the cognitions of responsibility and ego controls comprise a psychological analogue to what has been called the "moral will."

The preceding model bears considerable similarity to the one proposed by Rest in Chapter 2. Although Rest's model identifies nearly the same psychological functions as does ours, its purpose is somewhat different. The major difference is that we do not try to integrate studies from various psychological traditions. That is the strength of Rest's approach, and were we to do so, it is doubtful our conclusions would differ substantially from his. Rather, our goal here has been to explore the extent to which one particular set of constructs, moral stage and moral type, illuminate the judgment-action process.

REFERENCES

Baier, K. *The moral point of view: A rational basis of ethics* (Rev. ed.). New York: Random House, 1965.

Berkowitz, L. *Development of motives and values in a child.* New York: Basic Books, 1964.

Blasi, A. Bridging moral cognition and moral action: A critical review of the literature. *Psychological Bulletin, 1980, 88,* 1–45.

Blasi, A. Bridging moral cognition and moral action: A theoretical perspective. *Developmental Review, 1983 in press.*

Brown, R., & Herrnstein, R. *Psychology.* Boston: Little, Brown, 1975.

Colby, A., Kohlberg, L., Gibbs, J., & Lieberman, M. A longitudinal study of moral judgment. *Monographs of the Society of Research in Child Development, 1983, 48*(1–2).

Colby, Kohlberg, et al. *The Measurement of Moral Judgment.* New York: Cambridge University Press, 1984 (in press).

Frankena, W. K. *Ethics.* Englewood Cliffs, N.J.: Prentice-Hall, 1963.

Galon, D. *The theories of Kohlberg and Lonergan.* Unpublished doctoral dissertation, Ontario Institute for the Study of Education, 1981.

Gilligan, C. *In a different voice: Psychological theory and women's development.* Cambridge, Mass.: Harvard University Press, 1982.

Gilligan, C., & Belenky, M. A naturalistic study of abortion decision. In R. Selman & R. Yando, *Clinical development psychology.* San Francisco: Jossey-Bass, 1980.

Grim, P., Kohlberg, L., & White, S. Some relationships between conscience and attentional processes. *Journal of Personality and Social Psychology, 1968, 8,* 239–253.

Haan, N., Smith, M. B., & Block, J. Political, family and personality correlates of adolescent moral judgment. *Journal of Personality and Social Psychology, 1968, 10,* 183–201.

Hare, R. M. *Freedom and reason.* New York: Oxford University Press, 1963.

Hartshorne, H., & May, M. A. *Studies in the nature of character* (3 vols.). Vol. 1, *Studies in deceit;* Vol. 2, *Studies in self-control;* Vol. 3, *Studies in the organization of character.* New York: Macmillan, 1928–1930.

Kleinberger, A. Theories of moral action. *Journal of Moral Education,* 1982, *11,* 147–158.

Kohlberg, L. From is to ought. In T. Mischell (Ed.), *Cognitive development and epistemology.* New York: Academic Press, 1971. Reprinted in L. Kohlberg, *The philosophy of moral development.* San Francisco: Harper & Row, 1981.

Leming, J. S. An exploratory inquiry into the multi-factor theory of moral behavior. *Journal of Moral Education,* 1976, *5,* 179–188.

McNamee, S. Moral behavior, moral development and motivation. *Journal of Moral Education,* 1978, *7,* 27–32.

Milgram, S. *Obedience to authority: An experimental view.* New York: Harper & Row, 1974.

Peters, R. S. *Ethics and education.* Glenview, Ill.: Scott, Foresman, 1968.

Piaget, J. *The moral judgment of the child.* London: Routledge & Kegan Paul, 1932.

Rawls, J. *A theory of justice.* Cambridge, Mass.: Harvard University Press, 1971.

REFERENCE NOTE

1. Helkema, K. *The development of the attribution of responsibility. A critical survey of empirical research and a theoretical outline.* (Research Reports, Department of Social Psychology.) Unpublished manuscript, University of Helsinki, 1979.

CHAPTER 5

The Relationship of Moral Atmosphere
to Judgments of Responsibility

ANN HIGGINS, CLARK POWER, AND LAWRENCE KOHLBERG

Interventions in moral education based on a cognitive-developmental approach and on the structural-psychological theory of individual moral judgment development have been tried in prisons, halfway houses, and elementary and secondary schools since 1970. The core of these interventions were group moral discussion of hypothetical and practical dilemmas and democratic governance. The evaluations done usually reported individual moral-judgment-stage change. This is the first report of an evaluation of the moral atmosphere of three alternative democratic high schools and their three companion high schools. This chapter utilizes the distinction between hypothetical classical dilemmas and practical dilemmas introduced by Leming and the distinction between deontic or justice reasoning and responsibility reasoning introduced by Gilligan in the analysis of individual moral judgment. Second, this chapter describes and discusses the moral atmosphere of each school in terms of the existence and development of sociomoral collective norms and the valuing of community. Three student case studies and preliminary group results for four of the six schools are presented.

In the preceding chapter, Kohlberg and Candee hypothesized that between a deontic judgment of rightness or justice and a situational decision to act morally there is an intervening variable or process of judgment of responsibility on real-life decisions. Our discussion of judgments of rightness and responsibility is embedded in our discussion of the way in which each judgment is influenced by the moral atmosphere of a group or institution such as a school.

In Chapter 4, it is hypothesized that a judgment of responsibility is a mediating bridge from a deontic judgment of rightness and justice to moral action. In the Milgram experiment, for instance, it was found that higher-stage subjects quit shocking the stooge victim because of a judgment of responsibility, asserting that what was going on was their responsibility, not just that of the experimenter, despite the experimenter's assertion that he would take the responsibility for shocking the victim. Moral action usually takes place in a social or group context, and that context usually has a profound influence on the moral decision making of individuals. Individual moral decisions in real life are almost always made in the context of group norms or group decision-making processes. Moreover, individual moral action is often a function of these norms or processes. For example, in the massacre at My Lai during the Vietnam War, individual American soldiers murdered non-combatant women and children. They did so not primarily because, as individuals, their moral judgment that the action was morally right was immature, or because, as individuals, they were "sick" in some sense; they did so because they participated in what was essentially a group action taken on the basis of group norms. The moral choice made by each individual soldier who pulled the trigger was embedded in the larger institutional context of the army and its decision-making procedures. Their decisions were dependent in large part on a collectively shared definition of the situation and of what should be done about it. In short, the My Lai massacre was more a function of the group "moral atmosphere" that prevailed in that place at that time than of the stage of moral development of the individuals present. The realization of the important role that moral atmosphere or group norms play in individual moral action has led us to hypothesize that in many cases the best approach to moral education is one that attempts to reform the moral atmosphere in which individual decisions are made. This hypothesis has guided our interventions and research in the schools and prisons.

In the research reported here comparing judgments of responsibility and the moral atmosphere of democratic alternative high schools and traditionally governed high schools, we hypothesized that the democratic school students would both make more responsibility judgments and make them at a higher stage than would the regular school controls. There were two reasons we expected this. First, participatory democracy puts sociomoral decisions in the hands of the students, giving them a greater sense of responsibility for school-related actions. Second, participatory democracy, we believed, helps create a sense of the school as a caring community. Students would develop shared or collective norms of helping, of trust, and of active participation on behalf of the group, norms supported by a sense of community or of a valued sense of group solidarity and cohesion. Students' practical judgments of responsibility, we believed, would derive from their perception of the moral atmosphere of the school, that is, from their perception of the school's norms and the school's sense of itself as a community.

Having outlined our educational evaluation aims and hypothesis, we should add that our theoretical interest lay in developing concepts and measures that would bridge moral psychology and sociology. According to Durkheim's *Moral Education* (1925/1961), the classroom or school group creates collective norms and attachments to the group that are group phenomena *sui generis.* We believed him. We thought a Stage 3 collective norm is not the same thing as an average of individuals' stage judgments at Stage 3. In a school promoting moral development, collective norms would be formulated at a stage that was the leading edge for the group, and adapting to these norms would stimulate those students whose individual stage was lower to grow (Kohlberg, 1980, 1981; Power, 1979). Still more basically, we thought by building collective norms and ideas of community at a higher stage we would promote morally better student action.

In this chapter we discuss the moral judgment of groups of high school students about how they would act if certain prototypical high school dilemmas occurred in their school. One purpose of the research was that of formative educational evaluation, which had as its aim not only evaluating the effects of an intervention program but also providing categories of analysis that can be used conceptually to change and guide the ongoing intervention program. In our own work this means that the categories we use indicate the existence, sharedness, and strength of prosocial, moral norms and evidence of whether and how members of a school value it as a moral community.

1. PREVIOUS RESEARCH

Before presenting the method and results of our research on high schools, we need a brief review of previous work in the field on which we have tried to build. The three areas reviewed represent the three categories of variables used in our study: (1) the kinds of dilemmas, (2) the kinds of judgments, and (3) the influence of the moral atmosphere on moral reasoning.

A. Classical and Practical Moral Dilemmas: The Leming Study

The first scores in Table 5.3 are the stage scores of deontic judgment on standard dilemmas like the Heinz dilemma, which taps what we shall call *classical* moral judgments. The Standard Issue Scoring method used has proved to be useful for measuring individual longitudinal changes in a variety of cultures and subcultural settings. The very abstractness of the standard moral dilemma situations helps make them a standard test stimulus having similar meanings to individuals living in various cultural worlds. Their focus on what someone in general, Heinz, *should* do minimizes nonmoral personality and situational variations in responses that might be brought out by the question, What would you do? As a result, it yields a good picture of the student's moral judgment *general competence,* regardless of variations in personality and situation that might influence his or her specific moral judgment *performance.*

In addition to being abstract and hypothetical, and in addition to asking for *should* and not for *would* answers, the standard dilemmas are primarily dilemmas of justice. They pose a conflict between the rights of one person (Heinz's wife) and that of another (the druggist). Alternately stated, they oppose one social norm (respecting property) to another social norm (respecting life). The resolution of such justice conflicts requires reference to a principle, such as the utilitarian principle of the greater good or the justice principle of equal respect for each person. The rules or principles just cited are those found at Stage 5, but each stage has its characteristic rules or principles of choice.

In our study of democratic schools, we were less interested in students' general moral judgment competence about justice than we were interested in how students actually made real-life moral decisions in action. Research reviews by Blasi (1980) and by Kohlberg and Candee (Chap. 4) show that classical moral judgment correlates with, or predicts to, moral action in naturalistic and experimental situations. These correlations, however, tell us little about the process of moral decision making or about moral judgment in action.

Leming (1973, 1976) started exploration of a somewhat different method for studying moral judgment related to action, the method of studying "practical," as distinct from "classical," moral judgment. According to Leming, the standard dilemmas tap classical moral judgment for two reasons. First, it is classical because of the type of dilemma—abstract hypothetical dilemmas rather than dilemmas representative of the respondents' life space, that is, more "real-life" dilemmas. Second, it is classical because it asks for deontic or prescriptive moral judgment, and a deontic judgment alone. It asks, Should Heinz or anyone have stolen the drug, was he right or wrong? In contrast, says Leming, practical decision making is in the deliberative mode, What will or would you do if you were in Heinz's situation? This mode is future oriented, it is concrete (What would *you* do), and it is descriptive (What *would* you do), not simply prescriptive (What *should* you do?).

Real moral decision making is not only a prescription but also a description of facts of the situation and of the self's needs and motives and those of others in an integrated deliberative practical judgment. In calling the judgment elicited by the standard test prescriptive, we may elaborate and call them, in the terms of moral philosophy, deontic (Frankena, 1973) judgments of the right, or judgments of duty and obligation.

Our reasons for calling classical moral judgments deontic will become clearer after we report Leming's actual findings. Leming set up four cells to represent his basic practical-classical distinction. One cell involved classical dilemmas with prescriptive moral reasoning; one with classical dilemmas with deliberative reasoning; one with real dilemmas with prescriptive moral reasoning; and one with real dilemmas with deliberative reasoning. Leming interviewed 60 7th- and 12th-grade students, filling all four cells for each student. He used three classical (standard hypothetical) dilemmas and three practical (or more everyday real-life) dilemmas. The first practical dilemma centered on a choice involving deception of one's parents in order to go to a party. The second dilemma dealt with the issue of cheating on a school assignment, and the third with a peer group conflict. Leming's results were just what he and common sense might expect. First, Leming had little difficulty in stage scoring practical judgment, using the Kohlberg 1972 Clinical Issue Rating System. Even though the stage descriptions were meant to classify prescriptive reasoning about justice, Leming had little difficulty classifying pragmatic exchanges in the peer group or family as Stage 2, or concerns about hurting the feelings and expectations of others as Stage 3. Stage scores in classical moral judgment correlated well with other classical dilemmas ($r = 80$), less well with deliberative judgments on the classical dilemmas ($r = 70$), and least well with deliberative judgments on the real dilemmas ($r = 60$) (Leming, 1976). Of more importance, Leming found that practical judgment was systematically lower than classical judgment. Students scoring Stage 3 in classical moral judgment were often Stage 2 in practical moral judgment. This result corresponds to the commonsense expectation that classical moral judgment taps highest competence, the moral "high road," whereas more real-life practical judgment is more likely to take the "low road." It is plausible to believe that Leming's assessment of practical judgment is more likely to represent performance, that is, real-life moral decisions, than is assessment of classical moral judgment.

B. Responsibility and Deontic Reasoning on Practical Moral Dilemmas: The Gilligan and Belenky Studies

In 1976 Carol Gilligan and Mary Belenky reported in preliminary form the results of their clinical interviews with women in the process of making the decision as to whether to have an abortion. Not only were their interviews of Leming's practical-reasoning type but they also were not typically framed as deontic justice dilemmas. The framing was left to the subjects. The dilemma was typically not framed by the women subjects as a justice conflict between the fetus's right to life and the mother's rights violated by the existence of an unwanted child; rather, they were typically framed as conflicts of caring and responsibility. Gilligan and Belenky interpreted that these caring and responsibility judgments emerge directly from intrinsically valued relationships or connectedness of persons, not from balancing individual rights through reciprocity and contract. In addition to dilemmas of justice, our high school students also faced these dilemmas of caring or responsibility. Caring dilemmas, as studied by Gilligan (1977), Eisenberg-Berg (1976), and Mussen and Eisenberg-Berg (1977), put in conflict individual responsibility for the care of the self and social responsibility for the care and welfare of another person or a group. The intrinsically moral quality of relations *per se* suggested by Gilligan and Belenky and Eisenberg-Berg is somewhat like Durkheim's belief that the sheer existence of a solidary group creates moral responsibilities, obligations, and aspirations.

Gilligan (1977) builds partly on H. Richard Niebuhr's *The Responsible*

Self (1963), which suggests that in addition to a "civic" deontological rules and justice orientation and a teleological or utilitarian orientation, there is a third "responsibility" orientation, the responsiveness of a social self in a network of relations with other selves.

Drawing on Gilligan, we have in Table 5.1 outlined the elements of a responsibility orientation or a responsibility judgment. Lyons (1982) has developed a complex and reliable method for classifying orientations to personal moral dilemmas as either care oriented or rights oriented, or a mixture of both. She has found that males tend to respond more in the rights orientation and females more in the care orientation but that a majority of both males and females show use of both orientations.

The coding system developed by Lyons based on Gilligan's research was not available at the time we scored our school dilemmas, nor did the distinctions we wished to make exactly correspond to the Gilligan and Lyons notion of two independent moral orientations of rights and of care. Instead, we thought that deontic judgments of rightness were often embedded in judgments of responsibility but that judgments of responsibility went beyond deontic judgments in a number of ways.

In designing our school dilemmas, we enlarged the sphere from our classical dilemmas of justice to dilemmas of care, responsibility, and altruistic action. We also sensitized ourselves to listening to practical judgments made in the language of responsibility as well as in the deontic language of rightness and justice. Gilligan, Lyons, and Langdale (Note 1) have just begun exploring definitions of stages in the responsibility or care orientation. With the need to complete our project, we made up a rough scoring manual for Stages 2–4 for both deontic and responsibility judgments for school practical moral dilemmas. The criteria and rules that we used to define and score judgments of responsibility and a tabular summary of the responsibility stages on our practical school dilemmas are given in Table 5.1.

C. Moral Atmosphere: The Scharf and Hickey Studies

At the same time Leming conducted his study, Kohlberg, Scharf, and Hickey (1972) conducted a different study pointing in the same direction, although the interpretations at the time were different. The starting point of the Scharf (1973) study was observations in conducting moral discussion of real and hypothetical dilemmas in a group at the Cheshire Reformatory. Inmates' judgments and reasoning appeared to be higher concerning hypothetical dilemmas, both the standard test dilemmas and the hypothetical group discussion dilemmas, than were their judgments about real Cheshire Reformatory dilemmas. Furthermore, the way they judged prison dilemmas in the group discussions was different from the way they reported making decisions when they were out of the group and back on the cell block.

To test these observations, Scharf (1973) designed a set of real-life or practical prison dilemmas and gave them to both the discussion group mem-

TABLE 5.1. Criteria for Judgments of Responsibility and Stages of Responsibility Judgments

A. Judgments of responsibility go beyond deontic judgments in one of four ways:

1. Judgments that consider the needs and welfare of the other as an individual where the other's welfare seems to be a matter of a right or claim the other has or where it is a matter of not harming the other's welfare is a deontic concern. Judgments that consider filling the other's need when it is not based on a right or claim or where it is a matter of enhancing his or her welfare, not just preventing harm, is a responsibility concern.

2. Judgments of responsibility consciously consider the involvement and implication of the self in the action or in the welfare consequences to the other.

3. Judgments of personal moral worth (aretaic) of the kind of self the actor wants to be (perfecting character) or would be if he or she failed to perform the action (judgments of blame, guilt, loss of integrity) are judgments of responsibility when explicitly used as a basis for action rather than rights or obligations.

4. Judgments that use an intrinsic valuing of social relationships such as friendship or relationships of community as justification for performing a moral action are judgments of responsibility.

B. Stages of responsibility judgments:

Stage 1. Responsibility and obligation are seen as being the same. The person feels compelled to fulfill the commands of superiors or authority figures or the rules given by them.

Stage 2. Responsibility is differentiated from obligation from this stage onward. The person is responsible only to and for himself or herself and his or her welfare, property, and goals.

Stage 2/3. There is a recognition that everyone is responsible to and for themselves, their welfare, property, and goals. Persons who are irresponsible or careless lose some of the right to have themselves, their welfare, and so on, respected. For example, being careless mitigates the right to have one's property respected as well as justifying a lessened concern for the person's welfare.

Stage 3. Responsibility for the self is to do the "good" thing, to live up to generally known and accepted standards of a "good person." Responsibility to others is limited to those with whom one has a personal relationship and is defined as meeting their needs or promoting their welfare.

Stage 3/4. Responsibility is seen more as a process for maintaining and enhancing feelings of closeness and affection in personal relationships. Being irresponsible is defined as "hurting the other's feelings" within a relationship and is considered a valid basis for a lessened concern of the other's welfare.

Stage 4. Responsibility is seen as a mutually binding set of feelings and agreements among people in relationships, groups, or communities. Being responsible for the self means one must act out of dependability, trustworthiness, and loyalty regardless of fluctuating feelings among people. Irresponsibility on the part of those people within the same group does not mitigate concern for their welfare or rights by other group members.

bers and to control group prisoners involved in a larger study. Like the Leming practical dilemmas, the prison dilemmas elicited much "would" or deliberative judgments as well as eliciting some deontic rights and duty judgments. If Leming found Stage 3 classical moral judgments on the standard dilemmas giving way to more Stage 2 judgments on the practical dilemmas, Scharf found this effect in spades in the prison. He found that "none of the 34 inmates scored higher on the prison dilemmas than on the standard non-prison dilemmas. Of the 16 inmates characterized as Stage 3 on non-prison dilemmas, for example, 11 were rated as Stage 2 on the prison dilemmas. Inmates tended to see relationships with other inmates in Stage 2 instrumental terms. Inmates were seen as 'ripping' each other off, 'ratting' on their friends and 'punking' weaker inmates" (Kohlberg, Scharf, & Hickey, 1972, p. 6).

At the time these researchers did not think clearly of what their findings might mean for moral deliberation and action in general. Instead, they saw it as a statement of what they called the moral atmosphere of the prison. More generally, it indicated that practical moral judgment is not simply a product of a fixed property of the individual, his or her moral competence, but is a product of the interaction between his or her competence and the moral features of the situation, what we also term the "moral atmosphere" of the social situation in which he or she makes decisions.

In our view, the Stage 2 practical reasoning of the prisoners with Stage 3 competence in classical moral judgment was more a function of the prison environment than of the prisoners as personalities. We would characterize the real environment of prison guards and inmate peer groups as a Stage 2 environment or moral atmosphere, and inmates' Stage 2 practical judgments were a realistic adaptation to it. Again then, the Scharf study got closer to action or performance stage, but by tapping something that mixes the level of the environment with the level of individual moral judgment. The Scharf study addressed the moral atmosphere component of practical moral judgment but did not elaborate a systematic method for its study, a task taken up in the present research.

2. METHODOLOGY OF THE HIGH SCHOOL STUDY

A. Samples

The research project included samples of between 20 and 30 students from each of six high schools. The results reported in this chapter are preliminary, including about two-thirds of the students from only four schools.

Three of the six groups of students attended public alternative schools within the larger high school. The other three attended the regular high school counterparts of these alternative schools. The three alternative schools made and enforced rules and settled issues of fairness in a weekly community meeting based on participatory democracy—one person, one vote, whether teacher or student. The school-wide democratic meeting had 60–90 participants, depending on the size of the alternative school. It was preceded by a small group discussion of the moral issues in the decisions to be made, discussions with 10–20 students and a teacher leader.

We expected and found individual moral stage change on the standard hypothetical justice dilemmas in the alternative school students compared with controls in the regular high schools. The upward change in individual moral reasoning was about a quarter stage per year for the alternative school students in two of the three schools. This is the expected change from a good moral discussion program. Such change, however, was not the focus of our research interest. Our focus was on developing two related kinds of assessment: first, an assessment of the presence of and stage of judgments of responsibility on the real school dilemmas, and second, an assessment and comparison of the differences in the moral atmosphere between the alternative schools and their companion traditional high schools.

B. Types of Dilemmas

Table 5.2 presents the four school dilemmas used in the present study. All of the four dilemmas used in the current study we have classified as practical dilemmas as defined by Leming; that is, they ask about situations in the students' own school, and they ask how students think they would reason and act and how their peers would reason and act as well as how they should reason and act.

TABLE 5.2.   The Practical School Dilemmas

1. Caring Dilemma

The college Harry applied to had scheduled an interview with him for the coming Saturday at 9:00 A.M. As the college was 40 miles away from Harry's town and Harry had no way of getting there, his guidance counselor agreed to drive him. The Friday before the interview the guidance counselor told Harry that his car had broken down and was in the repair shop until Monday. He said he felt badly but there was no way he could drive him to his interview. He still wanted to help him out, so he went to Harry's homeroom and asked the students if there was anyone who could drive Harry to the college. No one volunteered to drive him. A lot of students in the class think Harry shows off and talks too much, and they do not like him. The homeroom teacher says he has to take his children to the dentist at that time. Some students say they cannot use the family car, others work, some do not have their licenses. One student, Billy, knows he can use his family car but wonders whether he should do something for Harry when the few students in class who know him best say they are busy or just cannot do it. Besides, he would have to get up really early on a Saturday morning, the only morning during the week he can sleep late.

1.   Should Billy volunteer to drive Harry to the college? Why or why not?

2. Restitution Dilemma

Tom took the money. When Mary returns to the classroom she looks into her pocketbook and notices the 20-dollar bill is missing. She goes to the teacher and reports what has happened. The teacher asks the person to return the money, but no one does. Zeke, a friend of Tom, saw Tom take the money.

1. Should Zeke persuade Tom to return the money? Why?
2. If Zeke tries to persuade Tom to restitute and Tom will not, should Zeke report Tom to the teacher?
3. If no one in the class admits to taking the money or knowing who did it, what should the teacher do? Why?
4. Would there be a general feeling or an expectation in your school that everyone should chip in? Are people supposed to chip in?
5. Would you expect all members of your school to chip in? Would you feel that any member of your school because he or she is a member of your school should chip in? Why?

3. Stealing Dilemma

When Mary arrived at her history class, she noticed that although the students were all there, the teacher had not arrived. She sat down for a few seconds but decided to chat with a few of her friends in the hall until the teacher came. She opened her pocketbook, pulled out a letter she wanted to show her friends, and ran out of the classroom, leaving her pocketbook unsnapped and lying on her desk. Tom, a student in the class, looks into Mary's pocketbook and sees a 20-dollar bill. He thinks about taking the 20-dollar bill from her pocketbook.

1. What do you think a student like Tom would do in a situation like this? Why?
2. Should Mary have been trusting like that in this situation, or should she have been more careful?

4. Drug Dilemma

Before the junior class trip the faculty told the students that the whole class had to agree not to bring or use alcohol or drugs on the trip. If students were found using drugs or alcohol, they would be sent home. The students knew that without faculty approval they would not be able to have their trip. The students said in a class meeting that they all agreed to these conditions. On the trip, several students ask Bob, a fellow student, to go on a hike with them to the lake. When they get to the lake, they light up a joint and pass it around.

1. Should Bob refuse to smoke? Why or why not?

The first two dilemmas we have labeled as prosocial discretionary, following the use of the concept "prosocial" put forth by Eisenberg-Berg (1976) for labeling hypothetical dilemmas given to school children. We call them discretionary because although the actions involved are usually considered to be good, the carrying out of these actions is not usually considered a duty or obligation. The first example is the caring dilemma.

The second example involves a class decision about whether collectively to restitute to a member of the class for the money stolen from her pocketbook by an unknown member of the class. This involves a prosocial and discretionary action by the other members of the class for the victim.

The third dilemma is a mandatory justice dilemma that asks whether anyone should or would steal money from a purse lying open and unattended in a classroom. Obviously, in a dilemma such as this there is consensual agreement by most students that it would be wrong for the protagonist to steal money for reasons of justice, that is, that it is a violation of the property rights of the victim. Even though a deontic justice judgment that it is mandatory not to steal is made, it is possible that a practical judgment to steal could be made by the self or for other students.

The fourth dilemma about the use of marijuana comes close to the type that Turiel (1980) has classified as conventional. In this dilemma the prescription of not smoking arises from a particular organizational school rule rather than from inherent moral justice considerations of violating the rights of other individuals. Our drug dilemma does not fit the strict definition of conventionality offered by Turiel, for laws have been made against it on the grounds that smoking marijuana is inherently harmful to the smoker. This inherent harmfulness, however, is questioned by many adolescents and adults today.

C.   Variables of Individual Moral Judgments and Choices

There are six variables used to describe the individual's ways of moral reasoning. Variable 1 is the stage score (and moral maturity score) for the classical standard moral dilemmas (Forms A or B). The remaining five variables are all categories of responses to the four practical school dilemmas described in the previous section. Variable 2 is a stage score of deontic reasoning. Variable 3 is a stage score of responsibility reasoning. Both of these are "moral judgment" scores assigned to material determined to be in either the deontic or the responsibility orientations according to the criteria in Table 5.1. Each individual, then, can have three moral stage scores but will always have at least two, one based on responses to the standard dilemmas and one based on responses to the school dilemmas.

Variable 4 is the proportion of the use of responsibility judgments over all judgments made in the school dilemmas and is reported as a percentage.

Variables 5 and 6 are the frequencies (in percentages) of making the prosocial (should) moral choice for oneself (Variable 5) and of predicting that one would act in the prosocial way across the four school dilemmas (Variable 6).

These variables are listed in Table 5.3 in the same order as presented here. That table gives both case study and group results.

D.   Variables of the Moral Atmosphere

There are seven variables we have constructed to describe and analyze the moral atmosphere of a school. In this chapter we define and describe them in terms of how they appear in individual school dilemma interview material. We should note here that five of these variables were first constructed using group community meeting transcripts as the data base. Only the first two variables are unique to the individual interview data.

Table 5.4 presents both the case study and group results of the perception of the moral atmosphere for the following seven variables in the order described herein.

TABLE 5.3. Summary of Results for Four Schools: Group Medians of Individual Moral Judgments and Choices

Variable	Brookline High School	(Jay)	School-Within-A-School	(Sarah)	Cambridge High School	(Rob)	Cluster School	(Betsy)
1. Median classical hypothetical moral judgment stage	3/4 (318 MMS[a])	(3/4) (317 MMS)	3/4 (330 MMS)	(3/4) (335 MMS)	3 (287 MMS)	(3/4) (321 MMS)	3 (305 MMS)	(3/4) (345 MMS)
2. Median practical school deontic stage	3	(3/4)	3/4	(3/4)	2/3	(2/3)	3	(3)
3. Median practical school responsibility stage	2/3	(2/3)	3/4	(3/4)	3	—	3/4	(3/4)
4. Proportion of all judgments that are responsibility judgments	12%	(75%)	55%	(66%)	3%	(0%)	46%	(75%)
5. Frequency of prosocial choice for self	75%	(50%)	86%	(75%)	66%	(50%)	83%	(100%)
6. Frequency of predicted prosocial behavior for self	61%	(50%)	77%	(75%)	63%	(50%)	74%	(75%)
Number of students	10		16		15		20	

[a] Moral maturity score.

85

TABLE 5.4. Summary of Results for Four Schools: The Moral Atmosphere

Variable	Brookline High School	(Jay)	School-Within-A-School	(Sarah)	Cambridge High School	(Rob)	Cluster School	(Betsy)
7. Frequency of perceived prosocial choice for others	34%	(0%)	81%	(75%)	45%	(50%)	84%	(100%)
8. Frequency of predicted prosocial behavior for others	26%	(0%)	67%	(50%)	34%	(25%)	58%	(75%)
9. Median degree of collectiveness of norms (1–15)	4	(2 and 5)	11	(12)	4	(1 and 6)	13	(14)
10. Stage of collective norm as represented at median degree or above of collectiveness	3	(2/3)	3/4	(3/4)	2/3	(2/3)	3/4	(3/4)
11. Modal phase of norms	0	(0)	4	(5)	0	(0)	4	(4)
12. Median degree of community valuing (1–4)	1	(0)	3	(3)	0	(1)	3	(4)
13. Median stage of community valuing	2	—	3/4	(3)	2/3	(2/3)	3	(3/4)

Variables 7 and 8 are the frequencies in percentages of students' perceptions of their peers' prosocial *should* choices and a prediction of whether their peers *would* actually act in the prosocial manner across the four school dilemmas.

Variables 9, 10, and 11 are three related ways of characterizing the prosocial moral norms highlighted in the four dilemmas. They are norms of caring or helping, of restituting collectively, of trusting and of upholding property rights, and of upholding the community's rules against drug use. Variable 9 is a measure of the degree to which a norm is collectively shared by members of a school *because* they are members of the school. The scheme for categorizing norms by degree of collectiveness is given in Table 5.5. Variable 10 is the stage of the norms as represented at the median degree of collectiveness or above. Our research assumes that a group norm can be perceived as being at a certain stage that is not necessarily the same as the average stage of individual judgments relevant to that norm. The last variable concerned with norms, Variable 11, is a measure of the strength of the expectations a group has that its norms will be upheld. We call this the phase of the norm. Because phase is the measure of the strength of group norms held in common, norms held only by individuals as personal values are given a phase score of 0. In terms of our scoring rules, this means that norms categorized between 1 and 6 on degree of collectiveness have no phase.

TABLE 5.5. Degree of Collectiveness of Norms

1.	I—Rejection	No one can make a rule or agreement in this school that would be followed or taken seriously.
		Descriptive. I as an individual. No group constituency.
2.	I—Conscience	An action in accordance with the norm should not be expected or demanded by the group because it should be left to each individual's free choice.
		Prescriptive. Could be descriptive. I as an individual.
3.	I—No awareness	Does not perceive the existence of a shared norm concerning this issue and does not take a position pro or con about the group developing such a norm. Also does not have an individual norm concerning this issue.
		Descriptive. I as an individual. Group constituency.
4.	I—Individual	An action should be performed that is in accordance with the norm where this action is not defined or implied by membership in the group. There is no suggestion that the task of the group is or should be to develop or promote the norm.
		Prescriptive. I as an individual. Constituency is universal, applied to people in the group as much as to people outside the group.
5.	I—Individual ambiguous	An action should be performed that is in accordance with the norm where this action is implied by membership in the group.
		Prescriptive. I as an individual. Constituency is ambiguous but seems to apply to people in the group more than to those outside.

TABLE 5.5 (Continued)

6.	Authority	An action should be performed because it is expected or demanded by the teacher or administrator whose authority derives from his or her status or the law that makes the teacher a superior member of the group.
		Prescriptive or Descriptive. Teacher as authority. Group constituency.
7.	Authority—Acceptance	An action should be performed because it is expected by authority or law with the clear implication that the group accepts this authority and thinks promoting and upholding the norm is in the interest of the group's welfare.
		Prescriptive. Teacher as authority. Group constituency. The speaker perspective is the individual speaking as if he or she and others have internalized the norm.
8.	They—Aggregate (I disagree)	They, the group or a substantial subgroup, have a tendency to act in accordance with a norm in a way that the individual speaker does not share or disagrees with.
		Prescriptive or Descriptive. I as a member of the group. Group constituency.
9.	I and they—Aggregate	They and I have a tendency to act in the same way in accordance with a norm.
		Prescriptive or Descriptive. I and they as members of the group. Group constituency.
10.	Limiting or Proposing I	The speaker thinks the group or all members of the group should follow or uphold this norm better or should have this new norm. (This category overlaps with Phase I—Proposing.)
		Prescriptive. I as a member of the group. Group constituency.
11.	Spontaneous—Collective	They or they and I think that group members should act in accordance with the norm *because* they feel naturally motivated to do so due to the sense of belonging to the group.
		Descriptive. They and I as members of the group. Group constituency.
12.	They—Limited collective	They think that group members should act in accordance with the norm without the speaker identifying himself or herself with that normative expectation. The speaker can differentiate his or her own normative perspective.
		Prescriptive. They as members of the group. Group constituency.
13.	I and they—Limited collective	Both I and they, as members of the group, think that group members should act in accordance with the norm.
		Prescriptive. I and they as members of the group. Group constituency.
14.	Implicit—We collective	The members of this group think that all of us should act in accordance with the norm.
		Prescriptive. Speaker perspective is group member qua group member.
15.	Explicit—We Collective	We, the members of this group, think that we should act in accordance with the norm.
		Prescriptive. We (explicitly stated), members qua members. Group constituency.

The two remaining variables are Variable 12, the degree of community valuing, and Variable 13, the stage of community valuing. Degree of community valuing is a four-point scale roughly categorizing the extent to which members of a school value their school as a community for its own sake. This measure is described in Table 5.6. The stages of community valuing are given in Table 5.7.

3. STUDENT CASE ILLUSTRATIONS OF THE METHOD

The following three cases are prototypical members of three of the schools studied. These students' Standard Form moral judgment scores are all the same and are close to the averages for their groups. We quote from these cases to illustrate how the practical school dilemmas are scored and the meaning of the variables listed in the preceding sections.

The students are from Brookline High School, Cambridge Rindge and Latin School, and the Cluster School of Cambridge, Massachusetts. Their individual scores appear in parentheses beside the scores for their groups in Tables 5.3 and 5.4. These tables also include the scores of a prototypical student from the Brookline alternative school, School-Within-A-School, although considerations of chapter length precluded discussion of that case.

A. The Case of Jay

Jay is a 10th-grader in the regular Brookline High School, a school composed primarily of adolescents from middle and professional classes. Most of the students in this school are white and most are either Jewish or Irish-Catholic. Of the 10% black minority, most are bused to the high school.

TABLE 5.6. Degree of Community Valuing

I.	Instrumental extrinsic	The school is valued as an institution that helps the individual to meet his or her own academic needs.
II.	"Esprit de corps" extrinsic	The school is valued as an institution that helps the individual and that the individual feels some loyalty toward as manifest in team spirit and support of teams or groups in school.
III.	Spontaneous community intrinsic	The school is valued as the kind of place in which members feel an inner motivation to help others in the group community and the community generates special feelings of closeness among members.
IV.	Normative communal intrinsic	The school as a community is valued for its own sake. Community can obligate its members in special ways, and members can expect special privileges or responsibilities from the group and other members.

TABLE 5.7.   Stages of the Sense of Community Valuing

Stage 2

There is no clear sense of community apart from exchanges among group members. Community denotes a collection of individuals who do favors for one another and rely on one another for protection. Community is valued insofar as it meets the concrete needs of its members.

Examples:

The community is like a "bank." Members meet to exchange favors, but you cannot take more than you give.

Stage 3

The sense of community refers to a set of relationships and sharings among group members. The group is valued for the friendliness of its members. The value of the group is equated with the value of its collective normative expectations.

Examples:

1.   The community is a family in which members care for one another.
2.   The community is honorable because it helps others.

Stage 4

The school is explicitly valued as an entity distinct from the relationships among its members. Group commitments and ideals are valued. The community is perceived as an organic whole composed of interrelated systems that carry on the functioning of the group.

Examples:

Stealing affects "the community more than the individual because that is what we are. We are not just a group of individuals."

On the classical hypothetical moral dilemmas Jay was Stage 3/4. This transitional stage was the median stage for the regular Brookline High School comparison sample.

In the classical dilemmas Jay demonstrates a sense of justice obligating him to keep contracts and trusts even to unrelated strangers based on golden rule reciprocity. His sense of obligation to help an unrelated stranger in the Heinz dilemma is very different from his response to the first practical school dilemma, the caring dilemma. In answering this dilemma, Jay equates obligation with responsibility and concludes that he is not responsible to or for a stranger. See Table 5.2 for the dilemma stories.

Should Billy volunteer to drive Harry to college?

I don't think he has any obligation. If I was in his place, and I didn't know the kid too well, if I wanted to sleep late, I don't feel that it is my responsibility to go drive somebody to their interview, it is up to them, they are responsible. If I were going there, if I had an interview there at the same time, sure I would. But if I had the opportunity to sleep late and didn't know the kid at all, I wouldn't.

Why is it not a responsibility?

It's not really that you are obligated to a person because you are more re-sponsible to yourself and your actions. I know I have been through this year, a whole mess of garbage with my friends about driving around since I got my license. People seem to think as long as you have a car they have a ride, and in my opinion it doesn't operate that way. If I wanted to give him a ride, I will give him a ride, if I am going there and they want to go there. It is my car and I am the one who is driving, and I don't see why I should give him a ride.

You think you shouldn't give them a ride?

It doesn't mean I shouldn't give them a ride, but if I don't know them well enough, I think just out of protection for myself and my property, I wouldn't. I think people may say that being responsible to yourself is more important than other pople. I think there is an extent where you put yourself first. And when you believe in putting yourself first, like I do, or try to at least, I don't feel I should be obligated to do somebody else's work, especially if I don't know them, I don't think I should give them a ride.

Jay helps us to understand the relation between two kinds of judgment, deon-tic judgments of duty and judgments of responsibility.

We could say one has a responsibility to drive Harry without implying Harry has a right to be driven. *Responsibility* is sometimes a stronger word than *duty,* sometimes a weaker word. Responsibility is weaker in the caring dilemma in that one may have some responsibility to drive Harry even though prosocial caring for the other is supererogatory, driving is an altruistic act be-yond the call of duty. *Responsibility* may be a stronger word than *duty* as in a justice dilemma. A stranger dying in the Heinz dilemma may have a right to live, and one may have a duty to maintain the right, but one would not or-dinarily be said to have a responsibility for the stranger's life in the sense one does for one's spouse's life.

Jay's introduction of his idea of responsibility into the caring dilemma helps us make sense of the discrepancy between the moral stage or level of his response to that dilemma and his response to the Standard Form moral dilemmas.

In the caring dilemma Jay understands full well the Stage 3 niceness of helping Harry. But he makes a Stage 2/3 judgment of individualistic respon-sibility in making his decision. A judgment of responsibility, as Gilligan points out, depends on the positing of a social bond or relationship as neces-sary. Jay posits a relationship of friendship but defines it in Stage 2/3 reci-procity terms. He says, "I think it really depends on the relationship of a per-son to the person who needs a ride. If they are good friends I don't think he has an obligation. I think it would be nice and I know if it was my friend, if it was an important interview, he would do the same for me, then I would do it." As noted before, a brief summary of our definitions of stages in judgments of responsibility is given in Table 5.1.

We think that responsibility judgments are a species of practical judgment; they are not readily elicited by the standard justice dilemmas. Jay speedily falls into psychological or *would* language in explaining his idea of responsibility in the caring dilemma. Responsibility language is at the intersection between prescriptive moral structures and the descriptive language of an acting self.

The question remains, however, of whether Jay's Stage 2/3 response to the caring dilemma is due to his practical moral judgment being lower than his classical moral judgment or whether it is because his responsibility judgments are lower than his deontic judgments. In our opinion, it is the latter case. We hypothesized that the stage development of an orientation or judgment of responsibility lags behind development of deontic judgments if there is a discrepancy between the two. In the caring dilemma Jay makes only a judgment of responsibility. We find Jay is consistently at a lower stage in his judgments of responsibility than in deontic judgments as we move from a caring situation to a justice situation, stealing, in which he makes both types of judgment.

In responding to the practical school dilemma of stealing, the third dilemma, he says, "I would leave the money there because I respect people's property because I expect them to do that to my property. I know it is a big temptation but its her money, she earned it however way she did. Besides it being against the law, it's also respect of a person's property, and you don't have any right to take it just because you want it. Otherwise we would have a pretty sick society with no laws and with chaos." Jay's use of deontic justice reasoning in this response is indicated by his use of rights, of the golden rule, and of the need to maintain social order. We score this as deontic Stage 3/4 consistent with his standard moral judgment stage.

Jay's Stage 2/3 responsibility reasoning comes out in the stealing situation in his response to the restitution dilemma, asking about responsibility for restitution to Mary, the victim of the theft. In reply to the idea of the whole class chipping in to help Mary because the thief is unknown, he says, "No, because there are two reasons. One because it was Mary's fault or lack of responsibility by leaving her purse out. She was too trusting. The second thing is why should I pay for what somebody else did? Why should I get involved?" Jay also feels other students would not want to chip in. He says, "The same thing, why should they pay for what other people are doing, or other people's lack of responsibility that it got stolen."

Jay's lower-stage (2/3) judgments of responsibility compared with his higher-stage (3/4) judgments of justice are closely connected to his perception of the moral atmosphere of the high school. According to Jay, the high school lacks collective norms for caring and responsibility and lacks a sense of community. He is asked on the caring dilemma, "Should the school have some kind of agreement or understanding that someone should help out someone else?" In response he says, "I think this school really lacks that. It lacks in togetherness, I think. Nobody really takes pride in the school except a few who are good students or very good athletes. Where people don't take pride in something, go out of their way to help each other, the community doesn't really benefit. It doesn't promote the welfare of the school."

Jay thus tells us that there are no collective norms of helping and little sense of community in his school. He responds in a similar way on the stealing dilemma. Asked, "Would you express your disapproval and try to find out who took Mary's money?" Jay answers, "It depends. I wouldn't go much out of my way, again it's her responsibility . . . in this school people care too much for themselves, and they wouldn't really go out of their way to do something. We have a lot of things stolen from lockers. Nothing seems to get done about it. In that sense I guess nobody really cares. There is a lack of trust or caring about other people's property in this school."

Jay's sense of the nonexistence of collective norms of trust and helping and his sense of his fellow students' lack of feeling or valuing community are scored in our moral atmosphere manual as 1 on the scale of the degree of collectiveness of norms displayed in Table 5.5 and as 0 on the scale of degree of community valuing presented in Table 5.6.

To summarize, we have presented Jay to give some feeling for the differences between deontic and responsibility judgments and to highlight the way in which these different modes of judging usually appear on the practical school dilemmas.

To illustrate the constructs of moral atmosphere we will compare two students from Cambridge, Betsy, a student of the Cluster School, a just community alternative school, and Rob, a student at Cambridge Rindge and Latin, the regular high school.

B. The Cases of Betsy and Rob

Betsy and Rob are both 10th-graders and both scored Stage 3/4 on the hypothetical classical moral dilemmas. These students are one-half stage higher on individual moral judgment than the median of their groups, which were Stage 3. Both Betsy and Rob are middle-class students in schools where at least half of the students are working class. Ethnically, Cambridge Rindge and Latin School was 25% black and 10% Hispanic and other minorities, and Cluster School was half black and half white in 1979, when these interviews were done.

In answer to why people in her school should help out on the caring dilemma, Betsy says: "Yes, they should because Cluster is a community. Because you have a responsibility to the kids in this school, even if you don't like them all that much, you are in school and you're with them every day, you know, you are supposed to think of them as part of the school and part of the community, so you should do it."

Betsy clearly expresses the value of community. We categorized her response as being at Degree 4, the normative communal level (see Table 5.6). We see this way of thinking about community in her idea that the school is a community that expects members to help one another because they are all members of the same group. This idea implies an awareness and valuing of community that creates moral obligations and norms. The interviewer asks: "What does it mean, it does sound kind of corny, because it sounds like a cliché when you say it, we are a community, so we are supposed to help each other?" Betsy says, "Because everyone is supposed to be one, it is our school, it is not a school that all these separate people go to that don't care about each other."

Betsy's response indicates three aspects of this level of community valuing. First is the idea that a community implies a strong degree of unity, a oneness or solidarity. Second, it expresses the idea of personal identification with the group and its objectives: "It is our school." Third is the feature that membership in the group means mutual caring about one another as group members.

On the caring dilemma she also clearly indicates the existence of a shared or collective norm of helping. She says, "Anyone who is in Cluster knows they should help out . . . there is a general feeling and everyone knows that."

Should someone help out?

Yes, they should because Cluster school is a community. Because you have a responsibility to the kids in this school. You are supposed to think of them as part of the school and part of the community, so you should do it.

Betsy's response depicts a group with a high degree of collective norm, Degree 14 (see Table 5.5). Her statement exemplifies the three aspects of the highest two levels of the collectiveness of the helping norm. When Betsy says, "you are supposed to," she is speaking as one member of a collective to other members of the collective, and she is representing the point of view of the group as a whole. This aspect of her response we call "speaker's perspective," a perspective ranging from speaking from the standpoint of oneself as an individual to speaking from the standpoint of *we,* the members of the group. At the highest level, speaking from the point of view of the group becomes explicit, taking the form of "we think we should . . ."

Betsy is Degree 14 because her command of "you have a responsibility to the kids in this school" does not come from her as an individual but is a statement from the perspective of the group representative of the collective norm. The speaker perspective defines the group *for* whom the subject is speaking or representing. The group constituency defines the group membership of the persons *to* whom the subject is speaking or prescribing a rule or action. In this example, it is clear to whom Betsy is speaking; she is prescribing to the members of the Cluster School. In our system, constituency is either individual or a specified group. Degrees 1–4 represent the individual as the constituent, and Degrees 5–15 specify a particular group as the constituency.

The third aspect is that the norm is stated prescriptively in terms of an obligation at the higher levels. We distinguish norms that are prescriptive from norms that are aggregate or stated as descriptive of the behavior of individuals or groups. Aggregate norms reflect a "statistical tendency" rather than a clearly shared idea of obligation.

In contrast with Betsy, Rob, a student of the regular Cambridge High School, does not see a shared valuing of community, but it is not clear whether he sees the school as a valued organization serving learning and other goals. He individually values the school but thinks that others do not: I don't consider this school a community. Too many people hold grudges against each other, because maybe they look different or act different. Or some kids come to school to be with their friends or to be stoned, and some kids come to do work. Like the kids who get stoned might stand around and see someone with a lot of books walk by and laugh. But they won't laugh when graduation comes. No, most people think of themselves, really.

How do you think thinking about the community would affect that?

If they did think about it, I don't really know, because I don't know if they ever did, like I said only people in committees and stuff would think about it and talk about it, and those would be a small minority.

In handling issues about respecting other people's property and trusting other people, do you think Cambridge Rindge and Latin School is really a community?

Well not really, because in a way like we own this school and a lot of kids mess it up. Like write on the walls, there is no need for that, there is paper to write on. I don't know, some people do and some people don't. I don't really know the percentage.

These comments indicate that Rob is Degree 1 in his thinking about the value of the school (see Table 5.6). He, as an individual, attaches some value to the school as an organization and says, "in a way like we own this school and a lot of kids mess it up." He feels some ownership of the school and finds vandalism or injury to it offensive. He also values its major function, academic learning, even though he sees that many other students do not. Thus, there is a contrast between his individual valuing of the school as an organization and his perception of the attitudes of most of the students in this regard. Moreover, Rob does not perceive any shared norm of helping. He believes that it would be a good thing to have a shared norm to help but does not believe that it exists. When asked if his school should have a shared agreement to help out, he says: "Yah, right. Like it is not a law, but everybody knows that it is good to help someone out. But people just don't care about anyobdy else." Going on the theme of a lack of a sense of community and caring at the high school, he comments that "seventy-five percent of them wouldn't care."

Why?

They are worried about their own problems probably.

Rob himself as an individual holds a norm of helping, but he is conspicuously aware of the discrepancy between his individual norm of helping and the absence of any collective norm of helping.

What should the agreement be and why should it be such an agreement?

It's really—it should be an agreement with yourself, you know. It is like, I have strong feelings toward other people. I don't like to think bad things and I never say anything bad about anybody, and it is more of an agreement with yourself than with anybody, you couldn't make an agreement with somebody about something like this.

Not only is Rob aware of the discrepancy between his individual norm of helping and the lack of any collective norm, but also his response indicates that he thinks it is impossible to develop shared moral norms on issues such as helping. This is scored as Degree 1 on our scale, explicit rejection of the possibility of developing a shared norm (see Table 5.5).

The statements by Rob that "I just believe in helping people" and "it should be an agreement with yourself" demonstrate clearly that he is speaking only for himself rather than from a "we" perspective, as is involved in the higher levels. His responses indicate that his idea that one should help is not defined in terms of a specific group, like members of the school, who should follow the norm and be the persons toward whom help is directed. He sees that any "good person" would hold this norm for himself or herself. His norm does not define a group constituency, a bounded group of people where responsibilities are felt toward one another. For Rob, the idea of helping is not obligatory or prescriptive but is a positive value that is based on a concern or caring for others. When this concern is absent, he sees no possibility for expecting someone to help out another person. Accordingly, Rob's conception of the norm of helping is nonprescriptive.

Although Rob does not see a positive collective norm of helping, he does perceive a counternorm in this situation that makes helping an unpopular student disapproved of by the peer group.

What would you do?

I would wait till after class, I would keep it quiet so nobody might know about it, and then I could help the kid. Then nobody would say anything to me, because they would not know about it.

Rob's feeling that he would help but in a way so that others did not know about it indicates he is concerned about disapproval for helping, presumably because of the existence of a peer group norm making it "uncool" to associate with or aid an unpopular student.

For example, when Rob says he would be secretive about helping, he is responding to his daily observation that students do not help their unpopular classmates. The consistency of his observation shows both Rob and ourselves that there exists an *aggregate* counternorm (Degrees 8 and 9). This aggregate norm of helping influences Rob's behavior, but it is not obligatory in the same sense as Betsy's articulation of the norm of helping. Explicit shared agreements in a group have obligatory force, whereas the power of statistical or "average" behaviors do not. Aggregate norms arise out of a concern to fit into the average behavioral pattern of one's peers.

Assigning the degree of collectiveness or sharedness to the way Betsy and Rob perceive the norm of helping in each of their schools still does not tell us the extent to which the norm is upheld by either the students or his peers. Table 5.8 describes another dimension in the perception of school norms, the dimension of phase of commitment to upholding the norm. The phase of the norm came to be defined when we were observing Cluster School's community meetings in terms of the development of its norms over time.

In our observations of the development of collective norms from meeting to meeting and from year to year in the Cluster School, we identified a dimension of phase of commitment to and institutionalization of the norm that could be distinguished from the existence or degree of collectiveness of the norm itself. Our scheme describes the evolution of collective norms going through distinct phases from the time they are first proposed to the time they are expected and upheld.

We designed a set of questions about phase intended to form a Guttman scale. In a Guttman scale, saying yes to a question implies having said yes to all the lower items of questions in the scale. For example, the highest point in our Guttman scale of phase is expressed willingness publicly to sanction a member for violating a norm. The Guttman scale notion implies that anyone who says yes to this, for example, Phase 6 willingness publicly to express disapproval to a member for violating a norm says yes to all less extreme phases of commitment to the norm.

On the caring dilemma, Betsy says that the Cluster School holds its collective norm of helping at Phase 6. She says, "They would disapprove. . . . I think the kids would be very mad at him if he didn't do it. They would have said something [to Billy] . . . because of why it's important to do it [that is, to help] and why they would bitch at him for not doing it."

Comparing Rob's responses on the caring dilemma with Betsy's responses, we said that he perceives his school as having no shared expectation of helping. It is always the case that when a norm is perceived to be at a low degree of collectiveness (Degree 6 or below), the phase will be 0 or nonexistent. On the caring norm, Rob is Degree 1 and says, "You couldn't make an agree-

TABLE 5.8.   Phases of the Collective Norm

Phase 0:   No collective norm exists or is proposed.

Collective Norm Proposal

Phase 1:   Individuals propose collective norms for group acceptance.

Collective Norm Acceptance

Phase 2:   Collective norm is accepted as a group ideal but not agreed to. It is not an expectation for behavior.
   a.   some group members accept ideal
   b.   most group members accept ideal

Phase 3:   Collective norm is accepted and agreed to but is not (yet) an expectation for behavior.
   a.   some group members agree to collective norm
   b.   most group members agree to collective norm

Collective Norm Expectation

Phase 4:   Collective norm is accepted and expected. (Naive expectation)
   a.   some group members expect the collective norm to be followed
   b.   most group members expect the collective norm to be followed

Phase 5:   Collective norm is expected but not followed. (Disappointed expectation)
   a.   some group members are disappointed
   b.   most group members are disappointed

Collective Norm Enforcement

Phase 6:   Collective norm is expected and upheld through expected persuading of deviant to follow norm.
   a.   some group members persuade
   b.   most group members persuade

Phase 7:   Collective norm is expected and upheld through expected reporting of defiant to the group.
   a.   some group members report
   b.   most group members report

---

ment with somebody about something like that." When he was asked, "Should there be an agreement?" he said, "It wouldn't get followed anyway." These statements tell us three things: that there is not existing agreement in Cambridg Rindge and Latin to help (a Phase 3 idea); that there is no shared ideal of helping (a Phase 2 idea); and that Rob feels it would be unrealistic to propose such an agreement (a Phase 1 idea).

The remaining concepts in analyzing "moral atmosphere" using individual interview material are the stage of the representation of the collective norm and the stage of the representation of community valuing. We define the stage of representation of the collective norm as the stage the individual uses to explain how most people in the school understand the meaning of the particular norm. Betsy represents the stage of Cluster School's collective norm of caring as being 3/4. She says, "Because you have a responsibility to the kids in this school, even if you don't like them all that much, you are supposed to think of them as part of the school and part of the community, so you should do it." Furthermore, Betsy understands the school community in a transitional 3–4 sense, as being an entity separate from the individuals who compose it. Betsy's response illustrates that both the norm of caring and the value of community can be stage scored. The stages of the valuing of community are presented in Table 5.7. Although we distinguish for analytical purposes an individual's stage of the collective norm and the stage of community value, on any particular school dilemma these are almost always the same.

As we discussed earlier, speaker perspective is important in defining the degree of collectiveness of a group norm. It is equally important in determining what responses in an interview are stageable representations of the collective norm rather than simply the individual's own stage of reasoning. The speaker perspective defines *for* whom the subject is speaking or representing. Thus, it helps us identify the material representative of the collective norm. When a subject, like Betsy, speaks *to* the group on *behalf* of the group and does so prescriptively, we identify and use that material as indicative of the *collective* norm. Material isolated in this way, furthermore, generally has clear stageable characteristics. In other words, the way we assess the structure or stage of the collective reasoning is parallel to the way we assess the structure or stage of an individual's reasoning.

After Betsy prescribes that Cluster School members should uphold their own norms of caring, she then states an exception when she as an individual would not uphold this norm. She says, "The only way I would say he shouldn't help him is if he was a creep and he really did something rotten to him in the past, if he showed he didn't care about Billy or anyone else, then I wouldn't help him out." In this statement Betsy is prescribing only for herself; she is specifying for herself the conditions and reasons for which she would not uphold the norm under certain circumstances. Her individual reasoning in this case is Stage 3. She feels no obligation to help someone who has in the past violated the group's shared expectations of caring.

Contrasting Rob's interview with Betsy's, we know there is no collective stage of a norm of helping because, as Rob tells us, there is no such collective norm. He does this in two ways. First, in response to the question "Should there be an agreement about helping?" Rob says, "Yeh right . . . like it is not a law but everybody knows that it is good to help somebody out but people just don't care about anybody else; . . . it is more of an agreement with yourself than with anybody; you couldn't make an agreement with anybody about anything like this." In his response Rob denies the possibility of even establishing a collective norm in Cambridge Rindge and Latin and tells us that he can speak only for himself. Thus, there is no collective norm of caring to be staged. This material is, however, stageable; it reflects Rob's own Stage 3 reasoning that good people should try to help others, a stage score assigned to his individual norm of helping.

Remembering that Rob did report an aggregate counternorm in his school, however, one that said it is "uncool" to be seen helping an "unpopular" student, he represents it as being moderately collective (Degree 8) and at a very high phase (Phase 6). He believes people would actually say he should not help if they saw him doing it. Although assigning stage to counternorms is ambiguous because they are descriptions of behavior often given without any justification, frequently we feel we can assign guess stage scores. In this case Rob is representing a counternorm against helping that seems to be Stage 2 or 2/3. The important point is that we and Rob agree that it is clearly a lower stage than his own individual norm of care, which is Stage 3. Rob's representation of the stage of community valuing is also 2 or 2/3. He describes the school as an institution legitimately used by some for their own academic ends and abused by others for arbitrary and personal reasons.

Turning to Rob's and Betsy's responses on the school dilemma about collective restitution, we will quickly run through our assessment procedure. When Betsy is asked:

Would there be a general feeling or expectation in the class that everyone should pitch in 50¢?

Yes, because the reason why is it is just easier that way, first of all, and if something like that is going to happen at the school, the school should be responsible for it, the kids.

Why is that fair?

It is fair because if everyone gets away with stealing and no one cares here, then it just can't be a good place, first of all. If people think everything is everyone else's tough luck and it is too bad that happened, then this place would not be a very caring place. Stealing from someone in the community is just like stealing from the community.

Would that make it an unfair place?

Sure, it would make it a very unfair place.

Why?

Because some people have better luck than other people. Some people have more or less and some people are bigger and can get their way more and if that is the way it worked, then it would be very unfair.

If the teacher asks the kids to chip in and some kids say they will not, what should they do?

They should chip in. But if they won't, they are not really in a community, they don't care. You have to do what the majority wants to do, or else we would have no school and it would be very unorganized and nothing goes right.

From these responses, we say that there is an explicit shared norm of collective restitution at Degree 14. Betsy speaks prescriptively as a member of the community in explaining that the norm should be upheld in order to affirm the community qua community. Thus, the degree of community valuing is 4. The phase of this norm is not explicitly stated, but we know it is at least Phase 4, that Betsy expects people to act consistently with the majority vote to chip in. The norm of collective restitution and the degree of community valuing as represented by Betsy are both Stage 3/4. She argues that because individuals in the school may have differential advantages, the school must be equally responsible to all its members and the way to be responsible is to act according to the majority will.

Rob, on the other hand, has very little to say about collective restitution or even about what the teacher could do to help the victim of a classroom theft to get her money back. Moreover, although Rob has made the deontic judgment that it is wrong to steal, it does not help him decide whether he would report a friend who did steal:

Do you think Zeke should report Tom for the theft?

If he is his friend, he won't. I don't know.

No one in the class admits to taking the money or knowing who did, what should the teacher do?

He can't really do anything. There is nothing he can do.

If you were in Zeke's position, would you try to persuade your friend to return the money?

Definitely, because I don't just care about myself, I care about other people, probably the girl doesn't care about the money either, but just cares that somebody had the gall enough to take it right there in the room, you know. I'd persuade him to give her the money back for that sake, too.

If your friend refused to return the money, would you report him?

No.

Why not?

Because he did it, I don't know. I don't feel obliged to do it, I don't feel I should.

Should you report him?

I guess so, I'm not really sure, Zeke should I guess.

Why?

Because it [stealing] is against my conscience, it is against what I believe in.

Should the class all chip in to repay Mary her money?

No.

Why not?

Because the class didn't steal it, just one person did.

What would you do?

If I was in the class and it got stolen, I would just ask everybody, I wouldn't accuse anybody. There is nothing I could really do except for that.

Should a good member of your school be willing to chip in?

No.

If there was an agreement that students should do that, would most students chip in willingly?

No, not willingly.

Do you think this school should have an agreement that everyone should chip in in situations like this?

Nope.

Again Rob tells us there is no collective norm of restitution of any form in his school. He does reiterate his individual norm (Degree 4) of caring about other people, here scored as Stage 3. From Rob's responses, we learn that the moral atmosphere of the regular high school does not contain any ideas or norms of restitution. Thus, no degree of collectiveness, stage, phase, or degree of community valuing scores can be assigned for this dilemma. From Rob's answers on the stealing dilemma, we hear again about his individual norm against stealing, represented at Stage 3 and at Phase 5, an expression of personal disappointment that stealing occurs in his school.

When asked whether he should or would be trusting in his school, he says:

Would you be as trusting as Mary about your possessions?

I have been bringing a skateboard to school and I have really been thinking about leaving it in my locker, because I know someone in the voc ed school that I went to for a year, they used to break in the lockers all the time and I kind of never used a locker for that reason and I only use a locker for my books. I was—when nobody was looking, I put my skateboard in there, because I don't trust some people.

Do you think you should be trusting about leaving stuff in this school?

You should be, but you can't be.

Why can't you be?

Because there are people who do steal and people who will steal outside of school will do it in school, too, because I know people who have done it.

The norm of trust is scored as Degree 1 of collectiveness, an explicit rejection of the possibility of having a shared norm of trust. Therefore, the phase is 0. The degree of community valuing implicit in this passage is 0, no feeling that the school is valued even as an educational institution to foster individual academic achievement. The stage of reasoning Rob uses to describe his school and his own lack of trust we can loosely call Stage 1/2.

E. Summary Data for Brookline and Cambridge

Looking at Table 5.3 and 5.4, which report the median scores for each of four groups in the school dilemmas, we see that the differences between Jay and Betsy and Rob are prototypical of the difference between democratic alternative school students and regular high school students on responsibility reasoning and on the moral atmosphere for the four schools.

The downward stage discrepancy evident for the regular high school students illustrates the relevance of the distinction we have made between classical and practical reasoning (Table 5.3). These students did not use their highest or best moral reasoning when thinking about real-life dilemmas in the context of their own schools. We attribute this finding to the lack of democratic discussion and decision making, to the lack of collective and relatively high stage group norms, and to the lack of valuing the schools as communities. We now turn to the comparative results on the variables that operationalize these components of the moral atmosphere.

Table 5.4, which gives summary results for the four schools and four average students, lists the proportion of students in each school that make the choice of social responsibility over the individual responsibility choice. In terms of the content of choice rather than the mode of judgment about it, there was a moderate tendency for the democratic schools to lead students to make the prosocial choice as opposed to the individual choice.

When we asked what each student should or would do, we considered that to be a part of the evaluation of individual judgments. When we then asked what they thought their peers should or would do, make the prosocial choice or not, we move to consideration and evaluation of the moral atmosphere of each school. In the democratic schools, over 80% of the responses of the students showed that they believed their peers felt they should act prosocially, whereas in regular high schools about 40% of the responses indicated that students believed their peers felt they should act prosocially.

In predicting their peers' behavior, about 60% of the democratic school students' responses indicated that they felt their peers would act consistently with their prosocial choice. In the regular high schools, about 30% of the responses showed that students believed their peers would act prosocially.

The disparity between answering for themselves and for others is interesting. Whereas the majority of regular high school students make the prosocial choice for themselves, less than half, or one-third, feel their peers would make the prosocial choice. This phenomenon seems to be an example of "pluralistic ignorance." In other words, most students in the regular high schools say they would help but do not believe many of their peers would help. Seeing their peers as different from themselves and in some sense as less responsible, we think, is in part a result of the school environment that provides few opportunities for discussing and creating explicitly shared norms.

In the democratic schools, most students report that they themselves would make the prosocial choice and act on it. They also report that most of their peers would do the same. This congruency between students' perceptions of others and their self-reports is evidence that pluralistic ignorance can be overcome through open democratic discussion. The relationship of judgments of responsibility to moral action as discussed by Kohlberg and Candee in Chapter 4 seems to us to be reflected in our own results. That there were equally high percentages of judgments of responsibility and predictions of prosocial moral action for others and themselves suggests that such judgments create a way of thinking that leads to moral action. Additionally, we feel that a positive moral atmosphere provides the context in which students feel it makes sense to think in terms of responsibility and to act morally toward their peers and teachers.

There are sharp differences between the democratic school students and the regular high school students in the frequency of use of responsibility judgments. Although half of the responses of alternative school students were in the responsibility mode, only 5–12% of responses made by regular high school students were classified in this mode.

Looking at the median stage scores for deontic and responsibility reasoning on the school dilemmas, we see that in both modes the regular high school students' reasoning was one-half to one stage lower than the stages used by democratic alternative school students (see lines 2 and 3, Table 5.3). This result is striking because the median classical moral judgment scores were the same within each pair.

For the degree of collectiveness of norms, Table 5.4 shows that neither regular high school has truly collective norms. The predominance of a score 4 indicates that the students held only individual norms about caring, trust, and so on. In contrast, students in both democratic schools articulated strongly shared norms at Degree 11 for School-Within-A-School and Degree 13 for Cluster School. Table 5.5 describes this difference. Most students in the former school felt norms should be upheld because of positive feelings and motivations that they saw as generated spontaneously by being in a close and caring community. Cluster School students saw the norms as morally prescriptive and as generated by a collective decision process.

The median stage of the Degree 4 individual norms is 3 for Brookline and 2/3 for Cambridge Rindge and Latin School, in both cases, one-half stage lower than the median stage for each sample on the classical hypothetical dilemmas. The stage of the collective norms for both democratic schools was 3/4; this is the same or higher than the median stages of both on the classical hypothetical dilemmas.

The results mean that when students reason individually about school norms, they tend to formulate them at a lower stage. In contrast, when students through explicit discussion formulate truly collective norms, they do so at a higher stage, sometimes a half stage above that of most students in the group.

Degree of community valuing and its median stage give parallel results for the four schools. Cambridge Rindge and Latin High School students indicated on the whole that they did not value their school even as an educational institution. The score is 0. Brookline High School students mostly valued their school as an educational institution, a place to go to meet their own academic needs. The score was 1. Both alternative schools were intrinsically valued as communities by their students, as is indicated by a score of 3 on degree of community valuing. The stage of community valuing scores reflect these differences. Brookline and Cambridge students' conceptions of their schools as Stage 2 and 2/3 places is consistent with not valuing or instrumentally valuing their schools. School-Within-A-School and Cluster students conceptualized their communities in Stage 3/4 and 3 terms, respectively. This also is consistent with the expressed valuing of their communities as enabling and promoting caring, trusting, and sharing relationships.

In summary, the democratic school students were higher than their regular high school controls in the content of their school dilemma choices, favoring prosocial responsibility; in their mode of judgment, making judgments of responsibility; and in their stage of judgment. We believe that these differences reflect real differences in moral action in the schools, a belief we support in a detailed history of the alternative schools that we are now writing. We interpret these differences in practical moral judgment as arising from the differential moral atmospheres of the democratic and comparison schools. The democratic schools have a high sense of collective prosocial norms and a strong sense of community. The methodology that we have described is useful for studying the moral atmosphere not only of the school but also of the work place and the family. Pilot extensions of the methodology for these other institutions are now underway.

REFERENCES

Blasi, A. Bridging moral cognition and moral action: A review of the literature. *Psychological Bulletin,* 1980, *88,* 1–45.

Durkheim, E. *Moral education: A study in the theory and application in the sociology of education.* New York: Free Press, 1961. (Originally published, 1925.)

Eisenberg-Berg, N. *The development of prosocial moral judgment and its correlates.* Unpublished doctoral dissertation, University of California, Berkeley, 1976.

Frankena, W. K. *Ethics* (2nd ed.). Englewood Cliffs, N.J.: Prentice-Hall, 1973.

Gilligan, C. In a different voice: Women's conceptions of self and morality. *Harvard Educational Review,* 1977, *47,* 481–517.

Gilligan, C., & Belenky, M. A naturalistic study of abortion decision. In R. Selman & R. Yando (Eds.), *Clinical-developmental psychology.* San Francisco: Jossey-Bass, 1980.

Kohlberg, L. Exploring the moral atmosphere of the school. In L. Kohlberg, *The meaning and measurement of moral development.* Worcester, Mass.: Clark University Press, 1980.

Kohlberg, L. *Essays on moral development* (Vol. 1): *The philosophy of moral development.* San Francisco: Harper & Row, 1981.

Kohlberg, L., Scharf, P., & Hickey, J. The justice structure of the prison: A theory and intervention. *Prison Journal,* 1972, *51,* 3–14.

Leming, J. S. *Adolescent moral judgment and deliberation on classical and practical moral dilemmas.* Unpublished doctoral dissertation, University of Wisconsin, 1973.

Leming, J. S. An exploratory inquiry into the multi-factor theory of moral behavior. *Journal of Moral Education,* 1976, *5*(2), 179–188.

Lyons, N. *Two orientations to morality; Rights and care: A coding manual.* Unpublished doctoral dissertation, Harvard University, 1982.

Mussen, P., & Eisenberg-Berg, N. *Roots of caring, sharing and helping.* New York: Freeman, 1977.

Niebuhr, H. R. *The responsible self.* New York: Harper & Row, 1963.

Power, F. C. *The moral atmosphere of a just community high school: A four-year longitudinal study.* Unpublished doctoral dissertation, Harvard University, 1979.

Scharf, P. *The moral atmosphere of the prison and an intervention to change it.* Unpublished doctoral dissertation, Harvard University, 1973.

Turiel, E. The development of social-conventional and moral concept. In M. Windmiller, N. Lambert, & E. Turiel (Eds.), *Moral development and socialization.* Boston: Allyn & Bacon, 1980.

REFERENCE NOTE

1. Gilligan, C., Lyons, N., & Langdale, S. Personal communication, 1982.

PART THREE

Stage-Structural Constructivist Approach

CHAPTER 6

Self-understanding and Moral Development from Childhood to Adolescence

WILLIAM DAMON

This chapter considers morality and the self as two separate conceptual systems and traces the development of each from childhood to adolescence. A developmental scheme of self-understanding during this age range is presented, and major features of moral development during the period are described. Changes in the two conceptual systems are compared and contrasted, and an analysis of how the two systems interact at various developmental levels is offered. The main point is that beginning in early adolescence there is a transformation of the relation between the two systems. Prior to adolescence, the organizing principles of the two conceptual systems are constructed in such a way that makes coordination between the two impossible in many instances. For example, the self during childhood is construed physically and actively. This excludes consideration of one's moral interactions and beliefs in one's self-concept, despite the rich and lively moral sensibilities that children express while making moral judgments. The resulting split between the two conceptual systems frequently leads to opposition between the conceived interests of the self and the conceived demands of morality, as can be seen from common childhood inconsistencies in moral judgment and conduct. This split is resolved during adolescence, when changes in each system open the way for new forms of integration between the two. For example, the self is now conceived socially and psychologically, which leads to the self becoming more defined in moral terms. One's moral interests and self-interests become more clearly defined and connected to each other, and a greater awareness of their mutual influence and interrelation emerges. To illustrate the developmental changes described in this chapter, selections from the protocols of two subjects in a longitudinal study of self-understanding are quoted.

The research described in this chapter was supported by a grant from the Spencer Foundation.

Depending on one's orientation toward it, morality can be seen either as antithetical to one's self-interests or as an essential ingredient in the fulfillment of the self. In one extreme position, morality may be viewed as an externally induced constrainer of the antisocial, yet very real, desires of the self. In an opposite but equally extreme position, morality may be viewed as the safest and most gratifying route toward one's enlightened self-interest. Most personality theories take a position somewhere in between these two extreme positions. Classic Freudian theory, for example, holds that morality is a necessary part of civilized social living, which has its own rewards; but that submission to moral standards will inevitably conflict with some deep inclinations of the self, thereby leaving some residue of personal discontent (S. Freud, 1922/1960).

For all persons, there are times when moral obligation demands real sacrifice. Conversely, there are times when one's choice to act morally, and one's moral beliefs, enhance one's social relations and yield important benefits for one's sense of self-worth. There is no simple answer to the metaethical questions asked of themselves by so many persons at various times in their lives: Does it do me any good, as an individual, to act morally? If so, what?

Developmentalists naturally assume that the way a person answers these questions has something to do with the person's developmental level, and I shall do nothing in this chapter to undercut this sensible assumption. But developmental level of *what?* Of moral judgment? This, indeed, may be the claim of theories such as Kohlberg's that consider one's moral perspective to be inextricably tied to one's total perspective on oneself in relation to society (Kohlberg, 1969, and Chap. 4 in this book). But I would like to present here an alternative position: that morality and the self are separate conceptual systems that may or may not be coordinated for any particular individual during certain periods of development. This means that a person's level of moral judgment does not determine the person's views on morality's place in one's life. To know how an individual deals with this latter issue, we must know about not only the person's moral beliefs but also the person's understanding of self in relation to these moral beliefs.

One implication of this alternative position is that persons with the same moral beliefs may differ in their views on how important it is for them to be moral in a personal sense. Some may consider their morality to be central to their self-identities, whereas others may consider it to be peripheral. Some may even consider morality to be a force outside of the self, a socially imposed system of regulation that constains or even obstructs one's pursuit of one's personal goals. In such cases, morality may even be viewed as antagonistic to one's "real self," at least at times.

I wish to make it clear that I do *not* claim that one's moral conceptions are totally irrelevant to the question of how important morality is to the self. Certainly there are moral positions from which it is impossible to deny one's personal moral responsibility in many instances. Kohlberg's higher stages describe some examples of such positions. A radical separation of such moral positions from the self cannot be maintained by any coherent type of thinking, barring distortions or rationalizations of one's moral principles. Nevertheless, even though the nature of one's moral beliefs do place certain conceptual limits on how one resolves the problem of morality's role in one's personal life, there is still considerable variation possible within these limits. In other words, moral beliefs in themselves often do bear some implications for how and when they must be used in one's personal life, but these implications are at most only partial solutions to the problem. For some individuals at some phases of life, the implications may be so ill-defined that they offer little guidance at all. In fact, one of the themes of this chapter is that during some periods of development self and morality operate as two distinct conceptual systems with little direct bearing on each other. At other times there is more integration and reciprocal influence between the two. The transition from childhood to adolescence marks one shift from a state of separation and noncoordination to a state of relative integration between the two systems. There are, no doubt, other parallel shifts later in life, but this chapter shall focus on this early one.

It should be evident that the way in which one views morality's role in the self influences greatly the course of one's moral conduct. If it is true that two individuals can have similar moral beliefs but that the first individual sees morality as central to one's self-identity and the second sees it as peripheral, we would expect a greater readiness toward moral action from the first individual. This person would no doubt have a greater tendency than the second individual to construe life situations as moral in nature. The first individual would see moral problems in a wide variety of life situations and would believe that the self's role in such situations is to act as a moral agent. In that way one's inclination toward moral action may be influenced by one's orientation toward oneself and one's situations. That is, if one believes that one's morality is an essential part of oneself, one is more likely to assume a moral orientation toward life situations. If one believes morality to be a minor ingredient in one's own makeup, or if one sees no connection at all between oneself and one's moral obligations, one is less likely to experience life situations as in nature and is therefore less likely to assume moral responsibility in them.

THE SELF AS A PSYCHOLOGICAL CONSTRUCT

In this chapter I shall refer to the *self* as a conceptual system of the same epistemological status as morality. That is, it is a psychological concept, constructed by individuals to organize part of their life experiences, just like any other concept. The self, therefore, is not synonymous with "personality," does not have "its own" motives, thoughts, wishes, or independent means of functioning "within" the person. It is not a "regulator" of other action external to itself and does not occupy a privileged role or executive position deep inside the individual. It is a construct, no more and no less, whose domain is the individual's experience of personal identity. As such, the construct is useful in helping the individual establish a coherent knowledge of one's physical and psychological nature, as well as a knowledge of one's unique position in the social world. Sarbin (1962) has offered a similar definition of self:

> The interbehavioral field of the human can include perceptions and cognitions referable to objects in the external world, and perceptions and cognitions referable to his own body, to his own beliefs, his own statuses, and so on. . . . The self is one such cognitive structure or inference. [p. 11]

As William James long ago pointed out, the self is inherently a *dualistic* concept, in that it is both subject and object at the same time. This was James's notion of the "I" and the "Me," which he summarized as follows:

> Whatever I may be thinking of, I am always at the same time more or less aware of *myself*, of my *personal existence*. At the same time it is I who am aware; so that the total self of me, being as it were duplex, partly known and knower, partly object and partly subject, must have two aspects discriminated in it, of which for shortness we may call one the *Me* and the other the *I*. [1892/ 1961, p. 43]

George Herbert Mead (1934) referred to this duality as the peculiarly "reflexive" nature of self when he wrote that the self is "an object to itself" (p. 136).

James predicted that the "I" aspect of self-duality would prove elusive to empirical study, precisely because of its indeterminate nature. It is difficult to observe or characterize a phenomenon that is totally subjective and that therefore may change unpredictably from moment to moment. Also, unlike the somewhat circumscribed nature of the "Me" (which is mainly the collection of definitions that one and others construct for one's self), the "I" potentially incorporates all of a person's interactions with the world. The "I" enters into all of a person's experience, for it determines the unique nature of all the person's interpretations of events, people, and things. James's conclusion was that inquiry into the "I" was best left to philosophical rather than psychological analysis and that psychologists interested in self-concept should focus on the "Me."

But Mead offered a constructive solution for psychologists who would hesitate to deny their discipline access to a major aspect of self. Mead suggested, in effect, approaching the "I" through the "Me" by studying individuals' *knowledge* of their own subjective selves. This suggestion amounts to focusing the empirical study of self not on self in all its duality but rather on *self-understanding*. The "Me" is, by definition, the understanding of self as object, so that the study of the "Me" is by nature the study of self-understanding in one of its aspects. Extending such study to the "I" means in addition exploring individuals' understanding of self-as-subject. Self-understanding, then, includes in this comprehensive definition an individual's knowledge and reflections on the "self-as-known" as well as on the "self-as-knower," on both the "I" and the "Me" features of self. We shall use this definition in this chapter.

CHILDHOOD MORALITY AND SELF-UNDERSTANDING

By the end of childhood, there is a strong sense of basic moral principles as applied to everyday interpersonal situations. In particular, children acquire during the childhood years principles of justice like equality and reciprocity. By age 10 or so, a child is typically able to coordinate these principles with one another and to apply them flexibly to a range of peer-group and adult-child situations.

In my own research, I have used situations requiring "fairness," as in distributive justice, as an index of how children use moral principles. Generally, I find that children around the age of 6 begin prescribing equality of treatment as a means to fairness; a bit later reciprocity in the form of compensation for merit or deserving develops; and by age 10 or 12, both principles are elaborated and integrated with each other. Equality by age 10 includes both a present dimension (equal treatment), a past dimension (make up for prior deprivation), and a future dimension (provide equal opportunity). Reciprocity includes both indirect compensations (for work, need, talent) and direct pay-backs (tit for tat, as in Kohlberg's Stage 2). In my research I have offered examples of how children are able to coordinate these principles of equality and reciprocity in the context of distributive justice judgments (1975, 1977, 1980).

Now children do not *always* express such principles in their moral discourse. If children are presented with conflicts of authority drawn from the adult world, as in the case of Kohlberg's dilemmas, they are likely to acquiesce to the press of adult constraint and keep their moral principles to themselves. This is why we find Stage 1 responses to the Heinz dilemma all through childhood. But, as a number of developmentalists back to Piaget have demonstrated (Damon, 1977; Piaget, 1932/1965; Youniss, 1980), Stage 1 obedience has little to do with the lively "other morality of the child," expressed often in peer settings and based on principles of equality, cooperation, and reciprocity. That this "other morality" exists as a robust phenomenon is by now beyond question: It may be easily generated from practically any child through various child-study techniques (see Damon, 1977).

The split between the two moralities of the child, however, provides us with a clue about the nature of social knowledge during childhood. It is common but noteworthy to see a child profess unquestioning obedience to adults on the one hand and in the same breath to insist that no sharing with a friend would be wrong, despite what one's parents say. Such phenomena abound in the childhood years, arising from incompatibilities between the conceptual principles that serve peer relations as opposed to the conceptual principles that serve adult-child relations. As Youniss (1980) had pointed out, it is only when children finally apply the principles of mutuality and cooperation that they have learned in the peer context to their interactions with adults that these incompatibilities are resolved. This resolution, which occurs sometime in adolescence, opens the door for new kinds of intimacy and equal exchange between parent and child. But prior to adolescence there is no conceptual basis for integrating these two contexts for social interaction.

Another key conceptual split found during childhood is between children's self-understanding (as defined earlier) and their moral principles. In my current investigation of self-understanding from childhood to adolescence, I focus on the characteristics that children use to define themselves. My interviews present children with a number of self-definitional questions of the type, What kind of person are you? or How could you describe yourself? In addition, I ask questions about self-interest (What do you want in life: what are your hopes and aspirations?), about self-development (How did you get to be the way you are? How could you change?), and about self-in-relation (What are you like with your parents, with your friends?). From these questions I receive a series of self-statements that can be analyzed according to a developmental scoring manual based on the scheme presented in Figure 6.1.[1]

The logic of this scheme is as follows: People at all ages have some knowledge of the physical, active, social, and psychological aspects of themselves, but this knowledge changes in nature throughout development. Such changes are represented in the vertical dimensions (the columns) of Figure 6.1. These changes reflect some of the trends noted in this review: in particular, the increasingly volitional and self-reflective quality of self-understanding, and the tendency toward integrating and systematizing one's self-conceptions. In addition to these "vertical" trends, there is an ontogenetic movement that favors, respectively, the active, social, and psychological aspects of self as the child becomes the adolescent. This movement is reflected in the diagonal (bold type) of Figure 6.1.

Finally, there are "horizontal" relations between the parallel developmental levels of the four aspects of self outlined in Figure 6.1. These horizontal relations are conceptual linkages to the self-statement that emerges as dominant for any given level. In other words, the four aspects of self-knowledge are linked at each developmental level because they share a common characteristic deriving from the dominant conception of self at that level. This "dominant" conception is shown in Figure 6.1 as the box along the diagonal. Thus, at each new level a new aspect of self assumes dominance and lends its characteristics to parallel-level conceptions of other aspects of self. At Level 1, therefore, all self-understanding is to some extent physicalistic in the sense that it is chiefly descriptive of surface features. That is, even

---

[1] Interviews and scoring manual for self-understanding development are available on request from the author.

Developmental level	Physical self	Active self	Social self	Psychological self
4	Physical attributes reflecting volitional choices, or personal and moral standards	Active attributes that reflect choices or personal and moral standards	Moral or personal choices concerning social relations or social personality characteristics	**Belief systems, personal philosophy, and self's own thought processes**
3	Physical attributes that influence social appeal and social interactions	Active attributes that influence social appeal and social interactions	**Social personality characteristics**	Social Sensitivity, communicative competence, and other psychologically related social skills
2	Activity-related physical Attributes	**Capabilities Relative to others**	Activities that are considered with reference to reactions (approval or disapproval) of others	Knowledge, learned skills, motivation, or activity-related emotional states
1	**Bodily properties or material possessions**	Typical behavior	Fact of membership in particular social relations or groups	Momentary moods, feelings, or impulses

FIGURE 6.1. Conceptual foundations of physical, active, social, and psychological self at four developmental levels during childhood and adolescence.

115

when concerned with the self's actions, social interactions, or emotions, it treats these only taxonomically and descriptively, as if they were physical objects. Similarly, at Level 2 each of the four aspects are to some extent treated actively; at Level 3, socially; and at Level 4, psychologically. The qualifier "to some extent" is necessary because each of the four aspects still retains its unique substance at each level. For this reason, we have rejected a one-dimensional developmental sequence that would proceed from physical to active to social to psychological in favor of the multidimensional model of genetic relations outlined in Figure 6.1.

Empirical results from two rounds of longitudinal testing have shown that children younger than age 12 rarely express Level 3 or 4 self-statements. Generally their understanding of self is confined to physicalistic or active notions, although there is some mention of Level 1 or Level 2 social and psychological characteristics. This means that social self-statements during childhood are confined to comments about one's group memberships or one's activities with others ("I am the kind of person who belongs to the Boy Scouts"; "My friends like me to play baseball with them"). Psychological self-statements during childhood are confined to expressions of mood ("I feel cranky in the mornings sometimes"), or comments about one's activity-related cognitive states ("I am always anxious to do a good job"; "I don't know very much about fixing bicycles"). Rarely are Level 3 statements in any of the self-schemes expressed during childhood, and almost never are Level 4 statements expressed.

It should be clear even from the sketchy outline presented in Figure 6.1 that moral self-statements are one signal of Level 4 and rarely appear in prior levels. The only real exception is some mention of reciprocal moral responsibilities sometimes made in the context of Level 3 social-relational self-statements. But morality does not become a dominant characteristic of self until Level 4, and Level 4 statements are not found in any frequency until middle adolescence.

Childhood self-understanding, therefore, is largely characterized by physical and active self-statements that have little to do with moral principles. When children describe what they are like, they use categories derived from the material or active world. They refer to their bodily properties, to where they live, to their clothes, to the kinds of activities that they typically engage in, and to general characteristics of self pertinent to these activities (such as "I'm athletic" or "I'm smart"). Social and psychological statements about oneself, when they are made, are mostly descriptions of their group memberships or their internal states and capabilities. There are few childhood statements concerning how the self interacts with others, and fewer still concerning the child's moral beliefs. Yet, as we know from direct studies of social interaction and moral development during childhood, children do have deeply held and frequently expressed moral principles.

This lack of integration of the moral self into children's self-understanding can be further found in children's statements concerning their self-interests.

Wishes, hopes, and aspirations during childhood almost always focus on material or action opportunities. Children wish for more money, a new car, a trip to South America. In some cases they wish for changes in their internal states, like "being happy." But during childhood we find few wishes with moral implications, either of a direct sort (such as a wish for improvement in the lot of others) or in terms of one's own makeup (such as a wish for a stronger moral character or a finer set of moral beliefs). Nor do children see morality as one of the features of themselves that changes or that makes them the way they are.

Even in our "self-in-relation" questions we get little sense that children see morality as playing an important role in their interpersonal transactions. They speak of activities commonly engaged in, of emotional states (excitement, love) shared by them and another, but almost never of interactions centered around concerns of justice, responsibility, or the welfare of others.

The split between children's morality and their self-understanding, particularly as regards their views on self-interest, also can be seen in a series of studies that Randy Gerson and I conducted on children's moral conduct (Damon, 1977; Gerson & Damon, 1978). We found that in a real-life situation that provides children opportunities to further their self-interest, children will often hedge on their moral principles in favor of that self-interest. The situation that we used was a distributive justice task in which four children were asked to make bracelets for us and then were rewarded with 10 candy bars. The children's task was to decide how to split fairly the candy among themselves. We had different age groups, ranging from 4 to 10, representing the various developmental levels of childhood justice.

The pull of self-interest was evident throughout the results of these studies. Children at all ages tended to demand more candy for themselves than for others, except in one control condition: a hypothetical version of the bracelet-making task, with cardboard rather than real candy bars, in which children to the ratio 3:1 offered more candy to others than to themselves. It is true that children at the lower developmental levels of justice were more self-oriented than were those at the higher levels, indicating that moral principles did play a role in mitigating self-interest. But this was an indirect role, as the following finding indicates: As could be predicted by our distributive justice sequence, children reasoning at Level 1–B and above, unlike children lower than 1–B, often chose solutions based on merit (give X more of the candy because X made the most and worked the hardest). Yet they did so only under one condition—when they themselves were the one who had made the most, thus "owning" the claim to merit and being in a position to benefit from this claim. So the higher-level justice principle of reciprocity through merit, which the younger children did not have access to, was used in the service of self-interest. Use of this justice principle still changed the nature of the solutions: Whereas the younger children's solutions were often blatantly self-interested (they might grasp seven candy bars for themselves "because I want all these"), the older children constructed self-interested solutions with some precision and some balance. Those who had a claim to merit awarded themselves a carefully chosen extra proportion, and those who were in no position to claim merit argued for an equal solution. Thus, even though the footsteps of self-interest could be found throughout the decisions of all age groups, there were also marks left by the developing principles of justice.

The two systems, morality and self-interest, interact in various ways as children at different developmental levels construct their real-life decisions. But it seems clear that although these conceptual systems may interact to influence one another, they are essentially uncoordinated in any systematic sense during the childhood years. Children may hedge their behavior for moral reasons here or there, but they do not consciously attempt to balance the wishes of the self with the demands of justice. In our studies, only at the oldest age group (10) did we see some real consistency between hypothetical moral judgment and actual conduct in the bracelet-making task. It was some indication that the self-interest and morality were beginning to be integrated conceptually, for it means that (1) children were able to anticipate the realistic pull of self-interest while making hypothetical moral judgments; (2) they were able to deny their self-interest in favor of their moral judgments during the real-life task; or (3) some combination of both. Whichever is the case, the older children's consistency indicates that they could now appreciate the problem that the interests of the self are often incompatible with the demands of justice. Burton (1963, and Chap. 11 in this book), in his reanalysis of the Hartshorne and May data (1928–1930), has found a similar move toward moral consistency at the end of childhood. Without some conceptual integration between the two systems of morality and self, there will always be some irregularity and inconsistency of behavior, for one cannot predict which system will be operative in any given context. This split led our younger subjects to inconsistency between what they said one should do and what they did. Once the split between the two systems is resolved, we should expect less vacillation in judgment and conduct, because there is a new awareness of the complex relation between morality and self-interest.

ADOLESCENT MORALITY AND SELF-UNDERSTANDING

Most investigators of adolescent morality have noted at least two changes from the childhood years. First, the adolescent becomes sensitive to the expectations and opinions of others in society. One's "reputation" becomes a focal concern, and the moral aspect of one's reputation becomes primary. Associated with this, the adolescent realizes that others expect to assume responsibility for the welfare of others, particularly others in close relation with oneself. Fulfilling this responsibility not only means living up to the expectations of others in one's social network but also is necessary to bolster or enhance one's reputation. Such concerns are the basis of Kohlberg's Stage 3 (Kohlberg, 1976) and have been described as well by other writers on adolescent morality (A. Freud, 1958; Hoffman, 1980; Hogan, 1975).

The second noted development in adolescent morality is its ideological flavor. As Piaget himself briefly described in his moral judgment book (1932/1965), and as countless others have since then documented, adolescents love to weave theories of every kind, philosophical, political, and moral. These theories are often taken quite seriously, with the result being a new coherence of judgment and opinion, deriving from an arduously thought-out system of beliefs. In the moral realm, the ideologies vary from adolescent to adolescent, but there are some recurring themes that have been noted by Kohlberg (1971), Turiel (1974), and others (Colby, 1978). Among these are relativism, utilitarianism, perfectionism, asceticism, and even mysticism. Perhaps at no other time in life, at least for most individuals, are such doctrines so extensively articulated and so purely held. This ideological morality begins in early adolescence but blossoms most fully during the college years.

In the development of self-understanding during adolescence, there are two major shifts that provide a basis for conceptual integration with adolescent moral thinking. The first shift is the emergence of a social personality perspective on self at Level 3. The self is now viewed in the context of its social-interactional characteristics: I am how I act with others. A manner of social interaction generally has moral implications. For example, being helpful, generous, open, suspicious, all are morally relevant characteristics of one's social interactional self. This connection between social-interactional style and morality is inevitable because morality is a major regulator of social interactions. Thus, the Level 3 conception of the self in social interaction quite naturally calls forth an awareness of the moral side of the self. This is in contrast to Level 1 and 2 conceptions of self, for purely physicalistic or active conceptions bear few directly moral implications.

The second developmental shift in self-understanding during adolescence also provides a conceptual mesh with adolescent moral thinking, though at a later age during adolescence and for different reasons. This is the shift toward a definition of self based on one's belief systems, personal philosophy, and moral standards. The adolescent, as I noted earlier, weaves complex ideological theories of a moral type as well as of a philosophical, personal, and political type. Not only do adolescents weave such theories, they also take them seriously. In fact, these theories become a critical material for the definition of self. When an adolescent says "I am a Moonie," "I am a pacifist," or "I believe in the American way," these statements often represent layers of well worked out conceptual belief. Such statements often reflect the main organizing principles of the adolescent's self-conception. The system of belief that they represent may be the centerpiece of the adolescent's personal identity. Such conceptual systems, if extensively elaborated (as many adolescents tend to do), reach into every aspect of the adolescent's behavior and belief. They can guide the choices and interpretations of adolescents in every sphere of life. It goes without saying that they have moral implications, for many of these belief systems are themselves fundamentally moral in nature.

During adolescence, therefore, we see an integration of previously segregated conceptual systems: morality and the self. What were once "partial structures," to use Piaget's term, now become coordinated to form a more wholistic system of knowledge. The unity of the two is still not complete, because there are always aspects of the self, however nondominant, that defy a moral perspective, and vice versa. But there now are at least two new bases for integration between the systems: first, the social-interactional perspective of early adolescence, and second, the ideological perspective of later adolescence. These bases for integration establish increasing coherence and communication between the systems and provide the conditions for greater regularity of thought and conduct. As I noted earlier, this integration does not resolve all splits between social-cognitive structures for all time, but it does represent one critical developmental advance.

For the remainder of this chapter, I shall illustrate the changes that I have described by quoting two subjects in my present longitudinal study of self-understanding in children and adolescents. These two subjects are both in the process of making the childhood-to-adolescent shifts described earlier. These quotes were taken from interviews conducted with these subjects at two ages: first, when the subjects were 11 and 12 years old, and second, two years later, when they were 13 and 14 years old. These children, therefore, were just leaving childhood and entering early adolescence at the time of our two longitudinal testings.

Paul, age 12 at our initial testing, provides us with an example of the first developmental shift noted earlier. When Paul was interviewed at Time 1, he generally relied on physical, active, and material categories to describe himself and his personal aspirations. When asked the first question about how he would describe himself to somebody else, Paul referred to his height. Later in the interview, Paul spoke about his physical strength and about his "looks," including hair and eye color. He talked about changing himself by lifting weights and making himself more "tough." As for his wishes and aspirations, the following dialogue gives a sense of Paul's focus on material goods and activities:

What would you wish for?   *A minibike.*

OK, a minibike.   *A new house. And money.*

And money? OK, why would you wish for a minibike?   *'Cause they look fun. I've ridden on one with a friend. They look fun.*

OK, so you think it would be a fun thing to do, ride a minibike around.   *Uh huh.*

OK, and why would you want a new house?   *'Cause our house is old.*

OK, your house is pretty old. OK, so why would you want a new one?   *'Cause new houses are nice.*

OK, what do you mean nice?   *We would have more things like there may be a swimming pool in that house that we don't have in our other house.*

OK, so you'd want a house with a swimming pool?   *Yeah.*

And why else would you want a new house?   And why would you want money?   *'Cause you can buy a lot of things with money.*

OK, would you want a real lot of money or what?   *Yeah.*

OK, so you can buy things with money, right?   *Uh huh.*

Why else would you want money?   *So I could go on trips.*

OK, so you could go on trips. OK.   *Travel.*

Why would you want to go on trips and travel?   *To see the world.*

OK, why would you want to see the world?   *'Cause the world is interesting, all the different places.*

OK, good enough. OK, are those the things that you hope for most in life: a minibike, a new house, and money?   *Yeah, except I don't want a minibike when I'm older.*

OK, why don't you think you'll want a minibike when you're older?   *'Cause I'd be too big for it.*

OK, so you'd be just too big for it to be able to ride around on it.   *Yeah.*

OK, why are those the things that you hope for most in life?   *'Cause I like 'em the best.*

OK, is there anything else that you hope for in life besides a minibike, a new house, and money?   *My health.*

Your health?   *Yeah, I want to move to Florida.*

OK, you want to move to Florida.   *And that's all really.*

OK, why do you want to be healthy?   *'Cause I don't want to be sick with a disease or something.*

OK, why not?   *'Cause you can't do anything if you have a disease that's bad.*

OK, why do you want to move to Florida?   *It's nice down there.*

Have you been to Florida?   *Yeah.*

And you really like it? OK, what makes it nice for you?   *The weather.*

OK, the weather.   *And it's just an exciting place to be.*

OK, what do you find exciting about it?   *Everything really. I like going in the swimming pool, and the beaches. The water is warm there. There's a lot of sharks though.*

OK, what do you think the most important things are that are good for you?   *I can't think of anything. Uh, living a good life. Like going traveling and all instead of just sitting home and growing old.*

OK, so living a good life is important.   *Having a good time.*

Even at Time 1, Paul did refer occasionally to aspects of his "personality" and to his capacity for social relations. For example, he said that he was "fun to be with" and "not dumb." But at Time 1, these occasional comments were overshadowed by Paul's focus on his physical, material, and active self.

By the time of the next interview, Time 2, Paul's social and personal characteristics had become his main concern. Paul was now 18 months older, and the difference in the quality of his self-understanding is striking:

What else can you say about yourself, besides that you're a good person? *Well, I guess I'm helpful, kind.*

What do you mean by you're helpful? *Well, I help people if they have problems in school, if they need help in math or whatever. And I help a lot around the house.*

It that important to you that you're helpful? Does that matter to you? *It does some.*

Why is that important to you that you're helpful? *It encourages you.*

What do you mean? *It makes you feel good that you can help someone else do something.*

How come you think it makes you feel good that you can help someone? *Just knowing that you helped someone with something that they didn't understand or couldn't do. You just feel good.*

OK, did you say "kind" afterwards? *Yeah.*

What do you mean by kind? *Well, I'm not mean. I'm not rude to anyone. I don't sass the teachers in school.*

Does that matter to you? Is that an important part of you? *Yeah.*

Can you think of anything else to say about yourself, what kind of person you are? *I'm fun to be with I guess. You can have a good time.*

What do you mean you're fun to be with? *Well, you have a good time wherever you go.*

Is that important to you that you're fun to be with? *Yeah, 'cause I mean you have more friends 'cause you're fun to be with.*

Why is this important to you to have more friends? *'Cause you'll be more popular and all the kids will accept you to be in the in crowd.*

Why is that important? *To be in the in crowd? Because if you're not, you're like an outcast. They make fun of you, and they'll do different things.*

Is there any other reason besides that they make fun of you? *It's just fun to be in with all the other kids.*

OK, fine. Can you tell me something that you're not? *I'm not mean.*

Is there anything else you didn't say before? *I'm not unthankful for anything. I'm glad that I have, you know, but I do want more stuff but I'm not—*

But you're not unthankful? *No.*

Why is that important? *I don't know.*

Why do you think it's an important thing to say about you? Why does it matter that you're not unthankful? *Because people that aren't thankful, they just take things and they don't care what they do with 'em. Like someone that buys you a car, you really don't care if you get into an accident. But if you buy it yourself, it's your own money and you really care about it.*

Why else is it important to be thankful? *I guess when you're thankful, you make someone feel better because they're really happy that you thanked them for what you got.*

OK, why is it important for you to make people feel better? *It just makes you feel better to have other people feel good, so they'll know that I'm thankful.*

In the preceding dialogue, Paul refers to his helpfulness and charity to others, a notion that emerged for the first time on the Time 2 interview. This, of course, is a notion based on one's social and moral interactions with others. Paul also repeats a theme that was present at Time 1, that he is "fun to be with." But now Paul expands this theme in some important ways. First, he makes note of its implication for social acceptance (he will not be an "outcast"), and second, he notes its implications for his sense of moral reciprocity (the need to be thankful so that others will "feel good").

Finally, Paul includes among his wishes and aspirations the desire to be more "good-natured." In the space of 18 months, therefore, Paul's statements about himself and his aspirations have changed in a consistent direction. These statements increasingly reflect Paul's awareness of the social personality aspects of himself. Inevitably tied to this social personality focus is an awareness of his moral interactions. In particular, Paul makes note of his kindness, helpfulness, gratitude, and good-naturedness. These characteristics do not constitute a systematic or well-integrated moral philosophy, but they do indicate a concern with the moral quality of one's social relations. This concern emerged as a significant part of Paul's self-understanding between the ages of 12 and 14. In our longitudinal sample, we have observed similar changes in the self-understanding of many other young adolescents at around this same age.

The second subject that we shall consider here started out at Time 1 at about the same place that Paul reached in his Time 2 interview. We shall call this second subject "Ben." At Time 1, Ben was also 12. The following quotes from Ben's Time 1 interview demonstrate the already-dominant focus on social-personality characteristics in Ben's self-understanding:

Exactly. What about your personality? What do you mean? What do you like about your personality? *I think I'm rather friendly. Like I would go up to anyone and just talk to them and, you know, I'd help them. But like kids who don't help me I don't really feel the obligation to help them. I would if they really needed it, but say if someone who never helped me asks me for a pencil, I would give him the pencil. If I had one I'd like to shove it in my pocket and say "I don't have a pencil." I wouldn't like to tell him that I don't have a pencil at all.*

I think I'd still not want to hurt people's feelings. I really feel so bad 'cause, like, it's happened to me so many times—it doesn't happen, like, it's not, like, every day. I don't want to give you the impression that every day I go out and lots of people make fun of me. You're gonna' sit down at Clark and listen to this tape and say "That poor kid." That isn't the thing; it's just, like, you know, it's happened to me before and I know the feeling. Like when you go upstairs and you just sit there and you realize that you're not doing things that other kids are doing. And I don't like to do that to other people.

I don't judge people usually, unless it's really something severe. 'Cause, like, I really feel bad for people 'cause it's happened to me before. As a matter of fact we had this project to do in a team and there was this one girl—her name is Leah Goldchine; she's in my music class—and no one would pick her for the group. And I hate groups anyway 'cause they're so, you know. So I felt so bad for her and I don't judge people like that 'cause she doesn't really have that great a personality and she's kind of shy. So I brought her into our group. You know, I'm like that. I don't like the way people judge people. And, like, I don't like the people, 'cause people do that at my age, you know. They're there if you don't play sports you don't belong like and I don't like that. 'Cause it's happened to me and so I don't like doing it to other people.

In these statements, Ben shows an awareness of the social and moral implications of his behavior. His manner of interacting with others is clearly primary to his sense of self. But, like Paul at Time 2, Ben has not worked out a consistent belief system that he associates with his self-identity. Rather, his self-understanding is based on the specific nature of his social personality and on the social and moral interactions that his personality characteristics foster.

On the occasion of Ben's Time 2 testing, Ben's self-statements had a different quality. He now had worked out a personal belief system based on moral views toward honesty and self-sacrifice. In addition, Ben had integrated these beliefs into his own idiosyncratic attitudes about humor. The result is a unique blend of moral and personal self-statements that Ben can truly call his own. Because this belief system is both coherent and absolutely distinct to Ben, it is well suited for establishing Ben's personal identity. Of course, Ben will need to make further choices and syntheses before he has formed a consolidated identity in the Eriksonian sense, but at the time of our second longitudinal interview, he seemed well along on his way there.

Tell me what you're like. *I don't know. I think I'm basically, like, honest. I don't like people that aren't honest. Pretty good-natured. I don't know. Maybe nonconformist. I think people that lie or something like that must have something to cover up. Like I've never known anyone that it's compulsive, you know, it's just so compulsive for them to lie. It's like on soap operas or something like that; it's just that unreal, someone that lies like that. You know, a one-sided person that lies like that. I don't know how to explain it. Like someone that cheats and stuff like that. I like being honest like with yourself and with everyone. 'Cause, you know, if you're a bad person, lying, is like—that's how I'd label someone. If they lied, they would be a bad per-*

son to me. *Like they could be, in the eyes of everyone else, like, the best per-son in the world, but if I knew, like, they were lying or cheating, in my eyes they wouldn't be. Whereas it would be the opposite; like it could be some criminal who never told a lie, you know, if he was brought on the jury stand and said, "I did it," then I would consider him all the more man or person to say he did it, to admit his fault like that.*

OK could you summarize that and say what that says about what kind of per-son you are?   *I don't know. I guess, like, I respect people more if they re-spect themselves. So if you cheat, you're not, like, respecting yourself. You're not giving yourself, you know, yourself a chance. I think if you don't like yourself, then no one else will like you. 'Cause you know, what's there to like about you if you don't even like yourself. So if you like yourself you won't abuse yourself, you won't do things like that and you won't cheat. Because if you like yourself, you like what you're doing without the good or bad mark. It shouldn't shock you that much. Unless there's some pressure to do well, like that. So it all goes back to, like, you have to like what you're doing and everything else from there.*

When I'm friendly, it's more like, you know, to tell people that it's all right to be yourself. Not necessarily don't conform, but just whatever you are just, you know, be happy with that. Don't, like, you know, try to prove anything for anybody; just be yourself. So I'm not an overly bubbly person that goes around, "Hi, how are you?" you know like that. That makes me sick. But, you know, just if someone wants to talk to me, you know, sure. I wouldn't, like, not talk to someone. Just anybody, you know, I'd say hi to. Like that.

I think the total giving of something to, like, one idea is really—especially a good idea. Like if you're gonna devote yourself to, you know, massacres of people, then that's not too good. But if you're gonna, like, devote yourself to the good of people, totally devote yourself then, you know, I think that's great. I don't know. It's hard for me to say. 'Cause it ties into, like, my re-ligion. So, I don't know, it's not really my belief; it's just been, like, what I've been brought up with. I would think that would be, like, very good to do that. You know, like that. And people like comedians I like very much, you know, like "Saturday Night Live," like Gilda Radner and them, Chevy Chase because they can really make you laugh and I think laughter is really im-portant.

Why is laughter important?   *Because people take things too seriously. I think so many times, like, I mean things should be taken seriously. I don't think we should all sit there and laugh at everything, you know, the econ-omy's going downhill, you know, and just laugh about it. But I think laughter is very, like important too, to be a good person. You have to know when to laugh. I think there's a right time to laugh, you know. But I think it's very important at some time to laugh, you know. Especially laugh at yourself. I think you have to be able to, like, look at yourself and see something's funny and, you know, laugh about it. I think that you'd be closer to yourself if you can laugh at yourself and view yourself objectively. I know a lot of people who could never laugh at themselves. They'd get really, you know, mad if you laughed at them. Whereas me, if I did something stupid, I'd, like, always laugh at myself. Sometimes I may seem crazy, but I do. I think it's important. I don't think, like, you should always be laughing, but I think a good sense of humor is needed to get along. I think, you know, if you never had a sense of humor, I don't think you could really survive in a world like this where so much bad news is always cropping up. And then I think it's important to have, like, you know, like, a little time when you can laugh. That's probably what I mean when I say, you know, to affect a lot of people at one time. Just something where you could take them away from the problems of the world for a little while, you know, through whatever medium or whatever. And just, you know, give them time to forget the problems and everything. 'Cause, I think, if you didn't have that time there'd be a lot of insane people going around.*

There are, yes, there are.   *But that's, like, probably what I mean. So I guess when I grow up I want to be Mother Theresa and Chevy Chase.*

OK, that's an interesting combination.   *No, those are the two characteristics from the two. I wouldn't want to be, like, so religious that it would divide me from people. That happens a lot. You get, like, a lot of old priests and stuff who view, if you're not Catholic, you know, that's the old saying, the old joke, if you're not Catholic you don't go to heaven or whatever. But that's, like, so absurd, you know. What is heaven anyway? I don't even know. So I think that's crazy. The only reason why I even have a religion is to, like, pacify me. You know, a time when I can, you know, I don't know, put my troubles into someone else's hands. And just, you know, feel that they're resolved. Or if I do something bad, just to talk to someone and just get them resolved and know that they're forgiven or whatever. That would be my only reason. Like I don't think that, you know, I don't take it as strongly as some people do, so medievally, I guess, so mystic. I don't believe it in that way. I just think, you know, it's just something that I use to pacify my needs like that.*

REFERENCES

Burton, R. Generality of honesty reconsidered. *Psychological Review*, 1963, *70*, 481–499.

Damon, W. Early conceptions of positive justice as related to the development of logical operations. *Child Development*, 1975, *46*, 301–312.

Damon, W. *The social world of the child.* San Francisco: Jossey-Bass, 1977.

Damon, W. Patterns of change in children's social reasoning: A two-year longitudinal study. *Child Development*, 1980, *51*, 1010–1017.

Freud, A. Adolescence. In R. S. Eissler et al. (Eds.), *Psychoanalytic study of the child* (Vol. 13). New York: International Universities Press, 1958.

Freud, S. *Civilization and its discontents.* New York: Norton, 1960. (Originally published, 1922.)

Gerson, R., & Damon, W. Moral understanding and children's conduct. In W. Damon (Ed.), *New directions for child development* (Vol. 1). San Francisco: Jossey-Bass, 1978.

Hartshorne, H., & May, M. S. *Studies in the nature of character* (3 vols.). Vol. 1, *Studies in deceit;* Vol. 2, *Studies in self-control;* Vol. 3, *Studies in the organization of character.* New York: Macmillan, 1928–1930.

Hoffman, M. Moral development in adolescence. In J. Adelson (Ed.), *Handbook of adolescent psychology.* New York: Wiley, 1980.

Hogan, R. Theoretical egocentrism and the problem of compliance. *American Psychologist,* 1975, *30,* 533–540.

James, W. *Psychology: The briefer course.* New York: Harper & Row, 1961. (Originally published, 1892.)

Kohlberg, L. Stage and sequence: The cognitive-developmental approach to socialization. In D. Goslin (Ed.), *Handbook of socialization theory and research.* Skokie, Ill.: Rand McNally, 1969.

Kohlberg, L. Moral stages and moralization. In T. Lickona (Ed.), *Moral development and behavior.* New York: Holt, Rinehart and Winston, 1976.

Mead, G. H. *Mind, self, and society.* Chicago: University of Chicago Press, 1934.

Piaget, J. *The moral judgment of the child.* New York: Free Press, 1965. (Originally published, 1932.)

Sarbin, T. A preface to a psychological analysis of the self. *Psychological Review,* 1962, *59,* 11–22.

Youniss, J. *Parents and peers in child development.* Chicago: University of Chicago Press, 1980.

CHAPTER 7

Moral Identity:
Its Role in Moral Functioning

AUGUSTO BLASI

The general issues of this chapter concern moral action and the relations be-
tween moral cognition and moral action. Specifically, the chapter will focus
on the role of identity in mediating moral knowledge and practical moral de-
cisions. From this perspective, the problem of moral action becomes a ques-
tion of self-consistency.

Three central psychological concepts and their functional articulations will
be discussed. The first is the concept of self-identity and the importance that
morality plays in it (self-as-moral). The role of morality in one's identity is
viewed as a dimension of developmental and individual differences. The sec-
ond, the concept of responsibility, is understood here specifically as an exten-
sion of one's identity into the domain of action. The third is the concept of
self-consistency, which becomes integrity in the area of morality.

Both the theoretical and the practical implications of the identity approach
to moral development and moral functioning will be analyzed.

The relations between moral knowledge and moral action represent a central
issue for a philosophical as well as for a psychological understanding of
moral functioning and moral development. This question, however, has received relatively little theoretical attention, even among cognitive-developmental psychologists. This is particularly clear when one considers the
amount of energy and the degree of conceptual sophistication that has been
devoted to the understanding of moral reasoning and of the development of
cognitive moral structures. Chapter 4, by Kohlberg and Candee, is an important but rare attempt to address the issue from a cognitive-developmental
perspective. This state of affairs is also surprising because there is a widespread skepticism, among psychologists and philosophers alike, concerning
the motivational power of cognition. A cognitive-developmental solution to
the problem of moral functioning remains not only incomplete but also theo-

retically unconvincing, unless it is shown how moral understanding is indeed a motive for action.

Recently I (Blasi, 1980, 1983) presented a model, labeled "self model," which attempted to deal, in a tentative and sketchy way, with both consistency and inconsistency between moral judgment and moral action. In it I hypothesized (1) that the outcome of moral judgments becomes, at least in some cases, the content of judgments of responsibility; in other words, that the agent, having decided the morally good action, also determines whether that action is strictly obligatory for him or her; (2) that the criteria for responsibility (in the sense of strict obligation) are related to the structure of one's self, or to the essential definition of oneself; (3) that the motivational basis for moral action lies in the internal demand for psychological self-consistency; and (4) that moral action will be more likely to follow moral judgment if the individual has the ability to stop defensive strategies from interfering with the subjective discomfort of self-inconsistency.

In this chapter I will focus on the self, the core element of the self model, and will further explore its nature and its role in moral action. In Chapter 6 Damon presents a research project aimed at describing the development of the self in children and adolescents. His findings seem to be perfectly compatible with my understanding of the role of the self in moral functioning. My chapter, however, does not present empirical data; it focuses, instead, on certain conceptual features of the moral self, which will be globally designated by the term *identity*. The advantage of the term *moral identity* may not necessarily lie in its conceptual clarity. Within the Eriksonian tradition, however, this concept is more or less consistently used to refer to certain psychological processes and has acquired certain properties that, when properly understood, seem to be necessary in a complete theory of moral functioning.

This chapter will raise two questions, one in each of the two main sections. First, what is meant by moral identity and what are the advantages of introducing this concept in the scheme of moral action? Second, what are the relations between moral cognition and moral identity? In this second section, as a way of introducing the problems that identity raises for a cognitive-developmentalist, two noncognitive approaches to the moral self will first be discussed: the ideal self of psychoanalysis and the self-regarding sentiment of McDougall. With the help of these two contrasting views, a cognitive solution to the issue of moral identity will be very briefly outlined.

The general framework of this chapter, therefore, is frankly cognitive. In other words, I assume that it is impossible to understand the moral quality— positive or negative—of an action without resorting to the agent's judgment, that moral judgments reflect the individual's general understanding of himself or herself, other people, social relations, and situations, and that this understanding can and does change as a result of the development of one's intelligence and of richer and more complex experience with the social world. Admittedly, a great deal is being assumed, considering the importance that these ideas have in the development of my argument. Because these assumptions are mostly philosophical in nature and are aimed at defining the moral phenomenon, however, their discussion seems to be unnecessary and out of place in the present context.

MORAL IDENTITY

There are three characteristics of identity that not only seem to be central in Erikson's account (particularly in *Insight and Responsibility, 1964*) but also are useful for my purposes: First, identity is experienced as rooted in the very core of one's being; second, identity is described as involving being true to oneself in action; third, it is associated with truthfulness, namely, with respect for one's own understanding of reality. The latter two meanings are part of the cluster of characteristics by which Erikson defines fidelity, the human virtue that is intimately associated with the development of identity. My use of this concept of identity is somewhat opportunistic: Erikson's descriptions of these characteristics are useful for my purpose, independently of the overall theoretical context in which they are embedded and from which they derive their specific Eriksonian meaning.

One of the most frequently heard criticisms of the contemporary emphasis on moral reasoning is that moral understanding and moral knowledge give a rather abstract and lifeless perspective on the moral reality. The doubts that moral reasoning may be reliably tied to moral action seem frequently to reflect the same kind of bias with which life and soul are associated only with emotions and desires. Erikson (1964) himself appeared to imply a similar view, when he distinguished between ethical or moral ideas ("nobility and rectitude as cultivated by moralities," p. 211), on one hand, and what he calls "virtues" or "strengths," on the other. The first, by themselves, are "nonvital," "despirited" superstructures and need the latter in order to acquire not only psychological roots but also validity and actuality. "Virtues," instead, are vital, "essential," "animated," and "spirited" qualities, originating from the convergence of "unfolding capacities with existing institutions" (p. 142); they exercise the function of giving human beings the same sense of rootedness that animals possess as a privilege of nature (p. 117). Ethical ideals will provide strength and trustworthy guidelines for adapting to the real world only to the extent that they are built on, and integrated with, the substructure and the rock bottom of these inherent natural strengths.

McDougall (1936), as we shall see, starting from very different assumptions, arrived at a similar conclusion: Moral ideals are powerless if they are not rooted in a moral self. Thus, despite different theoretical frameworks, a common belief is stressed, a belief that also seems to be shared by common sense: Morality is more a characteristic of the agent than of either action or thinking; the ultimate source of goodness lies in good will, and good will is at the core of what a person is.

In this chapter, then, identity is considered equivalent to the essential self.

Each individual, beginning relatively early in development, has an image, a perception, a scheme, or a theory of himself or herself (all these terms are awkward; none captures precisely the type of reality to be conveyed), being at the same time a principle of cognitive organization and the source of a special class of motives, the self motives.

The self is not simply a collection of characteristics, traits, or percepts; it is an organization of self-related information in which the various elements are brought together according to certain principles of psychological consistency. The organizing principle, varying from person to person, determines the order and the hierarchy among the characteristics that are included in the self, along such metaphorical dimensions as central peripheral, deep superficial, important unimportant, and so on. It also defines what could be called the essential or the core self, namely, the set of those aspects without which the individual would see himself or herself to be radically different; those so central that one could not even imagine being deprived of them; those whose loss would be considered and felt as irreparable.

Defined in this manner, identity includes at least some elements of the ideal self and functions as the ideal principle of action. Understanding that a specific ideal is a goal for one's becoming already involves a restructuring of the very core of the actual self, introducing in it a new principle of tension between what one understands and what one does. The seemingly curious psychoanalytic expression "identification with one's self" (Sandler, Holder, & Meers, 1963) begins to make sense when it is understood to indicate that parts of the actual representation of oneself have acquired the function of self ideal.

Although already implicit in what has been said, it may be useful to point out explicitly that the psychological construct of self-perception and similar constructs, which have been guiding empirical work in this area, are a feeble if not distorted version of the reality that is suggested by the term *identity*. This is so even when attempts are made to capture the organizing aspects of self-perceptions. The essential self or identity cannot be found simply, or mainly, in what one says about oneself, particularly through the framework of checklists, rating scales, and questionnaires. One would have to uncover the unverbalized, and to some extent unverbalizable, assumptions that underlie what one says about oneself and about others, the decisions one makes, the emotions one experiences.

Much of this material may be unconscious (though not necessarily in the Freudian sense of the term), may appear in fantasy, in day and night dreams, and may elicit the whole range of defenses. One can think of experiences such as the sense of futility and waste in one's life, of uselessness of one's work, of incompetence in one's chosen field, of inadequacy in one's love. People's essential selves may vary; however, one should get to this level of analysis to even hope to find it. Anything less would be "lifeless" and "despirited," in the sense that Erikson gave these words.

Identity, as has been described here, is relevant to moral functioning in two ways. First, being moral, being a good person, being fair and just in a general sense, may be, but need not be, a part of an individual's essential self. From a psychological perspective, it seems plausible (or at least not impossible) that some people's identity does not include morality (see Chap. 6). In fact, one can hypothesize for morality different degrees of centrality in people's identities. The individual who lacks a moral identity will still understand and use moral speech, will be able to make moral judgments and to engage in discussions about the appropriateness of certain moral decisions and the validity of certain moral criteria. However, a moral perspective will play no significant role in his or her life, in the decisions that really matter, in the fundamental outlook on the world and on history, or in eliciting strong emotions and deep anxieties. Second, one can hypothesize that different moral aspects characterize the moral identity of the individual who does have one; where one person sees compassion as being essential to his or her identity, another emphasizes instead fairness and justice; where one considers obedience as a central ideal, another stresses moral freedom.

Moral identity, in sum, both in its general and in its specific aspects, can be looked at as a dimension of individual differences. Quite possibly, some of these variations are developmental in nature. It should not be surprising if moral identity cannot be found before a certain age, even when moral reasoning and cognitive moral criteria are already present. Similarly, it is not improbable that one's moral identity undergoes changes, for instance, from focusing on obedience as a central virtue to emphasizing loyalty and, finally, moral autonomy. There are, at present, no data directly relevant to the preceding hypotheses, with the possible exceptions of anecdotal, biographical, and clinical materials. In fact, there are no readily available methods by which these hypotheses could be empirically addressed. But the questions are clearly empirical, and adequate methods are not beyond our empirical imagination.

From my present perspective, moral identity is directly related to moral action, providing one of its truly moral motives. As already mentioned, one aspect of fidelity, the basic virtue that Erikson considers as inherently tied to the development of identity, consists of a concern with being authentic and true to one's self in action. In my self model (Blasi, 1980, 1983), the connection between moral identity and action is expressed through the concepts of responsibility (in the sense of strict obligation to act according to one's judgment) and integrity. These two concepts are closely related and derive their meaning from a view of moral action as an extension of the essential self into the domain of the possible, of what is not but needs to be, if the agent has to remain true to himself or herself. Responsibility, in this sense, stresses the self as the source of "moral compulsion." Integrity, instead, emphasizes the idea of moral self-consistency, of intactness and wholeness—all essential connotations of the self as a psychological organization. Neither of these ideas is new. Over a century ago, the French philosopher J.-M. Guyau wrote: "Thought, action—they are at bottom identical. And what is called moral obligation is, in the sphere of the intellect, the sense of this radical identity; obligation is an internal expansion, a need for completing our ideas by making them pass into action. Morality is the unity of the being" (quoted in Baldwin, 1899, p. 56). It should be added that moral cognition and moral action are not the same; their relation is not a matter of fact but is a matter of obligation and depends on the unity of the self.

MORAL IDENTITY AND MORAL COGNITION

The second section of this chapter is much more controversial and is more on the side of philosophy than on the side of psychology. It raises questions concerning the cognitive nature of the moral self and the functional relations between moral judgment and moral identity. The issue is important for a cognitive approach to moral functioning and development; it also has some practical implications, particularly with regard to the origin and the transformations of moral identity.

The problem can be stated as follows: If, at least in some instances, moral judgment, derived from cognitive criteria and other cognitive considerations, is not sufficient to motivate moral action, but requires motives originating from within one's identity, what becomes of the cognitive basis of moral action? To use a concrete example, two hypothetical individuals may share the same structure of moral reasoning but are characterized by a different identity with respect to morality (e.g., the first has but the second lacks a moral identity). In a specific situation, the first man behaves consistently with both his moral judgment and his moral identity, whereas the second behaves in a way that is inconsistent with his moral judgment but not inconsistent with his identity. In this and similar cases, can we still maintain a cognitive approach to the understanding of morality? Can we say that moral understanding is functionally related to moral action? Or should not we say, in contradiction with the premises of this chapter, that structures of moral reasoning are ultimately sterile and play no real significant role in moral functioning? In sum, is it possible to make one's moral understanding alive, full-blooded, animated, and rooted in one's deeper psychological nature without losing in the process its cognitive characteristics?[1]

Anticipating a later discussion, a cognitive solution will be possible to the extent that the essential self is sensitive to, and indeed biased toward, cognitive considerations, not only in moral decisions but also in setting up goals and ideals for itself, namely, in constructing its very self. First, however, I will illustrate the risks presented by a psychological approach to morality that is based on the self and on identity. Of course, the assessment of risk depends

---

[1] The conflict between moral judgment and identity is problematic for a cognitive theory of moral functioning in a way that other conflicts—for example, between moral judgment and hedonistic desires, or between moral reasoning and career ambitions—are not. The reason is that moral consistency can be understood only as a part and within the broader domain of self-consistency, and not in opposition to it; one type of consistency cannot be pursued at the expense of the other.

on the assumption adopted in this chapter that reason is of the essence of morality and cannot be eliminated without destroying the moral phenomenon itself. I will do so by commenting on the psychoanalytic theory of the ideal self, or one version of it, and McDougall's (1936) concept of the self-regarding sentiment.

Freud's (again, in some interpretations of his thinking) and McDougall's views share two characteristics: Both attempted to anchor morality in the total personality of the individual and looked skeptically at a morality that relies on abstract ideals; they both constructed the moral personality around a core of instinct-like impulses and their transformations. The differences, however, are as important as the similarities: Freud's basic motive (in the version discussed here) concerned hedonistic desire; McDougall relied instead on social needs, particularly on the need for social acceptance and approval, while rejecting egocentric and hedonistic needs as inadequate to account for the truly moral experience. Echoes of McDougall can be found in Chapters 13 and 16 in this book.

From the perspective of the present chapter, the aim and the interest in comparing psychoanalysis and McDougall's theory are to show that the risks involved in a self-based approach to the psychology of morality lie not in the type of needs or instincts that one places at the core of the self, but in the noncognitive, nonrational nature of needs and instincts. Social impulses are frequently considered higher, and more obviously moral, than hedonistic needs; this was certainly McDougall's (1936) opinion (see particularly pp. 162–164). To the extent that the social self is not a response to understanding and reason, however, to this extent a moral functioning based on the self seems incompatible with a cognitive-developmental account.

The Psychoanalytic Ideal Self

It is well known that Freud did not leave a coherent account of the moral agencies, that is, an account in which ego, conscience, superego, and ego ideal are clearly defined and clearly distinguished from one another. My comments follow the reconstruction that Sandler et al. (1963) gave of one such agency, the ideal self, on the basis of Freud's own writings and of later psychoanalytic discussion. The purpose here is not to offer a reliable account of what Freud really thought or said, but to discuss one way of approaching moral functioning from the perspective of the self.

According to the Sandler et al. (1963) account, the ideal self is one element of the representation of oneself that is constructed on the basis of three contents: a very early identification with the "admired object" (frequently the father); identification with the "ideal child," namely, with the "parents' ideal of a desirable and loved child, as perceived by the child" (p. 154); and identification with the self, namely, with those earlier shapes of the self that were associated with a high degree of narcissistic gratification.

These authors also point out the special "economic gains" (measured, namely, on the basis of libidinal gratification) that derive from constructing the ideal self on the identifications just described: By internalizing compliance to the authority, the child "gains a feeling of being loved"; by identifying with the admired object, "he can love and admire himself as he does the object" (p. 153); the third identification, finally, is a direct attempt "to restore . . . the primary narcissistic state of the earliest weeks of life" (p. 156). In sum, the construction of the ideal self is guided by the wish to obtain as much libidinal gratification as possible, either by way of primary narcissism or by way of secondary narcissism.

Thus, instinctual self-love is the motivational spring guiding the construction of the ideal self. Moreover, the specific shape that the ideal self acquires in any situation, including situations in which a moral decision is called for, is "a compromise between the desired state of instinctual gratification and the need to win the love of, or to avoid punishment from, authority figures, internal or external. The ultimate criterion at any given time is an economic one" (p. 153).

Other later influences will affect the ideal self, but its stable core will be mostly unconscious and will be based "upon the ideals created in childhood" (p. 155). Knowledge and reality are indeed given a role, but only a prudential one: Their function is not to shape ideals, but simply to make the individual aware of his or her own limitations and potentialities as well as of the possibilities for gratification offered by the environment.

When this psychoanalytic account is stripped of its metapsychological terminology, it appears quite similar in its essential message to other, more familiar, views of morality: Moral standards in the best of cases (namely, by comparison with the aggressive and limiting superego morality) are based on the self and on the ideal for the self; the latter is rooted in the most natural and vital of needs, the need to obtain love and the most intensive pleasure that is possible; at its best, morality cannot be but a form of self-interest. Therefore, so-called higher virtues, disinterested ideals (and these would include several stages suggested by cognitive theories of moral reasoning), have no grounding in real human substance and should be suspiciously regarded as hypocritical and devious maneuvers to serve one's self-interest.

It should perhaps be added, parenthetically, that ego-psychoanalytic theorists, when they attempt to balance the previous account of morality by adding certain cognitive-developmental principles such as those of Jean Piaget or Lawrence Kohlberg, frequently do not seriously consider the constraints that are presented by an instinctual view of the self and of the ideal self. Rationality and truth are not brought back in by relying on the "economic principle," that is, on the best possible compromise between truth and instinctual self-interest.

McDougall's Self-regarding Sentiment

In McDougall's (1936) system, the concept of self-regarding sentiment plays, with regard to moral action, the same roles that the ideal self plays in the preceding psychoanalytic account. The self-regarding sentiment is said to integrate within it the moral sentiments, namely, those emotional orientations that lead to moral judgments, and, most important, to provide the motivational force for moral action. On one hand, it motivates the acceptance of rules and of the moral tradition; on the other, it informs volition and sustains the determination to pursue moral ideals despite strong contrary desires. In contrast, moral inconsistency and backsliding are explained on the basis of a weak self-regarding sentiment.

Therefore, the self is, in its emotional substance, the center of moral functioning. Moral victories are achieved because "the personality as a whole, or the central feature or nucleus of the personality, the man himself, or all that which is regarded by himself and others as the most essential part of himself, is thrown upon the side of the weaker (but moral) motive" (McDougall, 1936, pp. 206–207).

But what is the self-regarding sentiment? It is a sentiment, first of all, namely, an organized system of emotions and tendencies, a cluster of affects and impulses, centered around a specific object. In this case, the object is the idea of self. As the self originates in social interaction and maintains throughout life a structure that reflects its origin, the emotions and motives that constitute the self-regarding sentiment are mostly social in nature: admiration, awe and reverence, altruistic feelings and sympathy, and particularly shame and pride, self-respect and self-satisfaction. From these originate the two central motives: search for social approval and avoidance of social disapproval. In turn, the roots of the self-regarding sentiment lie in primitive, essentially inborn, instincts: passive sympathy, the gregarious instinct, and the instincts of self-display and self-subjection.

McDougall rejected very strongly any attempt to reduce the self-regarding sentiment and morality to a concern with punishments and rewards and to material interests. On the other hand, he thought that people's desire for social approval has such a degree of intensity as to be unexplainable on rational grounds. Here lies the living source of that type of morality that is specifically human.

Of course, cognition is also important; emotions and motives require an idea, the idea of self, in order to be clustered together and are modified with the changes that this idea undergoes. However, as McDougall (1936) writes, "The relation between the cognitive disposition and the emotional dispositions comprised within a sentiment is that the latter remain the conative-affective root of the whole system . . . furnishing to it the energy, 'drive,' conative force or interest by which all thinking of the object is sustained" (p. 438). His views on this matter are particularly clear when he discusses the role and the nature of moral judgments.

McDougall (1936) realized the limitations of a moral system based on social approval and was aware that a higher type of moral functioning can occasionally be observed, namely, a moral functioning in which "man . . . is capable also of standing up against public opinion and of doing what he judges to be right in defiance of it" (p. 183). A central factor that characterizes this level and makes it possible is moral judgment. But moral judgments are also said to originate from emotions and sentiments.

There are, in fact, two kinds of judgments: The first is purely classificatory and consists in applying to concrete instances emotionally charged labels that are provided by one's society (lie, theft, etc.); this judgment does not proceed from emotions. By contrast, the second kind of moral judgment, called original moral judgment by McDougall and corresponding approximately to moral reasoning in contemporary cognitive-developmental theory, is a result of sentiments, particularly of abstract moral sentiments (e.g., love of justice, love of truth, hatred of deception). It seems that emotions of this type depend on, and originate from, certain kinds of understanding. According to McDougall, however, they are acquired from absorbing the finer aspects of one's moral tradition, through the admiration (another sentiment) of those exceptional individuals who embody them. Much, of course, is left unexplained in this account: How does one recognize the more refined aspects of a tradition? According to which criteria are certain people judged to be exceptional and worthy of admiration? How is it possible to make original judgments that go beyond the tradition of one's society?

In sum, McDougall's central explanation of moral strivings lies in the self-regarding sentiment, which he considers to be structured around the search for approval and the emotions that are associated with it. He saw the need for a postconventional morality, to use Kohlberg's term, and for personal autonomy. He was able to describe these characteristics, but he was unable to account for them and to transcend the level of moral praise and blame. From my understanding, the central reason for McDougall's failure lies in the assumptions that moral judgment is noncognitive and that reasoning is powerless to affect the emotive core of the self.

CONCLUDING REMARKS

It was argued, first, that it is important for a psychological theory of morality to study the relations between moral action and personality and to recognize that a morality that actually works, not only in this or that action but also in one's life in general, must be rooted in some form of identity. Erikson's approach through the idea of a naturally unfolding set of "virtues," the psychoanalytic approach, based, in the version presented here, on the ideal self, and McDougall's self-regarding sentiment are all attempts to ground morality in the nature of the psychological being. The notion of moral identity was aimed at the same purpose.

It was pointed out, then, that an attempt to establish morality on personality runs the risk of eliminating from morality what seems one of its essential characteristics, namely, its being based on judgment and reason. Neither Freud nor McDougall avoided this risk. Erikson's position is more ambiguous in this respect, mostly because it is not clear to what extent his virtues depend on a genuine understanding of and not simply on adaptation to our social world.

All these views share the idea of a naturally occurring morality, namely, of a morality spontaneously evolving from natural impulses, basic instincts, and the like. One could blame, then, the "naturalistic" approach of these theories for eliminating from morality the foundation of reason. But it is not clear what "natural" and "naturalistic" mean, or what would be contrasted to these terms. I certainly do not suggest an unnatural or a supernatural morality.

As already mentioned, moral functioning inevitably becomes divorced from reason and truth when morality derives from the self, personality, identity, or similar constructs, *and* when personality, identity, or the self are impervious, in their basic structure, to the influence of reason. The dilemma is this: If moral identity is based on natural impulses, egoistic or social, one loses the cognitive basis of morality; if cognition and reason are stressed as establishing moral motives, one risks losing the person as the center of morality. It would appear, then, that the only hope of grounding morality on the essential self without losing morality's reason is to hypothesize that the self's very identity is constructed, at least in part, under the influence of moral reasons.

The steps could be the following:

1. General moral structures would be constructed through social interactions and would reflect a genuine understanding of the social reality, namely, an understanding that is, in principle, independent of one's personality biases, objective, and open to revision as a result of better and more complete evidence and experience.
2. General moral structures would influence the construction of more concrete ideals of actions and ideals of agents.
3. This would lead, in turn, to the construction of an ideal moral self and, eventually, to the moralization of the self and personality.
4. At this point, the self, partially constructed under the influence and the guide of moral reason, could become, itself, the source of concrete moral judgments. These judgments would be grounded on one's identity but would also be cognitive and genuinely moral. Fundamentally, however, the direction of influence would be from moral understanding to moral identity, rather than the other way around, as Freud, McDougall, and possibly Erikson seemed to think.

Of course, the crucial question is, Can the self and identity be influenced in their shape by knowledge and truth? This question is as yet unanswered, at least through research data. Leaving this issue aside for the time being, I am suggesting that the self and identity *should* be influenced by knowledge and truth; that one should not be indifferent as to whether one has a moral identity or not, or as to the type of moral identity that one has; that the construction of such an identity is indeed a genuine moral issue, more important than altruism, honesty, or truthfulness; and, finally, that morality and the good life, to use a Kantian distinction, cannot be separated.

REFERENCES

Baldwin, J. M. *Social and ethical interpretations in mental development*. New York: Macmillan, 1899.

Blasi, A. Bridging moral cognition and moral action: A critical review of the literature. *Psychological Bulletin*, 1980, *88*, 1–45.

Blasi, A. Moral cognition and moral action: A theoretical perspective. *Developmental Review*, 1983, *3*, 178–210.

Erikson, E. H. *Insight and responsibility*. New York: Norton, 1964.

McDougall, W. *An introduction to social psychology*. London: Methuen, 1936.

Sandler, J., Holder, A., & Meers, D. The ego ideal and the ideal self. *The Psychoanalytic Study of the Child*, 1963, *18*, 139–158.

CHAPTER 8

Resolving Conflicts in Friendship: The Development of Moral Understanding in Everyday Life

MONIKA KELLER

This chapter deals with the morality of intimate interpersonal relationships. It analyzes the emerging interpersonal-moral understanding of conflict in a friendship. Friendship is seen as a paradigmatic relationship in which we can study the developmental roots of interpersonal morality. Moral development is seen as the development of a "moral orientation." This "moral orientation" encompasses various aspects including an awareness of the moral aspects of situations, the consequences of the violation of obligations (moral feelings), and the necessity for moral discourse as well as the necessity for justification and restitution in the case of violation of obligations.

These aspects of a moral orientation are analyzed developmentally in children's practical and moral reasoning about a friendship conflict.

Recent years have witnessed a shift of interest within moral development research in the cognitive-structural tradition from the structure of deontic judgment to the justification of responsible action in social situations. Following Kohlberg (1976), moral development research in the 1970s viewed morality mainly in terms of justice and fairness. More precisely, researchers focused mainly on changing structures of deontic judgments, that is, judgments involving rights and duties (Frankena, 1973). Such judgments of obligations

This research is part of the Project Child Development and Social Structure carried out by the Centre of Development and Socialization in the Max Planck Institute for Human Development and Education in West Berlin in cooperation with the Department of Social Science of the University of Iceland. I wish to thank Wolfgang Edelstein for helpful comments on this chapter and Michael Maute and Michael Mönnig for contributing to the construction of the levels. I also wish to thank the German Research Foundation (DFG), who supported this research with a career development grant.

are "absolute": They define what is right for any person under the conditions of a specified, hypothetical dilemma and are based on the notion of universal moral principles. For Kohlberg, following Rawls (1971), the principle of justice takes precedence over other principles because it represents the highest degree of structural elaboration and, therefore, of assimilatory adequacy.

Recently, however, researchers have begun to focus on moral judgment structures in terms of their relevance to or function in practical moral decisions. This focus has broadened the scope of moral development research in several ways. Blasi (1980, and Chap. 7 in this book) has shown how judgments of responsibility (i.e., the obligations accepted by a moral self in action) mediate between abstract moral judgment and actual moral decision making (see also Chap. 4). Gilligan (1980), deeply concerned with practical moral decision making in highly stressful real-life situations, attempted to base an alternative conception of morality on an ethics of care; for her, the pivotal concepts are concerns and responsibilities rather than rights and obligations (see Chap. 19). As opposed to the public and abstract issues in the dilemmas of traditional moral research, Gilligan's dilemmas depict highly concrete, particular, and intimate situations in self-other relationships.

These approaches all have in common an attempt to *contextualize* moral judgment—in various types of social interaction, specific self-other relationships, and differing performance conditions of the self. Within such a framework, types of moral dilemmas that have been neglected in the Kohlberg tradition emerge. Whereas the classical moral dilemma calls for the resolution of a conflict of duties, these dilemmas often depict a situation in which desires conflict with obligations. This is the structure of many morally relevant conflicts of everyday life. Furthermore, these approaches broaden the scope of morality from morality as justice to a morality of the good life (Frankena, 1973) involving principles of supererogation. These dilemmas deal with nonobligatory acts that are oriented toward the welfare of others (Eisenberg, 1982). Such acts go beyond what is required by principles of duty (Rawls, 1971; Richards, 1971). In contrast to a tradition uniquely concerned with deontic judgments, sympathetic concern and altruism are perceived to be morally relevant from this perspective.

THE MORALITY OF INTERPERSONAL RELATIONSHIPS

The research presented here is related both to Kohlberg's work and to the other approaches mentioned. It addresses the development of a morality of interpersonal relationships that can, at the same time, be conceptualized as the development of a moral self. By moral self, we refer to the awareness of the moral aspects of interpersonal relationships, a "moral orientation" (Melden, 1977; Richards, 1971) toward others with whom the self is seen to stand in a moral relationship.

Interpersonal conflicts in everyday life relate to morality whenever they involve the evaluation of self's and others' behaviors, motives, and feelings with regard to rules and principles about both what is right and reasonable in terms of justice or fairness and what is good in terms of ideals of self and relationships. Thus, within interpersonal relationships, ethics deal with how interests and claims "should be pursued and whether they sometimes should not be pursued, remembering always their pursuit in a world of relationships" (Emmet, 1966, p. 53).

The morally relevant expectations that govern people's interactions arise in self-other relationships and can be seen as products of the developmental transformations of the self-other relationship. Therefore, the cognitive and affective understanding of relationships and the naive theories about what it means (morally) to stand in a relationship (Hamlyn, 1974) are seen to form the basis for the development of an understanding of concepts of obligations and responsibilities in relations. Given the intricate connection between the system of moral rules and the system of interpersonal relationships, it appears plausible to investigate the developmental origins of moral rule systems within particular, intimate, and affectively meaningful relationships. Among these, friendship has a special status.

Blum (1980) characterizes friendship as a special moral relationship of "concern, care, sympathy and the willingness to give oneself to the friend which goes far beyond what is characteristic and expected of people generally. The caring within a friendship is built upon a basis of knowledge, trust and intimacy. . . . In genuine friendship one comes to have a close identification with the good of the other person" (p. 69).

The developmental literature on friendship convincingly shows that qualities of friendship as described by Blum are a relatively late achievement in development (Damon, 1977; Selman, 1980; Youniss, 1980). An understanding that the self is part of an ongoing relationship that involves deep mutual emotional sharing, caring, and concern for another person appears to be an achievement of early adolescence (Selman, 1980).

Astonishingly enough, friendship has received little attention from a moral perspective. This holds true for moral philosophy as well as for moral development research. Only recently, Youniss (1981) has argued that friendship represents a prototypic relationship in which the development of rules of fairness and of sympathetic concern can be studied. In agreement with Piaget (1932/1962), he sees friendship as a symmetric relationship that, in contrast to parent-child relationships of unilateral constraint, allows for the development of a morality of reciprocity.

The aim of the research presented here is to analyze the normative aspects of interpersonal relationships, using friendship as the specific example. Our approach is indebted to Kohlberg, as our moral dilemma involves justice as fairness. Yet, the concept of justice only partially covers the range of morally relevant aspects of relationships, which is why Gilligan's work presents a challenge. In addition, our research derives from Selman's (1980) work on perspective-taking and friendship. We share with Selman the notion of a deep structure of self-other relationships as elaborated in his concept of perspective-taking. The developmental levels of friendship described by Selman (1980) provide a general framework for the analysis of the normative and moral implications of friendship emerging from a situation of conflict between friends. Instead of centering on the descriptive understanding of friendship, however, we focus on the development of moral awareness—the ability to see the moral implications of an interpersonal conflict in a relationship. It is the ability, to paraphrase Thomas (1932), to define a situation as moral and deal with the consequences of such definition.

MORAL DEVELOPMENT AS DEVELOPMENT OF A "MORAL ORIENTATION"

According to Melden (1977) and Richards (1971), moral development can be seen as the formation of a "moral orientation." It is an orientation

> in which we exhibit appropriate sensitivities in thought, feeling and action towards others out of a concern for them as we go about in our affairs in ways that affect their and our own interests. It is this moral concern for others as persons, rather than principles and priority rules, which provides us with a rationale for resolving many or most of the moral conflicts that arise, easily and without hesitation. [Melden, 1977, p. 18]

The development of a "moral orientation" involves both *cognitive* and *affective-motivational* aspects. On the cognitive side, it presupposes knowledge of the moral rules and principles that are relevant for social interaction. Reuss (Note 1), referring to Hare (1952), points out the role of imagination in morality. The cognitive component of imagination relates to the anticipation of consequences of one's morally relevant decisions for self and others. In this sense, imagination is based on social cognitive abilities. It further includes the development of a repertoire of interaction strategies to compensate for consequences resulting from the violation of obligations and responsibilities toward others.

The affective-motivational component of imagination relates to the extent to which anticipated consequences of the self's actions for others are emotionally meaningful for the self or, more generally, to the extent to which the self is willing to deal with others' interests and concerns as if they were his or her own. It also includes a motivation to compensate for the violation of obligations and responsibilities. Thus, as various authors have pointed out, feelings of sympathy and concern for others form an important motivational base for the moral regulation of actions (Blum, 1980; Hoffman, 1977, and Chap. 16 in this book). Similarly, Peters (1979) has argued that morality encompasses broad dimensions of a "moral self," including motives, emotions, attitudes, and dispositions. Thus, we can see moral awareness or a moral orientation as a response to other persons in which we take the others' weal and woe into account.

COMPONENTS OF A MORAL ORIENTATION

From a constructivist point of view and, particularly, in the tradition of symbolic interactionism (Mead, 1934), the development of a moral orientation involves a variety of processes: first, the process of defining situations with regard to the moral rules and principles they contain; second, moral feelings, or the awareness of consequences when obligations or responsibilities have been violated; and third, moral discourse, which is the process of negotiating conflicting claims, obligations, expectations, and interests.

1. The moral definition of the situation. In most moral development research the interpretation of the situation in terms of the moral rules and principles involved has been taken for granted. But given that situations of everyday life are ambiguous in principle (Turner, 1962), actors must reconstruct them in terms of their moral and nonmoral meaning (Cooney, 1978; Damon & Gerson, 1978). The implications of such a constructivist approach become even stronger when situations are less idealized and pure than Kohlberg-type dilemmas with regard to the conflicting values and principles involved. The interpretation of the situation involves aspects of social-cognitive, moral, and ego functioning. As Denzin (1980) has pointed out in response to the "over-cognitive conception of man" in symbolic interactionism, the process of defining the situation involves interpretations based on intense feelings as well as on deliberate cognitive interpretations.

2. Awareness of the consequences of violating obligations and responsibilities: moral feelings. The development of a moral attitude also implies certain forms of feelings where others have been treated unfairly or where self has violated other's rights or failed in responsibility to other persons. Whether such violation results from "competing moral considerations or from factors for which the person may or may not be directly responsible, the person must bear the appropriate moral burden and show an appropriate concern towards the other person" (Melden, 1977, p. 20). This concern involves feelings of remorse and regret. Feelings of shame are related to the failure to live up to one's self ideal and identity (Richards, 1971; Thrane, 1979). They lead to the blaming of the self and thus stimulate the self to act differently on other occasions. Feelings of guilt can be seen as related to the act of having violated reciprocity principles and thereby having treated others unfairly. Guilt feelings thus become the basis for compensation and moral restitution to those who have been treated unfairly and irresponsibly.

3. The Negotiation of Conflicting Claims: Moral Discourse. The negotiation of conflicts in relationships requires the application of moral rules and principles under the constraints of practical situations. It implies taking into account the psychological particularities of the situation and of the persons dealing with one another in conflicts of interest, goals, expectations, and obligations and considering the moral and practical consequences of self's and other's decisions for their ongoing relationships. Thus, the process of weighing priorities in light of possible consequences in the course of practical decision making is an integral part of moral reasoning. Again, both cognition and affect are involved.

The process of moral decision making in which the moral actor hypothetically takes the perspective of others in order to find (morally) adequate solutions to everyday situations involves others with whom the actor can join in a moral discourse in order to find a solution that is acceptable to all parties concerned. The capacity to engage in moral discourse can thus be seen as a significant part of moral development that has only recently emerged as a topic of interest (Gilligan & Murphy, 1979; Youniss, 1981).

Moral discourse involves *justifications* whenever practical decisions violate obligations. According to Singer (1958), this justification means giving reasons that outweigh obligations. Such justifications can be used in a moral dialogue in which the practical decision is negotiated. But they can also be used as practical explanations following moral transgressions (Döbert & Nunner-Winkler, 1978; Sykes & Matza, 1957). In all cases, justifications can be used as defensive maneuvers whether serving to deny the negative consequences of the act (justification) or to reject personal responsibility (excuses) (Keller, in press).

Moral discourse may also involve action strategies designed to make up for violations and thus to restore the moral relationship between self and other by asking forgiveness or by offering various forms of material or psychological compensation. Selman (1980) has described such forms of compensation as strategies of conflict resolution.

DEVELOPMENT OF A MORAL ORIENTATION IN REASONING ABOUT A FRIENDSHIP CONFLICT: THE EMPIRICAL RESEARCH

The developmental levels of moral orientation presented in the following section have been derived from preliminary analysis of selected cross-sectional and longitudinal data from 140 children between 7 and 13 years old. The scoring of the complete data set according to the system presented here is currently underway.

The conflict situation presented to the child is a slightly modified version of Selman's (1980) friendship story and involves conflicting interpersonal moral norms as well as hedonistic needs and desires. The hero of the story has promised to see his or her best friend on a given day. The hero, however, is tempted to accept an invitation to a movie coming from a third child. The movie happens to be exactly at the same time as the scheduled visit promised to the friend. The story gives further details on which the child can focus selectively: The friendship has a long history; it is an intimate friendship. The two friends have a special arrangement to meet on a particular day every week. The promise given was for this special day. The friend wants to play records and talk some things over with the hero (there are hints that the friend may be experiencing some trouble). The new child who invites the hero to a movie and to hot dogs and soda has only recently moved into the neighborhood and has not yet made friends. The hero and the new child seem to like each other, but the old friend does not like the newcomer.

Structurally, the story can be analyzed in terms of both the conflicting interpersonal moral norms it contains and the basic moral principles underlying the situation. Specifically, three norms are involved:

1. Contractual norms, represented here by the moral institution of promising.
2. Norms of particular interpersonal relationships, represented here by the particular, intimate relationship of friendship.
3. Norms of general interpersonal relationships, referring here to general obligations such as altruism.

In addition, three fundamental moral principles apply to the situation (Rawls, 1971; Richards, 1971):

1. The principle of fairness or reciprocity as a principle of duty, seen here in the issue of keeping or breaking a promise.
2. The principle of truthfulness (Habermas, 1976) as a principle of duty, seen here as the issue of whether or not to lie when an obligation has been violated.
3. The principle of beneficence as a principle of supererogation, seen here as the responsibility to help someone in need.[1]

The structure established by these principles constitutes the conflict background built into the story. After reading the story to the child, the researcher conducted a semistructured interview lasting about 45 minutes. Its purpose was to evaluate how children define the situation, giving their naive theoreti-

---

[1]The two principles of duty relate to a moral institution or a social practice that is of benefit to everyone. They are fundamental to the regulation of social interaction in terms of mutual orientation and trust in relationships. The failure to act according to these principles therefore is a violation of a relationship of trust. The third principle refers to nonobligatory acts of sympathy and kindness toward others. According to Richards (1971, p. 205), these acts range from kindness toward others as part of daily routines to the benevolence of a personal friendship. Assuming a moral attitude, in all cases of violation of these principles the mature moral actor has to bear his or her burden of guilt or shame and the obligation to restore the relationship.

cal assessments of decision, reasons for decision, consequences of decision, and consequences of consequences. The overall goal was to evaluate:

1. The child's spontaneous sensitivity for the interpersonal-moral aspects of the situation.
2. The components of the child's moral orientation as revealed in how children try to maintain, reestablish, or subvert a moral balance in an ongoing relationship while weighing moral and nonmoral concerns.

The *cognitive-developmental analysis* presented in the following sections describes the emerging rule system of interpersonal moral obligations seen in these interviews. The analysis addresses the question of how the growing awareness of what is morally good and right influences practical argumentation about actions in a hypothetical conflict. The rule system described was inferred from those normative aspects of actor's and other's situation that the child takes into account when thinking about action choices, the reasons he or she gives for these choices, the consequences derived from these choices in terms of moral feelings, the nature of justifications and restitutions, and the evaluation of practical decisions in terms of moral adequacy.

DEVELOPMENTAL LEVELS OF INTERPERSONAL MORAL REASONING

In the following section the levels of interpersonal moral understanding are described. An overview of these levels is given in Table 8.1. The description follows the order of the columns in the table. Developmental changes in the following aspects are discussed in turn: (1) the *definition of the situation;* (2) the *reasons* given for the *practical decisions;* (3) the *consequences* of violating friendship obligations for the *friend;* (4) the consequences of violating friendship obligations for the *actor* (moral feelings); and (5) aspects of an imagined "moral discourse" between the friends, for example, *strategies of justification and restitution* to make up for or avoid the consequences of violating obligations. In the column on the left side, Selman's (1980) levels of friendship are presented. They form the framework for the interpretation of the levels of interpersonal moral reasoning elaborated here.

There are two types of moral conceptualization of the situation possible at all the levels above Level 0; The first is the interpretation of the dilemma in terms of the conflict between *duty and desire* where an obligation toward the friend is perceived as conflicting with a desire related to the hedonistic quality of the offer from the new child;[2] the second is the interpretation in

---

[2]The situation is never interpreted as an obligation toward the new child conflicting with a hedonistic offer (toys) from the friend.

TABLE 8.1. Levels of Interpersonal Moral Reasoning

Level of friendship[a]	Interpretation of Situation	Practical Judgment (Reasons for Decision)		Consequences of Violation of Friendship Obligation		Moral Discourse or Rebalancing
		Consistent with Friendship Obligation	Inconsistent with Friendship Obligation: Desire; Obligation	For Other or Relationship	For Self (Moral Feelings)	
0. Physicalistic	Self's desires	Self's hedonistic desires	Desire: self's hedonistic desires	Object-related feelings (left out from fun)	Pragmatic concerns	No understanding of justification; compensation
1. Unilateral	Self's desires or other's desires or feelings	Anticipated consequences of action for friend	Desire: weighing of choices in terms of hedonism: obligation: avoidance of negative feelings	Interpersonal feelings (left out from interaction); termination of interaction	Empathetic concerns (consequences of action for other); fear of consequences (physical action)	Justification as informing about action; concealment of action; material compensation
2. Fair-weather cooperation	Self's obligation or other's expectation (quality of relationship)	Self's obligation related to promise; friendship	Desire: exceptionality of situation (good opportunity) obligation: obligation to help	Violation of expectations (feeling betrayed); termination of friendship	Interpersonal or normative concerns (guilt over betraying reciprocity or veridicality); fear over termination of friendship	Perceived necessity of information; asking permission; asking forgiveness; concealment of action (explicit lying)
3. Intimate friendship	Self-other relationship of mutual concern over time, trust, loyalty (psychological particularities of situation)	Self's obligation related to moral self and ideal of friendship (being a trustworthy person or friend)	Exceptionality in context of relationship (hypothetical role switch) desire: opportunity obligation: to integrate into friendship	Betraying as violation of friendship loyalty; moral evaluation of actor's personality; diminution of friendship	Guilty conscience over breach of trust in relationship; shame over moral inadequacy of action	Perceived necessity of negotiating decision, of justifying decision through reasons, or of reassuring of solidarity in communication

[a] From Selman, 1980.

148

terms of *conflicting obligations* (conflict of duties) that result from the relationship with the friend or the promise given as well as from the relationship with the new child (helping). These two types of conceptualization are constructed in specific ways at each developmental level.

Level Zero

At this first level, there is no awareness of an obligation of the self toward another (friend) to whom the self is bound interpersonally and morally through friendship and promise. The *definition of the situation* is premoral. The choices are perceived from a purely hedonistic perspective (fun quality of the offers). The situation is predominantly perceived in terms of objects and actions and not in terms of relationships. The actor's self-centered desires and wants (related to the hedonistic offers) are the main elements of the situation. Sometimes the concept of an intentional subject having choices is not yet established.

These hedonistic desires become *reasons for the decision.* The decision involves weighing the desire to see the toys or the pleasure of playing with the toys or with the friend against the desire to get soda and hot dogs or to have a party.

Children at this first level are aware of the *consequences* of the decision to go to the movie *for the friend.* They know that the friend will feel bad if the actor does not come to visit. But these negative feelings are not related to the violation of an obligation. They are, rather, interpreted as resulting from the frustration of the friend's hedonistic wants (feeling bad over not getting to go to a movie or over being bored at home). Also, the negative consequences of such a decision for the friend are not yet an integral part of the actor's decision making; they are simply seen as its inevitable consequences. *Consequences* of the decision to go to the movie *for the actor* (self's perspective) again are not yet related to the violation of an obligation. With a decision to go to the movie the actor feels basically good (because he or she gets to go to a movie), or he or she may have pragmatic concerns over the adequateness of the choice in terms of fun (maybe the movie was not so good).

As there is no awareness of the violation of a moral norm, there is no need to *justify* the decision in the full meaning of the concept as "giving reasons that outweigh an obligation." The decision to go to the movie is seen as unproblematic. There is neither a need to hide the action or the reasons for the action from the friend nor any perceived need for restitution of the balance in the relationship.

Level One

At this level, the relationship of friendship becomes part of the *definition of the situation.* The conflicting interests of the friends are perceived against the background of such a relationship. The actor is now situated in an interpersonal world where the interacting subjects have their own needs, interests, goals, and feelings. A concern for other's "inner world," not present at Level 0, emerges. The main elements of the situation are now perceived as conflicting desires, needs, interests, and feelings (as consequences of choices). There is now a clear sense of subjectivity and agency in the sense that decisions are made with a growing awareness of consequences for self and other. Other's wants and feelings are considered, if only as obstacles to one's own intentions.

Thus, the *reasons for the decision* to visit the friend are no longer the purely hedonistic ones as at Level 0. It is rather aspects arising from the relationship itself (liking the friend, liking to be with the friend, the fact of being friends) that gain the status of reasons for decision. To this are added interpersonal concerns such as the friend's invitation or the avoidance of negative consequences for the friend (not leaving the friend out, not making the friend stay alone). Relationships, however, are defined by their affective quality rather than in obligational terms. If hedonistic desires become the motive for the decision to go to the movie, there is an explicit weighing of choices in terms of fun for the self (it is so much fun to go to a movie, much more than to see toys). But in contrast with Level 0, these reasons are not used as justifications to the friend. In addition, aspects of the new child's situation now may emerge as reasons for decision. These can be nonmoral qualities (interest in the new child, wanting to get to know the new child), quasi-moral qualities (the appropriateness of accepting the new child's invitation), or interpersonal concerns related to the new child's psychological situation (he or she is alone, not wanting to exclude the new child). In these quasi-moral concerns, we see a rudimentary beginning of weighing priorities. The situation is now interpreted as a conflict of interests and expectations. But this process of weighing is still insufficient and unbalanced with regard to obligations toward the friend.

The *consequences* of going to the movie *for the friend* are now interpreted in terms of the relationship between actor and friend. That the friend would feel bad or sad because he or she has invited the actor and wants the actor to come or has prepared everything and is looking forward to the visit (concept of expectation) is now considered. The awareness of the frustration of the friend's interests is linked to an anticipation of friend's physical retaliation (hitting, not playing with the actor anymore). This awareness of the other's interests and feelings as well as the other's external reactions toward the self ties in with the judgment of *consequences for the actor* (self) related to the decision of going to the movie. The actor may become empathetically concerned over the consequences of his or her decision for the friend (feels bad about the decision because friend is home alone). Another type of predominant concern relates to the consequences for the self (the friend will be angry with the actor, will hit him or her, be his or her enemy, or not play anymore).

An awareness appears that the action of going to the movie, whether for hedonistic or for altruistic reasons, is at least partly problematic and violates the interpersonal balance in the ongoing relationship with the friend. This awareness goes along with a perceived need for *acts of restitution*. Such strategies of conflict resolution tend to be "physicalistic," compared with the more psychological strategies at higher levels (e.g., inviting the friend to a movie next time).

The awareness of the problematic aspects of the decision to go to the movie for hedonistic reasons can lead to an intentional attempt to conceal the action from the friend. The two predominant motives for such a strategy are the avoidance of the friend's interference with the decision (friend would start arguing and then actor would miss the movie) and the avoidance of negative consequences for the self after the action has been performed (not telling anything because friend would be so angry). When the situation is constructed such that the friend asks about the course of events, the action may be reported in a rather "factual way" (he or she went to a movie) *without* reference to one's egoistic wants as at Level 0. Use of these strategies can be seen as an indication of the awareness of the moral inadequacy of the action of going to the movie (especially if the motive for the decision is hedonistic).

Level Two

At Level 2, the friendship as an ongoing interaction over time is part of the *definition of the situation*. Children begin to take into account the special nature of the friendship by picking up psychological details of the story presented: The friends have known each other for a long time; it is their special meeting day; the old friend does not like the new child. These aspects of the situation have a special meaning with regard to expectations and obligations in a friendship. It is only at this level that the promise comes in the focus of the argumentation as an obligational commitment of the self to the friend.

The promise gains special salience on the background of general friendship expectations. Only at this level is there a beginning understanding of the reciprocal nature of promising as outlined in theories of morality. There is an awareness now that through giving a promise an obligation is created. This obligation gains further importance in the context of the specific situation given, as defined by the interpretation of the psychological details of the relationship mentioned earlier. Thus, the friend not only wants the actor to come (as at Level 1) but also expects the actor to come. Not living up to this obligation is now perceived as betrayal.

The actor's commitments as well as the expectations resulting from these commitments can become *reasons for the decision* to visit the friend: One does not want to betray or cheat the best friend one has known for such a long time and to whom one has made a promise. Other types of reasons have to do with the anticipated consequences for the actor or the friend of the violation of obligation.

Awareness of the obligations and expectations related to friendship and promising creates a motivational "press" to justify a decision that violates the perceived obligations. Earlier, this aspect was noted as "giving explanations that outweigh the obligations." Yet by Level 2 mere reference to hedonistic needs is no longer accepted as sufficient reason in such a case. The decision to go to the movie is now justified by the exceptionality of the situation (e.g., such a good opportunity, the movie plays only this day). These justifications are also used in moral discourse as practical explanations given to the friend as legitimate reasons for the decision to go to the movie.

Again, prosocial or altruistic motives can form another group of reasons for the decision to go to the movie (conflict of duties). In such cases the special neediness of the new child is taken into account and interpreted as an obligation to help someone who is lonely and has not yet established friendship. Even when recognizing the special obligations toward the friend, the subject may grant priority to altruistic obligations that are implicitly understood as outweighing the promise given to the friend. (In these cases—which are rather few—intense conflict over the choice is observed.)

The *consequences for the friend* that result from violating obligations are now interpreted in a more interpersonal and moral way than at Level 1: The betrayal of friendship makes the friend feel hurt, disappointed, and left out. The friend is seen as morally disapproving of the decision to go to the movie because of the obligation contracted through the nature of the friendship, the promise given, or his or her aversion toward the new child. The friend's anger or sadness over this decision is based on his or her disapproval of the betrayal. As a consequence, the friend is seen as considering terminating the friendship.

The *consequences of the decision for the actor* are now conceptualized as interpersonal and moral feelings. The self's feelings are tied to the representation of the other in the self. The actor is concerned about the other's feelings (empathic concerns) and is worried over a possible loss of the relationship with the friend. But at this level we also observe the beginning of self-evaluation: a moral self evaluating its own actions according to moral criteria (feeling bad over having cheated). Besides the awareness of violating obligations and responsibilities, another source of moral feelings emerges at this level: a beginning awareness of the norm of truthfulness as an obligation not to lie to the friend about one's intentions or actions. Violation of this norm leads to guilt feelings (actor feels bad because he or she did not tell the friend about going to movie).

The awareness of the moral inadequacy of betraying the friend again leads to *rebalancing* by performing acts of restitution. The strategies used here indicate a more psychological understanding of the situation than seen in Level 1. They include asking forgiveness, strategies of integration (bringing the friend together with the new child), or making the friend understand the action by giving reasons, although compared with Level 3 the latter is still limited. But again there is an alternative strategy as well: The awareness of the moral inadequacy of the action may lead to a tendency to conceal the action from the friend. The Level I strategy of concealing the action is sup-plemented by giving nonveridical reasons, that is, by explicitly lying (I had to go downtown with my mother). This is a form of justification by which responsibility is denied and the moral balance subverted. A predominant mo-tive for such strategies is fear of the consequences, at this level tied to the loss of friendship. Guilt feelings related to lying are an indication of the awareness of the obligation to be truthful.

Level Three

As at Level 2, the friendship relation is part of the *definition of the situation* at Level 3. But now friendship is seen as a system of shared expectations in-volving mutual commitments over time, implying trust, reliance, and a special concern for each other's needs and feelings at a much deeper level than at Level 2. More subtle particularities of the friend's psychological situation are taken into account as meaningful criteria for practical decision making: That the friend *wants to talk* to the actor receives the interpretation that he or she has special needs that are emotionally significant for the actor. Within the definition of friendship as intimate mutual concern, the friend's needs and feelings represent special obligations to the actor.

In comparison with Level 2, where the structuring of the situation is guided implicitly by moral obligations, at Level 3 these obligations become more explicit. Actions can be evaluated from a "third-person" perspective (Selman, 1980), implying the notion of what one morally ought to do (Mead, 1934). A *moral self* is established such that the child takes a pre-scriptive attitude toward actions. This moral orientation refers to rules of fairness and to self ideals of how good, loyal, and trustworthy persons or friends should act toward each other. The keeping of the promise to the friend is seen as an obligation that cannot be changed arbitrarily. Thus, *rea-sons for decision* to visit the friend are stated as "moral" reasons referring to expectations deriving from friendship and promise (if hero has promised the friend, he or she must go, it would be unfair not to go). Reasons for action are tied to a moral self, to one's self ideal (not wanting to be a traitor or promise breaker), and to the anticipated moral feelings if obligations were violated (hero would feel guilty, have a guilty conscience). Another type of reason for this decision relates to the concept of "trust" (friend would not trust hero anymore if he or she would not go to him or her).

With regard to *consequences,* a violation of the obligation toward the friend is now conceptualized as betrayal of trust, confidence, and loyalty. *Moral feelings* arising from such anticipated violation of obligation are feel-ings of *guilt* (resulting from the breach of trust) and *shame* (resulting from acts that are inconsistent with one's moral self-ideal). It is only at this level that children spontaneously make use of the concept of a "guilty conscience." The actor is conceptualized as taking a moral perspective on his or her action (hero is thinking about what he or she did right or wrong). The violation of the obligation no longer goes along with the anticipation of a termination of the friendship but rather signals an attrition of the degree of friendship (being less good friends, trusting each other less).

Given the understanding of friendship as intimate sharing of feelings at a much deeper level than at Level 2, the general understanding of the promise as morally binding again gains special ascendancy. There is a definite moral awareness of the necessity of communication with the friend about any change of intentions, implying that not keeping the promise presupposes agreement of the promise (the friend). This moral awareness often leads to a spontaneous proposal for a *moral discourse* with the friend to negotiate the keeping of the promise and to find common solutions that integrate the needs of all parties involved. Such discourse now takes into account the particularities of the friend's situation and personality (how friend reacts to talking to him or her, what kind of person he or she is). Attempts are made to assure the friend of affection and solidarity and of the value of the ongoing relationship. The justifications given for wanting to go to a movie with the new child define exceptionality within the context of the friendship. The child may make use of a more flexible role switch as a means of considering possible actions and reactions from the viewpoint of others (e.g., asking friend, What would you do? What would you have done in this situation?). Justifications are designed to establish consistency between action and obligation. Thus, the self's hedonistic desires may be interpreted as one's rights (it should be possible to go to such a good movie once, or to accept such a good offer). The same type of justification is given in the case of altruistic motivation, where an appeal is made to the friend to accept the exceptionality of the situation because of the obligation to integrate a newcomer into a network of friendship. Both forms are based on the possibility of a mutually shared understanding of each other's perspectives. They go along with various types of *conflict resolution strategies,* which are all based on communication as a means toward finding a solution that is acceptable to everybody involved or capable of reestablishing trust and intimacy.

Even though truthfulness toward the friend is the predominant strategy at this level, there are forms of nontruthful interaction as well. These consist of conscious attempts to hide the violation of trust and reciprocity by lying to the friend. Although the same type of justification may be offered the friend as at Level 2 (had to go downtown with my mother), another type of practical explanation that functions as an excuse (the friend would have done the same, or everyone would have acted like this) emerges. Thus the actor denies responsibility for the action (Keller, in press). As a result of the awareness of the moral inadequacy of such behavior, rather intensive feelings of guilt and shame may arise. They may even take the form of psychosomatic reactions (tummy ache). They need not lead to any restructuring of the action, however. Rather, it seems that despite theoretical knowledge about standards of friendship, such standards remain external and are not applied to the self as obligatory (Blasi, 1980).

Level Four

There are some aspects in our data that point to the direction of what would have to be conceptualized as a Level 4, but there are not yet enough data to justify fully describing this level. It seems that only at that level can concerns be weighed against each other systematically according to priorities (if the friend really needs the hero, then he or she must go, but if the situation is not that urgent, the friend should accept that the hero visits friend later). The *legitimacy* of the friend's needs is weighed against the legitimacy of one's own needs, defined as one's rights on the basis of the relationship and one's obligations that transcend the initmate friendship. There is an assumption of mutual understanding for each other's claims and obligations that can be negotiated in a "rational" way. This understanding implies a beginning conception of autonomy, where persons are seen as having complex needs and being embedded in multiple networks of relationships. The friends must take each other's needs into account as well as their obligations toward each other and toward third persons. Thus, the friend would also have to give up what might be his or her "rights" in the light of legitimate claims of the self or more legitimate claims of another person. The friend then is seen as having a moral obligation to take the other's situation into account.

CONCLUSION

The developmental levels described here were constructed on the basis of children's reasoning in discussing the dilemma. Although data analysis is not yet complete, it is clear that there are both general age-related trends and large individual differences. Future empirical analysis will have to deal with the issue of structural consistency within the various components of the moral attitude. Theoretically, we would postulate an underlying deep structure of organization that ties the components together in an equilibrated system. This consistency would result from the *unity of the situation* the child is dealing with. All the components analyzed represent different aspects of one course of action. This assumption differs significantly from cognitive-developmental research, where "domains of experience" (Turiel, 1978, and Chap. 15 in this book) or "issues" (Selman, 1980) have been seen as relatively independent achievements. Given the theoretical assumption of structural consistency, we will have to understand empirical inconsistency as cases of *disequilibrium*. This imbalance, then, represents the dynamic side of development, a side not evident in the structural analysis. This disequilibrium provides the motivational force for cognitive reorganization.

I will summarize by focusing on some of the aspects mentioned that we consider necessary elements of a more encompassing conception of morality. The theoretical analysis shows that the definition of the situation is clearly related to the child's structural level of interpersonal and moral understanding. There appears to be a systematic relationship between the level of understanding and those normative aspects of the situation that the child takes into account spontaneously. To put it differently, touching on and elaborating certain aspects of the conflict presented is in itself an indicator of a certain level of interpersonal moral understanding or the normative construction of self-other relationships.

Across developmental levels there is growing awareness of the psychological meaning of situations. The psychological particularities of situations and persons are elaborated, and consequences of practical decisions are taken into account when making choices. Extrapolating from the empirical data base to mature forms of moral decision making, moral rules, or principles are increasingly considered in the light of the particularities of the situation in which self's and other's interests and claims have to be weighed.

The achievement of Level 3 appears to be a milestone in this development. The reflexive role-taking that constitutes Level 3 becomes the basis for the development of a moral self in the form of "How will I appear to others?" The self is regarded in terms of moral rules that are no longer external to itself but that have become part of self-expectation. Thus, morality has become part of the self-definition (see Chaps. 6 and 7). This is a milestone in development because particular experiences and expectations within particular relationships are transcended. An awareness emerges of an objective interpersonal system outside the subjective self that has claims on the person. This system consists of rules of fairness and ideals of self and of friendship.

The understanding achieved at Level 3 is taken to be the basis for the perceived necessity of "moral dialogue" as the means for solving moral conflicts as well as for reestablishing moral balance when obligations have been violated. In the mature form of this dialogue others are seen as having the same moral responsibility that the self has. Thus, the promisee, despite the right conferred on him or her through the promise given, is credited with the obligation to reflect this right in the light of the particular situation at hand. He or she must be prepared to give up his or her rights for claims that are entitled to enjoy precedence. At the same time, he or she also has a responsibility to forgive the violation of obligations if the situation warrants it. Thus, Level 3 seems to be the point in development where the particular is beginning to be linked to the universal. Yet clearly the universal emerges from particular experience, although, dialectically, particular experiences can be conceptualized only in terms of the universal they both generate and presuppose.

REFERENCES

Blasi, A. Bridging moral cognition and moral action. A critical review of the literature. *Psychological Bulletin*, 1980, *88*, 1–45.

Blum, L. A. *Friendship, altruism and morality*. London: Routledge & Kegan Paul, 1980.

Cooney, E. *Social cognition development: An experimental intervention in the elementary grades.* Unpublished doctoral dissertation, Harvard University, 1978.

Damon, W. *The social world of the child.* San Francisco: Jossey-Bass, 1977.

Damon, W., & Gerson, R. P. Moral understanding and children's conduct. In W. Damon (Ed.), *New directions for child development* (Vol. 1). San Francisco: Jossey-Bass, 1978.

Denzin, N. K. A phenomenology of emotion and deviance. *Zeitschrift für Soziologie,* 1980, *9,* 251–261.

Döbert, R., & Nunner-Winkler, G. Performanzbestimmende Aspekte des moralischen Bewußtseins. In G. Portele (Ed.), *Sozialisation und Moral.* Weinheim: Beltz, 1978. (English version can be obtained from authors.)

Eisenberg, N. The development of reasoning regarding prosocial behavior. In N. Eisenberg (Ed.), *The development of prosocial behavior.* New York: Academic Press, 1982.

Emmet, D. *Rules, roles and relations.* Boston: Beacon Press, 1966.

Frankena, W. *Ethics* (2nd ed.). London: Prentice-Hall, 1973.

Gilligan, C. Justice and responsibility: Thinking about real dilemmas of moral conflict and choice. In C. Brusselmans (Ed.), *Toward moral and religious maturity.* Morristown, N.J.: Silver Burdett, 1980.

Gilligan, C., & Murphy, M. Development from adolescence to adulthood: The philosopher and the dilemma of the fact. In W. Damon (Ed.), *New directions for child development* (Vol. 2). San Francisco: Jossey-Bass, 1979.

Habermas, J. Was Heißt Universalpragmatik. In K. O. Apel (Ed.), *Sprachpragmatik und Philosophie.* Frankfurt: Suhrkamp, 1976.

Hamlyn, D. W. Person perception and our understanding of others. In T. Mischel (Ed.), *Understanding other persons.* Oxford: Basil Blackwell, 1974.

Hare, R. M. *The language of morals.* Oxford: Oxford University Press, 1952.

Hoffman, M. The development of altruistic motivation. In C. B. Keasey (Ed.), *Nebraska Symposium on Motivation* (Vol. 25). Lincoln: University of Nebraska Press, 1977.

Kelles, M. Rechtfertignngen. Die entwickenne praktisches Erklärmyen. In W. Edelstein & J. Habermas [Eds.], Soziale Interaktion ünd soziales versteheu. Frankfurt: Suhrkamp, 1984 (English version: Children's justifications of moral transgressions. Competence and performance aspects. Can be obtained from author.)

Kohlberg, L. Moral development and moralization. In T. Lickona (Ed.), *Moral development and behavior.* New York: Holt, Rinehart & Winston, 1976.

Mead, G. H. *Mind, self and society.* University of Chicago Press, 1934.

Melden, A. S. *Rights and persons.* Berkeley: University of California Press, 1977.

Peters, R. S. Virtues and habits in moral education. In D. B. Cochrane, C. M. Hamm, & A. C. Kazepides (Eds.), *The domain of moral education.* New York: Paulist Press, 1979.

Piaget, J. *The moral judgment of the child.* New York: Collier, 1962. (Originally published 1932.)

Rawls, J. *A theory of justice.* Cambridge, Mass.: Harvard University Press, 1971.

Richards, D. A. J. *Reasons for action.* New York: Oxford University Press (Clarendon Press), 1971.

Selman, R. L. *The growth of interpersonal understanding.* New York: Academic Press, 1980.

Singer, M. Moral rules and principles. In A. J. Melden (Ed.), *Essays in moral philosophy.* Seattle & London: University of Washington Press, 1958.

Sykes, G. M., & Matza, D. Techniques of neutralization: A theory of delinquency. *American Sociological Review,* 1957, *22,* 664–670.

Thomas, W. I. *The child in America.* New York: Knopf, 1932.

Thrane, G. Shame. *The Journal for the Theory of Social Behavior,* 1979, *9,* 139–166.

Turiel, E. Social regulations and domains of social concepts. In W. Damon (Ed.), *New directions for child development* (Vol. 1). San Francisco: Jossey-Bass, 1978.

Turner, R. H. Role-taking: Process versus conformity. In A. M. Rose (Ed.), *Human behavior and social processes.* London: Routledge & Kegan Paul, 1962.

Youniss, J. *Parents and peers in social development.* Chicago: University of Chicago Press, 1980.

Youniss, J. Moral development through a theory of social construction: an analysis. *Merrill-Palmer Quarterly,* 1981, *27,* 385–403.

REFERENCE NOTE

1. Reuss, S. *Autonomie und Vernunft: Die mögliche Begründungsfunktion analytischer Moralphilosophie für die Moralerziehung.* Unpublished manuscript, Max Planck Institute for Human Development and Education, Berlin, 1980.

CHAPTER 9

Cognitive Stages of Interaction in Moral Discourse

FRITZ OSER

This chapter introduces the concept of cognitive levels of moral interaction and presents some of the major findings of an experimentally designed intervention study in which 120 discussion groups were confronted with three treatments:

1. *Provision of information on the moral problem to be discussed (complexity stimulation)*
2. *Provision of rules of justice*
3. *Provision of guidelines for an optimal course of discussion (strategy stimulation).*

The impact of these treatments on the cognitive level of interaction and the communicative compactness of interaction are demonstrated with regard to three different kinds of moral problems. From the clear empirical support of the central hypothesis, finally, some conclusions for moral education are drawn.

When a group of individuals attempts to resolve a moral dilemma, the most salient problem is the one of coordinating meaning. What strategies are available? How can we distinguish between optimal and suboptimal forms of moral discourse in such a dilemma situation without evaluating only the result of the process? When participants introduce arguments, how can we evaluate the rationality of these arguments within a given context of discourse?

There are two sets of theories from which partial answers to these questions can be derived. The first type of theory generates a set of *philosophical*

This research was supported by the Swiss National Foundation.

criteria or prerequisites for the so-called ideal speech situation (Habermas, 1973, 1976; Miller, Note 1). The most important criteria are (1) equal opportunity to share in communicative speech acts, (2) equal opportunity to question the validity claims of statements, (3) a level of communication involving full reciprocity, and (4) full exchange of general norm-referenced expectations. This set of theories is used only as a frame of reference for an ideal communicative situation.

A second set of relevant theories describes models of *psychological* structures of judgment (Doise, Mugny, & Perret-Clérmont, 1974; Kohlberg, 1976; Selman, 1980). These models attempt to answer the following questions: What do individuals at different ages decide in a critical communicative situation, and how do they reason about the decision? They do so by positing cognitive structures that serve the functions of assimilation and accommodation. Structures are observed in the context of verbal material produced by single persons usually solving a set of social problems. Structures are measured using scoring procedures that call for semantic consensus (i.e., scoring manuals).

Both approaches, the philosophical concept of an ideal speech situation and the psychological concept of individual structure, resolve only part of the problem. In the group discussion of a moral dilemma, the coordinations of arguments constitute a system of elements and relations on a given interactive level that possesses a certain level of complexity and particular process characteristics. Although the criteria defined by Habermas are important elements in the process of solving moral problems through interpersonal discourse, they are not sufficient for differentiating among qualitatively different types of interactions. They are relevant for analyzing social conditions of structures but not for analyzing the structures themselves. Although the theory of communicative speech acts does partially attend to process, the structural-psychological approach, for the most part, disregards interpersonal processes. Individual contributions to the solution of a moral dilemma are of interest as far as they can be viewed as a result of a history of individual socialization (i.e., a consequence of past interaction). But the interactional process that takes place in a moral dilemma situation is more than a summation of individual reasoning. It is a system of interrelated, structurally objectivated reasoning. This system may represent different levels of cognitive legitimation.

There are certain requirements for generating a system on a particular level. Our research reveals some of these requirements and thus provides steps toward a theory of moral interaction.

GROUP STRUCTURE

Instead of confining ourselves to the judgment of individuals, we regard it as necessary to take a closer look at the system of the interactional process discussed earlier. From this perspective, individual arguments are considered part of a group action that establishes rules and strategies. Members of a group generate elements of social structure, which have to be detected in the pattern of a living discussion situation. This pattern is not merely the sum or average of aggregated individual judgments, it is something else; it is a "group structure." As Piaget (1977) says, it is "a system of relations each of which generates, as a relation, a transformation of the terms which it relates" (p. 29, translated by author).

This system emerges almost as if it had always been there, but it is new nevertheless; it has its own structure, its own economy, and its own representation. The system can be represented at higher and lower levels.

The term *group structure* refers to the arguments produced in the group, which favor or refute a given position. These arguments contain a certain moral complexity, which we will describe later as levels of interaction. We have found that the description and formal representation of such interactive levels are more easily assessed than are individuals' cognitive structures. Our work has shown that significantly less material is furnished in statements coming from individual interviews and that when found, such material is generally of a unilateral type. Few supporting arguments are naturally available in individual interviews, for the incentive to further reasoning is provided by continued interviewer questioning. In comparison, real-life sociomoral problems are frequently solved in a group context (family, peer, school, associations, etc.). Therefore, we hypothesize that a group's system of relations can be extracted structurally from spontaneous interaction in situations of sociomoral problem solving. The characteristics of this system are neither identical to nor necessarily on the same level as the cognitive structure of the participants taken singly, as is implied by the additive model.[1]

On the basis of discussion material and the so-called in-depth study method, we have tried to define levels of interaction (cognitive stages of moral discourse), which I shall present in the following discussion. (We use the words *level, stage,* and *perspective* interchangeably. *Perspective* refers to the way in which a group reveals the characteristics of an interactional level.) By using the constructs of "adequacy" and "transformational complexity," we ascertain that higher-level group interactions contain numerically more

---

[1] Kohlberg and his associates also feel that the individualistic, product-oriented description of structures of moral problem solving should be expanded to encompass a community concept (cf. the Just Community Approach, Power & Reimer, 1978; Power, 1979; Kohlberg, Note 2; and chap. 5 in this book). In the work done in this theoretical tradition, the judgment structure of a single individual is of less interest than the judgment of a whole group. Kohlberg calls the judgment structure of a whole group its "moral climate." By this means, the relationship of a person to collective normative values is measured. The person's "sense of community" is considered to be a kind of Stage 2 or Stage 3 ideology of a group. Note, however, that although Kohlberg uses discussion protocols of a community, he focuses only on the judgment of individuals and not on the interrelations on the system of their moral judgments themselves.

moral arguments. Moreover, we also observe the emergence of a completely different quality of interaction that cannot be explained merely by verbal competency or the amount of moral arguments. "Levels of interaction" are ways of "communication coordinating complexity." We hypothesize that the qualitatively different levels (perspectives) are hierarchical and sequential. Nevertheless, individuals can act on different levels depending on the kind of situation. "Levels of interaction" will here be conceived as the way the group structure is articulated and the way problem-solving strategies for moral dilemmas form the perspective of justice.

The most simple level is that of complete instrumentalism. We define it as the "functional perspective": Participants in a communicative situation outline solutions without questioning its moral legitimation.

The second stage or perspective is characterized by the belief that knowing the facts will guarantee the rightness of decision. Because persons at this stage attempt to confront facts, this stage can be defined as the "analytical perspective."

Only the third stage, the "normative perspective," provides for the question of moral justice. Different rules, values, and norms of justice suggest different interpretations of facts.

At a fourth stage, finally, groups solve a moral problem on the basis of an ethical-philosophical conception that is interpreted in view of its application.

These four levels or perspectives of interactions have been elaborated in greater detail, with each major perspective composed of two sublevels:

1. Functional perspective
    A. The discussion is limited to considering a set of solutions to the moral problem. Questions or additional facts are rarely presented.
    B. The discussion remains narrowly outcome oriented. Conditions and reasons (consequences, intentions, causal relationships) that function only to confirm one's initial position are given. A hierarchy of proposed solutions becomes possible.
2. Analytical perspective
    A. The analysis of facts and needs is central to the discussion. The participants believe that a moral decision is based on facts only.
    B. The systematic analysis of intentions, consequences, and general causal relationships is also central to the discussion. These arguments gain an importance of their own. A hierarchy of arguments may be achieved.
3. Normative perspective
    A. Discussion focuses on the moral norms, rules, and principles that underlie the individual's system of values. Proposed solutions (Perspective 1) and the analysis of those solutions (Perspective 2) merely accompany or result from the discussion of norms or principles.

    B. Moral rules and moral norms are criticized; that is, they are nei-
ther simply accepted nor simply refuted. They are considered as
constitutive of the group's sociomoral system, and they are criticized on this basis. The ability to universalize a norm becomes an
end in itself.

4. Philosophical perspective (authentic moral perspective)
    A. A particular universal moral principle is discussed on the grounds
of moral philosophy. Criticism of norms, discussion of principles,
proposals for deductions, analysis of how theory is translated
into practice, and so on, emerge and evolve.
    B. Several theories of moral philosophy are critically analyzed in
order to clarify one's own position. Criticism of norms, analysis
of facts, and proposals for solutions are seen in the light of such
theories.

Each of these perspectives can appear on a second dimension, the level of
"communication compactness." This process variable indicates how inten-
sively the speakers refer to each other. Three levels (I, II, III) of "communicative compactness" are presented:

    I. The participants in a discussion rarely take one another into account.
One proposition is counterposed to another. Evaluations can be only
indirectly deduced from the questions and assertions at hand (private
speech or egocentrism of each participant).

  II. The participants in a discussion take one another into account intermittently. The aspects treated become the units of communication.
Within these units the coordinative complexity is high; values are
made explicit and can be inferred from this phase of discussion.
Communication is uninterrupted for each of the same segments devoted to a given content.

 III. The different units of communication (cf. II) are mutually related to
one another. Values relating to a single aspect (or discussion phase)
are fully clarified. The shared propositions show that every participant adopts a value aspect that has been discussed among all the
participants.

With regard to our four major perspectives of interaction and the additional distinctions, a few comments are in order: First, these perspectives or
levels claim validity only for the discussion of conflicts in which moral norms
and sociomoral principles are meaningfully involved. What Habermas calls
a "practical discourse" consists, among other things, in the formation of a
consensus and the representation of interrelated arguments in which empirical laws are of no particular relevance. In this sense, the objects of such
discussion are real interpersonal dilemmas. Second, though the stages postu-

lated here claim descriptive validity (this is impressively documented by protocols of discussion among high school students), a critical evaluation must be supplemented by a justification on the basis of philosophy and a theory of communication. Third, the postulated developmental nature of the levels of interaction has not yet been proven. Possibly, longitudinal studies will call for a number of refinements. Fourth, it is important to note that there are really two dimensions to these levels: the levels of interaction themselves and the levels of the communicative relatedness of the participants.

We will present three short examples of the different perspectives (levels). The problems we discuss deal with distributive justice (e.g., distribution of goods or gratifications under restrictive conditions).

The sample answers are taken, for the first example, from a discussion of the problem of how to distribute two free tickets for a movie among three students. Who should get one? What would be a just distribution of the tickets in a group consisting of more than three persons (Oser, 1981, p. 58)?

The first number and letter on the right of each segment of communication refer to the levels of interaction. The numbers I, II, III refer to communicative compactness. The numbers on the left indicate the number of the student in the group. Discussions were conducted in French and are translated here.

A. Example for Perspective 1

Student Number			Notes
3:	I would like to see if someone already is planning for something else; then I wouldn't give him the ticket.	1AI	Students bring different proposals; the others do not discuss them. The counter proposal is the coordinating part.
2:	One could also take the money for the tickets and go to the public swimming pool.	1AI	
1:	One could bring back the tickets and distribute the money.	1AI	
3:	And then, one could go somewhere else.	1AI	Student 3 starts with an analytical prospect, is hindered, and joins the functional level.
2:	One could buy something with that money.	1AI	
3:	We could go to the movies together, then, our friends are with us. Alone, it's boring.	1BI	Consequences are brought in only to back the proposals.

Student
Number   Notes

2:	What do you mean?	
1:	We could sell the tickets and share the money.	1AI
2:	But we have already got the tickets.	
3:	We could offer somebody the ticket, somebody who has nothing else to do and who has no TV at home.	1AII
2:	Yes, we could do that.	
1:	We could distribute them by throwing a coin.	
3:	But in that case, the person who does not get it would get angry.	1BII
2:	I would check the possibility with the TV.	1AI

The examples for Stage 2 interaction are taken from a discussion about a mother who "sold" her baby in times of great financial stress and years later sees her child again and goes to court in order to get her child back.

B. Example for Perspective 2

Student
Number   Notes

1:	If that mother loves her child and if she wants the child to be happy and healthy, she should notice that it is better for the child to be with its real parents, and to know nothing; consequently she should note that it's better for the child to have its real parents.	The first statement is a proposal for a solution to the problem. The differences with Perspective 1 are borne out by the many conditions that mark the analytical pattern of coordination. These conditions (if a, b, c, d . . . , then y) prove that facts and values are taken into account when making a decision. All these facts and values are related to the life of the child. Until now,
2:	But I think that the mother has never properly loved her child, because she has given him away. And I think that the child wouldn't love his mother,	

Student Number		Notes

because the adoptive parents are like the real ones. The child has been in that family since he was a little baby.

4: You should also consider the circumstances: The mother had no money, she couldn't bring that child up. Of course, she shouldn't have given him away. Perhaps her parents would have taken care of the baby, or a friend. During daytime the mother could have left the baby there and fetched him after work. I think she felt she had to lead her own life too.

3: Perhaps she had already lived with her grandmother and she didn't want to accept an additional person in the house.

2: If the baby had been in a home for infants, the mother would have had to pay for him, so it is just the same as before.

2BII

nobody has proposed the rule of providing the best conditions for development to those most in need, in this case the baby. But the analysis has prepared the students to discover such a rule.

The last statements are typical ways of analyzing the social context at this level. Analysis is limited to presenting arguments concerning the suitability or rightness of justifications, of reasons within the situational perspective.

The next examples take us back to the discussion about the just distribution of two tickets for a movie. But now the discourse is conducted at Perspective 3 (Oser, 1981, pp. 115ff.).

C. Example for Perspective 3

Student Number		Notes

3: And this rule: Justice means that one isn't afraid afterwards. What do you think of this?

4: I don't like it as much as the other one, [the rule that those with the best grades and the best achievements would get the tickets]. One cannot help it if one isn't good at school.

The patterns of the structural interaction refer to rules or standards of justice. The students take a stance. They indicate whether they would like to apply the rule or not. The review of a rule constitutes the act that regulates the moral competency of the

Student Number		Notes

3: Oh! It's no good to reward the lazy pupils. What do you say to that?

2: Of course there are pupils who are lazy. But these just don't want to study. For that reason one shouldn't give them a ticket.

group. The member's interests are not only compared and weighed against each other, as in the analytical perspective, but also subordinated to a moral rule that has yet to be found.

4: Do you think it's okay that the teacher has to agree to this, or what do you think?

1: That is none of his business. If someone were skipping school, I would surely agree that he tells him.

3: Okay.

1: But otherwise, it's really none of his business.

3: No, it isn't. And now I'm referring to the sentence: "Justice means . . ." I think that the expression *just* shouldn't be used in that context. *Just* means "equal" in the sense that everybody gets an equal share and everyone is equally disadvantaged. But couldn't we use another word for *just,* for example, *disadvantaged?* Or, for example, everyone gets an equal share? Then, the sentence would be: If you act so that you are not afraid afterwards, means that everybody gets an equal share.

At the same time, it is important to find out if the students' proposals contradict that moral rule. The speech acts are of the same kind as before: refutations, confirmation, new proposals, and extensions, but the structural mode has changed completely.

3BII

1: But, when don't we need to be afraid?

3: Yes, I wonder.

1: Finding a common solution . . .

3: Yes, everybody would agree.

We have not encountered examples of Perspective 4 among high school students. Possibly, these students do not have the logical prerequisites for a Level 4 interaction.

EXPERIMENTAL STUDY

The construct of a group's cognitive structure of interaction can best be demonstrated by an intervention study that we have conducted. In this study we attempted to find out about the factors that determine the levels of moral problem solving in groups. The study consisted of a multifactor experiment in which not individuals but groups of individuals were the subjects, that is, the unit of analysis. These were high school students, aged 15, from 42 classes of schools in two Swiss cantons. They had a fairly homogeneous middle-class background.

Variables

The dependent variables are the "cognitive levels of moral interaction" and the levels of "communicative compactness." There were five independent variables or factors:

The type of problem discussed

The school class of the students

Three kinds of interventions or treatments, designed to influence the course of the interaction

Conditions of Group Communication

The first treatment was called "stimulation of cognitive complexity." Under this condition, the discussion group was provided with a short text like those teachers usually give: for example, "think of the consequences of your proposal for a solution, consider the intentions of people, or consider the effects of mentioning a particular proposal for a solution."

The second treatment consisted of a set of rules of justice that the group was asked to consider when finding a solution of the moral problems. These rules were, generally speaking, modeled after Kohlberg's stages of morality. The rules were again presented as a short text so that the group could make free use of them.

The third treatment was a "guideline strategy," that is, an intervention designed to help conduct an orderly discussion. The outline defined in a step-by-step fashion what the group was to do (successive selection strategy).

The first treatment was expected to stimulate Perspective 2; the second, Perspective 3; and the third treatment was expected to influence the degree of communicative compactness.

Types of Moral Problems

The first problem, in which two tickets for a movie play were to be distributed justly among the group members (always more than two), is a problem of distributive justice. Although this problem led to considerable conflicts, it offered the chance to discover an optimal solution that pleased everyone involved (conflicting optimization type problem).

The second problem involves the selection of three applicants for a job as an architect. The candidates differ with regard to such factors as practical and theoretical qualifications, general job aspirations, reputation, and socioeconomic status. Each person was portrayed as having a rather balanced pattern of favorable and unfavorable qualities. Thus, the problem is of the "conflicting choice" type. As one of the applicants is preferred, the chances of the other two approach zero.

The third dilemma involves the classical Solomon problem. A baby is given away for adoption because the mother is poor. The child is happy with his new parents. After some time, the mother wants her child back. She engaged the adoptive parents of her child in a court trial. This problem implies that an option for the natural rights leads to rejection of social justice and vice versa.

Analysis

The unit of analysis is the entire transcript of the discussion of each group. For reasons of economy, a total of 120 protocols were randomly selected from a total pool of 336. Each discussion was rated by two trained raters. The correlations between the two ratings were $r = .94$ for the level of interaction and $r = .62$ for the level of communicative compactness.

Because the experimental factors consisted of three types of problems, five school classes, and two states for each of the three treatments (given or not given), the experiment had a partly nested $3 \times 5 \times 2 \times 2 \times 2$ design. Consequently, a multivariate analysis of variance that tested various hypotheses about the impact of any of these factors or combinations on the level of moral interaction was conducted.

Hypotheses

We tested the following hypotheses:

1. Those groups that did not receive any treatment will more frequently discourse on Level 1, relative to the treatment groups.
2. Those groups that receive additional information about the problem (stimulating complexity) will operate on Level 2, relative to other groups.
3. Groups that are supplied with principles of justice (rules) will discourse on Level 3.
4. Groups that receive guidelines for discussion (strategy) may be expected to show no effect with regard to the stage of interaction.

5. Groups that receive guidelines for discussion (strategy) may show differences in levels of communicative compactness, although the direction of differences cannot be predicted.
6. The type of problem will affect the level of interaction, although the direction of effect cannot be predicted.

Findings

The findings are, in the order of these hypotheses:

1. A considerable number of groups stayed on Perspective 1, in particular when no treatment was given. This is true mainly for those groups that discussed problem number one.
2. Results concerning the second hypothesis were in the expected direction. Discussion groups that received additional information (stimuli of complexity) improved in analytical discourse moving, on the average, from Level 2A to Level 2B. The difference of one-half level is, however, not statistically significant. Perhaps younger children would have confirmed the hypothesis more clearly. Fifteen-year-olds often interact on Level two from the outset and hence cannot be expected to gain much.
3. The third hypothesis was supported most clearly. Supplying the group with rules of justice raised the interactional structure a whole stage, namely, from 2A to 3A (from $\bar{x} = 3.11$ to $\bar{x} = 5.02$), which is highly significant ($F = 142.765$, d.f. $= 1,50$, $p < .0001$) (see Figure 9.1).

It is important to note a theoretically as well as statistically significant exception to the success of this treatment. If presented together with additional factual information about the problem to be discussed (Treatment 1), the effect of rules is considerably reduced (see Figure 9.2). These treatments seem to interfere with each other. This effect remains even if the students have more time in discussion than the other groups.

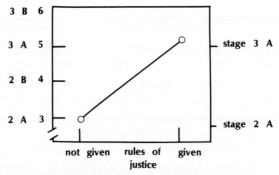

Figure 9.1.   The effect of the treatment "rules of justice."

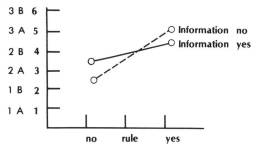

Figure 9.2. Combined effect: complexity by rules.

4. Guidelines for discussion (strategy) had only a weak positive effect on the level of moral interaction.

5. They have, however, a clearly demonstrable impact on the level of "communicative compactness" ($F = 50.84$, d.f. $= 1,50$, $p < .0001$). The means (1.94 and 2.31) also show that without this intervention most groups discuss a moral problem on the second level of compactness (Level II); that is, the arguments and rebuttals are divided into thematic periods.

6. Finally, as expected, differences in structure of interaction arose because of the type of problem discussed. Problem 1 (optimization type) produces, on the average, the lowest level of interaction (the so-called functional orientation) (see Figure 9.3). Problem 2 turns out the "lowest" solutions in terms of $F = 4.10$, d.f. $= 2$, 50, $p < .02$. Means for level of compactness are Problem 1, 2.10; Problem 2, 2.05; Problem 3, 2.23. One reason for this finding may be the higher level of frustration evoked by Problem 2.

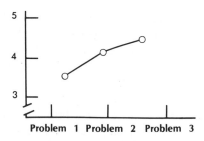

Figure 9.3. Effect of type of problems on stage of interaction.

CONCLUSIONS

These results support the notion that, besides individual levels of moral judgment, levels of interaction in a group of individuals may be profitably addressed by educational research.

1. Among the empirical results, two are most impressive: First, consider the impact of rules of justice on the cognitive stage of interaction. Through this treatment most discussion groups could be moved to the level of considering moral norms when solving their problem. Note that the individual participants afterward also showed a marked increase in their stage of moral judgment as measured by a moral preference test (for more details, see Oser, 1981, pp. 396ff.). Second, consider the impact of guidelines (strategy) for discussion on the level of communicative compactness of interaction. With this treatment, the discussion of moral problems was demonstrably modified toward greater interactive coordination among the participants.

The findings of our research taken together suggest a number of conclusions with regard to the educational relevance of levels of interaction:

2. It can no longer be the sole aim of a moral education curriculum to encourage students to communicate without guidance and to be expected to arrive at a "good" solution to the dilemma. The meaning of "effectiveness" of moral education must be reinterpreted. The aim of moral education must be to foster the acquisition of a higher level of interaction and to improve what Piaget has called interactive economy or what we refer to as communicative compactness. This goal cannot be achieved through orders, indoctrination, or algorithms of learning. On the contrary, the stimulation of structure-forming components is necessary. Hence, the teacher should not only be supplied with ends and analysis of relations between ends and means but also be made aware of the hierarchy of interactional stages. If students successfully solve moral dilemmas in Stage 3 without any further treatment, then the overarching goal has been reached. The methods for accomplishing this goal would be the same as those developed by Fenton (1976).

If the object of stimulations is rules of justice, it is by no means certain that students will use them. But when they do use them, the course of the moral discussion is structurally quite different. Where this is not the case, one could object that the experiment was tautological; that is, a discussion of rules is required, and consequently, rules are used more often. But the solution is not that simple, for when rules are provided as an aid for discussion, the discussion becomes "moral" in a much broader sense: Suddenly, it becomes important that justice is related to just rules, and thus to rational arguments about rules instead of being limited to feelings or social facts alone.

3. When guidelines for discussions are provided, the students engage in discussion for longer periods of time and the economy of interaction is improved. The level of interaction, however, is not affected. Students reflect about the process of their interaction, categorize, summarize, give overviews, and so on, and pattern the entire course of their interaction. This compactness, too, is a cognitive variable. But it is "empty" if a higher structural level of interaction is not stimulated at the same time. This aim is missed by teachers who focus on the optimization of instruction through technical aids and strategies only.

4. Although the effects due to the type of problem are interesting and may give rise to some stimulating speculations about the interrelationship between it and the level of interaction, these differences are contaminated by the treatments. The impact of the problem content must be recognized, yet it is small compared with the impact of the interventions. This is not surprising, because, for example, the discussion of rules soon becomes abstracted from the particular content of the problem (retention effect). From an educational point of view, this implies that as soon as stimulating effect of a treatment is operative, the kind of problem, the width of the problem space, or the usage or acquisition of information are not decisive for the process of moral interaction. The heuristics of levels of interaction are equally meaningful for all four stages regardless of content specification. This applies to both aspects of interaction. The effects of combined treatments show, however, that the teacher would be better off to employ only one treatment at a time. Two treatments together tend to distract students from achieving a "higher" level of interaction rather than to produce additive effects.

These preceding four points have important implications for the education of teachers. Our findings, so far, suggest a didactic process model for solving moral problems. As a central feature, this model relies on the hierarchical order of cognitive levels of moral interaction, as well as on the stimulating effect of certain structure-forming treatments.

REFERENCES

Damon, W. *The social world of the child.* San Francisco: Jossey-Bass, 1977.

Doise, W., Mugny, G., & Perret-Clérmont, A. N. *Social interaction and the development of cognitive operations.* Env. J. Soc. Psychol. 1975, 5(3).

Fenton, E. The cognitive-developmental approach to Moral Education. In Social Education, 4, 40, 1976, p. 187–193.

Habermas, J. Wahrheitstheorien. In *Festschrift für W. Schulz.* Pfullingen: Neske, 1973.

Habermas, J. *Moralentwicklung und Ich-Identität.* In J. Habermas, *Zur Rekonstruktion des historischen Materialismus.* Frankfurt: Suhrkamp, 1976.

Kohlberg, L. *Moral stages and moralization. The cognitive developmental approach.* In T. Lickona (Ed.), Moral development and behavior: Theory, research, and social issues. New York: Holt, Rinehart and Winston, 1976.

Oser, F. *Moralisches Urteil in Gruppen. Soziales Handeln. Verteilungsgerechtigkeit.* Frankfurt: Suhrkamp, 1981.

Piaget, J. Etudes sociologiques. Genève: Droz, 1977.

Power, C. *The moral atmosphere of the school: A method for analysing community meetings.* Unpublished doctoral dissertation, Cambridge University, 1979.

Power, C., & Reimer, J. *Moral atmosphere: An educational bridge between moral judgment and action.* In W. Damon (Ed.), *New directions for child development* (Vol. 2). San Francisco: Jossey-Bass, 1978.

Selman, R. L. *The growth of interpersonal understanding.* New York: Academic Press, 1980.

REFERENCE NOTES

1. Miller, M. *Argumentation als moralische Lernprozesse* (Working Paper). Unpublished manuscript, Max Planck Institute, Starnberg, 1980.

2. Kohlberg, L. *Cognitive-developmental theory and the practice of collective education* (Working Paper). Unpublished manuscript, Harvard University, 1973.

The author is grateful to Rich Shavelson who helped design the study. He also thanks Daniel Candee for correcting his English.

PART FOUR

Learning-Behavioral Developmental Approaches

CHAPTER 10

What Develops in Moral Development?

ROBERT M. LIEBERT

The prevailing literature on moral development has been dominated by two related propositions: (1) there is a universal progression of stages or levels in human moral development, and (2) there are universal moral principles, found at the end of the progression, the cultivation of which will elevate the human condition. A critical review of research, theory, and logic shows that neither of these propositions is tenable. The available data themselves can be explained by a less romantic and more parsimonious biofunctional account that stresses the development of moral sophistication. *The interplay of motivation and experience brings an increasingly profound grasp of the indirect and long-term consequences of one's words and deeds and, accordingly, increasingly farsighted actions in pursuit of individual self-interest. Contrasting implications of the two views for the conduct of human affairs are discussed.*

Morality is broadly concerned with how people deal with one another and with prescriptions and proscriptions regarding interpersonal relationships and transactions. The buzzword of morality is *should,* which is surprisingly ambiguous in that it may convey obligation, duty, propriety, or expediency. Those interested in moral development ask whether and how an individual's dealings with moral issues change with age and experience. The question, What develops in moral development? is likewise an encompassing one, referring both to observed changes in morally relevant words and deeds and to the underlying psychological processes that account for the changes.

In approaching the question of moral development, two different paradigms, the absolutist and the relativist, have guided theory and research. In this chapter I critically review the two major propositions of the absolutist paradigm, outline an alternative relativist account of the available data, and compare the two paradigms in terms of their social and political implications.

THE ABSOLUTIST PARADIGM

The prevailing literature on moral development has been dominated by two related propositions: (1) there is a universal progression of stages or levels in human moral development, and (2) there are universal moral principles, found at the end of the progression, the cultivation of which will elevate the human condition. Taken together, these two propositions form a paradigm in Thomas Kuhn's (1962, 1970) sense. That is, they constitute a framework for examining and understanding moral development and invite "normal" research of a technical nature, designed to extend but not challenge the paradigm.

The absolutist paradigm has its roots in the psychological literature in the writings of William McDougall, who viewed humans as prewired with a moral instinct, which unfolded gradually according to nature's plan. McDougall envisioned stages of moral development to parallel the concept of physical stages of growth that had worked so well for nineteenth-century biology. According to McDougall (1908):

> We may distinguish four levels of [moral] conduct, successive stages, each of which must be traversed by every individual before he can attain the next higher stage. These are (1) the stage of instinctive behaviour modified only by the influence of the pains and pleasures that are incidentally experienced in the course of instinctive activities; (2) the stage in which the operation of the instinctive impulses is modified by the influence of rewards and punishments administered more or less systematically by the social environment; (3) the stage in which conduct is controlled in the main by the anticipation of social praise and blame; (4) the highest stage, in which conduct is regulated by an ideal of conduct that enables a man to act in the way that seems to him right regardless of the praise or blame of his immediate social environment. [p. 186]

McDougall's scheme of increasing moral goodness based on an innately programmed universal sequence set the direct precedent for the contemporary absolutist paradigm, and his basic scheme is uncannily like the one promulgated by moral absolutists today.

How successful is the paradigm? Surprisingly, it has been exposed to relatively little critical review, perhaps because there seems to be an inherent appeal to the notion that all human beings move naturally and invariably toward some higher goodness. Moreover, it is romantically appealing to believe that the problem in most human conflicts over power and resources can somehow be resolved by reaching out to "natural justice" and to "universal moral principles." In the following two sections I critically review the empirical and logical status of the two major propositions that lie behind the absolutist strategy, approaching the issues as a tough-minded, empirically oriented developmental psychologist rather than as a moral philosopher.

Is There a Universal Progression of Stages or Levels in Human Moral Development?

Most of the evidence bearing on this question comes from research on hypothetical moral dilemmas. In such research, subjects are presented with a hypothetical situation and asked to offer a moral judgment regarding the actors or their actions. The term *moral judgment* encompasses a number of quite different specific measures. All of the measures are, however, intended to tap the subject's underlying "moral reasoning" and to demonstrate that the basis for such reasoning changes in a stagelike way. Although research on moral dilemmas can be traced back to the late nineteenth century (Johnson, 1962), it is the work of Jean Piaget and Lawrence Kohlberg that has made moral dilemma research famous.

Problems with Piaget's Work

According to Piaget, there is a natural shift in moral development coincident with or shortly after the cognitive transition from preoperational to operational thought at about age 7. The shift is said to be such that the child begins for the first time to consider and utilize information about subjective intent in making moral judgments that involve others.

The data on Piaget's theory of intentionality present an object lesson in the importance of careful methodology and rigorous thinking. Piaget presented subjects with a pair of vignettes involving protagonists whose actions varied in both their intentions and in the consequences they brought and asked children which protagonist was naughtier. One such story pair involved John and Henry. According to the stories:

> John was in his room when his mother called him to dinner. John goes down and opens the door to the dining room. But behind the door was a chair, and on the chair was a tray with 15 cups on it. John did not know the cups were behind the door. He opens the door, the door hits the tray, bang go the 15 cups, and they all get broken.

In contrast:

> One day when Henry's mother was out, Henry tried to get some cookies out of the cupboard. He climbed up on a chair, but the cookie jar was still too high, and he couldn't reach it. But while he was trying to get the cookie jar, he knocked over a cup, the cup fell down and broke.

Both Piaget's own data and many subsequent studies, including a study by Bandura from a different theoretical perspective, indeed seemed to show that very young children tend to judge the naughtiness or wrongness of acts solely on the basis of consequences and that a significant shift occurs between the approximate ages of 6 and 8 so that the intentions of the actor and related subjective considerations come to be given some weight for the first time (Bandura & McDonald, 1963; Johnson, 1962; MacRae, 1954). It has now become apparent, however, that the original Piagetian method, though it may produce quite reliable results, is plagued with artifacts that render the original interpretation of the data conceptually invalid. Inasmuch as I have reviewed these problems elsewhere (Liebert, 1979), I will limit myself here to a description of what is perhaps the most telling empirical critique, namely, that in Piaget's method the conceptual dependent variable (relative weight given to intentions and consequences) is confounded with the *order* in which information about intentions and consequences is presented. The importance of this possible order effect is demonstrated in three studies (Austin, Ruble, & Trabasso, 1977; Feldman, Klosson, Parsons, Rholes, & Ruble, 1976; Nummendal & Bass, 1976), all of which have shown that children are more likely to take an actor's intentions into account when they learn of the actor's intentions *after* they learn about the consequences of the act (he broke 15 cups, though he did not intend to do so) than they are if they hear about the intentions before they learn of the consequences (he did not intend to do so, but he broke 15 cups), as in the traditional Piagetian format. Thus, younger children may seem to place no importance on an actor's intentions because they have forgotten what the actor's intentions were rather than because they are unconcerned about intentions per se. This interpretation receives relatively strong support from the Austin, Ruble, and Trabasso (1977) study, in which 5-year-old children were found to be just as likely to make moral judgments on the basis of intention as were 10-year-old children *when all children had the stories repeated to them until they could remember all the important details about those intentions and consequences.* Moreover, as would be expected, the younger children required considerably more repetitions than did the older ones in order to recall the stories accurately. Thus, the observed difference between older and younger children's moral judgments turns out to rest on strictly cognitive grounds and does not reflect an additional change in underlying values or moral understanding.

Problems with Kohlberg's Work

Like Piaget, Kohlberg has attempted to demonstrate a universal progression of moral development by reporting the results of moral dilemma research. Unlike Piaget, however, Kohlberg has focused on the moral justifications offered by his subjects rather than on their moral judgments. By moral justifications I mean the explanations or rationale that a subject offers to justify his or her moral judgment or moral conduct in a given situation, usually elicited by the question, Why?

In Kohlberg's research, moral justifications have been obtained most often through a Moral Judgment Scale, which presents nine interdependent situations, each presenting a moral dilemma. Situation 3 is the most famous:

> In Europe, a woman was near death from a special kind of cancer. There was one drug that the doctors thought might save her. It was a form of radium that a druggist in the same town had recently discovered. The drug was ex-

pensive to make, but the druggist was charging 5 times what it cost him to make the drug. He paid $400 for the radium and charged $2,000 for a small dose of the drug. The sick woman's husband, Heinz, went to everyone he knew to borrow the money, but he could only get together about $1,000, half of what it cost. He told the druggist that his wife was dying and asked him to sell it cheaper or let him pay later. But the druggist said, "No, I discovered the drug and I'm going to make money from it, so I won't let you have it unless you give me $2,000 now." So Heinz got desperate and broke into the man's store to steal the drug for his wife.

Q. Should Heinz have done that? Why?

Situation 4 continues:

The drug didn't work, and there was no other treatment known to medicine which could save Heinz's wife. So the Dr. knew she had only about 6 months to live. She was in terrible pain, but she was so weak that a good dose of pain-killer like ether or morphine would make her die sooner. She was almost crazy with pain, but in her calm periods, she would ask the Dr. to give her enough ether to kill her. She said she couldn't stand the pain and she was going to die in a few months anyway.

Q. Should the Dr. do what she asks and give her the drug that will make her die? Why?

As is well known, Kohlberg (1958) concluded from the moral justifications offered by 10-, 13-, and 16-year-old boys that moral development follows an invariant universal sequence of three broad levels—preconventional, conventional, and postconventional—which are remarkably similar to the stages suggested by McDougall. His subsequent research and writings have continued this view.

Kohlberg (1976) now claims that his theory is "true" in the sense that "any one who interviewed children about moral dilemmas and who followed them longitudinally" (p. 47) would come to see the same levels as he did, emerging in an invariant sequence. This claim is quite remarkable because Kohlberg's own report of his only longitudinal data, a follow-up of his initial sample, actually shows relatively little systematic change over time, and one of the clearest findings seems to be that a number of the subjects displayed a lower level of moral reasoning than they had in high school (Kohlberg & Kramer, 1969).

Other studies cast further doubt on the empirical validity of Kohlberg's invariant sequence hypothesis (Holstein, 1976; Turiel, 1966). Turiel (1966) attempted to induce experimentally shifts in the stage of moral reasoning of seventh-grade boys by exposing them to reasoning that was either "above" or "below" their preexperimental stage by one or two stages. Turiel predicted that exposure to a stage one above "their own" would be most effective in shifting his subjects' moral reasoning, deriving the prediction from Kohlberg's hypothesis of an invariant sequence. Although Turiel and others have taken his results as providing clear support for Kohlberg's theory, Kurtines and Greif (1974) have correctly pointed out that Turiel actually failed to support his prediction at even the minimal level of statistical confidence; the difference between the plus-one and minus-one training groups was simply not significant ($.05 < p < .10$).

Holstein (1976) studied 53 families, longitudinally obtaining data from both parents and from a son or daughter who was age 13 at the first assessment and age 16 at the second assessment. Holstein failed to find the stepwise progression among individual stages required by Kohlberg's theory, even though she used his moral dilemmas and scoring methods. What is more, large percentages of subjects regressed from higher to lower stages across the three-year period, and these shifts were about equally likely to occur among both genders and for both parents and adolescents. Thus, again, Kohlberg's hypothesis regarding a universal, invariant sequence in moral justifications was not supported.

Are There Universal Moral Principles?

Plato raised the issue of whether some rules, standards, or principles are better than others in an absolute sense, and the question has continued to be debated by philosophers ever since. Although the claim that there are universal moral principles is hardly a new one, however, Kohlberg has certainly added a new dimension to the issue by asserting that he has now scientifically tested and validated the proposition.

The essence of Kohlberg's argument is (1) that the most advanced people in every time and place have independently come to the same moral principles, and (2) that these principles can be seen to arise as the natural end point of the universal progression in moral development that his work has shown. This argument enjoys neither empirical nor logical support.

Anthropological studies provide no support for the proposition that there are universal moral principles. To the contrary, it has been found that norms, standards, and values as to what is good, right, or moral vary widely from one culture to another. With the possible exception of the incest taboo (Murdock, 1949), the substance of human moral belief seems to share *no* moral precept that could properly be called universal (Benedict, 1934/1958; Ferguson, 1958; Garbarino & Bronfenbrenner, 1976; Robertson, 1947). In fact, it has been observed that there is "scarcely one norm or standard of good conduct that, in another time and place, does not serve to mark bad conduct" (Melden, 1967, p. 7).

Kohlberg is also mistaken in claiming that there exists an independent consensus among philosophers on the truth of the moral scheme he has expounded. As his critics have noted repeatedly, this claim is based on a very selective reading of the philosophical literature. (Who could deny that the forceful arguments of Nietzsche and Machiavelli are anything less than postconventional and reflective in terms of their philosophical caliber?)

Kohlberg's argument for universal moral principles also contains a fundamental logical error. The notion that postconventional moral reasoning, as expressed in data such as Kohlberg's, is in some absolute way superior to other levels or types of moral reasoning is based on the wrong assumption that developmental change can be equated with improvement. This supposition is based on the logical error in which an *observation* (some behaviors temporally precede others in development) is converted into a *characterization* (later developing behaviors are more advanced than earlier developing ones), which in turn is converted into an *evaluation* (more advanced behaviors are better than less advanced ones). The fallacy can be seen by turning away from moral reasoning to a parallel example that can be approached with less confusion between the logic of the equation and the appeal of its conclusion.

There seems to be little doubt that human beings are more likely to develop vasocirculatory illness in middle age than in adolescence and that one major reason is structural changes in the heart and arteries that are an invariable part of the metamorphosis of human development. It can also be said that hardened arteries represent a more advanced developmental state than supple arteries, and longitudinal data show convincingly that persons with hardened arteries almost invariably had supple arteries at an earlier time in their lives, whereas the reverse pattern never occurs. But none of these relationships, however arranged, suggest that logically it is better to have hardened arteries, or that hardened arteries are superior to supple ones. As this example shows, there is no logical connection between observed sequence in development (however invariant or universal the sequence may be) and the relative desirability or quality of individual stages in the sequence. Evaluation invariably involves preference, and preference is invariably relative.

THE RELATIVIST PARADIGM

The notion of universal or absolute truths reflects the nineteenth-century conception of natural science, which presumed that absolute knowledge was, in principle, within the reach of human capability. This view is no longer taken seriously. Philosophers of science, stimulated by advances in theoretical physics, have shown that natural phenomena are necessarily observed and understood relative to some position in time and space, and never in any absolute sense.

Like moral absolutism, moral relativism is not a new idea, but it has taken on some new dimensions with the advent of psychological theory and research. Moral relativism finds expression today through the modern cognitive-behavioral approach.

The Cognitive-Behavioral Approach

The cognitive-behavioral perspective approaches moral development from the point of view of the individual person, a biological organism whose verbal and substantial behavior is shaped by the same basic law of effect that governs the activities of all living beings. The approach assumes that appropriate responsiveness to environmental consequences is the fundamental mechanism of biological adaptation. Verbal and substantial behavior within the moral sphere, like all behavior, is under the direct influence of both objectively and subjectively perceived or anticipated consequences. Any such behavior is intended to gain reward, avoid punishment, win praise, or secure some other advantage within the payoff matrix of social interaction. It is not a romantic expression of moral goodness or principled thinking.

The Central Role of Cognitive Factors

Modern cognitive behaviorism recognizes the obvious intellectual capacities of the human being, including our remarkable ability to transmit, process, and store information for later use. It also recognizes that future consequences are often anticipated or inferred and that future expected outcomes can be represented cognitively in the present and thus can be hypothesized to influence future behavior. A person's moral judgments, moral justifications, or personal conduct may be influenced by the cues the person is given before or while confronting a moral dilemma, and these cues may be interpreted by the person as having implications about the actual payoff matrix that prevails in this situation. The person will also have available information gleaned from the observation of others in similar situations and may be knowledgeable about a variety of societal norms (not always consistent with one another) that can be brought to bear on the situation.

Moral Sophistication

According to the cognitive-behavioral view, what develops in moral development is moral sophistication. *Moral sophistication* is the general term for knowing how to pursue one's own long-term self-interest effectively, through both direct and indirect means. As a result of the interplay of cognitive development and social experience, humans achieve an increasingly profound grasp of both the direct and immediate and the indirect and long-term effects of their words and deeds. This knowledge is integrated into new levels of practical understanding, which, in turn, determine what we say and do.

Thus, moral development is a matter of learning *what* the moral standards and norms of one's society are, of determining *how* and *when* they are applied, including *by whom, to whom,* and *with which* short-term and long-term consequences. A human being can learn that one is expected to make (or can benefit from making) lofty moral pronouncements in certain circumstances, and a human being can learn that immediate short-term losses can be in his or her own self-interest if they lead to larger, long-term gains. This remarkable cognitive capacity underlies and can account for the full range of moral reasoning and conduct. A great strength of this analysis is that it lends meaning to the apparent inconsistencies in moral reasoning and personal conduct that have troubled other theorists and plagued researchers who consider inconsistency in the moral sphere to be embarrassing. When it is recognized that the functional situation (and not "principles") underlies expressed moral judgments, then seeming inconsistencies between a person's words and deeds are immediately explicable in terms of the differing sets of contingencies that prevail for each.

Age and Other Demographic Variables

There is little doubt that the moral justifications offered by both children and adults are related to age, gender, social class, IQ, and other demographic variables. The cognitive-behavioral approach interprets these relationships as reflecting differences in the information, knowledge, and experience possessed by various demographic groups rather than differences in their underlying level of goodness. Moral maturity, from the cognitive-behavioral perspective, involves the expression of increasingly farsighted efforts to live pragmatically and pursue one's own self-interest.

Situational Factors Assumed to Influence Expressed Moral Reasoning

From the cognitive-behavioral perspective, the term *moral reasoning* as currently used in the literature is quite misleading. Subjects in studies involving moral dilemmas provide the examiner with a representation of their reasoning. Such representations are likely to be influenced by the full range of demand characteristics present in the situation, and thus it is a serious error to equate the representation of moral convictions given to an examiner with the convictions, beliefs, and decision-making guidelines actually held or used by the subject. Indeed, perhaps the single most important difference between the absolutist cognitive-developmental and relativist cognitive-behavioral approaches is that the latter approach draws a theoretical distinction between how decisions are made and how they are justified, based on differential patterns of expected consequences.

Moral Reasoning and Personal Conduct

Moral reasoning would be of no interest to society if it were unrelated to personal conduct, a fact clearly recognized by moral absolutists. Kohlberg (1970) has put the view nicely: "A moral principle is not only a rule for action but a reason for action" (p. 70). Nevertheless, research within the absolutist paradigm has shied from research on conduct and has hesitated to predict or explain the relationship between expressed moral reasoning (words) and actions that affect the welfare of others (deeds). Determining and explaining the actual relationships that exist between moral reasoning and personal conduct is a major goal of the cognitive-behavioral approach.

An important difference between the absolutist and the relativist views involves their expectations on the relationship between moral words and moral deeds. From the absolutist point of view, it would seem critical that moral justifications and declarations on the one hand and moral actions, on the other be consistent. In contrast, a relativist cognitive-behavioral view would not generally expect the two types of responses to converge. A range of examples, including investigations guided both by the cognitive-developmental and cognitive-behavioral perspectives, support the relativist position and illustrate the actual relationship between what is said and what is done in the moral sphere.

Personal Conduct and Kohlbergian Moral Stage

Two important studies have examined the relationship between level of moral reasoning as measured by Kohlberg's scheme and actual personal conduct.

Haan, Smith, and Block (1968) compared the percentages of college males at various Kohlbergian stages who were actively involved in the free speech movement sit-in at the University of California at Berkeley during the 1960s. Despite that participation was apparently construed by these authors as a principled act, over half of their Stage 2 subjects were involved, compared with 18% of their Stage 3 subjects and only 6% of their Stage 4 subjects. In fact, the two groups that were most similar in their activist behavior were those who scored primarily at Stage 2 and those who scored primarily at Stage 6, a similarity that is dismissed by the authors with the claim that Stage 2 subjects were involved because of a concern "with their individual rights," whereas Stage 6 subjects "were more concerned with the basic issues" (p. 198).

Podd (1972) placed undergraduate men who had been classified on the basis of their responses to Kohlberg's dilemmas as at preconventional, conventional, or postconventional levels of moral reasoning into a situation almost identical to the one created by Milgram (1963), in which subjects are asked to give ever more painful (and ultimately dangerous) shocks to another person in a supposed experiment dealing with the effects of punishment on learning. Contrary to prediction, there were no differences among subjects' willingness actually to administer shocks as a function of moral reasoning level, nor were postconventional subjects less likely to administer severe shocks than were preconventional subjects. Among subjects who terminated the experiment rather than continuing to shock the victim, however, postconventional reasoners explained their behavior with more altruistic reasons than did preconventional reasoners.

Altruism

So-called altruistic behaviors are often held out as the evidence that absolute moral principles can transcend relative self-interest. The data themselves, however, suggest that farsighted self-interest, moral sophistication, and prevailing circumstances can more completely and parsimoniously account for the actual data.

Consider the following instructive juxtaposition of facts. When adults are asked if they are willing to make a sacrifice in the future, a remarkable degree of "altruism" is evidenced. Schwartz (1970), for example, found that a majority of his adult subjects stated they were willing to donate their bone marrow to a complete stranger even after being warned that the donation would involve a general anesthetic, a day in the hospital, and soreness for several days thereafter. On the other hand, when the opportunity for self-sacrifice is at hand, altruistic intentions are invariably harder to find. Contrast Schwartz's findings with those of Darley and Bateson (1973), who asked students at Princeton Theological Seminary to volunteer to give a lecture for a small sum of money, with half of the students being asked to lecture on the good Samaritan parable while the others were to lecture on job opportunities for seminary graduates. As each volunteer walked across campus to give his lecture, he came upon a man slumped in a doorway, coughing, groaning, and in obvious distress. Most of the seminary students did *not* help the victim in this situation, and neither the topic on which they were to lecture nor the value they placed on religious commitment was associated with helping. In fact, according to Darley and Bateson, one of the seminary students "going to give his talk on the parable of the Good Samaritan literally stepped over the victim as he hurried on his way" (p. 107). The only factor that seemed to influence helping in this situation was the amount of time each student believed he had before his lecture was to begin; those who believed they had to hurry were less likely to help than were those who believed they had ample time and thus could afford to stop.

Cheating

As with altruism, a close examination of the cheating literature shows that self-interest rather than principles governs its occurrence. The likelihood of cheating is a function of the perceived likelihood of detection, the magnitude and importance of the gains that successful cheating will bring, and the anticipated consequences if caught cheating. Age- and IQ-correlated patterns of cheating appear to result from the way in which these factors are weighed and combined by the individual rather than from differences in the underlying belief systems of those of different ages or intelligence levels.

An early study by Howells (1938) suggested that students are less likely to cheat on a test when they think cheating can be detected than when they think cheating is "safe," and numerous subsequent experiments have confirmed that cheating is strongly influenced by risk and the possibility of detection. Thus, cheating is less likely to occur when students are asked to write their answers in ink than when they are asked to answer in pencil (Canning, 1956) or when cheating involves turning around instead of merely glancing forward (Atkins & Atkins, 1936).

The relationship between age and cheating appears to depend strongly on the type of cheating situation involved, as would be expected if cheating is viewed as a result of shifting age-correlated patterns of self-interest. Thus, on tests in which academic achievement appears actually to be measured, the tendency to cheat seems to *increase* with age (Feldman & Feldman, 1967), whereas in gamelike situations cheating appears to *decrease* with age (Grinder, 1964; Medinnus, 1966).

There is overwhelming evidence that among children IQ and cheating are negatively related (Canning, 1956; Hartshorne & May, 1928; Hetherington & Feldman, 1964; Johnson & Gormly, 1972; Nelsen, Grinder, & Biaggio, 1969). That brighter children cheat less does not necessarily mean, however, that in any fundamental way they are more honest. As Burton (1976) points out, the major influence of IQ may be in permitting the child to recognize more quickly that cheating may be detected, or it may be that less bright children are motivated to cheat as the only way to attain success that would otherwise not be within their grasp. Johnson and Gormly (1972) found that among fifth-grade boys and girls, high-IQ children were significantly less likely to cheat than were low-IQ children when the probability of being detected was high; however, when it seemed certain that the cheater could probably go undetected, IQ was unrelated to cheating.

CONTRASTING IMPLICATIONS OF THE TWO PARADIGMS

The two paradigms differ markedly in their implications for the conduct of human affairs.

Moral Education

Moral education within the absolutist paradigm aims to cultivate the child's ability to make moral judgments and offer moral justifications at what are taken to be "higher and more desirable levels of moral thought." Insofar as the individual is believed to be destined to take an invariable journey through a fixed sequence of stages, one by one, considerable attention is given to ways of thinking and value systems that the individual is expected ultimately to discredit and discard. At the same time, the individual is implicitly encouraged to make moral judgments about self and others, fostering a belief in moral superiority, which I shall discuss later.

In contrast to the absolutist paradigm, the relativist paradigm assumes that the best way to ensure that the child will display any desired response is to teach the response explicitly, model it consistently, and reinforce it reliably. Available evidence strongly suggests the efficacy of these procedures. Lickona (1971, cited in Lickona, 1976), for example, found that an adult "simply telling the child straight out that a judgment based on intentions was right, and explaining why this was so" was more effective than any of three more elaborate methods designed to stimulate underlying moral structures. In addition, the same direct and explicit approach was the only one that led children to generalize from intentionality in physical damage done (the focus of training in all conditions) to intentionality in children's lying (for which they had not been trained).

Likewise, it has been shown repeatedly that standards such as honesty are most strongly fostered by exposure to models whose actions are consistently honest, whereas exposure to dishonest models promotes dishonesty, especially when the dishonesty is apparently rewarded. Children exposed to models who proclaim the virtues of honesty or generosity and then act in a dishonest or stingy fashion are likely to imitate the hypocritical package *in toto,* having learned from the adults around them to preach one course of action and practice another (Liebert, 1973).

Moral Superiority versus Moral Sophistication

The relativist and absolutist paradigms differ in their answer to the question with which we began, namely, What develops in moral development? For the relativist, it is moral sophistication; for the absolutist, it is moral superiority. The answers lead to entirely different world views.

The absolutist views lends itself easily to the claim that some individuals and groups (as well as some causes) are morally superior to others. Thus, among the discoveries claimed for the absolutist paradigm is that males, persons of European extraction, the better educated, and the more intelligent tend to be more morally advanced than females, non-Europeans, the educally disadvantaged, and the less intelligent (cf. Shweder, 1982).

Like many other absolutist claims, these tend to be an artifact of sloppy method. Consider, for example, the claim that males are morally more advanced than females. The conclusion is based on presenting female and male subjects with "identical" moral dilemmas—in which all of the protagonists have been male. A study in England by Bull (1969) points up dramatically the error of limiting moral dilemma stories in this way. Bull studied the development of moral reasoning and analyzed children's moral justification roughly as Kohlberg had done but presented female subjects with stories involving female characters and male subjects with stories involving male characters. Employing this methodology, he reached the conclusion that female children at any given age are not less but *more* morally advanced than males— a phenomenon that he attributed to girls' earlier maturation and greater verbal facility.

There are significant dangers in legitimating *any* claims to moral superiority. History teaches us to be extremely apprehensive whenever someone claims that they have come upon an absolute moral truth. It is under the banner of absolute moral truths and universal principles that all manner of violence and destruction has been waged.

The concept of moral superiority *is* promulgated by the absolutist cognitive-developmental approach in both explicit and subtle ways. Consider, for example, Kohlberg's use of value-laden epithets in association with the "lower" (e.g., *good boy, nice girl*) and "higher" (*principled moral reasoning*) stages. The implication is that persons who justify their hypothetical moral choices in lofty terms are operating from deeply held convictions and principles, whereas all other individuals are automatons blindly following codes or conventions in which they do not really believe or that they do not even understand.

Such general characterizations easily lead to specific characterizations that amount to *ad hominem* arguments and extreme intolerance and elitism. Whereas being at a low level of moral development is a status that discredits one's opinions and judgments and calls into question the motives of one's actions (it is stigmatizing), being referred to as "morally mature" or at a "high" or "principled" level of moral development confers a veritable halo of noble purpose. All of this is reminiscent of William Saroyan's observation many years ago in his penetrating novel *Rock Wagram:* "Each man is a good man in a bad world, as he himself knows."

In contrast, viewing moral development in terms of increasing moral sophistication leads to healthy skepticism about moralistic claims and breeds tolerance and pragmatism in dealing with others and constructing workable social and political arrangements. Witness the presumption that each party will attempt to pursue his or her own self-interest, one of the fundamental presumptions of the law, which reflects not a philosophical bias but is rather the product of what has been honed by practical human experience. Similarly, the eminently successful political concept of checks and balances, in which it is clearly presumed that unless restrained each party would be expected to pursue its own self-interest, is highly successful as a principle for interpersonal interaction. Finally, the relativist perspective is in keeping with the political writings of Thomas Jefferson and Thomas More, both of whom stress the idea that in order to produce a smooth-running society one must first *grasp the nature of self-interest* and then construct political and social arrangements with a watchful eye to how self-interest can be expressed within the system. Such realism is in my view preferable to idealism and illusion.

REFERENCES

Atkins, B. E., & Atkins, R. E. A study of the honesty of prospective teachers. *The Elementary School Journal, 1936, 36,* 595–603.

Austin, V. D., Ruble, D. N., & Trabasso, T. Recall and order effects as factors in children's moral judgments. *Child Development, 1977, 48,* 470–474.

Bandura, A., & McDonald, F. J. The influence of social reinforcement and the behavior of models in shaping children's moral judgments. *Journal of Abnormal and Social Psychology, 1963, 67,* 274–281.

Benedict, R. *Patterns of culture.* New York: New American Library, 1958. (Originally published, 1934.)

Bull, N. J. *Moral judgment from childhood to adolescence.* Beverly Hills, Calif.: Sage, 1969.

Burton, R. V. Honesty and dishonesty. In T. Lickona (Ed.), *Moral development and behavior: Theory, research, and social issues.* New York: Holt, Rinehart and Winston, 1976.

Canning, R. Does an honor system reduce classroom cheating? An experimental answer. *Journal of Experimental Education,* 1956, *24,* 291–296.

Darley, J., & Batson, C. From Jerusalem to Jericho: A study of situational and dispositional variables in helping behavior. *Journal of Personality and Social Psychology,* 1973, *27,* 100–108.

Feldman, N. S., Klosson, E. C., Parsons, J. E., Rholes, W. S., & Ruble, D. N. Order of information presentation and children's moral judgments. *Child Development,* 1976, *47,* 556–559.

Feldman, S. E., & Feldman, M. T. Transition of sex differences in cheating. *Psychological Reports,* 1967, *20,* 957–958.

Ferguson, J. *Moral values in the ancient world.* London: Methuen, 1958.

Garbarino, J., & Bronfenbrenner, U. The socialization of moral judgment and behavior in cross-cultural perspective. In T. Lickona (Ed.), *Moral development and behavior: Theory, research, and social issues.* New York: Holt, Rinehart and Winston, 1976.

Grinder, R. E. Relations between behavioral and cognitive dimensions of conscience in middle childhood. *Child Development,* 1964, *35,* 881–893.

Haan, N., Smith, M. B., & Block, J. Moral reasoning of young adults: Political-social behavior, family background, and personality correlates. *Journal of Personality and Social Psychology,* 1968, *10,* 183–201.

Hartshorne, H., & May, M. A. *Studies in the nature of character* (Vol. I): *Studies in deceit.* New York: Macmillan, 1928.

Hetherington, E. M., & Feldman, S. E. College cheating as a function of subjects and situational variables. *Journal of Educational Psychology,* 1964, *55,* 212–218.

Holstein, C. B. Irreversible, stepwise sequence in the development of moral judgment: A longitudinal study of males and females. *Child Development,* 1976, *47,* 51–61.

Howells, T. H. Factors influencing honesty. *The Journal of Social Psychology,* 1938, *9,* 97–102.

Johnson, C. D., & Gormly, J. Academic cheating: The contribution of sex, personality, and situational variables. *Developmental Psychology,* 1972, *6,* 602–605.

Johnson, R. C. A study of children's moral judgments. *Child Development,* 1962, *33,* 327–354.

Kohlberg, L. *The development of modes of moral thinking and choice in the years ten to sixteen.* Unpublished doctoral dissertation, University of Chicago, 1958.

Kohlberg, L. Education for justice: A modern statement of the platonic view. In N. F. Sizer & T. R. Sizer (Eds.), *Moral education,* Cambridge, Mass.: Harvard University Press, 1970.

Kohlberg, L. Moral stages and moralization: The cognitive-developmental approach. In T. Lickona (Ed.), *Moral development and behavior: Theory, research, and social issues.* New York: Holt, Rinehart and Winston, 1976.

Kohlberg, L., & Kramer, R. Continuities and discontinuities in childhood and adult moral development. *Human Development,* 1969, *12,* 93–120.

Kuhn, T. S. *The structure of scientific revolutions.* Chicago: University of Chicago Press, 1962.

Kuhn, T. S. *The structure of scientific revolutions* (2nd ed.). Chicago: University of Chicago Press, 1970.

Kurtines, W., & Greif, E. B. The development of moral thought: Review and evaluation of Kohlberg's approach. *Psychological Bulletin*, 1974, *81*, 453–470.

Lickona, T. Critical issues in the study of moral development and behavior. In T. Lickona (Ed.), *Moral development and behavior: Theory, research, and social issues.* New York: Holt, Rinehart and Winston, 1976.

Liebert, R. M. Observational learning: Some social applications. In P. J. Elich (Ed.), *The Fourth Western Symposium on Learning: Social learning.* Bellingham, Wash.: Washington State College, 1973.

Liebert, R. M. Moral development: A theoretical and empirical analysis. In G. Whitehurst & B. Zimmerman (Eds.), *The functions of cognition and language.* New York: Academic Press, 1979.

MacRae, D., Jr. A test of Piaget's theories of moral development. *Journal of Abnormal and Social Psychology*, 1954, *49*, 14–18.

McDougall, W. *Social psychology.* Boston: John W. Luce, 1908.

Medinnus, G. R. Age and sex differences in conscience development. *Journal of Genetic Psychology*, 1966, *109*, 117–118.

Melden, S. I. *Ethical theories.* Englewood Cliffs, N.J.: Prentice-Hall, 1967.

Milgram, S. Behavioral study of obedience. *Journal of Abnormal and Social Psychology*, 1963, *67*, 371–378.

Murdock, G. *Social structure.* New York: Macmillan, 1949.

Nelsen, E. A., Grinder, R. E., & Biaggio, A. M. Relationships among behavioral, cognitive-developmental, and self-report measures of morality and personality. *Multivariate Behavioral Research*, 1969, *4*, 483–500.

Nummendal, S. G., & Bass, S. C. Effects of the salience of intention and consequences on children's moral judgments. *Developmental Psychology*, 1976, *12*, 475–476.

Podd, M. H. Ego identity status and morality: The relationship between two developmental constructs. *Developmental Psychology*, 1972, *6*, 497–507.

Robertson, J. M. *Morals in world history.* London: Watts, 1947.

Schwartz, S. Elicitation of moral obligation and self-sacrificing behavior. An experimental study of volunteering to be a bone marrow donor. *Journal of Personality and Social Psychology*, 1970, *15*, 283–293.

Shweder, R. A. Liberalism as destiny. (Review of Kohlberg's *The philosophy of moral development*, Vol. 1.) *Contemporary Psychology*, 1982, *27*, 421–424.

Turiel, E. An experimental test of the sequentiality of development stages in the child's moral judgments. *Journal of Personality and Social Psychology*, 1966, *3*, 611–618.

CHAPTER 11

A Paradox in Theories and Research in Moral Development

ROGER V. BURTON

The definition of the domain of moral development is the problem posed. Much current work in moral development based on moral reasoning eliminates many prototypical moral acts, a situation seen as a paradox in this area of research. Rather than assume that more desired moral conduct follows an increase in moral judgment, and therefore that the conduct component of morality can be treated with benign neglect, the theoretical model proposed in this chapter is that action, affect, and cognitions are essential factors determining moral development and that all three factors must be studied together for an adequate conceptualization of moral development.

How to define the domain of moral development is the problem posed in this chapter. The main point of the discussion is that much current work in this area defines morality in such a way that a prototypical moral response lies outside the realm of moral discourse.

The dominant theoretical orientation in studies of morality at this time (as the chapters in this book exemplify) is the study of moral judgment and reasoning. Although the behavioral component in these cognitively focused conceptions of morality is recognized, moral conduct is assumed to follow from advancing stages of moral thought. It follows, therefore, that direct measurement of moral action is tangential to the core of these studies of moral development and is treated with benign neglect.

In contrast, the argument is made here that a *developmental* perspective of morality requires a definition of the domain that makes conduct and judgment equally important. Judgments or verbalized decisions about abstract moral dilemmas, or responses to questionnaire items—no matter how specific to actual conduct situations—are insufficient for assessing moral development.

Nancy Johnson's cogent and constructive comments on an early version of this chapter are gratefully acknowledged.

A short historical analysis sets the stage, showing how the current state of affairs has come about, why the concentration on moral reasoning waxed as the focus on behavior waned. The implications of reliance on conscious verbal material for assessing moral development are then discussed. This reliance has led to the paradox in research of moral development, a paradox in which the most common, everyday moral situations are excluded by definition.

A portrayal of the development of moral self-control is used to show how much learning of moral decisions may occur at very young ages, before children are capable of verbally expressing the complex issues involved in the situation. Furthermore, much of this early learning may be critical in determining moral conduct at later ages. And, from this developmental perspective, it is seen that moral reasoning for these frequently occurring moral situations is a product of the action taken, not of the executive component.

Two contrasting models, one in which the flow is from action to cognitive structure, and the other, from cognitions to behavior, are compared. The analysis indicates that neither position is sufficient and that a model that attempts to establish how cognitions and actions are linked through a developmental sequence of experiences is needed. The position is taken that many prototypical moral decisions manifested in moral conduct are made unconsciously. Any conscious rationale for such an act must come after the action has occurred, and yet the act exemplifies mature moral behavior. For this kind of moral action to occur, it is argued that some form of punishment is a necessary part of the socialization history of the individual and that some trace of the affective component of this punishment is still present when the moral situation occurs, producing a decision so rapidly that there is no awareness a moral dilemma was even experienced. Also considered are the cognitive factors involved in classifying situations, information processes that become critical in developing generality of morality and that link together moral reasoning and conduct.

To summarize, I suggest a four-step theoretical model as necessary for studying moral development, a model that shifts from initial emphasis on conduct to an increasing emphasis on thought and reasoning. This model is proposed as a rapprochement between the behavioral and cognitive-developmental orientations. Despite the increased attention paid to cognitive factors in moral development, and the tenet that these factors may become a critical link in the determination of consistency of conduct, the conceptual path for the proposed solution to the paradox given in this chapter requires overt action as the ultimate criterion for an assessment of moral development.

HISTORICAL ANTECEDENTS

The two major traditions for studying moral development are the behavioristic orientation of Hartshorne's and May's *Studies in the Nature of Character*

(1928, 1929, 1930) and the moral-reasoning orientation of Piaget's *The Moral Judgment of the Child* (1932). Although much current research seems to be tied to those two classics in psychology, it is surprising that at the time of their publication they generated so few follow-up investigations. Hartshorne's and May's emphasis on situational specificity and their conclusion that there is no unified character trait of honesty seems to have implied to many behaviorally oriented investigators that it was a waste of time to study moral development because moral traits did not exist as organized inner entities in individuals. For Piaget, the reception in the United States was indifference, apparently due to the unfamiliar terms and difficult writing style as well as to the domination in American psychology of the learning-theory orientations of Edwin Guthrie, Clark Hull, and Edward Tolman with their experimentally controlled designs, measurement of specific responses, and statistical analyses.

Stimulated by the Freudian notions of identification and the internalization of superego and interest in studying the effects of child-rearing practices, investigators led by Sears, Maccoby, and Levin (1957) and Whiting and Child (1953) again turned their attention in the late 1940s and early 1950s to moral development. Although the data for many of these studies were based on verbal reports about behavior, the theoretical framework was a translation of the psychoanalytic concepts into a behavioral, learning orientation. The focus was on resistance to temptation and guilt, on overt responses and anxiety as drive. Clearly, the behavioral orientation was dominant in the area of studying morality.

Like a voice out of the wilderness—or out of the Midwest of Chicago—came Lawrence Kohlberg (1958), who was saying that Piaget was on the right track, that moral development was primarily a cognitive process, and that moral reasoning must be the focus of attention.

The ascendancy of this cognitive-developmental orientation over the behavioral-learning framework in the next 20 years was due to several factors occurring simultaneously. There were strong challenges within the behavioral camp itself that the dominant learning theories based on reinforcement principles were inadequate to account for important kinds of behavioral phenomena. Imprinting, species-specific behavioral predispositions, and different possibilities in associating certain stimuli and responses led many in the field of animal experimental psychology to look more closely at naturally occurring sequences of behavior rather than at the artificially delimited conditions usually used in studies of animal learning.

There was also accumulating evidence that the arousal of affective or emotional components in moral situations did not result automatically in either moral or deceptive action. The experiments using drugs to increase or depress sympathetic arousal (Nisbett & Schachter, 1966; Schachter & Latané, 1964; Schachter & Singer, 1962) or placebos to produce false expectations of pharmacological effects on emotional responding in moral situations (Dienstbier & Munter, 1971) showed that the cognitive context for emotional arousal or inhibition would lead to different overt responses. These experiments showed that the interactions between emotions, cognitions, and behavior are complex and that cognitive interpretations of the situation and of one's own affective states in the situation may be crucial in determining moral conduct (Dienstbier, Hillman, Lehnhoff, Hillman, & Valkenaar, 1975).

There was also a dissatisfaction with theoretical formulations whose major principles were based primarily on animal experimentation. If we were using animal experiments as analogues for establishing principles of human development, why not use humans for subjects as much as possible? This attitude was buttressed by an increasing awareness of the role of language, as discriminative cues (Aronfreed, 1968), semantic generalization (Burton, 1963), or second signal system (Luria, 1957, 1961) in the control and transfer of behavior. Animals do not have the same predilection to acquire and use language that humans have, so why continue to use animals to study an area in which language seems to play such a critical role?[1] Complementing this attitude was the attractiveness of Piaget's theoretical interpretations about human behavior that were based on direct observations of the behavior he wanted to explain, which was intellectual activity and development. Although students of development had for some time been aware of Piaget, this orientation was often not clearly understood or was slighted by the teacher. The American student who was interested and turned to Piaget's writing usually had little guidance in understanding the new terminology and concepts, until the appearance of Flavell's exegesis of Piaget's theory and work in 1963. By the time Kohlberg's (1964) chapter in the initial volume of *Review of Child Development Research* appeared a year later, the field was prepared to receive it with interest and understanding. Here was a theory of moral development based on responses of children of different ages to hypothetical moral situations. These were not studies using children as subjects to verify a finding based on an animal experiment.

Other developments in psychology not immediately related to studies of moral development also contributed to the waning of the behavioral orientation. Although different in many respects, the wave of cognitive psychology buttressed the cognitive-developmental orientation with its rejection of the animal learning models of the 1940s and 1950s. The interest was in central, cognitive processes themselves, not as hypothetical constructs between stimulus and response, but as the significant aspects of human behavior (e.g., Miller, Galanter, & Pribram, 1960). The questions were addressed to attempt to understand what was going on in the "black box," to study thinking and information processing directly. At the same time, the development of increasingly sophisticated computers and computer models of artificial intelligence permitted testing of alternative models of information processing. These

---

[1] This analysis should not be interpreted as the author's rejection of all animal experiments as bearing on moral development. For example, the studies of Solomon and colleagues (e.g., 1968) using punishment paradigms illuminate many complex issues in the development of moral conduct.

events were appealing, attractive, and exciting to researchers looking for un-plowed fields to explore. Somehow, the studies based on behavioral-learning formulations, even if well done, seemed old-fashioned, out of the mainstream.

These trends, both in developmental and general experimental psychology, all contributed to the current dominance of the cognitive-developmental orientation in studies of morality. The thrust of this cognitive orientation has been to focus on how people think and reason. How can we know what people are thinking? Ask them. Both Piaget and Kohlberg advocate the use of the clinical interview in order to obtain the data required to assess an individual's moral development. Furthermore, with each succeeding revision in the coding system, Kohlberg has moved increasingly toward the requirement that the individual clearly articulate a concept before being credited with it (Colby, Gibbs, & Kohlberg, 1980; see also Chap. 3 in this book). The data base then is both verbal self-report and manifest conscious material.

CURRENT PARADOX IN MORAL DEVELOPMENT RESEARCH

In addition to these two components being intrinsic to the method of the clinical interview and the scoring procedure, they have become required by the definitions of morality used by many investigators (see Chap. 7). It is just these requirements, conscious awareness of a moral dilemma and the verbal expression of elements of the conflict, that result in the current paradox of much research into the *development* of morality. The paradox is that the most common experiences in which a moral decision must be made are excluded by this operational definition.

To illustrate, the common types of moral decisions in everyday life are such things as telling the truth when we have been negligent and could easily get away with denying any responsibility for the damage, giving to the rightful owner something that we find and could pocket without risk, and telling a checkout clerk the correct price for an item when we might save money by lying. These are real situations that occur daily and are examples of what most people mean by moral situations. They involve lying, stealing, and cheating. And yet, for most socialized individuals, these particular situations are not experienced as conscious moral conflicts. There is no awareness of any dilemma. The decisions to own up to having been negligent, to give a found wallet to the owner without taking any money from it, and to tell the clerk the correct price occur without conscious thought. The decision in such instances is made so rapidly that any vestige of what was once a moral dilemma and felt conflict over the temptation to be deceptive is out of awareness, is now unconscious. Furthermore, as we shall portray, it is likely that these actions take place so automatically because of a learning history that includes punishment. By current definition, however, because there is no awareness of a moral dilemma, because there is no need to consider alternative choices and the reasons to justify them before making a decision and acting, and because coercion is a part of the developmental history of the action, these situations are excluded from the domain of morality (Kohlberg, 1976; Rest, 1983; see also Chap. 2 in this book). How can this be?

For those investigators working in the Piaget-Kohlberg tradition, morality is primarily a function of cognitive processes (see Chap. 4). Moral development is essentially a reflection of changes in the conceptions of justice and reciprocity. To be sure, moral conduct is acknowledged as a component of morality, and mature moral reasoning is theoretically required for mature moral behavior, but it is moral reasoning alone that identifies an individual's moral stage (Kohlberg, 1976; Rest, 1983; see also Chap. 3 in this book). We see an increasing number of publications in which success in moral development is based only on evidence that experience in a training program or in a "just community school" (Jennings & Kohlberg, 1983; Kohlberg, Kauffman, Scharf, & Hickey, 1975; Lickona, 1978) has led to an increase in stage of moral judgment. But is such evidence sufficient for an interpretation of success in moral development without any evidence that there is a parallel advance in moral behavior? The general theoretical framework of Piaget and Kohlberg, in which the translation of moral reasoning into moral action is supposed to occur, leads us to answer no (e.g., Kohlberg, 1964), p. 425). But the focus on moral reasoning has led to the current situation in which attention to conduct in the research itself is negligible.

ROLE OF BEHAVIOR IN INITIAL COGNITIVE DEVELOPMENTAL RESEARCH

For both Piaget and Kohlberg, however, there was originally interest in conduct as well as in judgments. Piaget (1932) initiated his study of moral development by observing children playing marbles. One of the most interesting observations in this classic study was the apparent contradiction between the age-related changes in perceptions of and compliance with rules. The young children in Stage 2 of playing a rule game perceive the rules as absolute, God given, and permanent and yet bend the rules at will in order always to win. The older children, in Stage 4 of rule games, understand the rules to be social conventions that can be changed if agreed on by the players. Nevertheless, they comply with the rules as a part of the game itself. The apparent contradiction is resolved by classifying the reasoning and the conduct of the older children as more mature than these two facets of moral development in the younger children. The morality of the older children, manifested in their understanding of and compliance with rules, contains elements of mutual respect and cooperation that are lacking in the authority-centered reasoning and egocentric behavior of the younger children. Just how these two components of moral development, knowledge of and compliance with rules, are linked together and tied to the development of moral judgment are questions most in need of continued exploration. Yet such questions involving cognitions and conduct have not been pursued by Piaget's followers (Burton, 1977).

Kohlberg (1958) began his work with a consideration of conduct when he selected delinquents, assuming that through an understanding of moral development he might gain knowledge of how to increase their level of morality so that they would become more law abiding. This assumption is also reflected in the more recent prison projects (Jennings & Kohlberg, 1983; Kohlberg et al., 1975; Scharf & Hickey, 1976). In general, however, the evidence on correspondence between moral judgments and controlled measures of moral conduct shows only small correlation. As the empirical data showing this lack of predictability from moral judgments to conduct have accumulated, there has been consistent moving away from attention to how and under what conditions are the links between reasoning and behavior forged. Although there are implied feedback loops in these presentations, the emphasis on top-down processes (i.e., reasoning to action) and conscious rationalizations have led to a huge corpus of literature on cognitive development with very little evidence of how it bears on the final link in the chain of "logic in action" (Kohlberg, 1964), the action being what a person actually does in a moral situation.

CUMULATIVE EVENTS IN LEARNING MORALITY

To capture a history of moral learning, let me delineate a brief scenario of events that commonly occur during early childhood, episodes that actually have occurred during the early years of my own daughters' lives.

After a wonderful time "trick or treating" with her older sisters on Halloween, Ursula, at a year and a half, was admiring all the candy she and her sisters had been given. When putting it away, Ursie started to put some of her sisters' candy into her bag. "No, Ursie, that's mine!" said one of the sisters, and I explained that she should put only her own candy into her bag.

A week later, when most of the candy was gone, the sisters found that some of their candy was in Ursie's bag. Hearing the fuss about "Not going to let you come into my room," and "That's stealing, Ursie," my wife intervened to see to it that Ursula returned the purloined loot and again explained about not taking her sisters' things. The next day, however, when my wife saw Ursula with her hand in a sister's candy bag, she said, "No, Ursula! You know you're not to take your sister's candy. Come out of her room now." Later I saw Ursula in her sister's room looking at the candy bag, and she looked up and said, "No, this is Maria's, not Ursula's," and walked out of the room to me. "Good girl, Ursie. You know you're not to take candy that's not yours."

About the age of 3 there was an episode in which a plastic toy was taken from a store, and Ursula had to return it immediately to the manager and say she was sorry. I again explained that taking it without paying was stealing and that she was not to do that. A few weeks after starting first grade, Ursula brought home a cartoon-character mechanical pencil with another child's name on it. After a painfully circuitous discussion at the dinner table, it finally came out that Ursula had "borrowed" the pencil, although the owner did not know it yet. We then explained about temptations, honesty, and how she would feel if it had been her pencil and another child had taken it, and her sisters talked about how no one likes a stealer.

Seven years later in Yellowstone Park, Ursula saw a wallet on the ground with money blowing out of it, frantically ran around gathering up the $20 bills, and finally mailed the wallet and its $485 to its owner in Montreal. When asked later if she had been tempted to keep any of the money, she looked nonplussed and said, "Dad! That would be stealing!"

This scenario portrays the kinds of cumulative events that my theory requires for the development of a prototypical moral action. Initially, Ursula wants the candy and takes it openly but is prevented from doing so by the power-assertive techniques of her sister. It was clear that the verbal distinction made in my explanation had much less impact on 18-month-old Ursula than did her sibling's physically retrieving the candy. In the next episode, her sisters' labeling her deception as stealing when expressing their displeasure, especially as they were normally very nurturant and affectionate to her, probably had more effect on her moral development at that age than did the more elaborate verbal explanation by my wife. Nevertheless, these kinds of experiences are conditioning some anxiety-arousing cues to both the perceptual interpretation of the situation and to the words being used when the reprimands occur. This autonomic arousal is theoretically the necessary motivational component for the cognitive interpretation of the situation to be implemented into overt action.

At the three- and six-year episodes, there is greater provision of cognitive structure in the explanations provided for exerting self-control when temptation arises. The explanations are not simply verbal elaborations of threats, but communicate at the child's level of understanding what to do in the situation and why. The general context of these experiences was still that an unpleasant experience occurred contingent on the unacceptable behavior. This recurrent pairing strengthens the conditioning of the autonomic arousal to the concepts expressed in the explanations and promotes the generalization of the action learned in this situation to other situations that are interpreted as being in the same class.

And in the final episode, the moral response occurs in what appears to be an automatic fashion. The situation was immediately interpreted as demanding picking up the wallet, gathering all of the money, and returning it all to its owner—all done without any awareness of temptation. When such temptation was suggested by my question, it seemed absurd to Ursula, for it was not considered an option in that situation. It is this type of experience that represents a prototypical moral decision in which the cognitive components depicted by Rest in Chapter 2—of interpreting the situation, formulating the appropriate course of action, considering the alternative actions, and committing oneself to the moral choice—occur out of awareness. It is also this kind of moral development that is more directly linked to amelioration of many contemporary social problems such as problems of drug use, delinquency, and crime—all problems of self-control.

THEORETICAL IMPLICATIONS

Empirical evidence supports this portrayal of a developmental shift from primary reliance on direct, noncomplex disciplinary practices with very young children to greater reliance on increasingly abstract verbal cues for training morality (Burton, Maccoby, & Allinsmith, 1961). The experimental studies show that when a rationale is provided to the child that serves to justify a prohibition and is more than just a verbal elaboration of the threat of punishment, intensity and timing of punishment interact and affect moral conduct very differently from instructions when no rationale is provided.[2] Placed into the developmental perspective delineated in this scenario, these specific experimental studies indicate that the required base of learning to inhibit temptations, to implement one's moral standards, is through direct techniques of differential rewards and punishments when the child is at a low level of cognitive development. With increasing cognitive development and the acquisition of symbolic control in the child, caretakers who are in tune with the child's changes rely more and more on cognitive structure in their training techniques, providing reasons that communicate to the child what should be done, when, where, how, and why.[3] These explanations are tailored to the child's ability to understand what is being said, a principle consonant with common sense as well as with the empirical evidence that children understand moral reasoning at their own level or slightly above (Turiel, 1966).

The emphasis in this developmental picture is that the cognitions that portray the child's conceptions of morality and that have directing power over behavior come about through actions in specific situations. Moral reasoning about stealing is being formed in the situations when training about stealing takes place. The behavioral experience has primacy in the development of cognitive moral reasoning. This hypothesis is clearly compatible with Piaget's dictum that the earliest structures develop out of the child's interactions with the environment and that subsequent structures develop out of existing structures interacting with current behavioral experiences. In much current cogni-

---

[2] These studies have been reviewed in detail in Burton, 1976.

[3] Observational learning and modeling processes are also major factors contributing to moral development. Discussion of these factors in the present context, however, would distract from the present argument. For a review of modeling affects relevant to moral development, see Burton, 1976, and Liebert and Poulos, 1976.

tive-developmental formulations, however, the direction of influence has changed. Now the hypothesis is that "to act in a morally high way requires a high stage of moral reasoning" (Kohlberg, 1976, p. 32). Structure has primacy, and the contents of specific interactions with environment are determined by the internal structure.

Another important theoretical issue portrayed in the Ursula scenario is that there is never a time when a moral action based on rights of others over one's own immediate gratification is completely independent of some traces of autonomic arousal previously associated with an aversive experience. Although it may appear that there is no affective arousal associated with the performance of a moral response, such as not taking money from the wallet, I believe there still is. The hypothesis is that as the child learns the required moral response and sees that it avoids the aversive consequences, it is performed rapidly so as to avoid the unpleasant feelings of the anxiety evoked by the situational cues. As this sequence becomes increasingly efficient, there is less autonomic arousal needed to be effective. Eventually, there is just the minimum arousal, which is so little that our current psychophysiological equipment cannot record it, yet our own physiological system is registering and reacting to it. Evidence to support this hypothesis comes from the experiments of Solomon and colleagues that showed that avoidance behavior continues to occur without any evidence of autonomic arousal and led to the proposal of "anxiety conservation" from such efficient performance (Solomon & Wynne, 1954). When restrained from performing the avoidance response, the affective behavior, manifested in obvious distress, reappears full blown. Also the increased deception in people administered an autonomic suppressor supports this hypothesis (Schachter & Singer, 1962).

Why does this portrayal require negative arousal when we can shape behavior so well with positive reinforcement? The reasons are both theoretical and practical. Behavior shaped solely through positive reinforcement remains flexible. There is no problem with the behavior becoming fixated and unresponsive to skillful use of differential positive reinforcement. For many kinds of behavior this is just what is wanted so that behavior continues to change as the conditions change. But in many moral situations, the immediate rewards are in the immoral options, such as lying, stealing, cheating, ignoring others' rights, being selfish, not going to the aid of someone in distress, and so on. In contrast, the positive reinforcement for ethical conduct tends to be delayed and modest, or not at all, because the moral choice is only what is expected. How is society to ensure that people will not turn to immediately self-serving deception to achieve material rewards, success, fame, or power, such as was demonstrated by the characters of the Watergate scandal? According to my theory, the negative affect maintains the moral behavior over the many instances of nonreinforcement. When reinforcement for moral behavior does come, it is often vicarious, in the form of seeing, hearing about, or reading of someone else who was honored for some moral action. Similarly, the negative affect associated with moral deception is reinforced when the mass media reports on someone who was caught and punished for a moral infraction. With the base of the early, direct learning experiences, these attenuated, vicarious reinforcements are sufficient to maintain and perhaps even strengthen the conditioned affect associated with the unethical behavior and to increase the tendency to perform the moral alternative.

The practical consideration is that it is important to avoid permitting a child to be rewarded by deceptive or unethical conduct. For example, had Ursula been able to consume her sister's candy each time she took some, to enjoy playing with the stolen toy, to keep the mechanical pencil, and to retain some of the money from the wallet, she would have experienced a strong and immediate reinforcement for behavior that is incompatible with the pre-scribed moral conduct in each of these situations. When children are small, their actions are often easily observed, even when they think their behavior is hidden or disguised. This situation permits parents to establish the negative associations with the misdeeds before the child is frequently reinforced by moral misconduct. If the misconduct is too frequently rewarded before pun-ishment is introduced, the conditions of intermittently rewarding and punish-ing the same behavior are likely to occur, conditions that experimentally result in behavior that is extremely difficult to extinguish or modify.

It is also important to build in positive reinforcement for moral responses during this early period of moral learning. For many prosocial, altruistic actions, it is easy to administer reinforcement by noting "You're a good child to share, to help, to be so kind." But for actions of self-control, of resisting temptation, it is more difficult. Witnessing Ursula's resisting the temptation to take the candy was a chance occurrence. Still, parents need to give positive reinforcement for acts of self-control so that a child does not become generally inhibited due to punishment for unacceptable behavior. In other words, al-though punishment is theoretically important to suppress the deceptive be-havior, desired moral action needs to be positively reinforced to ensure that all activity is not suppressed.

MORAL LEARNING PARADIGM

Where do all these considerations lead us? For some years, my students and I have been exploring how cognitions and behavior about moral situations can be linked together, how perceptions of a situation can set off a chain of cognitive processing and emotional arousal that terminates in a moral re-sponse. At present, the model that is being developed has four steps, not nec-essarily occurring as distinct links in the chain, but distinguished more for heuristic and theoretical purposes (Burton, 1976; Casey & Burton, 1982).

First, there is the necessity to condition the autonomic arousal to the cues present in the moral conflict situation. Aversive consequences are contingent on the performance or even more desired, on the manifested intent to per-form an unacceptable moral action. Thus the learning begins with an action, and the consequences of the action are conditioned anxiety. Initially, the cues conditioned to the anxiety are likely to be the physical cues of the situation as the child is young and not developed linguistically. With increasing age, the cues with most control become increasingly the verbal context.

The second step is concerned with the levels of abstractness in the verbal contexts. As research in concept development and class inclusion shows, concepts and their labels, what I call "critical terms," are hierarchically ordered in the number of instances included at each level in the arrangement. When very young, the world is divided into two major parts: "good" and "bad." "No, no" and "naughty" are also used to mean "bad" at this stage of infancy. Although these verbal cues gain control over the child's behavior, deterring or stopping performance of a specific act in the immediate situation, they do not contribute to the child's perceiving *new* situations as being in the same class. These terms are *too* inclusive to function for discriminative interpretation of new occasions in which the response to "no, no" is again applicable. In this context, these terms are highly specific to each situation. It is when more abstract terms directly related to the moral domain are used in the training situation that the child can respond to different moral situations in the same way. When the word *stealing* is applied to taking a sister's candy, then to somone else's toy, and so on, Ursula is learning that *stealing* means taking property that is not hers. On future occasions, if Ursula perceives the situation as fitting the class covered by stealing, regardless of the particular property or place involved, she is likely to be deterred and resist temptation.

In our studies, we have found that terms more abstract than *stealing, lying,* and *cheating* are not used in real-life training situations. Children around the age of 9 begin to understand the concept of dishonesty, but they have not had that term used to label unacceptable behavior when they were being punished. The concept is completely intellectual, with no affect associated with it. We were able to teach the children that *honesty* and *dishonesty* included many different kinds of moral behaviors, and they were then able to include cartoons depicting lying, stealing, and cheating in games and in classroom tests under that concept. That knowledge, however, had little impact on the consistency of their actual conduct in those moral situations. Such cognitive control was achieved by having children observe a videotape of a child being severely reprimanded for a rule infraction in a game when the term *honesty* or *dishonesty* was being used. Through vicarious, observational learning, the abstract concept acquired the anxiety-arousing properties required by our model and gained stimulus control—but not automatically, as indicated in the next step.

The model portrayed so far presupposes that the child will use the learned concept to interpret the moral situation and thus initiate the sequence. But we found that that does not just happen. The cognitive process required in classifying a situation must also be considered. The private event of labeling a situation with a concept has to be learned. The individual must recognize that the situation is one calling for a moral response. This becomes the third step in our model. After several studies we have found that to ensure that children actually use their knowledge of a concept to interpret a situation, they must be taught to talk to themselves and to use the critical term when they do so, what Meichenbaum and Goodman (1971) call self-instruction. In this procedure, the "teacher" models playing a game while repeating the rules aloud, followed by the child's imitating the teacher and receiving any needed assistance to ensure that the rules in which the critical term is embedded are actually said. The child then plays the game two more times, the first time just whispering the rules and the second time just thinking them. This training is to increase the likelihood that the child will actually use the critical term when interpreting a new situation that is a very different instance of the class of moral events in which direct tuition has occurred. To illustrate, if *honesty* is the critical term, the self-instructional training in a rule game is to promote the child's labeling other instances of honesty, such as stealing, lying, and cheating on classroom tests, with that term. According to our model, that initiates the chain of events that results in the moral response.

The fourth step in the sequence is the actual moral response. Without the evidence of an impact on action, the required end point, the model has little meaning. The behavioral evidence required is that the history of training portrayed in this model result in some consistency of moral conduct, not just the usual low level of generality across situations.

It is this requirement of generality that serves to bring together the behavioral and cognitive-developmental approaches to moral development. It is the cognitive structure or moral orientation that acts to produce the consistency in the overt behavior, and therefore investigations of how such integrated moral orientations develop are necessary. As the paradox delineated here indicates, however, the research and even the theory of much of this work in moral reasoning has become separated from the ultimate criterion for an assessment of moral development, which is what people do. There is obviously something wrong with a theory of moral development that avoids accounting for a prototypical moral situation by defining it as outside the domain. The model I have proposed recognizes and requires the development of hierarchically ordered conceptions of morality. But it also requires that the learning and use of those cognitive structures remain linked to action. Obviously, the model is incomplete, but it is a much-needed attempt to integrate strengths from both the behavioral and cognitive positions.

REFERENCES

Aronfreed, J. *Conduct and conscience: The socialization of internalized control over behavior.* New York: Academic Press, 1968.

Burton, R. V. Generality of honesty reconsidered. *Psychological Review,* 1963, *70,* 481–499.

Burton, R. V. Honesty and dishonesty. In T. Lickona (Ed.), *Research in moral development and behavior.* Holt, Rinehart and Winston, 1976, 173–197.

Burton, R. V. Interface between the behavioral and cognitive-developmental approaches to research in morality. In B. Z. Presseisen, D. Goldstein, & M. H. Appel (Eds.), *Topics in cognitive development* (Vol. 2): *Language and operational thought.* New York: Plenum, 1977.

Burton, R. V., Maccoby, E. E., & Allinsmith, W. Antecedents of resistance to temptation in four-year-old children. *Child Development,* 1961, *32,* 689–710.

Casey, W. M., & Burton, R. V. Training children to be consistently honest through verbal self-instructions. *Child Development,* 1982, *53,* 911–919.

Colby, A., Gibbs, J., & Kohlberg, L. *Standard form scoring manual.* Cambridge, Mass.: Center for Moral Education, 1980.

Dienstbier, R. A., Hillman, D., Lehnhoff, J., Hillman, J., Valkenaar, M. C. An emotion-attribution approach to moral behavior: Interfacing cognitive and avoidance theories of moral development. *Psychological Review,* 1975, *82,* 299–315.

Dienstbier, R. A., & Munter, P. O. Cheating as a function of the labeling of natural arousal. *Journal of Personality and Social Psychology,* 1971, *17,* 208–213.

Flavell, J. *The developmental psychology of Jean Piaget.* New York: Van Nostrand, 1963.

Hartshorne, H., & May, M. A. *Studies in the nature of character* (Vol. 1): *Studies in deceit.* New York: Macmillan, 1928.

Hartshorne, H., May, M. A., & Maller, J. B. *Studies in the nature of character* (Vol. 2): *Studies in self-control.* New York: Macmillan, 1929.

Hartshorne, H., May, M. A., & Shuttleworth, F. K. *Studies in the nature of character* (Vol. 3): *Studies in the organization of character.* New York: Macmillan, 1930.

Jennings, W. S., & Kohlberg, L. Effects of a just community programme on the moral development of youthful offenders. *Journal of Moral Education,* 1983, *12,* 33–50.

Kohlberg, L. *Development of modes of moral thinking and choice in the years ten to sixteen.* Unpublished doctoral dissertation, University of Chicago, 1958.

Kohlberg, L. Development of moral character and moral ideology. In M. L. Hoffman & L. W. Hoffman (Eds.), *Review of child development research* (Vol. 1). New York: Russell Sage Foundation, 1964.

Kohlberg, L. Moral stages and moralization: The cognitive-developmental approach. In T. Lickona (Ed.), *Moral development and behavior.* New York: Holt, Rinehart and Winston, 1976.

Kohlberg, L., Kauffman, K., Scharf, P., & Hickey, J. The just community approach to corrections: A theory. *Journal of Moral Education,* 1975, *4,* 243–260.

Lickona, T. Moral development and moral education: Piaget, Kohlberg, and beyond. In J. M. Gallagher & J. A. Easley, Jr., *Knowledge and development* (Vol. 2): *Piaget and education.* New York: Plenum, 1978.

Liebert, R. M., & Poulos, R. W. Television as a moral teacher. In T. Lickona (Ed.), *Moral development and behavior.* New York: Holt, Rinehart and Winston, 1976.

Luria, A. R. The role of language in the formation of temporary connections. In B. Simon (Ed.), *Psychology in the Soviet Union*. Stanford, Calif.: Stanford University Press, 1957.

Luria, A. R. *The role of speech in the regulation of normal and abnormal behavior*. New York: Boni & Liveright, 1961.

Meichenbaum, D., & Goodman, J. Training impulsive children to talk to themselves: A means of developing self-control. *Journal of Abnormal Psychology*, 1971, *77*, 115–126.

Miller, G. A., Galanter, E., & Pribram, K. *Plans and the structure of behavior*. New York: Holt, Rinehart and Winston, 1960.

Nisbett, R. E., & Schachter, S. Cognitive manipulation of pain. *Journal of Experimental Social Psychology*, 1966, *2*, 227–236.

Piaget, J. *The moral judgment of the child*. New York: Harcourt Brace, 1932.

Rest, J. R. Morality. In J. Flavell & E. Markman (Vol. Eds.), *Handbook of child psychology* (Vol. 3). New York: Wiley, 1983.

Schachter, S., & Latané, B. Crime, cognition, and the autonomic nervous system. In M. R. Jones (Ed.), *Nebraska Symposium on Motivation* (Vol. 12). Lincoln: University of Nebraska Press, 1964.

Schachter, S., & Singer, J. E. Cognitive, social, and physiological determinants of emotional state. *Psychological Review*, 1962, *69*, 379–399.

Scharf, P., & Hickey, J. The prison and the inmate's conception of legal justice: An experiment in democratic education. *Criminal Justice and Behavior*, 1976, *3*, 107–122.

Sears, R. R., Maccoby, E. E., & Levin, H. *Patterns of child rearing*. New York: Harper & Row, 1957.

Solomon, R. L., Turner, L. H., & Lessac, M. S. Some effects of delay of punishment on resistance to temptation in dogs. *Journal of Personality and Social Psychology*, 1968, *8*, 233–238.

Solomon, R. L., & Wynne, L. C. Traumatic avoidance learning: The principles of anxiety conservation and partial irreversibility. *Psychological Review*, 1954, *61*, 353–385.

Turiel, E. An experimental test of the sequentiality of developmental stages in the child's moral judgments. *Journal of Personality and Social Psychology*, 1966, *3*, 611–618.

Whiting, J. W. M., & Child, I. L. *Child training and personality: A cross-cultural study*. New Haven, Conn.: Yale University Press, 1953.

CHAPTER 12

Content and Structure in Moral Judgment: An Integrative View

MORDECAI NISAN

Theories of moral development have concentrated on either internalization of specific standards (moral content) or self-construction of general principles or orientation (moral structure). Analysis of early socialization and of the cognitive-developmental account of moral judgment suggests that it is necessary to ascribe to moral content an independent status in moral development and decision making, alongside the moral structures. Examination of subjects' responses to moral dilemmas suggests that the norms (standards of behavior, expectations, laws, etc.) and other components of moral content (like values, definitions, and beliefs) are not generated by the structure—the general orientation that characterizes the stage—but are culture dependent. A two-factor model of judgment is proposed, in which structure and content interact in a complex way but are essentially independent factors. According to to the model, the structure determines the choice and the interpretation of the norms and of other considerations that seem relevant in the situation, as well as the formal features of the reasoning (e.g., consistency). The content has a crucial role in determining moral decision but may also affect the structure, that is, the level of reasoning. It is suggested that the structure—the subject of the study of cognitive-developmentalists—indeed develops through the child's attempts to understand his or her social experience, whereas the content—the subject of study of social-learning students—is learned in an associative way through reinforcements and models.

A central controversy in the description and explanation of moral development is that between content and structure approaches. Content approaches suggest that morality develops through acquisition of specific behavioral standards, such as "Thou shalt not steal." The acquisition of standards is a special type of learning, involving a sense of obligation and affective responses. Different theories have suggested different mechanisms for this learning, including conditioning, identification and imitation (see Chaps. 10 and 11). Structural approaches, on the other hand, suggest that morality develops through the constant attempt of the child to understand the social world and to find effective solutions to conflicts encountered in his or her social experience. Through contemplating and understanding, the child formulates a general orientation regarding right and wrong, and this orientation, or structure, instructs his or her behavior in the various situations encountered. Thus, moral decisions of the individual are necessary conclusions derived from his or her structuring of the situation (see Chaps. 3 and 4).

These two approaches arose from different types of phenomena and, as one might expect, "fit" and "feel" better when viewed in this context. The content theorists have been impressed primarily by the well-developed codification in the moral domain, by the existence of clear, affect-laden standards of behavior that are explicitly and emphatically transmitted to children. In contrast, the structure theorists have been impressed mainly by the creative features of morality, by the ability of the individual to make decisions in novel and complex situations on the basis of definable principles; these decisions are perceived as obligatory, rational, and universally valid.

The two approaches have different implications in regard to moral development (Nisan, 1983), enabling the researcher to weigh the merits of each approach. This weighing process has tended to lead researchers in the field to select one approach and abandon the other. We propose that neither of the approaches provides a satisfactory explanation of moral judgment and that an integrated approach is required. In presenting our arguments, our starting point will be the structural approach, which we believe to have considerable theoretical strength and empirical support. We assume that moral behavior is based on moral judgment, that such judgment is based on a general structure, in the sense that the individual's moral considerations in different situations derive from and can be characterized by a unifying orientation or structure, and that there is a developmental order in the appearance of these structures. Given the foregoing assumptions, we shall attempt to demonstrate that the structural approach does not provide us with a complete and adequate explanation of moral development. We shall further suggest a two-factor model of moral judgment, including both structure and content. Our contention is that each of the approaches outlined earlier relates to a separate factor and that an integration of both approaches is necessary for a more complete explanation.

The body of the chapter will be divided into four sections. First, we demonstrate the need for an independent role of moral content, in the form of norms, within a structural analysis of moral judgment. Second, we identify and examine the various components of moral content, with the aim of tracing their origin; we see that they are not necessarily structurally derived. Third, we point to the role of the structure in moral decision making, leading us to the fourth part: a schematic presentation of a two-factor model of moral judgment, including both content and structure. In the conclusion, we advance the suggestion—further developed elsewhere (Nisan, in press)—that the content has an independent status, sometimes resisting the dominance of the structure.

THE NEED TO CONSIDER AN INDEPENDENT ROLE FOR MORAL CONTENT

Two types of considerations may lead cognitive-developmental students of moral behavior to consider the importance of moral content (i.e., of specific behavioral standards) in moral judgment: (1) an examination of moral socialization in childhood, and (2) an examination of the process of moral judgment (as described by the structural approach). The first examination suggests that it is reasonable to expect cultural standards to affect moral judgment. The second points out the inadequacy of the structural approach alone in explaining moral decision.

Moral Socialization in Childhood

In contrast to the development of conservation or hypothetical-deductive reasoning, which are not taught formally or directly, the teaching of moral standards is a focal point in socialization. From a very young age, children receive explicit instructions in regard to certain behaviors. The child is told not to hit, break, and so on. Moral socialization involves reward and punishment of the child, as well as modeling and identification (Sears, Raw, & Alpert, 1965). The result is a set of specific standards or rules that are quite well known by the child. Indeed, the mores of a culture are generally formulated in a specific manner, reflected by the way in which children are taught and how they are known to and expressed by the child. It is tempting to speculate that the level of rules ("Thou shalt not steal") is the "natural" intermediary level (e.g., between "Thou shalt not steal money" and the golden rule) in the sense that Rosch (1975) uses the term *level* in her treatment of concept learning.

In order to effectively inhibit behaviors deemed destructive in a given society that serve self-interest (Freud's "pleasure principle"), moral teaching must be very potent. And indeed socialization theorists have mentioned several features that make it a powerful, and to some extent irreversible, learning (e.g., its earliness, emotionality, frequency, and consistency). This learning is assimilated into the child's ways of understanding, as a structuralist would claim. It is undeniable, however, that the individual's conception of morality includes beliefs accepted from the outside world, from authorities he or she admires and believes to be knowledgeable in this field (as is true also for an adult's conception of the world, which includes "adopted" beliefs, e.g., that the earth rotates around the sun). Effects of socialization have been established in several domains (Goslin, 1969), and it seems reasonable to assume that the ongoing and affect-laden moral learning in childhood, focusing on standards of behavior, leaves deep traces in one's moral development. We therefore expect a degree of independence for established standards, as opposed to being just "aliment for the structures." The foregoing is, of course, only suggestive, and it brings us to the following analysis of the role of norms in the process of moral judgment.

The Role of Content in Kohlbergian Description of Moral Judgment

Even a superficial examination of Lawrence Kohlberg's approach will show its insufficiency in explaining moral judgment, and therefore in explaining moral development as well. The most obvious point is that the structures—or the stages—do not explain the direction of one's decision in a moral dilemma. Kohlberg claims that the highest stage does dictate a certain choice. Indeed, Kohlberg and Candee (Chap. 4 in this book) have shown that as one ascends the stages, the trend is toward greater agreement concerning the appropriate action. This may be true for some dilemmas but not for others, and even when it occurs, it may reflect cultural rather than structural effects. Indeed, in light of the long-standing disagreement among philosophers with regard to moral problems, it hardly seems reasonable to expect that high-stage structure can generate a clear-cut direction of decision in moral dilemmas. Furthermore, even if it were proven true that the highest stage dictates the decision, one would still seek explanations for choice in conventional stages, which, after all, constitute the modal stage of adults.

A clue for such an explanation is provided by an analysis of the structures, or stages, as proposed by Kohlberg. Such analysis reveals that each stage conveys the individual toward a certain class of behavioral standards, in accordance with its social perspective and logic. For example, in the second stage these are the standards related to and conveyed through concrete rewards and punishments, dictated by the holders of power; in the third stage they are the expectations of significant others; in the fourth stage, rules and laws of a more formal character; and in the fifth stage, rules and laws examined in light of agreed-upon principles within a social-contract framework. Thus, each stage directs the individual toward certain types of standards that are largely independent of the logic of that stage. Although the selection of one or another type of standard is anchored in the moral structure and derives from its logic, the specific content of the standards does not.

To further clarify this issue, we turn now to an examination of moral content. We shall look at its components and examine their relationship to the structure.

COMPONENTS OF MORAL CONTENT

In the present context, the term *moral content* refers primarily to internalized behavioral instructions regarding right and wrong, or, as we shall call them, norms. These norms may be explicitly formulated, as in laws and rules, or they may be implicit, as in the case of expectations of authority figures (parents, teachers, and various other leaders) or of peers. Whether explicitly or implicitly formulated, moral norms arise from external sources and are adopted, as opposed to being derived, by the child.

The learning of norms is unique in that the child comes to perceive them as objective data of a prescriptive nature, rather than as arbitrary instructions. In contrast with acquaintance with the moral norms of a foreign culture, the norms of one's own culture are perceived by the individual as representing the objective right and wrong. This attitude originates not only from direct injunctions with regard to right and wrong but also through an inferential process leading the child to conclude that a forbidden deed is wrong whereas the socially required one is right. Such an inferential process is based on the need for meaningful and consistent knowledge (e.g., Heider, 1958) and is reflected in Paiget's (1932/1965) finding that young children define "wrong" according to punishment and prohibition. The existence of such a process is also implied by some sociologists. Berger and Luckmann (1967), for example, suggested that institutionalized norms come to be perceived as rational and objective. According to this suggestion, conceptions of right and wrong are not inherent to humanity, but rather are culture dependent and are conveyed through the norms of a given culture.

The preceding position is discordant with Turiel's (1978; see also Chap. 15 in this book) interpretation of his findings that children as young as 5 years of age already recognize the distinction between moral issues, which are concerned with matters of justice and welfare, and issues of social convention, which are concerned with societal organization and coordination. Turiel's finding therefore suggests that moral norms are constructed by the child, at an early age, based on intrinsic aspects of the behaviors involved relating to human well-being and fairness. For this reason, behaviors prohibited by moral norms were judged by the children as wrong, even under conditions of lack of rules or laws forbidding such behaviors. It appears that the young child has already developed primitive moral structures, enabling him or her to derive norms and to make decisions accordingly. Turiel's account implies that moral norms, such as the definition of right and wrong, are not internalized from external sources and therefore are not culture dependent, but rather are "discovered" by the developing child. Our own research does not support these claims. Following Turiel's studies, we have investigated children's perceptions of social rules with four cultural groups in Israel: religious, nonreligious, and kibbutz Jewish children, and Muslim children. The children studied were in the first (6–7 years old) and the fifth (10–11 years) grades. Each child, individually interviewed, was presented with a number of stories recounting behaviors performed against the law or without the existence of a prohibitive law. The children were asked if the behavior was wrong, if so, to what extent, and what they thought the law should be. The results revealed that the children's distinction according to Turiel's criteria (whether a behavior is considered wrong even though there is no law prohibiting it, and whether they think there should be a law prohibiting it) is affected by cultural notions. The same behavior could be considered to be morally wrong (i.e., independent of existing law) by one group but not by another. For example, the bathing of boys and girls together was regarded as a serious sin (independent of law) by Muslim and religious Jewish children but not at all by kibbutz children. Referring to an adult by his or her first name was considered morally wrong by the Muslim children but only conventionally wrong (i.e., depending on a norm) by the other three groups. The classification of behaviors as right or wrong, the degree of approbation and censure, and the children's opinions as to what the law should be showed clear cultural differences (although not always easily explained). Our results suggest that at least some specific moral norms are culture dependent and not structurally derived.

Due to the basic human condition, some behaviors are universally prohibited among the different cultures. However, this cross-cultural agreement does not prove the claim that intrinsic features of acts are the source of their being judged morally wrong. On the other hand, cultural differences in moral perceptions, including viewing an act as wrong (independent of law) or mere convention, do support the claim that social norms determine perception of right and wrong.

Although the norm is the natural unit of moral content(in the sense that content is formulated and transmitted through norms), we can distinguish between various components of moral norms. These are generally implicit in the norms, but the components may also be formulated and perceived separately. For a better understanding of environmental influences on the moral content of the individual, it is useful to examine the relationship between different environments, or cultures, and components of the norm. Such an examination can be supported empirically. We have interviewed bright Israeli high school students about various moral dilemmas, some of which were taken from Kohlberg's test and some relating to other social issues such as emigration from Israel, censorship of movies, and so on. We were trying to uncover the links between the general structure, or principle, used by the subjects and the decisions arrived at. In order to maximize the variety of final decisions, we compared students from religious and nonreligious schools. Although the two groups did not differ in average level of moral judgment or in school grade-point average, there was great variety within, but more markedly between, the two groups in their choices. In our interviews we attempted to expose the origins of these differences, in order to discover implicit components of moral content. Analysis of the interviews identified several such components, which can generally be classified into evaluative and cognitive components.

Evaluative Components

Moral norms and judgments are based on value judgments; they represent evaluation of behaviors in terms of what Rokeach (1973) calls "terminal" values, particularly justice and welfare. A great deal of the variation in our subjects' decisions could be attributed to differences in value judgments. Thus, some of our subjects considered emigration from Israel to be morally wrong (e.g., because it undermines the existence of the nation and the culture), whereas for others it had no moral significance. Similarly, premarital sexual relations were considered morally wrong by some subjects but not by others. Such differences were found between adolescents at the same stage of moral judgment, including Stage 4/5 (using Kohlberg's old manual); thus, they reflect cultural variation in values. As many social philosophers contend, such differences cannot be rationally solved (Cohen & Ben-Ari, Note 1).

A related issue is that of hierarchy of values. Moral dilemmas, such as those used by Kohlberg, involve conflict between two or more values, the solution for which may require an ordering of priorities among the values. Such hierarchical ordering may be a part of the moral content of a culture. Sometimes it is explicit; one example is a frequent reply of Israeli children to the Heinz dilemma: "Life comes before everything else." This answer is based on an explicit cultural (religious) instruction, and it is not structural but is rather a norm (or content). More frequently, the hierarchy is conveyed only implicitly, such as in different ideologies with regard to values of freedom and equality. Differences in the priority of values were the basis of some of the variance in our subjects' decisions. Thus, although all subjects apparently agreed on values of national security, private rights, self-actualization, and obligation to one's people, they explicitly declared different orderings of these values. These differences were predictably related to subcultural background.

Ordering of values is included in Kohlberg's description of Stage 5. He suggests that ordering of values is dictated by the structure (as exemplified by the ordering of the values "life" and "property"). As mentioned previously, the continuous philosophical debate in relation to this issue and to commensurability of values, however, raises much doubt in regard to this claim. In any case, it is clear that prior to Stage 5 the hierarchy of values is culture dependent.

Another expression of this issue is the perceived gravity of different behaviors. Subjects of different ages understand and answer questions such as How bad is behavior X? or Which is worse, behavior X or behavior Y? when X and Y differ qualitatively. The replies to such questions appear to be systematically related to cultural expectations and norms. Thus Arab and Jewish children in Israel differ significantly and predictably in their rating of the gravity of disobeying father, going undressed in public, and so on. A more complex issue put to the children was that of individual misbehaviors that harmed the group, such as Daniel has not confessed to stealing an exam, thereby causing cancellation of a class trip. Kibbutz children rated this as a more serious offense than did city children, and as less serious than offenses intended to help a friend (such as, David stole stamps for a sick friend). These differences point to cultural effects on evaluation of gravity of an offense, a variable that is closely related to moral action.

Cognitive Components

Cultural norms imply and convey definitions or beliefs that are of central importance in determining moral decisions and behavior. Any adequate explanation of moral judgment must relate to these cognitive components, which are to a great extent culture dependent.

Two types of definitions emerged from our study: The first are definitions regarding the limits of required or prohibited behavior, such as the limits of parental rights and obligations toward children and vice versa, and of a citizen's obligation to his or her country. Although all subjects agreed on the norms themselves, subjects at the same Kohlbergian stage of moral judgment, even within the same culture, revealed a wide range of variation in their definitions of these norms. The second type of definitions regards the boundaries of the domain within which the moral obligations apply. For example, do they apply to a fetus or only to an infant or older child? The problem of definition is relevant even at advanced stages of moral judgment, as it appears to underlie such phenomena as slavery and murdering people outside one's tribe. History reveals that such definitions vary across time and place, although for the people involved they are always a given, that is, a derivation from the natural law.

Beliefs about the world are another component of moral content that has an effect on moral choice. Some norms are based on such beliefs and at the same time serve to transmit them, rendering them "facts." Such beliefs may be held independently of the norms, or they may be only inherent in a norm.

Thus, our subjects held different opinions about capital punishment, which were found to be related to their beliefs about human nature and the effects of capital punishment on potential terrorists and murderers. Similarly, some of our subjects were in favor of censoring pornographic and violent movies, based on their belief that watching such films tends to increase crime and violence. Beliefs such as these, which clearly underlie moral judgment, often stem from moral norms internalized by the individual. Thus religious students, who condemned acts forbidden by Jewish law, justified their attitude with the argument that these acts delay the arrival of redemption and are therefore destructive both to the individual and to society. Whether such beliefs are mere rationalizations makes no difference with regard to our contention: The essential points are that they do not derive from the structure and that they are important determinants of moral judgment.

We add here that the norm not only transmits definitions and beliefs but also helps to formulate social reality, determining new interpretations for behavior that have clear implications for moral judgment. Thus, the norm not to address an adult by his or her first name confers a certain social connotation on such behavior—it is designated as harmful. For example, our Arab subjects considered the use of first names to be morally wrong, independent of law, because for them it constitutes an insulting and hence harmful behavior. This example demonstrates that the distinction between intrinsically bad behaviors and those based on social convention is extremely shaky. The intrinsicality of physical harm, based on physiological data, is no more intrinsic than that of psychological harm, based on social-meaning data.

In conclusion, the analysis of interviews of subjects reaching different decisions although using similar structure (as measured by Kohlberg's stages) helped us to identify a number of components of moral content. These components, of the evaluative and cognitive types, are inherent in the norms and are transmitted by them, and each may affect moral choice. These components are "open," in the sense that they are not derived from the moral structure but are "filled in" by cultural expectations. Their content is not arbitrary, however, as shown by the systematic and consistent differences between the groups. This indicates that cultural norms and expectations are the source of these components of content.

STRUCTURAL EFFECTS ON MORAL DECISION

Our discussion of moral content has emphasized that norms, which have a crucial role in determining moral choice, are not entirely derived from the moral structure. If the structure were purely formal, however, having no effect on moral decision, its study would be merely an exercise in a form of thinking rather than in moral development. This is clearly not the case. The moral structures are not empty frameworks; they do have an effect on moral choice.

In the present context, the term *moral structures* refers to the stages of moral judgment as described by Kohlberg. Each stage represents a mode of perceiving relations between people and a conception of the optimal coordination between people holding differing expectations, desires, and claims. The structure, or stage, includes a variety of elements, along a spectrum ranging from criteria for evaluation of behavior to specific conceptions of human needs and values.

As stated previously, the moral structure is not purely formal. It suggests principles applicable to specific domains—interpersonal and social relations—and hence it must include certain content. This content relates to what is perceived as the invariants of human nature and social organization. Although some of these perceived "invariants" may be determined by environmental factors, as suggested earlier, there can be little doubt that many of the basic characteristics of humanity are not culture bound. These universals provide the content base of the structures. Indeed, each of the stages includes specific contents, from the predominance of concrete instrumental considerations in Stage 2 to the assumption of human equality in Stage 6 (Puka, 1980).

The contents of each stage reveals a coherence and an internal organization, suggesting a generalized orientation. We call it a structure so long as it serves as a basis for understanding a situation and a rationale for decision making. When a person "develops" into a higher stage, his or her previous rationale is integrated into a broader set of considerations and in this sense is transformed into a content. Thus, consideration of interpersonal reciprocity and sympathy, which serves as the main basis for judgment at Stage 3, constitutes only a part of the broader orientation of Stage 4, in which it is integrated into a more formal social perspective. This concept of a structure as being relative to the stage was suggested by Piaget (1970) regarding his stages of cognitive development.

The content features of the structure, as well as its more formal properties (contingent on its relationship to cognitive development), may provide it with an effect on moral content, including choice. We shall now examine the possible effects of the moral structure on components of moral content discussed earlier, which may be considered the foundation of moral choice.

The primary effect of the structure is probably its determinance of the relevant behavioral standards, consequent to the social perspective it dictates. At times, all the structures direct the individual to the same clear and explicit norms. In many cases, however, there are no explicit norms, or they are amenable to different interpretations, or there may be different or even contradictory expectations. In such cases, the structure determines (1) where to look for the moral standards, and/or (2) which expectation is valid, and/or (3) how the norm is interpreted. The resulting moral judgment and decision are based on these interpretations.

The following study provides an example of the role of structure in choice of valid expectations. Tenth-grade high school students were confronted with a dilemma concerning cheating on a matriculation exam. The dilemma presented was an actual event reported in the press: A teacher had helped his students with their exam so that the school would achieve higher academic standing. The problem thus presented a conflict between expectations of students and teachers, on one hand, and of law or society at large, on the other. The findings showed that a higher rate of students at Stages 3/4 and 4, as compared with lower stages, believed that the valid expectations were those of "society" and considered the cheating morally wrong.

In addition to selection of norms, moral structure also determines the norms' interpretation and thus affects their perceived meaning and validity. In contrast to the dilemma described earlier, in many cases the expectations of law, school, teachers, and students are in accord. Yet, there may be different perceptions as to the validity and boundaries of the agreed-upon norm. Such differences are exemplified in the following study: Adult members of a kibbutz were presented with Kohlberg's dilemmas and were also asked to name the people who most frequently took part in "extra-work," when requested in urgent situations (such as gathering tomatoes after a hot day). The results showed a significant relationship between moral judgment and "extra-work." Subjects revealing postconventional moral reasoning were chosen more frequently than were conventional-reasoning ones. On the basis of further interviews, it was concluded that only the postconventionals considered "extra-work" to be a valid obligation. These subjects held the social-contract point of view, rendering prescriptivity to a nondefined obligation.

The moral structure may also affect specific components of moral content. Analysis of the stages suggests that they may determine which values are taken into consideration in the moral decision situation. It appears that only from Stage 3 onward does the individual consider the value of interpersonal trust, which may lead to a decision that stealing a sum of money through cheating is worse than by robbery (one of Kohlberg's dilemmas). The value of social order is considered only from Stage 4. On the basis of his studies on political socialization, Adelson (1971) indicates that until the age of 13 children consider only consequences to individuals, not to the social system. This finding is in accord with the previous analysis.

A related aspect is the needs the individual takes into consideration in making moral decisions. The existence of a relationship between needs and development level has been suggested by several theorists (Harvey, Hunt, & Schroder, 1961; Loevinger, 1976). Kohlberg and Jacquette (Note 2) did indeed find a relationship between level of moral judgment and relative level of several needs measured by McClelland's system. Subjects at Stage 2 tended to be higher in need for power; at Stage 3, in need for affiliation; and at Stage 4, in need for achievement. Perception of needs is a primary criterion in evaluating the welfare of people and thus is an important determinant in decision making.

The effects of structure on the evaluative components of moral content, discussed earlier, have a cognitive side as well. Thus, one would expect the norm "Thou shalt honor thy father and thy mother" to be defined differently at different stages, according to the conception of human needs and values (e.g., at Stage 2 it will be mainly in concrete-instrumental terms, at Stage 3 in emotional and love terms, and so on). Apart from these effects on the definitions and beliefs that feed moral decision, however, there is also a more general, cognitive-style type of effect. This is the effect elaborated by Kohlberg. At the higher stages, we may expect a better ability to deal with more complex (e.g., multivariable) problems, a broader perspective, and more consistent application of logical rules. Thus, although the young child has intuitive structures of justice (e.g., Damon, 1977), when the child is confronted with more complex moral dilemmas, such as those of Kohlberg, this structure may not be apparent. One may speculate that the child is overwhelmed by the multiplicity of considerations and is rendered unable to apply his or her intuitive moral concepts. The higher the stage of moral judgment, the better the individual is able to use these concepts—that is, he or she is able to differentiate between more considerations relating to broader and more "abstract" social perspectives (Selman, 1980). In the same vein, more complex moral stages allow the individual to be less dependent on the literal norm and its implicit components; a broader perspective enables him or her to decide on the relevance of the norm and the appropriateness of its definition and interpretation, and he or she may even question the validity of the norm itself. Yet, we must reiterate the importance of the role of culture in this process. There is not enough empirical research in this area to permit us to speak definitively on this issue; however, human experience leads one to believe that the effect of structure on definitions and beliefs is quite limited; for example, it has not prevented some presumably high-stage people from subscribing to definitions of others as being subhuman.

This overview reveals the important role of moral structures in determining moral content and choice. Yet, we must bear in mind that the structure directs an individual to a *class* of expectations rather than to specific ones. Thus, for example, Stage 3 is characterized by valuing interpersonal relations and directs the individual to expectations of significant others. Culture (in its broad sense) will determine the nature of interpersonal relations, however, as well as the specific expectations of its people. Anthropological studies show wide variation in expectations, norms, values, and beliefs; it is this variation, rather than the unity detectable beneath it, that we focus on at this point.

The combined influence of content and structure on moral decision making becomes apparent on examination of the choices (as well as other components of moral judgment) across different stages and cultures. We have examined the data of a longitudinal and cross-sectional study in Turkey, including both city and village subjects (Nisan & Kohlberg, 1982). The results showed a significant effect of the stage on moral choice: The higher the stage, the more subjects tended to declare that Heinz should steal the drug (from one of Kohlberg's dilemmas; the actual Turkish story differed somewhat). Stage does not explain all variance in moral choice, however. In comparing subjects at the same stage from the city and from the traditional village, we found a significant difference between them: The villagers tended not to recommend stealing the drug. Examination of the interviews suggested that the difference between the cultures is related to moral content. In the village, stealing was considered to be a most serious sin, and even those who said Heinz should steal found it necessary to soften and reserve their decision.

A MODEL OF MORAL JUDGMENT

The foregoing has pointed to the roles of both content and structure in moral decision making. The discussion suggests that our present state of knowledge requires a two-factor model of moral judgment, the factors being content and structure—neither of which can be reduced by the other.

According to the suggested model, the moral system consists of (1) a general principle (structure), or orientation, regarding right and wrong, based on a certain mode of understanding social relations; and (2) an aggregate of specific standards (content) of forbidden and required behaviors, each of which is marked according to level of seriousness, conditions under which it should or should not be followed, and so on. Between these two basic and independent factors, the individual (with the help of culture) may construct any number of intermediary generalizations and rules, based on, and bridging, the two factors. Such intermediary rules serve to facilitate moral decision making, on one hand, and to rationalize and render the system coherent, on the other.

The moral system is activated when a behavior (planned or already performed) conflicting with the principle or a standard is perceived. The operation of the system requires a judgment and choice regarding the appropriateness of the behavior. The complete process may include the following phases: (1) examination of the behavior in light of the general principle (and of intermediary rules); (2) reference to the aggregate of standards; (3) quest for relevant information, as dictated by the principles and the standards; (4) re-examination of the behavior in light of the standards referred to, the information, the intermediary rules, and the overriding principle. Each behavioral alternative considered in the situation will undergo this process and will be compared with the others.

Our hypothesized process is a conceptual model; it is not intended to be a description of all (or even most) moral judgments. Phases of the model may be omitted, and the judgment process may not be sequential, as described here, but rather may involve parallel lines of judgment (with points of interaction). Indeed, we have suggested elsewhere (Nisan, in press) that in some cases the immediate response to an (already performed or merely contemplated) misbehavior is based on content alone, without reference to a general principle, and further that parallel to the structural judgment a partially independent judgment by content may occur.

The model calls for separate explanations of the developments of content and of structure. Without entering the metatheoretical issue of the relative merits of the two opposing approaches to socialization—social learning and cognitive developmental—we shall put forth the suggestion that each of the theories provides an explanation of one of the factors mentioned and that each approach is necessary to explain the development of one of the two factors. Although internalization theorists claim to have an adequate explanation of general principles of moral judgment (Liebert, 1979, and Chap. 10 in this book), they have dealt primarily, and more successfully, with explanations of specific norms. The learning mechanisms suggested by this approach, such as reinforcement and imitation, are related to specific behaviors, and most clearly their direct result is learning of norms or low-level principles.

Cognitive-developmental theory, on the other hand, relates to development of structures, or general principles, as a result of the individual's attempt to understand his or her experiences and to find solutions to the problems they pose. This explanation is not clearly relevant to learning of norms, which is based on acquiring affect-laden information about the social world. As previously argued, the content is somewhat arbitrary and does not derive logically from the interaction between the individual and his or her social environment, and certainly not in early childhood. Therefore, the learning of content is necessarily associative, at least in childhood, the most significant age for the acquisition of norms (though structuralists emphasize that the content is always assimilated into the existing structures).

The two-factor model seems adequate for explanation of both the universality and the variation found in moral judgment. Turiel (1972) claims that cross-cultural research showing universality in the stages of moral development does not support the claim that moral values are acquired through internalization of cultural contents. Turiel contends that although the internalization view of moral learning would predict cross-cultural differences in morality combined with intracultural commonality over different ages, cross-cultural findings show just the opposite: commonality across cultures combined with age differences within cultures. Internalization theorists, however, cite anthropological data apparently showing exactly what Turiel claims to be their prediction: commonality within a culture and variation across cultures. The apparent contradiction stems from the different classes of data used by the two factions. If one examines the norms, one is likely to find variation across cultures and commonality within a culture; when one examines the structure, one finds age differences within each culture but similarity in the structures across cultures.

Applying our model to a concrete example, such as Milgram's (1974) experiment, may help to point out its merits. The subject in this experiment is instructed to deliver an electric shock to another person. This order, of course, creates a moral dilemma, because it contradicts a moral principle and a specific moral norm (that one does not harm another person). The subject is thrust into a conflict between this norm and the norm of fulfilling the requirements of his or her role as a subject. The individual's decision is affected both by structure, which determines which norms are relevant and how to choose among them, and by the norms operating in the experiment. On receiving an instruction to deliver a shock, the individual examines the situation according to his or her principles. Stage 4 or 5 principles are likely to give precedence to the norm not to harm, and the subject will quit the experiment. Lower-stage principles may lead to preference for the authority and role-fulfillment norms, and the subject will continue. The social value of these norms, however, also affects the decision (at least of subjects in preconventional and conventional stages). Thus, in a society that places high value on obedience to authority and role fulfillment, subjects are more likely to obey the experimenter. For some citizens of prewar Japan, obedience to the emperor was the highest value and led apparently high-stage people to commit hara-kiri. On the other hand, in a society that places little value on obedience, we expect to find less, even in low-stage people. Studies have indeed found cross-cultural differences in rates of obedience (Milgram, 1974), as well as differences among people of different stages.

CONCLUSION

Starting from a structural view of moral judgment, viewing it as based on general principles developed through the child's attempts to find a coherent structure appropriate to his or her social experience, this chapter has attempted to emphasize the role of content in moral judgment. It was proposed that observation of moral learning in early childhood suggests the importance of specific standards of behavior, or norms, in moral development and judgment. An analysis of the structures described by Kohlberg, and empirically supported, shows that at each stage the individual refers to norms or expectations that do not derive from the structure. The norms that constitute the base of moral content include evaluative components (e.g., values, gravity of act) and cognitive components (definitions and beliefs). Moral content helps to explain the direction of choice in moral dilemmas, which cannot be entirely attributed to the structure. At the same time, we have also pointed out the contribution of the structure to moral choice, through its effect on choice of relevant norms, on their interpretation, and on the general approach to the moral dilemma.

The discussion of the role of content and structure led us to the conclusion that neither can be reduced to the other and that a complete explanation of moral development and moral judgment requires an integration of the two factors. Accordingly, a two-factor model of moral judgment was suggested, including both a moral structure and a moral content, that is, an aggregate of behavioral standards or expectations. The moral structure is said to "choose" and interpret the relevant content (norms). It was suggested that moral content develops through social learning, whereas the principles develop through cognitive structuralization.

The model may present a distorted picture of the role of content in moral judgment. It depicts the norms as secondary, as serving the structure and being tempered by it. This picture may not always hold true. Examination of a broad range of moral judgments, hypothetical as well as actual, reveals that the norms have an independent status; their effects are not completely dominated by the structures. We deal more broadly elsewhere (Nisan, in press) with four expressions of this independent status:

1. In some cases the role of the moral principle may be minimal; the decision is made mainly on the basis of a salient norm. Salience of norms can be manipulated, and we cite experimental evidence of its effect on decisions and presumably on the process of judgment.
2. Content, in the form of salient norms, values, and so on, may affect the level of judgment, that is, the structure used by the individual in his or her reasoning. For example, we show how changing the site of a moral dilemma, thereby raising the salience of a norm, changes the level of reasoning.
3. Content may affect the individual's beliefs about a situation. Examples are cited showing how the individual may distort the information and beliefs he or she holds about the situation in order to conform (either in choice or behavior) with a salient norm.

4. Even after a structural decision that is opposed to a salient norm has been made, the individual may feel uncomfortable (irrational guilt) about it, which may affect his or her later behavior, including in relation to the choice already made.

These four expressions of the independent status of norms may be seen as different levels of resistance of the content to be assimilated by the structure.

Our final point, regarding the uncomfortable feeling accompanying a decision that apparently violates a norm, may give us a cue to better understanding the functioning of norms. It appears that the content is dominated by affect, either that generated by social learning (see Chap. 11) or that by the empathic tendency (Hoffman, 1977, and Chap. 16 in this book). Norms have a script-type (Abelson, 1981) character; they constitute an organized whole that is responded to in a holistic undifferentiated manner, a manner characteristic of affective response. Zajonce's (1980) suggestions regarding the independent status of affect seem a good explanation of, and indeed are supported by, our observations of the independence of content.

REFERENCES

Abelson, R. P. Psychological status of the script concept. *American Psychologist,* 1981, *36,* 715–729.

Adelson, J. The political imagination of the young adolescent. *Daedalus,* 1971, *100,* 1013–1050.

Berger, P. L., & Luckmann, T. *The social construction of reality.* New York: Doubleday (Anchor Books), 1967.

Damon, W. *The social world of the child.* San Francisco: Jossey-Bass, 1977.

Goslin, D. A. (Ed.). *Handbook of socialization theory and research.* Skokie, Ill.: Rand McNally, 1969.

Harvey, O. J., Hunt, D. E., & Schroder, H. M. *Conceptual systems and personality organization.* New York: Wiley, 1961.

Heider, F. *The psychology of interpersonal relations.* New York: Wiley, 1958.

Hoffman, M. Empathy, its development and prosocial implications. In C. B. Keasey (Ed.), *Nebraska Symposium on Motivation* (Vol. 25). Lincoln: University of Nebraska Press, 1977.

Liebert, R. M. Moral development: A theoretical and empirical analysis. In G. J. Whitehurst & B. J. Zimmerman (Eds.), *The functions of language and cognition.* New York: Academic Press, 1979.

Loevinger, J. *Ego development.* San Francisco: Jossey-Bass, 1976.

Milgram, S. *Obedience to authority: An experimental view.* New York: Harper & Row, 1974.

Nisan, M. Two approaches to the development of moral judgment. In M. Nisan & U. Last (Eds.), *Between psychology and education.* Jerusalem: Magnes Press, 1983.

Nisan, M. The primacy of moral content. In L. Kohlberg & D. Candee (Eds.), *Recent research in moral development*. Cambridge, Mass.: Harvard University Press, in press.

Nisan, M., & Kohlberg, L. Universality and variation in moral judgment—A longitudinal and cross-sectional study in Turkey. *Child Development*, 1982, *53*, 865–876.

Piaget, J. *The moral judgment of the child*. New York: Free Press, 1965. (Originally published, 1932.)

Piaget, J. *Structuralism*. New York: Basic Books, 1970.

Puka, B. Kohlbergian forms and Deweyan acts: A response. In B. Munsey (Ed.), *Moral development, moral education and Kohlberg*. Birmingham, Alabama: Religious Education Press, 1980.

Rokeach, M. *The nature of human values*. New York: Free Press, 1973.

Rosch, E. Universals and cultural specifics in human categorization. In R. Brislin, S. Bochner, & W. Lonner (Eds.), *Cross-cultural perspectives on learning*. Beverly Hills, Calif.: Sage, 1975.

Sears, R. R., Raw, L., & Alpert, R. *Identification and child rearing*. Stanford, Calif.: Stanford University Press, 1965.

Selman, R. L. *The growth of interpersonal understanding*. New York: Academic Press, 1980.

Turiel, E. Stage transition in moral development. In R. M. Travers (Ed.), *Second handbook on research in teaching*. Skokie, Ill.: Rand McNally, 1972.

Turiel, E. Social convention and morality: Two distinct conceptual and developmental systems. In C. B. Keasey (Ed.), *Nebraska Symposium on Motivation* (Vol. 25). Lincoln: University of Nebraska Press, 1979.

Zajonce, R. B. Feeling and thinking: Preferences need no inferences. *American Psychologist*, 1980, *35*, 151–175.

REFERENCE NOTES

1. Cohen, E., & Ben-Ari, E. *Hard choices: The sociological analysis of value commensurability*. Unpublished manuscript, Hebrew University of Jerusalem, 1981.

2. Kohlberg, L., & Jacquette, D. *Level of moral judgment and relative strength of needs*. Unpublished manuscript, Harvard University, School of Education, 1980.

PART FIVE

Social-Personality
Theory Approaches

CHAPTER 13

Moral Action as Autointerpretation

ROBERT HOGAN AND CATHERINE BUSCH

This chapter places moral development within the context of personality development as a whole. We conceptualize personality structure in terms of three components: a self-image, images of what significant others expect of one during interaction, and behaviors designed to tell others how one would like to be regarded during interaction. From this perspective, moral conduct is a form of autointerpretation; it is conduct designed to maximize the disapproval of significant others in one's life. We then show how autonomous moral conduct can be interpreted in these terms. Finally, we offer data to support our theoretical claims.

For perhaps 30 years American psychology languished in the chilly embrace of logical positivism and behaviorism. According to *Psychological Abstracts*, for example, between 1930 and 1960 research on the topics of values and moral conduct was virtually nonexistent. Consequently, the emergence of moral development as a legitimate field of academic study was one of the more encouraging evolutions in the social sciences of the 1960s. It was encouraging because values are at the heart of the social process, and it is impossible to conceive of an intellectually valid social psychology that does not provide a persuasive account of how individuals develop their particular moral postures. Such an account is not possible from a traditional behaviorist perspective, but that point is beyond the scope of this chapter.

As the content of this book indicates, two theoretical viewpoints largely dominate moral development research today. These are cognitive-developmental psychology and modern social-learning theory. In their own ways, both traditions have substantially advanced our knowledge regarding various aspects of the moralization process. Nonetheless, there are sound theoretical reasons for trying to develop alternative perspectives. Our efforts along these lines are motivated by the belief that both the social-learning and the cognitive-developmental approaches to moral psychology are rather circumscribed in their theoretical focuses. Although we are also critical of many aspects of psychoanalytic theory, psychoanalysis, as a theoretical account of moral development, has the singular virtue of placing the moralization process in the context of personality development more broadly conceived. Because neither social-learning theory nor cognitive-developmental psychology was originally intended as a theory of personality, it is perhaps unfair to criticize them on the grounds of narrow focus. Let us simply note, then, that our perspective is unique in its attempt to consider moral development from the perspective of a systematic theory of personality.

In this chapter we provide an example of how moral development can be understood in terms of personality theory. The chapter is divided into four sections. In the next section we present a point of view on the structure of personality. This is followed by a section on personality development. The chapter then takes up the problems of autonomy and conformity. The last section of the chapter presents some preliminary data relevant to the claim that modern moral psychology contains a very interesting bias.

THE STRUCTURE OF PERSONALITY

Our viewpoint on personality is a blend of evolutionary theory and symbolic interactionism. Although the model bears a strong family resemblance to the views of James Mark Baldwin, Charles Cooley, George Herbert Mead, Theodore Sarbin, and Erving Goffman, it resembles most closely those of William McDougall (1908). Much of what we have done, in fact, is to recast McDougall in modern terms. McDougall was an able student of evolutionary theory who regarded human action as arising from a discrete set of biological impulses, which were themselves products of natural selection. Once expressed, however, these impulses become progressively divorced from their origins and, at the same time, hierarchically organized under the self concept. Although conduct originates in biology, it is quickly controlled by social influences.

Recent evidence from paleoanthropology suggests that Homo sapiens evolved as a group-living and culture-using animal. Our capacity for group organization and the successful transmission of culture (language, tools, shared wisdom) across the generations was a major key to our evolutionary success. Morality, as a means of regulating group life, becomes important in these terms.

A consideration of the evolutionary origins of our species suggests that morality serves not only a social-structural function—that is, it regulates group life—but also some powerful human needs. The reasons are as follows: Two innate human tendencies give a distinctive caste to human personality and social conduct. First, research on maternal deprivation (e.g., Bowlby, 1969) suggests that people have powerful needs for attention and approval and, conversely, should find criticism and censure highly aversive. Second, primate research (Hebb & Thompson, 1967) and experimental studies of neurosis (Mineka & Kihlstrom, 1978) indicate that people have strong needs for structure and order and find unpredictability and lack of control highly stressful. Taken together, these two human requirements suggest that people need to interact, but in structured and predictable ways. Morality serves these needs by organizing and regulating interaction at the level of individuals.

It follows from these comments that morality should be considered from two perspectives. In the social perspective, morality exists as an external and verifiable code of conduct, a set of rules that specifies mutual rights and obligations and prohibits certain grossly unsocial acts. In the individual perspective, morality is defined phenomenologically in terms of each person's subjective orientation to the rules and values of his or her culture. As a psychological study, moral development consists of tracing the nature and origins of these subjective orientations, which can be fruitfully approached from the perspective of personality development.

We proposed earlier that people need attention and interaction but that they also need structure and predictability. Consequently, social interaction tends to be rather carefully patterned and lawlike. Personality structure, as it develops over time, gives interaction its ritualized character. Consider the videotapes we have of 3-year-old children in a playroom. The children are filmed two at a time, and their interactions all have the same form: For a while the children bump around, not doing much. At some point, one of them will say, "Pretend you are Batman and I am Robin," or "Pretend this teddy bear is sick and you are a doctor." At that point the children begin talking in a reciprocal, dependent fashion, moving about and gesticulating in a way that depends on what the other is doing—in short, playing and interacting.

This example shows rather clearly that certain structural requirements are necessary before an interaction can take place. First, there must be a purpose or goal to the interaction, an external focus for the participants, and there must be roles to play. Thus, as Mead (1934) argued early on, roles are the vehicles for social interaction; outside of our roles we have little to say to one another. Second, by as early as 3 years of age children understand this process so well that they are able to play with it. So, when one little girl said to her boy companion, "Pretend you were the mommy and I was the daddy," the little boy would have no part of it. The girl, literally dancing with glee, persisted until the boy, on the verge of tears, threatened to "tell the teacher." At this point, the girl said she no longer wanted to play. Third, children's interaction is formally identical to adult interaction. Adults do not simply get together and boogie; they get together and do something. What they do is often irrelevant as long as there is a context for the interaction and people have roles to play.

The structure of personality can be described as follows: In each interactional context people have self-images, views of themselves that they would like others to credit them with. Their behavior in each situation can be seen, at least in part, as a form of autointerpretation; people act so as to tell others how they wish to be regarded. Indeed, sometimes people's actions are designed to tell others how they do not want to be regarded. Finally, people have images of what certain people, their reference groups or significant others, expect of them during interaction. Kelly (1955) called these images "role constructs." To summarize, the structure of personality can be conceptualized in terms of both fixed and variable components. The fixed components include certain innate tendencies; among the more important of these are needs for attention and approval and for predictability and order. Of the variable components of personality, three are fundamental. The first is one's self-image, the view of oneself that one would like others to believe. The second is one's repertoire of techniques of autointerpretation—the role behaviors one uses to explicate oneself to others. The third variable component is one's views of the expectations that significant others hold regarding one's social conduct.

PERSONALITY DEVELOPMENT

We have suggested that moral development should be conceptualized as part of the larger process of personality development and outlined a model for thinking about the structure of personality. The next question concerns how those personality structures evolve, which is the same as asking about personality development itself. Personality development passes through three broad phases, and the variable components of personality reflect one's experiences in each of these phases. The first phase of development, which ends around 5 years of age is largely concerned with working out one's relationships with authority and in the process acquiring the rules, values, and rudimentary knowledge structures—language, danger signs, the habit of obedience—necessary for survival. Core levels of self-esteem and attitude toward rules and authority come from this stage; these translate, of course, into self-images, into techniques for relating to authority figures, and into views of what those authority figures expect of one. Parents who are warm but controlling produce children who are self-confident but compliant, which defines maturity in a 5-year-old.

The second phase of development, which ends sometimes after puberty (but which may extend into early adulthood), is largely concerned with working out one's relationships with one's peers and in so doing developing respect for the expectations of others and for the notions of fair play, equity, and retribution. Social skills, peer-oriented codes of conduct, and a different self-image come from this second stage. In the first stage, children are essentially dealt their self-images by their parents; in the second stage, they must negotiate their self-images with their peers. The results are often quite different; for example, a child's self-image may change from mommie's precious darling at home to despised little fink in school. Autointerpretational tactics and notions about generalized social expectations derive from this process of peer interaction.

The third phase of development begins when one enters the world of work and starts a family. Here the problems of the past—learning to deal with authority and peers—are joined by the problem in identity. One must decide what kind of person one wants to be; one must develop a kind of "master self-image." At the same time, one normally begins articulating one's life goals and devising strategies for achieving those goals.

To recapitulate, one's self-images, methods of interacting, and visions of the expectations of others with regard to one's social conduct are shaped by one's developmental history. This history can be conceptualized as evolving through three phases: In the first, one must accommodate authority; in the second, one must deal with peers; in the third, one must establish a life-style. The foregoing is obviously a highly compressed overview of a complex series of psychosocial transactions. Because this presentation has been so compressed, there are some nuances that should be spelled out in a more didactic fashion. First, the three stages of development that we have described have clear moral implications. In terms of socialization theory, the first phase involves what the psychoanalysts call superego development. The middle phase entails what Mead (1934) called learning to adopt the perspective of the generalized other. The last phase concerns what Durkheim (1925/1961) and McDougall (1908) saw as the problem of autonomy.

Second, the key components of personality structure—one's self-image(s), autointerpretational strategies, and internalized reference-group expectations—are all cognitive schemas. At the same time, however, by early adulthood these cognitive structures are usually unconscious in the sense that one is not very reflective about them, that they influence behavior in ways that are often outside awareness. These cognitive structures are not unconscious in principle; rather, they are part of the unexamined world that we take for granted.

Third, this point of view on personality suggests that overt behavior ought not be taken at face value. People's actions, including the views they express during moral judgment interviews, are, at least in part, acts of autointerpretation, attempts to tell others how they would like to be regarded. Consider Kohlberg's well-known Heinz dilemma. What do responses to that dilemma mean? Are they a form of psychological X ray, a transparent projection of the structure of moral reasoning reflecting a kind of isomorphism between the organization of the psyche and each person's recorded verbal output? Or are they efforts by the respondent to project a self-image, to tell the interrogator how he or she wants to be regarded by significant others—and perhaps by the researcher? As a matter of fact, evidence is steadily accumulating that supports this second interpretation (Johnson, 1981; Johnson & Hogan, 1981; Mills & Hogan, 1978).

Finally, as a result of their developmental and social-learning histories, people differ in terms of the locus of the moral standards to which they are oriented. Some, the inner directed, are principally attuned to internalized standards of performance; as a result, they may strike others as being stubborn, independent, principled, and nonconforming. Some people, the other directed, are primarily attuned to the demands of the peer group. Like Snyder's (1974) self-monitoring persons, they will appear to be wishy-washy and conforming. Still others will be oriented to neither inner nor outer standards; responding to neither internalized standards nor peer expectations, they are the true aliens of any culture. Finally, some persons will achieve a nice balance between the demands of the inner reference group and the immediate social environment; we regard such persons as mature (see Hogan & Cheek, 1982, for a more detailed discussion of the "inner-outer" orientation to elements of social control).

THE PROBLEM OF CONFORMITY

A long tradition in American psychology holds that people who conform to ordinary social rules are not very bright, well adjusted, or moral (Hogan, 1975). The critical animus of psychoanalytic theory, for example, is directed against conventional morality as embodied in the superego. Persons whose superegoes are well developed are compliant, conscientious, sexually maladjusted, and neurotic; the goal of psychoanalytic therapy is to relax the burdens of a conventional conscience.

The justly famous conformity studies of Asch (1952) are interpreted in a way that is perfectly consistent with psychoanalytic theory. Persons who conform to group pressure in Asch's experiments are nervous, indecisive, and perhaps cowardly, and they grossly distort their perceptions of reality and their memories of Asch's experiment as well. Milgram's studies of obedience (1974) point to the same conclusion: persons who conform to the expectations of authority are at risk to commit gross crimes against strangers. Conformity is virtually equated with immorality and nonconformity with maturity. On the other hand, persons who refuse to conform are seen as well adjusted, intelligent, accurate in their perceptions of reality, and unwilling to inflict gratuitous pain on others. Finally, in Lawrence Kohlberg's well-known view of the evolution of moral reasoning we see the same themes. Persons who conform to social expectations or moral codes are, it is hoped, in a kind of developmental holding pattern, waiting for the time when they will be able to make judgments according to their own personal perceptions of certain abstract principles of justice.

There are two ways of interpreting this interesting tradition that extends from Freud to Kohlberg. The unsympathetic view is that these writers are trying to give intellectual legitimacy to their own antinomian and nihilistic tendencies and to their own hostility to rules. The second and more sympathetic view is that these writers are attempting to analyze the problem of autonomy, a topic that has engaged social theorists from Durkheim to the present. The concept of autonomy is used to explain cases where persons act in ways that some of us would regard as moral. An example would be Socrates, who ignored the pleas of his friends and poisoned himself as a way of affirming his belief in the principle of democracy. Acts of civil disobedience are often taken as examples of autonomous behavior.

Despite the importance of the concept, with the exception of a paper by Kurtines (1974), autonomy is to a large degree unanalyzed. How is it to be conceptualized? The notion is that by acting autonomously, one conforms to personal standards of conduct whose relationship to social norms is somehow irrelevant. McDougall (1908) thought autonomous behavior was the hallmark of maturity; he described it as an advance to the higher plane of social conduct. McDougall also suggested a possible psychological mechanism for this advance; it is reference-group theory—we act so as to maintain the good opinion of an internal review board, a panel of observers who exist inside our heads, whose praise we seek and whose censure we shun. In this model, we are still motivated to achieve social approval and avoid social criticism, but the locus of evaluation is internal rather than external.

McDougall's internalized reference group differs from Freud's superego in three ways. First, the Freudian superego is unconscious, whereas according to McDougall, we can spell out and even evaluate the demands of our reference group. Second, the Freudian superego is composed of the demands and expectations of one's father, more precisely, the demands and expectations as perceived by a 5-year-old child. McDougall's internalized reference group, on the other hand, includes teachers, valued colleagues, and other adult acquaintances. Finally, the Freudian superego is primitive and harsh, whereas McDougall's reference group is mature and flexible.

In McDougall's analysis, autonomous behavior is a specialized kind of conformity; it is conformity to an internalized group of evaluators. In this light, the polarity between autonomy and conformity turns out not to be clear-cut. People always conform; they differ only in terms of the group whose favorable evaluations they seek. Criminals, for example, are professional nonconformers. Close analysis, however, shows that, contrary to common belief, criminals care deeply about how they are regarded by their peers, and they carefully tailor their public behavior to the expectations of other malefactors. Academics are another group of professional nonconformers, although of a more cerebral variety. Like criminals, they also care deeply about how they are evaluated by their peers. Consequently, they cleave closely to standards of professional conduct and carefully maintain all the requisite properties, among which include being nonconforming and critical of the ideas of others.

This discussion suggests that the word *autonomy* is used in two quite different ways and that it is important to distinguish between them. On the one hand, there is the autonomy of Durkheim and Mead, which refers to autonomous conformity to the norms of a reference group. On the other hand, there is the autonomy of Asch, Milgram, and Kohlberg, which is the autonomy of nonconformity (although this nonconformity is somehow normative in intellectual and artistic circles). The former is the more general use of the term; the latter is a usage that is particular to contemporary social psychology. Conceivably, these two perspectives could be reconciled, but only after due regard is given to their coexistence.

INDIVIDUAL DIFFERENCES, PERSONALITY, AND MORAL CONDUCT

People differ in many ways. For our purposes, the theoretically significant ways in which they differ include variations: in the kinds of experiences they have had during development; in their moral phenomenology; in their reference groups; and in their methods and forms of autointerpretation. These variations border on ideographic chaos—how can one begin to find structure in all these parameters of variation? One solution is through type theory. As it turns out, there is considerable consensus regarding the number of personality types and how they are interrelated (Hogan, 1982). Perhaps the most heuristic and empirically well validated personality-type theory comes from the work of Holland (1973). He classifies the entire domain of personality in terms of six remarkably robust types, which he calls realistic, investigative, artistic, social, enterprising, and conventional.

Realistic types are practical, independent, introverted, and technically oriented; these include engineers and surgeons. Investigative types are theoretical, independent, introverted, and scientifically oriented; these include most research scientists. Artistic types are principled, creative, and nonconforming; these include philosophers and poets. Social types are idealistic, extraverted, and helpful; these include ministers and social workers. Enterprising types are extraverted, status oriented, and politically astute; these include lawyers and university presidents. Conventional types are well adjusted, careful about details, and financially oriented; these include accountants and insurance brokers. See Figure 13.1 for a visual rendering of this information.

These six types can be assessed with considerable reliability, and behind each type lies a distinctive constellation of self-images, autointerpretational tactics, and reference groups. At this point we make three claims: First, people can be classified in terms of their resemblance to the foregoing six personality types; this claim is in fact empirically well founded (Hogan, 1982). Second, each personality type can be characterized by a distinctive moral posture, defined in terms of what that type conforms to. Third, the moral posture that characterizes psychologists has been elevated by them to the status of moral maturity, but without any persuasive empirical or logical support for this elevation. We evaluated the second and third claims in the following way: We gave a group of 159 male and female undergraduates at Johns Hopkins University and Towson State University a battery of tests that included the following measures:

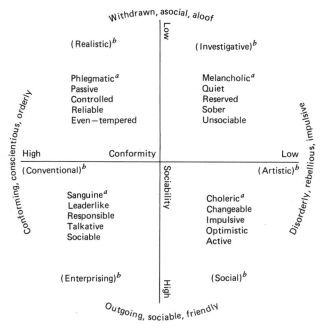

Figure 13.1. Circumflex models of personality structure ([a] = Eysenck's interpretation of Galen's types; [b] = Holland's types).

1. Holland's (1973) Self-Directed Search, a carefully developed and well-validated inventory, is designed to identify the personality types categorized by Holland.

2. The Socialization scale of the California Psychological Inventory (CPI) (Gough, 1975), which measures rule-following or delinquent tendencies, depending on whether scores are high or low, is perhaps the best-validated measure in the history of personality assessment.

3. The Empathy scale of the CPI (Hogan, 1969) is a well-validated measure of perceptiveness, interpersonal sensitivity, and role-taking skill.

4. The Independence of Judgment Scale (Barron, 1953), a measure of autonomy in the Asch, Milgram, and Kohlberg sense, was developed empirically against the criterion of yielding versus nonyielding in the original Asch conformity situation.

5. The Uniqueness Scale (Snyder & Fromkin, 1977), a measure of positive striving for uniqueness relative to other people, has three factors:
   (a) Lack of concern for others' reactions to one's different ideas, actions, and so on
   (b) Desire not always to follow the rules
   (c) Willingness publicly to defend one's beliefs

6.   A scale that asks about the degree to which a person bases his or her moral decisions on the rules and requirements of normative regulations, which we will call "Rules." This 14-item scale had an alpha reliability of .66.

7.   A brief scale that assesses the degree to which a person bases his or her moral decisions on a consideration of the feelings of others, which we will call "People." This 7-item scale had an alpha reliability of .51.

8.   A short scale that reflects the degree to which a person bases his or her moral decisions on principles or moral ideas, which we will call "Principles." This 8-item scale had an alpha reliability of .45.

These eight measures were intercorrelated, and the results are presented in Tables 13.1 and 13.2. We predicted that there would be a distinctive moral orientation associated with each personality type, and the data in the two tables support this prediction. Table 13.1 shows the relationship between the personality types and four measures of moral conduct that Hogan has used in his research for years. These are unusually well-validated indexes of moral action—Socialization predicts rule following or delinquency, Empathy predicts sensitivity to moral issues and people's expectations, Independence of Judgment and Uniqueness predict autonomous nonconformity in college students—so these correlations provide a sense of how moral conduct varies across the six personality types. Realistic, Investigative, and Artistic types (i.e., engineers, scientists, and humanists) are the persons most frequently found in academic environments. Table 13.1 indicates that these people are hostile to rules and conventions (negative correlations with Socialization), sensitive to moral issues (positive correlations with Empathy), and nonconforming (positive correlations with Independence of Judgment and Uniqueness). You will recall that the character type favored by Freud, Asch, Milgram, and Kohlberg is a person who is hostile to rules, principled, and nonconforming.

TABLE 13.1.   Correlations between Personality Types and the Variables Listed

Personality Type	Socialization	Empathy	Independence of Judgment	Uniqueness
Realistic	−.13	NS	NS	.21
Investigative	NS	.19	NS	.25
Artistic	−.11	.30	.18	.20
Social	.19	.34	−.18	NS
Enterprising	.14	.35	−.18	NS
Conventional	.18	NS	−.21	−.31

Note: $N = 159$.

Social, Enterprising, and Conventional types are more frequently found in the "real world" (i.e., they are social workers, politicians, and business people). These persons turn out to be well socialized, sensitive to moral issues, but conforming. You will remember that this character type is stigmatized by Freud, Asch, Milgram, and Kohlberg.

Table 13.2 describes the relationship between each personality type and four measures of moral thinking. The scales in Table 13.2 assess, in order, the degree to which one bases one's moral decisions on: (1) considerations of appropriate rules and procedures; (2) considerations of the needs and wishes of others; (3) considerations of principles; and (4) religious considerations. As the table shows, Investigative and Artistic types (i.e., academics) are hostile to rules and religion but keen on principles as guidelines for moral decision making. In contrast, Social, Enterprising, and Conventional types are willing to comply with tradition and are skeptical about principles as a basis for moral decision making.

These results are preliminary, generated for the purposes of this chapter and book. Moreover, the sample is very specialized—undergraduates—and the correlations are not very large. These results clearly need to be replicated with different groups. Nonetheless, we are impressed with the *consistency* of the results, given all the shortcomings of the data set. With the exception of the −.13 correlation between Realistic types and socialization in Table 13.1, none of the remaining 47 correlations disconfirms our initial predictions.

The data in these tables suggest that the Social and Enterprising types may be the most mature persons in that they show a balance of respect between the requirements of convention and authority and the needs of the individuals. In contrast, Investigative and Artistic types (which would include psychologists) are hostile to rules, nonconforming, and autonomous. This finding shows rather clearly that the moral orientation of psychologists corresponds to the image of moral maturity that comes from the writings of Freud, Asch, Milgram, and Kohlberg. Although it is comforting to think that people like ourselves are the best and most moral people in the world, such a conclusion is a little self-serving and not entirely credible.

TABLE 13.2.   Correlations between Personality Types and the Variables Listed

Personality Type	Rules	People	Principles	Religion
Realistic	NS	NS	−.26	NS
Investigative	−.14	NS	NS	−.14
Artistic	−.20	NS	.21	NS
Social	NS	NS	NS	.31
Enterprising	.22	NS	−.19	.23
Conventional	.20	−.29	−.26	.25

CONCLUSION

By way of a conclusion we will summarize the argument that we have out-lined here. The core of the argument is actually very simple; essentially, we made seven points.

1. A person's moral orientation—the way he or she reacts to rules, to others' expectations, and even to moral judgment interviews—is fundamentally related to the structure of that person's personality.
2. Personality structure reflects each person's developmental history; depending on the person's age, this may mean how the person deals with authority, with the expectations of his or her peers, or with the obligations of family and vocation.
3. The structure of personality can be defined in terms of three component structures:
   (a) Self-images, the views of oneself one would like others to believe
   (b) Autointerpretational tactics, typified forms of self-presentation that instruct others as to how we would like to be regarded
   (c) Internalized views of the expectations of significant others
4. People vary enormously in terms of these components of personality structure, but all that variety can be organized in terms of six personality types.
5. Each personality type has a characteristic moral orientation.
6. In a tradition extending from Freud to Kohlberg, psychologists have stigmatized conformity. In fact, however, everyone conforms; they merely differ in terms of the reference groups to which they conform.
7. The moral orientation preferred (i.e., described as mature) by psychologists in the tradition from Freud to Kohlberg turns out to be the moral orientation that characterizes those psychologists.

However the reader may feel about the merits of our role-theoretical account of moral conduct, several of our ancillary points seem quite valid. First, moral conduct is organically related to the structure of personality; this ancient psychoanalytic insight seems once again to be penetrating the consciousness of developmental psychologists. Second, psychologists are more similar to one another (in terms of their personalities) than they are, for example, to engineers or stockbrokers; that is, one can define a concept like the "modal personality" of psychologists. Third, there is a moral orientation that typifies the modal personality of psychologists, and psychologists seem disposed to call this orientation mature. Finally, although the moral character of competent adults clearly differs in maturity from the moral character of children or criminals, within the population of competent adults there are no moral grounds for preferring one kind of moral character to another. This introduces a note of relativism into our deliberations to which we see no alternative. The elitist posture of the field at present—that we *know* rather precisely what maturity looks like—is unacceptable.

REFERENCES

Asch, S. E. *Social psychology*. Englewood Cliffs, N.J.: Prentice-Hall, 1952.

Barron, F. Some personality correlates of independence of judgment. *Journal of Personality,* 1953, *21,* 287–297.

Bowlby, J. *Attachment and loss* (Vol. 2): *Separation.* New York: Basic Books, 1969.

Durkheim, E. *Moral education: A study in the theory and application in the sociology of education.* New York: Free Press, 1961. (Originally published, 1925.)

Eysenck, H. J. *The structure of human personality.* New York: Wiley, 1953.

Gough, H. G. *Manual for the California psychological inventory.* Palo Alto, Calif.: Consulting Psychologists Press, 1975.

Hebb, D. O., & Thompson, W. R. The social significance of animal studies. In G. Lindzey (Ed.), *The handbook of social psychology.* Reading, Mass.: Addison-Wesley, 1967.

Hogan, R. Development of an empathy scale. *Journal of Consulting and Clinical Psychology,* 1969, *33,* 307–316.

Hogan, R. Theoretical egocentrism and the problem of compliance. *American Psychologist,* 1975, *30,* 533–540.

Hogan, R. A socioanalytic theory of personality. In M. M. Page (Ed.), *Nebraska Symposium on Motivation* (Vol. 29). Lincoln: University of Nebraska Press, 1982.

Hogan, R., & Cheek, J. Identity, authenticity, and maturity. In T. R. Sarbin & K. E. Scheibe (Eds.), *Studies in social identity.* New York: Praeger, 1982.

Holland, J. L. *Making vocational choices: A theory of careers.* Englewood Cliffs, N.J.: Prentice-Hall, 1973.

Johnson, J. A. The self-disclosure and self-presentation views of item response dynamics and personality scale validity. *Journal of Personality and Social Psychology,* 1981, *40,* 761–769.

Johnson, J. A., & Hogan, R. Moral judgements and self-presentations. *Journal of Research in Personality,* 1981, *15,* 57–63.

Kelly, G. A. *The psychology of personal constructs.* New York: Norton, 1955.

Kurtines, W. Autonomy: A concept reconsidered. *Journal of Personality Assessment,* 1974, *38,* 243–246.

McDougall, W. *Social psychology.* London: Methuen, 1908.

Mead, G. H. *Mind, self, and society.* Chicago: University of Chicago Press, 1934.

Milgram, S. *Obedience to authority: An experimental view.* New York: Harper & Row, 1974.

Mills, C., & Hogan, R. A role theoretical interpretation of personality scale item responses. *Journal of Personality,* 1978, *46,* 778–785.

Mineka, S., & Kihlstrom, J. S. Unpredictable and uncontrollable: A new perspective on experimental neurosis. *Journal of Abnormal Psychology*, 1978, *87*, 256–271.

Snyder, M. Self-monitoring of expressive behavior. *Journal of Personality and Social Psychology*, 1974, *30*, 526–537.

Snyder, C. R., & Fromkin, H. L. Abnormality as a positive characteristic: The development and validation of a scale measuring need for uniqueness. *Journal of Abnormal Psychology*, 1977, *86*, 518–527.

CHAPTER 14

Steps toward a Comprehensive Theory of Moral Conduct: Goal Orientation, Social Behavior, Kindness, and Cruelty

ERVIN STAUB

A theory of personal goals and social behavior is summarized. How personal goals (and value orientations that provide the basis of moral goals) and aspects of the environment that activate goals combine in affecting behavior is discussed. Special characteristics of goals in the moral domain are considered. Research testing aspects of the model in the realm of prosocial behavior is described. The subjects with more of a prosocial value (goal) orientation were found more helpful in response to both physical and psychological distress.

The model is extended to antisocial behavior—violence, aggression, mistreatment of subgroups in a society. Activating conditions for aggression are discussed, both temporary and stable, including historical conditions. Ideologies that lead to mistreatment of people and scapegoating in response to activating conditions are examined. The psychological consequences of activating conditions and personal characteristics of individuals that make aggression in response to activation likely are also discussed. Anger and hostility, the effects of instigation on the self-concept, and feelings of injustice are some important consequences of instigating conditions. Value orientations, chronic frustration, mistrust and negative evaluation of people, and the learned enjoyment of others' suffering are among the personality characteristics that affect how people respond to instigating conditions. The nature of the self-concept and the self-other bond as important in kindness and cruelty is stressed.

The motivational theory is extended. The consequences of goals that are chronically frustrated, changing from desires to deficiencies, becoming needs that exert continuous influence, are discussed.

Preparation of this chapter was facilitated by National Institutes of Mental Health Grant No. 23886 to the author.

My associates and I have been working on a theory of personal goals for a number of years (Staub, 1978a, 1978b, 1980, 1982). The aim of the theory is to develop greater understanding of and greater ability to predict social behavior in general and prosocial behavior in particular. Traditionally, prosocial (and moral) behavior has been treated as something separate and apart from social behavior of other kinds. But people do not either behave prosocially or not behave prosocially—they usually act to benefit someone or to accomplish other aims. How is the aim selected, and what determines whether it is pursued in action? This is our major concern.

If one is concerned with people helping others, a major question is, Why is it that people so frequently do not help others in need? What is the psychology of passive bystanders? It is only one step further to be concerned with the psychology of perpetrators. How did the Nazis come to exterminate millions of people, what were the psychological processes that led to it and made it possible? What is the psychology of perpetrators of the disappearances in Argentina—both those in the government who make decisions and the direct perpetrators who perform violent acts? How does discrimination and violence against minorities come about? Are the determinants of such conduct similar to or different from acts of violence directed at people as individuals, not as members of groups? There has been surprisingly little connection between theory and research on the determinants or development of behavior that benefits others and those of behavior that harms others. Only limited attempts to connect these two realms have been made (Staub, 1971). My major purpose here is to expand the theory of goals and social behavior so that it will be applicable to both of these primary realms of moral conduct. Another purpose is to expand the theory in such a way that it will embody the great complexity of human beings, the influence of varied aspects and levels of their personality and environments, in determining moral conduct.

A primary concern is how individual characteristics—both value orientations, personal motivation that would move people toward, away from, or against other people, and characteristics of the self-concept—join with the life conditions of individuals (or groups) in leading to kindness or cruelty. The whole range of life conditions will be of interest: specific, limited situations; the more general conditions of the life of an individual (or group); and societal and historical conditions. These life conditions can, on the one hand, be the result of individuals (or groups) creating opportunities for themselves to fulfill certain motives, or, on the other, they can be imposed on people or result from unintended developments, sometimes arising out of the personality of individuals, other times not. Whatever their source, they can activate or inhibit kindness or cruelty, or the psychological processes leading to them.

In other words, in this chapter I am concerned with how kind and cruel behavior comes about; the values, motives, other individual characteristics, and psychological processes they give rise to that result in positive or negative conduct; and the role of the environment.

REVIEW OF THE THEORY OF GOALS

Personal Goals: The Role of Motivation

The theory presumes that humans are purposeful organisms who develop varied motivations, which will be called personal goals, in the course of their growth and development. Personal goals, when activated, can exert strong influence on behavior, partly by functioning as organizers of other personal characteristics that enter into influencing behavior. The word *goal* implies a preference for certain outcomes or end states or an aversion for certain outcomes and the desire to avoid them. Another characteristic of personal goals is a network of cognitions that is usually associated with a goal. It is certainly possible that the desire for some outcomes is primarily emotional, but usually there are conscious thoughts, beliefs, or values associated with the goal that make the outcomes desirable or aversive to us. These cognitions in part tune us perceptually to the kinds of circumstances that make it possible to satisfy our goal. They are also applied to the interpretations of situations or events. The cognitive network can lead to interpretations that give rise to affects—to active desire for the goal—and that motivate attempts to reach it. Thus, goals are cognitive orientations that are associated with the desirability of certain outcomes. More detailed discussion of these and other assumptions about the nature of goals has been presented elsewhere (Staub, 1978a, 1978b, 1980).

Personal goals can be activated by characteristics of the environment, either the external environment or a person's internal environment, his or her thoughts or imagination. The external environment can be described in terms of its activating potential for a particular personal goal. Depending on the activating potential of the environment and the extent to which the person possesses various personal goals, an environment may activate no goal or one, two, or more goals. When two or more goals are activated, they may conflict with one another when their satisfaction cannot be pursued by the same course of action. Alternatively, one of the goals may be dominant, or the goals may join with one another when a particular course of action can lead to the satisfaction of all of them. Sometimes helping another person can satisfy a prosocial goal, an approval goal—because helping others is a socially valued activity that often leads to approval and praise by other people—and even an achievement goal, for in the course of helping, a person can exercise skill, competence, or excellence. When two or more goals conflict with one another, action may be inhibited, or the conflict may be resolved.

Although in past presentations of the model, activating potential of the environment usually referred to the specific circumstances a person faced, such as someone's need, the opportunity to work on and do well on a task, or attack by another person, the environment has more general aspects as well. The stable life conditions of individuals may greatly vary in their activating potential for different goals. One person may live under conditions of frustration and deprivation, whereas another may be surrounded by indications of human need. The stable life circumstances may have a variety of consequences: They may change the position of a goal in the hierarchy of a person's goals, or they may affect the nature of the goal and its importance to the person. They may also affect the activating potential of the environment for certain goals. For example, being surrounded by the constant physical or emotional needs of others might reduce the power of such needs to activate prosocial goals. General historical conditions, the nature of circumstances of life in a society or during a historical period, can also act as activators of personal goals.

Environments and stable life conditions do not just happen to develop. To a smaller or greater extent, people shape their life circumstances as well as their immediate social circumstances, sometimes in order to make it possible to pursue important goals. As the preceding discussion suggests, the goals of individuals can usually be arranged in hierarchies, according to their importance. But such hierarchies are abstract, and living under certain conditions may represent relatively constant activation, either being the result of or influencing the position of goals in the hierarchy, or both.

Behavior according to this model is a joint function of situational influence and people possessing goals that might be activated by the situation. Beyond activated goals and the resolution of goal conflict, the role of supporting characteristics is important. Certain perceptual tendencies or capacities, such as the ability to process environmental cues quickly or to take the role of other people, can be important in affecting the likelihood of activation of some goals. Varied forms of competencies, such as subjective competence—confidence in one's ability to influence events (what has been described as variation in locus of control)—are likely to affect the execution of goals. Specific competencies can determine whether a person feels able and is actually able to perform acts needed to pursue some goal. The capacity to generate plans and strategies for action is another important competence. People may also vary in action tendency, the ease or difficulty of initiating and pursuing a course of activity, particularly under social conditions, when other people can observe and judge their actions (Staub, 1974).

So far in this model no differentiation has been made between personal goals relevant to self-serving conduct, where the outcome is self-gain, and personal goals that have moral relevance, that relate to the welfare of other people. Are there such differences? Conceivably, morally relevant goals are more generally active. Moral considerations can enter when any other goal is pursued. The pursuit of other goals may be contrary to moral goals, and consequently moral goals may produce conflict. It is questionable, however, whether this *breadth of applicability* makes morally relevant goals unique. For some individuals, other goals may have extremely broad applicability. Consider an achievement goal. It may be applied to academic work, to a job, to conversations with other people, to trying to initiate a relationship with a member of the opposite sex, and to almost any and all circumstances. Thus, although in actuality a prosocial or morally relevant goal may have wider ranges of applicability for most people than other goals have, the conceptual status of morally relevant and other personal goals need not differ.

A characteristic of goals just referred to can be of great importance from the standpoint of morality: their range of applicability. For some people, there may be a much wider range of activating conditions for morally relevant goals than there is for other people. For example, some people might have learned to apply their concern about others' welfare at times when another person is in physical need, but not in psychological distress; others might have learned to apply such concern only to people of certain kinds, perhaps people whom they think of as similar to themselves or as coming from the same ethnic or racial background.

Although the concept of range of applicability applies to all personal goals, it has substantial significance in the moral realm. As we know from history, from life experience, and recently from striking research evidence, human beings have a tendency for us-them separation, for a differentiation of in-group and out-group. Tajfel and his associates (1971) and subsequently many other researchers have demonstrated that such separation into us and them can come about on the most trivial bases. This research has shown that subjects who were told, on the basis of an aesthetic preference test, that they preferred the modern painter Klee to the modern painter Kandinsky later, in distributing resources, both favored people who presumably also preferred Klee and evaluated these people more favorably than they did those who favored Kandinsky. In other words, there is some discrimination against and devaluation of people in an out-group, even if the out-group is created on a superficial basis.

Although the tendency for us and them differentiation may be quite general, even universal, certainly individual differences exist. Individual differences can be embodied in value-goal orientations, or, alternately, people with the same value orientations can have different ranges of applicability of their moral values and goals to different groups of people. We have little knowledge, as yet, of which is the case. The extent to which the nature of a person's moral goal orientations and the range of applicability of these goal orientations are related or are independent is of substantial importance.

In any realm—achievement, approval, the moral realm, and so on—there is likely to be at least a small family of related goals, with members of this family defined by the kind of outcomes that they refer to, and perhaps more importantly by the associated networks of cognitions. For example, Durkheim (1925/1961) believed that some people are concerned with promoting the good and are inclined to respond to others' needs even if that demands a break with conventions, whereas other people are concerned with the maintenance of the social order. Hoffman (1970) found that some children, whom he called humanistic, seemed concerned with others' welfare and were willing to deviate from conventional rules and standards if it would benefit another person. Other children, whom he called conventional, tended to give legal and religious bases for moral judgments and tended to ignore extenuating circumstances for wrongdoing. The findings indicated that conventional children were concerned with both acting according to societal rules and with inhibiting some of their own impulses that they came to see as unacceptable.

Prosocial goals can have differing primary outcomes as their focus: person-oriented outcomes, such as benefitting other people and enhancing their welfare; outcomes related to the nature of society and the world in general, such as maintaining the social order, improving the world, and creating justice in the world; as well as self-related outcomes, such as living up to internal standards that prescribe helping others. I differentiated between two primary prosocial goals. One centers on feelings of duty and obligation, imposed by society and by principles that one has adopted or by the commandments of God. Duty orientation is based on internalized norms or standards. Another primary prosocial goal is more person centered. It is defined by three aspects of a cognitive network: (1) positive orientation toward other people, positive evaluation of human beings; (2) concern about—value placed on—others' welfare; and (3) a feeling of personal responsibility for others' welfare. A variety of research findings suggests that these dimensions of cognition (and affect) are important aspects of a prosocial goal of some generality and breadth (Staub, 1978a, 1978b, 1980). The first cognitive dimension or aspect seems psychologically to be a precondition for the other two. These three central dimensions of a cognitive network are characteristic of a value orientation that I called _prosocial orientation._[1] Research in which we attempted to assess such a value orientation, which is seen as giving rise to a prosocial goal that makes improving others' welfare a desirable outcome, will be described briefly.

Some Supporting Research

In three experiments we attempted to evaluate the joint influence of personal goals and activating conditions on behavior. A variety of tests that were intended to measure prosocial orientation were administered to subjects. Most of the tests were identical in the three studies, but some variation was also introduced. For example, Kohlberg's test of moral judgment was included in

---

[1] One of the convergences in research on moral behavior appears to be a recognition of the significance of a feeling of personal responsibility for other people's welfare. Social psychologists have long recognized this, although their concern has usually been the significance of responsibility focused on a person by circumstances. The role of responsibility as in administering shocks to other individuals (Milgram, 1974) or in helping others (Latané & Darley, 1970) has been recognized. I emphasized both the importance of responsibility focused on a person as a result of circumstances or of a person's competence or role and a feeling of responsibility that was due to individual characteristics (see particularly Staub, 1970, 1978a, chap. 3). As Chapter 4 in this book shows, the significance of responsibility is now also recognized in the cognitive-developmental approach to moral development. The separate scoring of moral reasoning for responsibility indicates the centrality accorded to the development of a sense of personal responsibility in relation to other people.

the first study, but its contribution did not seem special or unique enough to justify the time and effort demanded by administering and scoring the test. The tests included a measure of feelings of responsibility for others' welfare (Schwarz's ascription of responsibility for the self test); a test of Machiavellian orientation that included items to test both the perception of human beings or human nature as positive or negative and the tendency to engage in manipulative interactions with people; measures of social responsibility, of trust, and of interpersonal sensitivity; and some values from the Rokeach measure. Although these tests were administered in one case to males from Northeastern University, in another case to females at the University of Massachusetts at Amherst, and in a third instance to females at Brooklyn College, there was surprising similarity of the factor loading of each test on a factor that emerged in each factor analysis.

In the first study we found that subjects who scored high on this factor responded to a physically distressed confederate by being more likely to go into an adjoining room in response to sounds of distress; by being more likely to offer to go to Harvard Square to fill out a prescription; by also being somewhat more likely to engage in other forms of help in the course of their interaction with the confederate. Factor scores ("prosocial orientation" scores) were substantially related to our overall score of helpfulness ($r = .46$, $df = 115$, $p < .01$; Staub, 1974). In a second study, Feinberg (1977) found that in a high-need condition subjects with high prosocial orientation scores were more likely to look at and attend to a confederate (rather than to continue to attend to a task) who was in psychological distress than were subjects with low prosocial orientation scores. High need in this case was created by the confederate expressing feelings of distress that resulted from her boyfriend leaving her the day before, after a relationship of two years' duration, in the course of which marriage was considered. This difference between high and low prosocial orientation subjects in "nonverbal" helpfulness was not found in a low-need condition, where the confederate described, without apparent distress, the same experience as having occurred a year earlier. Interestingly, in this study subjects high on an achievement orientation and low on prosocial orientation were more likely to (1) attend to the task that they were supposed to engage in; (2) at the same time talk a very substantial amount to the confederate *in both the high- and low-need conditions;* and (3) express some dislike of the confederate in high need. These individuals, trying to attend both to the task at hand and to the person who initiated interaction with them, might have found their experience stressful and unpleasant when faced with a person in distress.

In a third study, Grodman (1978) found that female subjects with a strong prosocial orientation were verbally more responsive to a confederate in distress (the high-need condition described before). Prosocial orientation made less of a difference when the cost of helping subjects was greater, although high prosocial subjects still tended to be slightly more helpful than were subjects with a low prosocial orientation. These findings provide support for the conception that a particular value orientation, conceptualized here as embodying a personal goal, enters into the determination of positive action. The influence of an achievement orientation described earlier and additional findings of these and other studies discussed elsewhere (see Staub, 1978a, 1978b, 1980, 1982) provide further support for the overall conceptualization.

VIOLENCE AND CRUELTY: TOWARD A UNIFIED THEORY

In beginning to discuss the determinants of violence, cruelty, and aggression, I will rely to some extent on a historical-societal analysis. Later, I will return to the individual level. Some of the ideas that I will suggest apply, I believe, at both levels.

A good place to start is to consider the activating potentials for prosocial goals and aggressive "goals." The basic primary activating potential for prosocial behavior is the presence of some kind of need. There are many other conditions that modify or affect activating potentials (see Staub, 1980), but the existence of need, of distress, of the necessity or desirability to improve someone's well-being, is primary. A second sense in which need may exist is the need for help to accomplish a positive goal, to complete a task, to reach a desired end. Thus, a negative state, a state of deficiency, need not exist.

What are the activating potentials for aggression? Psychological theory and research findings have specified a number of them. They include frustration in the pursuit of one's accomplishment of goals and attack or threat of attack on one's self or on extensions of oneself such as one's family or property. They also include the expectation of frustration of one's goals, including hopes for the future, and attack or threat of attack on one's self-concept, self-esteem, or one's image of oneself. Many laboratory studies and theories based on them attest to the influence of these factors on aggressive behavior under the restrictive conditions of the laboratory. An examination of historical conditions gives substantial proof that these conditions also activate various forms of violence, aggression, and cruelty on a societal level.

IDEOLOGY AS A GOAL ORIENTATION

When extremely difficult historical conditions, conditions that represent attack or threat and create frustration in a society and its members, exist for an appreciable period of time, they sometimes give rise to ideologies. Ideologies can be regarded as embodying shared goals. They point to desirable outcomes and provide hope of a better life, a better future, sometimes for a particular group or a particular society and sometimes for humanity in general. Often they embrace superordinate goals under which many people can unite. In Germany, after World War I, an extensive period existed during which most or all of these activating conditions for violence were present. In addition to defeat in the war, which was unexpected (because the government and the military lied to the people about the progress of the war) and consequently highly frustrating for the population, the German people were subjected to what was regarded by them as a humiliating peace treaty. They experienced a revolution, an inflation in which money completely lost its value, the occupation of the Ruhr by the French, economic depression and political chaos, and violence in the streets between Nazis and Communists. The ideology Hitler offered them promised a better future, attested to the inherent superiority of the German people by claiming they had superior racial qualities, and offered them power and influence as a nation through the gain of territories for living space (and the subjugation of other peoples).

There are many examples in history of both heroic self-sacrifice and great evil done in the name of an ideology, including religious ideology, which promised the betterment of humanity. Frequently, some people are defined as interfering with the creation of a better world. In the case of religious ideologies, these may be adherents to another religion or heretics, individuals who hold somewhat different religious views from that of the orthodoxy. In the case of the Nazis, the Jews were defined as interfering with the creation of a better world due to their racial impurity. An ideology can stress the overwhelming importance of accomplishing its goals and propagate actions for this purpose that represent a clear reversal of morality. Proponents of ideologies often claim that the higher ideals that their ideology represents not only justify, but make necessary certain actions otherwise thought inconceivable. For example, here is what one Nazi had to say in his postwar testimony. He describes a conversation that took place at Belzec, one of the extermination camps:

> Doctor Herbert Leintner, who was here yesterday, asked me, "Wouldn't it be more prudent to burn the bodies instead of burying them? Another generation might take a different view of these things." I answered: "Gentlemen, if there is ever a generation after us so cowardly, so soft, that it would not understand our work as good and necessary, then, gentlemen, national socialism will have been for nothing. On the contrary, we should bury bronze tablets saying that it was we, we who had the courage to carry out this gigantic task!" [Chartock & Spencer, 1978, p. 12]

Although ideologies have often led to wide-ranging cruelties, it seems difficult to conceive of human beings engaging in the large-scale violence that the Nazis perpetrated just for the sake of ideology, for its own sake, so to speak, without seeing in this violence some pragmatic purpose. Gordon Allport wrote in *The Nature of Prejudice* (1954): "Hitler created the Jewish menace, not so much to demolish Jews as to cement the Nazi hold over Germany" (p. 40). It is apparently easier to see the generation of hatred and antagonism toward a group as "the Machiavellian trick of creating a common enemy in order to cement an ingroup" (Allport, 1954, p. 40), than to see it as being done out of hate or on the basis of ideology. Certainly, most persistent human behavior is multidetermined, both at individual and societal levels. Seemingly, however, an ideology provides an important goal orientation—embodying both an elaborate cognitive network and a specification of desirable outcomes—which can exert powerful influence on behavior.

The Role of Scapegoating

The activating conditions that I described earlier can also lead to scapegoating, to accusing some groups or individuals of responsibility in having caused the problems, the difficulties, the misfortune. As an initial step, scapegoating usually requires an us-them differentiation, the identification of some individual or group that is seen as different from the rest of the population that suffers from the instigating conditions. Scapegoats are likely to be selected on the basis of an already-existing devaluation of some group in a culture. This devaluation may be the result of existing social conditions that make this group appear inferior, embodying derogation of them. For example, some forms of discrimination that are institutionalized in the culture may define a group as less worthwhile. A long history of devaluation and the existence of an image of a group that embodies devaluation and is transmitted over time may also provide the basis for selecting scapegoats. Scapegoating represents both an added incitement to aggression and a mode of selecting victims.

To provide more contemporary examples of the role of ideology and the selection of scapegoats, recent history in Argentina may be considered. Perhaps as many as 15,000 people were made to disappear in Argentina in the last decade. These people were kidnapped, often tortured, and most apparently murdered. In Argentina, also, there were both very difficult economic conditions, a decline in the economy and inflation under Isabelle Peron, as well as political chaos and violence perpetrated to a large extent by leftist guerrillas or terrorists, but also by extreme right-wing groups. The military took over. Their basic view of the world, their ideology, was that of anti-Communism. There is reason to believe that in addition to involving self-interest—seeing Communism as a direct threat to the influence of the military—this ideology also involved a genuine belief in what is good for the country and the world. Apparently it was this basic view of the evils of Communism that led the military to create a system in which low-level operatives from the army could engage in kidnapping, incarceration, torture, and murder. Under these conditions, the targets that were selected included not only Communists and those who engaged in terrorist activity but also anyone who was regarded as having leftist leanings. People with liberal political views were also defined as an enemy of not only the system but also, as I am arguing, of the well-being of the nation and even the interests of humanity.

It is worthwhile to speculate that the relative economic distress that is currently experienced in our country, due to inflation and other factors, might have brought forth the Moral Majority. Historical analysis is necessarily somewhat loose. I am arguing, however, that difficult historical conditions of the kind that I described will give rise to groups or individuals representing ideologies that offer promise and hope, frequently at the same time defining some individuals as the enemy, as interfering with the welfare of the nation. For the Moral Majority, secular humanists are the enemy. Interestingly, secular humanists are described by them in terms somewhat similar to those Hitler used for the Jews. They are seen as the internal enemy, trying to subvert the country and its ideals and take over and establish their own rule.

One source of looseness of historical analysis is the difficulty in identifying the important or activating aspects of particular historical conditions. For example, in the Germany of the 1920s, in addition to the activating conditions that were noted, there was also a great deal of "moral chaos," perhaps due to the difficult life conditions. There was profound deviation from traditional German values in public life, such as otherwise "respectable" burghers dancing cheek to cheek in homosexual bars. Just as Germany's powerlessness and poverty deviated from and threatened a national self-image, so this moral chaos might have done so. The current fluidity and change in life-styles and values may be a contributing influence to the emergence and aims of the moral majority.

SOME PSYCHOLOGICAL CONSEQUENCES OF INSTIGATING CONDITIONS FOR AGGRESSION

1.   One result of instigating conditions for violence can be an internal state of anger and feelings of hostility that make the suffering of other people satisfying and a desired outcome. Findings in a variety of research studies show that when individuals are insulted, frustrated, or in some way attacked in laboratory studies, they favor and gain satisfaction from the suffering of those who inflicted distress or harm on them (see Staub, 1971, and Zillman, 1978, for reviews). The evidence seems to suggest that it is a relatively temporary condition: However, the instigation is usually limited in scope and temporary in nature, and the resulting aggression or the suffering imposed on the perpetrator creates a balance between the harm they caused and the harm they receive.

2.   The instigating conditions that were described have implications or consequences for the self-concept and self-esteem. A feeling of failure, of inability to achieve one's goals, of inability to protect oneself and one's family, or of inability to live up to important values can all result from the extended presence of these instigating conditions. The result can be a perception of attack on oneself, on one's concept of oneself or image of oneself. One function of scapegoating is that it relieves people of responsibility for their failure and the difficulties that result from economic problems or other threats or attacks on the self. If some others are responsible, others who are often seen as intentional perpetrators of the harm, then one is relieved of responsibility. Another function or consequence of scapegoating is that it unites people, it creates a kind of solidarity with an in-group that is confronted by the harmdoers, who are seen as the common enemy.

3.   The instigating conditions that were described can lead to a feeling of injustice, to a feeling of relative deprivation, if others do not experience the same conditions, and to moral outrage. They can lead to acts of aggression and violence to redress a real or imagined imbalance. The violence can both serve an emotional need and can be seen by the perpetrators as enabling them to achieve economic or social gains due them.

PERSONALITY CHARACTERISTICS AND THE EFFECTS OF INSTIGATION

Certain personal characteristics of individuals can make the impact of instigation for either prosocial action or for antisocial acts more or less likely. Here the focus will be on instigation for antisocial behavior.

1.   The prosocial orientation that was discussed earlier should diminish the impact of instigating conditions, or at least the likelihood of violent action. After all, this value orientation embodies both a concern for and a personal responsibility for others' welfare. As noted earlier, however, it is certainly possible that sometimes individuals or groups limit the range of applicability of their prosocial goal and define some people as falling beyond that range. Although no clear evidence is available, this limiting may be more likely to occur with a duty or obligation orientation, which allows exceptions. With such an orientation, individuals who somehow deviate from social norms or the standards embodied in the culture may be seen as falling beyond the range of applicability of obligation.

2.   Persons who suffer chronic frustration and dissatisfaction may respond more intensely to instigating conditions. Allport (1954), drawing on psychoanalytic thinking, suggested that such individuals may be more likely to displace their aggressive impulses and find some appropriate objects for expressing them. It is also likely that chronic frustration and dissatisfaction may make people susceptible to instigating conditions of lesser intensity. In discussing antisocial and aggressive behavior by aggressive delinquent youth, I suggested the importance of competence in achieving socially valued goals (Staub, 1971). A sense of competence, of the ability to bring about socially and personally valued goals and opportunities for doing so, would presumably be associated with less feeling of frustration and injustice. Fostering such competence, pointing to plans and strategies whereby personal goals can be achieved without aggressive means, may diminish aggression both by individuals and by cultures that experience difficult life conditions.

3.   Mistrust of other people, negative evaluation of them, and their derogation, may all contribute to a greater likelihood that instigating conditions will lead to aggressive action. Mistrust and derogation are not necessarily identical but most likely are often connected. People who mistrust others, who perceive their intentions as negative, may respond to actions that are not inherently injurious to them with self-defense or preretaliation. This can

be true of either individuals or social groups. Slavson (1965) described aggressive delinquent youth as highly mistrustful and tending to perceive others' actions as representing an attack on themselves. At the level of society, groups can perceive the actions or the very character of some other group as representing danger to them. In fact, governments, as Allport noted in the earlier quotation, frequently point to some group, often a minority, as a common enemy in order to shift enmity away from themselves or to create cohesion. We have seen in our own country that calling attention to an enemy will increase the popularity of a leader, even following failure. The *Mayaquez* incident is one example. The increase in John F. Kennedy's popularity after the Bay of Pigs fiasco seems another.

4.   The learned enjoyment of others' suffering represents another personality orientation that makes responsiveness to instigating conditions more likely. Although psychologists usually define aggression as behavior that intends to hurt, we have some difficulty in taking seriously the notion that for some individuals hurting others can be a source of satisfaction, a valued outcome. Some evidence for this is provided by a study of Hartman (1969), in which young delinquents who had a history of aggressive behavior responded to instigation with greater aggression after they observed the suffering of a boxer who was severely beaten in the course of a boxing match. Consistent with the findings of other studies, among nonaggressive delinquents the observation of the boxer's suffering reduced aggression in response to the instigation.

In order truly to understand how prosocial and antisocial behavior come about, in addition to value orientations and personal goals, we must consider the nature of the self and certain additional preconditions in either individual personalities or cultures and societies. These preconditions include the image of the world, in addition to the image of the self (for example, trust or mistrust, or more or less devaluation of some groups). They also include instrumental conceptions: strategies and plans for dealing with conflict, and both strategies and skills for pursuing desirable goals. At the personal level, children learning to resolve frustration with renewed attempts at achieving a goal (Davitz, 1952), or to resolve conflict with peaceful means such as discussion and compromise or aggressive means such as hitting and grabbing, can make a profound difference in their behavior. Some researchers proposed a "socialization void hypothesis," suggesting that some children, because of the nature of their experiences, including the family situation and exposure to aggressive but not to prosocial television shows, never learn prosocial means of resolving conflict and constructive means of regulating their everyday behavior, including task activities (Friedrich & Stein, 1973).

THE NATURE OF SELF AND THE SELF-OTHER BOND

In many ways kindness and cruelty are expressions of and are affected by the nature of the self-other bond. This is true even when kindness and cruelty are due to extrinsic reasons, such as being helpful to gain approval or engaging in aggression for instrumental gain. The self-concept and self-esteem, and other characteristics of the self, will affect the kind of bond a person is capable of or will usually enter. There is substantial evidence, for example, that when people receive negative feedback about themselves in the form of failure or in other ways, they will subsequently be less helpful (Rosenhan, Salovey, Karylowski, & Hargis, 1981; Staub, 1978). There is also evidence that when their concern about their performance, achievement, or self-representation is aroused (Berkowitz, 1970; Staub, 1978), people will again be less helpful. There are various ways to interpret these findings. One likely possibility is that when attention and concern are focused on the self, there is less attention to and concern about others' needs and welfare.

In addition, there is weighting of the relative claims of self and of other people. I proposed the concept of "hedonic balancing" to describe how this weighting occurs (Staub, 1978). The hedonic balancing hypothesis suggests that people will consider their usual state of well-being and compare their current state with it. Then they compare the discrepancy between their current and usual states with the discrepancy between the usual state of well-being of another person (which they may judge on the basis of their conception of people's welfare in general or their knowledge of this particular person's usual welfare) and the current state of this person's welfare. This hypothesis allows relatively complex predictions. For example, a person who is relatively happy may be usually more helpful, but his or her helpfulness will increase less when some experience results in a high level of subjective well-being. There is evidence that a customary level of self-esteem makes a difference. In a study conducted in Poland, when preadolescents' level of self-esteem was increased, due to extensive interventions, they perceived (or reported) to a greater extent another child's difficulties and need, which was presented to them on film (Jarymowitz, 1977).

In case of a negative self-image and low self-esteem, the need to protect or enhance the self may easily arise. This can be accomplished by cognitively diminishing (derogating) others, by denying one's own responsibilities through scapegoating, or by taking actual steps that will diminish others' welfare. Naturally, self-esteem alone will not determine how people respond to instigation. With a low self-esteem it is possible to react with withdrawal and avoidance, rather than with moving against other people in thought or action. Blaming and devaluing the self and other intrapunitive reactions are also possible. Value orientations, personal goals, action tendencies, the experience of chronic frustration of important goals, and other elements contribute to determining how people will respond to potential instigating conditions for either prosocial behavior or aggression.

Aspects of the self other than self-esteem can also be involved. For example, a moral orientation that focuses on the importance of inhibiting impulses has implications for the nature of the self. If anger, sexuality, or other impulses are not allowed as conscious aspects of the self, a variety of consequences becomes likely. The literature on the authoritarian personality

(Cherry & Byrne, 1977) focuses on the inhibition of such impulses as one aspect of the personality of authoritarian individuals. Although some of this literature is of questionable quality, the body of literature does point to certain personal characteristics that go together in some individuals. In addition to the inhibition of impulses, there also appears to be an orientation toward authority that is highly respectful. The words of authority are respected, accepted, and frequently obeyed. In contrast, those who are powerless are derogated by such "authoritarian" individuals. The unacceptability in oneself of such important feelings and desires, which are partly physiologically based and cannot be easily denied, can lead to projection, according to a psychoanalytic view, with the result that these impulses are seen in other people. Because they are unacceptable, they become a reason for punishing these people for the presence of these desires or impulses in them. This can happen through discrimination and violence.

THE PSYCHOLOGY OF DIRECT PERPETRATORS

A differentiation between people in various leadership roles who conceive of and propagate violent action and the direct perpetrators of violence may be useful. Leaders may propagate violent action on the basis of ideology or to enhance their power and influence and create cohesion among their followers.

What about direct perpetrators? Some of them may find themselves as the mistreatment of some individuals or groups begins in roles that make it part of their job or function to perpetrate violence. Prison guards or soldiers may become tools of disappearances, mistreatment, torture, and murder. To some extent, the psychological relationship between themselves and their victims that arises out of their roles, and to some extent obedience to authority, may predispose people in such roles to go with the tide and become perpetrators. As the prison study by Zimbardo, Haney, Banks, and Jafle (1974) suggests, "average" persons may come to mistreat others when a role as prison guard gives them power over other average, innocent people who enact prison inmates. The role of prison guard in relationship to inmates (and other role relations, such as police officer in relation to citizen) may give rise to us-them differentiation that together with the meaning of the prisoner role can easily lead to devaluation. In addition, prison guards are usually members of a fairly strict authority structure, and obedience to authority is likely to exert influence on their behavior.

Obviously, many direct perpetrators may be self-selected—often for initial acts less violent than acts they later perpetrate. The previous analysis suggested some of the personal characteristics of would-be perpetrators of mistreatment of minorities and subgroups in a population that lead them to their roles and activities. They may include a devotion to the ideology in the name of which violence is perpetrated; an authoritarian personality structure; a concern about maintaining justice in the world, in the sense of a just-world type reaction (Lerner, 1980), and a desire arising from this that people should receive punishment they deserve for misdeeds, real or imagined; an enjoyment of others' suffering, which I suggested before is characteristic of some individuals; a seeking and enjoyment of excitement that can be expressed through the kind of activities that are usually involved in the perpetration of violence; chronic dissatisfaction and frustration, which may give rise to self-other comparisons and anger and hostility; and value orientations that allow people to take on the role of direct perpetrators or lead them to such a role. Some support for the relevance of these characteristics is suggested by information about SS members, described by Steiner (1981). In interviews, former SS members described some of the following reasons for their joining and participating in the SS: attraction to and enjoyment derived from playing military or pseudomilitary roles; pragmatic or mercenary reasons, that is, to improve their existence or to gain tangible benefits; identification with the ideology that was presented to them as part of the SS; and the desire to become a professional soldier, which at the time was impossible because of the limit on the number of soldiers in the German army.

Finally, two additional components may be important in making it possible for direct perpetrators to engage in extreme acts of violence, such as the extermination of Jews in the Holocaust and of other people in the gas chambers. One of these was already mentioned: the role of ideology that leads to reversal of morality, so that the mistreatment of some individuals or groups is seen as serving a higher ideal. Another is the assumption of responsibility by leaders.

A feeling either of personal responsibility for others' welfare or that one is held responsible by society is strongly embedded in most people. Depending on a person's moral orientation, it may be stronger or weaker, and some people may be defined as outside the realm of the humanity whose welfare one is responsible for. Nonetheless, directly and personally inflicting extreme pain or murdering other people is still likely to activate in most people, at least initially, overlearned feelings of responsibility for others' physical well-being and life. The assumption of responsibility by leaders may be crucial to allow perpetrators to proceed. This is what happened in the Milgram (1974) experiments, where the experimenter told subjects to proceed in administering electric shocks and that he, the experimenter, would assume responsibility. This also happened with the Nazi perpetrators of genocide, who were told that their leaders, specifically Hitler and Himmler, would personally assume responsibility for their actions. At the same time, their actions were described as heroic conduct in the service of a higher ideal.

MOTIVATIONAL ORIENTATIONS AND PERSONAL CHARACTERISTICS REVISITED

The original theory described in this chapter was a theory of goals. In the moral realm different value orientations can give rise to different prosocial (or moral) goals. Goals are arranged in a hierarchy of importance. Their activation by aspects of the environment was stressed, but goals can also be self-activated by images and thoughts. Whether goals will be expressed in action also depends on varied supporting characteristics, such as competencies and perceptual orientations. To some extent these characteristics also affect the likelihood that goals are activated (Staub, 1980).

In the course of discussion of violence and cruelty, this theory was extended. A comprehensive theory of moral conduct requires additional elements, some of which were described in the course of the discussion and are more formally stated in the following paragraphs.

1. Ideologies can be an important basis of goal orientations in affecting morally relevant conduct. They can lead to actions that will potentially improve human welfare, but also to actions that will harm people who are seen as interfering, sometimes by their very existence, with desirable (both practically and morally) conditions in the world.

2. The nature of the self and of self-other bonds must be considered. A person's self-concept and degree of self-esteem and the extent to which all aspects of the self are accepted or some important aspects are denied can have important implications for the person's relationship to other people. What these implications are can vary and will be a function of other personal characteristics. For example, a low self-esteem can lead to personal distress, to feelings of negativity about the self. To some extent it will inevitably interfere with strong positive bonds to other people; the nature of the self has inevitable implications for the self-other bond. But whether difficulties with the self-concept and low self-esteem will make some individuals an easy prey to conditions that can give rise to us-them differentiation and derogation of other people and instigate hostility and aggression may depend on value orientations and moral goals as well. Similarly, the inability to accept certain characteristics in the self may lead to neuroses or may predispose people to turn against others.

3. A person's "operational system," knowledge about the world, the availability of plans and strategies for action, competencies in executing actions, and the like, also have implications for moral conduct. A well-developed person in these realms may be successful in pursuing important goals and less likely to experience frustration or threat to the self and to expectations for important outcomes. Such a person may also be more likely to respond to others' needs and to initiate action that will benefit others. The operational system can be very deeply rooted; some aspects of it can be described as a way of seeing the world, of conceiving what it is like and how people behave in it. Seeing the world as a place where aggressive behaviors are common and natural or as a place where helpful conduct is common and natural will have different consequences on what actions a person will contemplate in pursuing goals.

4. The earlier discussion and the summary in the preceding three paragraphs point to the need to expand the motivational conception embodied in

the theory of goals. In doing so, it seems worthwhile to differentiate between goals, needs, and unconscious motives. Goals as discussed in this chapter refer to specific outcomes or events that are desired and sought or outcomes and events that are aversive, with the object of the goal being their avoidance. Needs will be conceptualized as arising out of and representing deprivation. There may be two important kinds of deprivations. First, there can be physiological deprivation, the deprivation in sexual needs and desires and hunger and thirst, what has been conceptualized as primary needs. Such needs can be powerful, of course, when present. When they are normally satisfied, however, they frequently undergo substantial transformation and become goallike in character. For example, the gourmand travels far to find the best restaurants; acting out of a desire for satisfaction, he or she is motivated by a goal and not a need. Another source of needs may be chronic deprivation in the satisfaction of important goals. This assumes that when there is chronic deprivation the goal comes to be experienced as a deficiency, something that is needed, rather than a desired form of satisfaction. It is then likely that the experience of deficiency serves as an activator, so that the need exerts influence even without external activation. Even though the outcomes related to the goal originally were sought because they promised satisfaction, now the experience of this deficiency is primarily aversive. Alternatively, chronic unfulfillment can also lead to a loss of desire for relevant outcomes, to the goal losing its importance for the person. The earlier discussion also suggested the desirability of considering unconscious motivation. I discussed how one type of moral orientation may focus on the unacceptability of impulses such as hostility and sex, so that they will neither be accepted in oneself nor be allowed expression. As psychoanalytic theory persuasively suggests, such impulses do not disappear. They will continue to exert influence, sometimes in their projection onto other people, who then become legitimate objects of punishment. The recognition of their presence and of the need for their assessment and an examination of how they exert influence seem important.

In summary, in this chapter I discussed concepts that are important for understanding cruelty and kindness in a joint framework. A theory of goals or goal orientations was described. How personal goals, together with supporting characteristics and as a function of the environment, enter into the determination of social behavior, particularly prosocial behavior, was elaborated. In extending this conceptualization to cruelty, the importance of ideology as a goal was emphasized. The activating conditions for violence, aggression, and cruelty and that such activating conditions may be either temporary or created by historical conditions or stable life circumstances were briefly noted. Both psychological consequences of these activating conditions and the functions of aggressive responses were noted. In this context, the role of scapegoating was examined. The personal characteristics of individuals who would be particularly susceptible to instigating conditions were discussed. In addition to value and goal orientations, these included chronic frustration, mistrust, suspicion, and, as a consequence, frequent hostility to other people, as well as an authoritarian personality orientation. The important role of the self-concept and the self-other bond in kindness and cruelty were also discussed. Finally, the psychology of direct perpetrators was briefly examined, with the importance of the psychological consequences of being in certain roles, self-selection by personality, reversal of morality, and the assumption of responsibility by leaders. The discussion of cruelty suggested that in addition to goals, needs and unconscious motives are additional motivational influences that enter into determining behavior in general and cruelty and kindness in particular.

REFERENCES

Allport, G. *The nature of prejudice.* Reading, Mass.: Addison-Wesley, 1954.

Berkowitz, L. The self, selfishness, and altruism. In J. Macaulay & L. Berkowitz (Eds.), *Altruism and helping behavior.* New York: Academic Press, 1970.

Chartock, R., & Spencer, J. *The Holocaust years: Society on trial.* New York: Bantam Books, 1978.

Cherry, F., & Byrne, D. Authoritarianism. In T. Blass (Ed.), *Personality variables in social behavior.* Hillsdale, N.J.: Lawrence Erlbaum Associates, 1977.

Davitz, J. R. The effects of previous training on post-frustration behavior. *Journal of Abnormal and Social Psychology,* 1952, *47,* 309–315.

Durkheim, E. *Moral education: A study in the theory and application in the sociology of education.* New York: Free Press, 1961. (Originally published, 1925.)

Feinberg, J. K. *Anatomy of a helping situation: Some personality and situational determinants of helping in a conflict situation involving another's psychological distress.* Unpublished doctoral dissertation, University of Massachusetts, Amherst, 1977.

Friedrich, L. K., & Stein, A. J. Aggressive and prosocial television programs and the natural behavior of preschool children. *Monographs of the Society for Research in Child Development,* 1973, *38*(4, Serial No. 15).

Grodman, S. M. *The role of personality and situational variables in responding to and helping an individual in psychological distress.* Unpublished doctoral dissertation, University of Massachusetts, Amherst, 1979.

Hartman, D. P. Influence of symbolically modeled instrumental aggression and pain cues on aggressive behavior. *Journal of Personality and Social Psychology,* 1969, *11,* 280–288.

Hoffman, M. L. Conscience, personality, and socialization technique. *Human Development,* 1970, *13,* 90–126.

Jarymowitz, M. Modification of self-worth and increment of prosocial sensitivity. *Polish Psychological Bulletin,* 1977, *8,* 45–53.

Latané, B., & Darley, J. *The unresponsive bystander: Why doesn't he help?* Englewood Cliffs, N.J.: Prentice-Hall, 1970.

Lerner, M. *The belief in a just world. A fundamental delusion.* New York: Plenum, 1980.

Milgram, S. *Obedience to authority: An experimental view.* New York: Harper & Row, 1974.

Rosenhan, D. L., Salovey, P., Karylowski, J., & Hargis, K. Emotion and altruism. In J. P. Rushton, & R. M. Sorrentino (Eds.), *Altruism and helping behavior.* Hillsdale, N.J.: Lawrence Erlbaum Associates, 1981.

Slavson, S. R. *Reclaiming the delinquent.* New York: Free Press, 1965.

Staub, E. A child in distress: The effects of focusing responsibility on children on their attempts to help. *Developmental Psychology,* 1970, *2,* 152–154.

Staub, E. The learning and unlearning of aggression: The role of anxiety, empathy, efficacy and prosocial values. In J. Singer (Ed.), *The control of aggression and violence: Cognitive and physiological factors.* New York: Academic Press, 1971.

Staub, E. Helping a distressed person: Social, personality and stimulus determinants. In L. Berkowitz (Ed.), *Advances in experimental social psychology* (Vol. 7). New York: Academic Press, 1974.

Staub, E. *Positive social behavior and morality* (Vol. 1): *Social and personal influences.* New York: Academic Press, 1978a.

Staub, E. Predicting prosocial behavior: A model for specifying the nature of personality-situation interaction. In L. Pervin & M. Lewis (Eds.), *Perspectives in interactional psychology.* New York: Plenum, 1978b.

Staub, E. Social and prosocial behavior: Personal and situational influences and their interactions. In E. Staub (Ed.), *Personality: Basic aspects and current research.* Englewood Cliffs, N.J.: Prentice-Hall, 1980.

Staub, E. Notes toward an interactionist-motivational theory of the determinants and development of prosocial behavior. In E. Staub, D. Bar-Tal, J. Karylowski, & J. Reykowski (Eds.), *The development and maintenance of prosocial behavior: International perspectives.* New York: Plenum, in press.

Steiner, J. M. The SS yesterday and today: A sociopsychological view. In J. Dimsdale (Ed.), *Survivors, victims and perpetrators. Essays on the Nazi Holocaust.* Hemisphere Publishing, 1980.

Tajfel, H., Flamant, C., Billig, M. Y., & Bundy, R. P. Societal categorization and intergroup behavior. *European Journal of Social Psychology,* 1971, *1,* 149–177.

Zillman, D. *Hostility and aggression.* Hillsdale, N.J.: Lawrence Erlbaum Associates, 1978.

Zimbardo, P. G., Haney, C., Banks, W. C., & Jafle, D. The psychology of imprisonment. Privation, power and pathology. In Z. Rubin (Ed.), *Doing unto others.* Englewood Cliffs, N.J.: Prentice-Hall, 1974.

CHAPTER   15

Social Knowledge and Action: The Coordination of Domains

ELLIOT TURIEL AND JUDITH G. SMETANA

This chapter deals with the relations between social judgments and actions. Starting with the assumption that many behavioral situations are multidimensional, it is proposed that action is a product of the coordination of domains of social judgment. Behavioral situations are multidimensional in that more than one type of judgment is brought to bear on behavioral decisions. For example, social-behavioral decisions may include moral judgments of harm, rights and justice, and societal concepts (such as concepts of institutions, authority relations, customs, and social conventions). Therefore, the study of relations between social judgment and action requires analyses of the interrelations among domains of social judgments in interaction within the parameters of the situational context. Examples of behavioral data from studies including multiple dimensions are examined in order to illustrate how social actions stem from the coordination of domains.

Psychologists are fond of dualities. Dualities regarding thought and action, reason and culture, and social judgment and the content of social norms abound. Dualities of this sort are particularly prevalent in explanations of the social realms of psychological functioning. It is said that moral thought is discrepant from actual behavior and that people frequently fail to act in accordance with their ways of thinking about right and wrong. It is also said that reason is distinct from culture and that the force of culture or the collective will is often more powerful than the demands of reason. The content of social norms derived from one's culture can determine behavior in ways that are inconsistent with the conclusions derived from processes of reasoning. Further, a duality between moral judgment and self-interest that also makes for discrepancies between thought and action is said to exist. In some respects, the force of self-interest is not seen as independent of the force of culture because the self derives benefits from social approval and suffers

261

losses from social disapproval. In other respects, the force of self-interest is in conflict with social interest and obligation.

In contrast with the dualistic views, the position presented in this chapter focuses on the interrelations of social thought, social action, and cultural content. Structures of social thought are proposed to be central to individuals' relations to the social system and to their social actions. It is proposed that moral judgments are constructions stemming out of the child's actions in interaction with the social environment. Moral judgments, therefore, form a basis for dealing with concrete social experiences and are not dissociated from the individual's actions. In focusing on the interrelations of thought, action, and culture, it is proposed, first, that it is necessary to ascertain the different domains of social judgment constructed in the course of development. Of particular importance for the question of moral judgment and action relations, in addition to the development of moral judgments, is the development of concepts of cultural and social systems, including concepts of institutions, authority relations, customs, and social conventions. In separating domains of social judgment, a corollary proposition is that individuals do not take a unitary orientation to the social environment. Therefore, the study of the relations of social behavior to social judgments requires examination of the interrelations among domains of social judgment in behavioral situations. Social situations are frequently multifaceted in that more than one domain of judgment may be brought to bear on decisions and behaviors. In this context, behavior is viewed neither as the ultimate criterion of the validity of moral judgment assessments nor as in direct, causal relation with the individual's moral judgments. Actions in given situations are products of the interrelations of different types of social judgments, which may entail conflicts, coordinations, inconsistencies, and consistencies.

To understand the relations between moral judgment and behavior, nonmoral social judgments must be considered. With the availability of methods to distinguish individuals' moral and nonmoral social judgments, it becomes plausible to explore the interrelations of domains of judgment, in interaction with parameters of social situations. Research and disputation on the relations, or lack thereof, between moral judgment and behavior has had a long and checkered history. With few exceptions, the question has been put in causal and quantitative terms: To what extent does an individual's moral judgments or knowledge *lead to* corresponding behavior? It is our view that reformulation of the way the question itself is posed is a first step in research on what is still an inadequately understood and highly contested issue. As a means of providing the analytic framework for reformulating the question to account for interrelations among social judgment domains, we first consider some of the ways moral judgment behavior dualities and relations have been conceptualized and empirically investigated. This step is followed by consideration of research on both behavior and judgment that supports propositions regarding social judgment domain separations and their intersection in behavioral situations.

MORAL THOUGHT, ACTION, AND CULTURAL CATEGORIES

In the 1920s two large-scale and influential research projects on morality were conducted—one by Hartshorne and May (1928–1930) and the other by Piaget (1932). The methods and emphases of the Hartshorne and May research differed from those of Piaget, but in both projects relations between moral thought and moral behavior were examined. Hartshorne and May placed greater emphasis on behavioral measures than on measures of judgment; Piaget placed greater emphasis on measures of judgment than on behavioral measures. Hartshorne and May attempted to assess the extent to which moral knowledge is predictive of moral behavior ("the problem of the relation between what he says and what he does or would do"). Piaget attempted to examine correspondences between the organization of systems of judgment and the organization of systems of action. Hartshorne and May obtained findings that led them to conclusions different from those drawn by Piaget from his findings.

The main conclusion from the Hartshorne and May research relevant to our purposes was that behavior is not closely related to judgment. The findings came from correlations between behavioral measures of deceit and scores on standardized paper and pencil tests of "moral knowledge." The behavioral measures are well known. Close to 30 situations were used to assess cheating behavior. In most cases, subjects were placed in situations providing them with an opportunity to cheat on classroom tests, athletic contests, and party games. In a few cases, lying and stealing were measured. The moral knowledge tests were designed to assess the subject's awareness of moral standards of conduct. Responses to multiple-choice and true-false test items yielded quantitative assessments of subjects' moral knowledge, relative to presumed mature, adult standards. The correlations between moral knowledge test scores and behavior in specific situations were very low. Hartshorne and May did find a correlation of .50 between a general assessment of moral knowledge (i.e., pooled scores on all the moral knowledge tests) and scores on all the behavioral tests—hence the conclusion that, at best, there may be some general relations, of a moderate level, between what one knows and what one does.

In contrast with the Hartshorne and May approach, Piaget was concerned with the influences of action on judgment and judgment on action in the developmental process. It was proposed that the coordinations of actions and judgments are important influences on children's moral development. Although Piaget's research was in the main directed toward uncovering forms of judgment in children of different ages, he did a comparative analysis of children's behavior and judgments with regard to rules of games (Piaget, 1932, chap. 1). In the studies of behavior, or what Piaget referred to as the practice of rules, observations were made of children actually playing games (marbles and hide-and-seek) and responding to questions regarding the ways the games are played. In the studies of judgment, or what Piaget referred to as the consciousness of rules, children were interviewed about various aspects of game rules (e.g., origins, alterability, purposes). On the basis of these investigations, two parallel developmental sequences were formulated, one for the practice of rules and one for the consciousness of rules. Each sequence portrayed a shift from an external, egocentric, and heteronomous orientation to a cooperative orientation to rules as products of mutual agreements. The similarities between the levels of consciousness and practice led Piaget to the conclusion, which differed from that of Hartshorne and May, that judgment and behavior are interrelated.

The differences between the Piaget and the Hartshorne and May approaches were both methodological and theoretical. One major and obvious theoretical difference is in their respective constructs of moral knowledge or judgment. For Hartshorne and May, knowledge was defined as a quantitative dimension assessed by attitudes or conclusions reflective of adult standards. For Piaget, judgment was defined as a qualitative dimension reflecting the subject's organization of thought. Accordingly, Hartshorne and May used tests to derive a score that would represent the subject's degree of moral knowledge. Piaget, in contrast, used interview methods designed to obtain information on how subjects reason about moral problems. Correspondingly, the construct of moral behavior was conceptualized in different ways. Hartshorne and May treated behavior as a product (e.g., a child does or does not cheat). Piaget treated behavior as a product in association with an internal process and, therefore, examined patterns of action (i.e., in the application of game rules).

Another difference between the two approaches was in the conceptualization of thought-action relations. Posing the question in the causal form of whether or not judgment leads to action, Hartshorne and May assessed the degree of consistency in the two measures through correlational analyses. Findings of consistency would have been interpreted as indicative that behavior is determined by judgment, whereas the observed inconsistencies were interpreted as reflective of a dualism between judgment and behavior. In proposing that judgment and action are interactive, Piaget attempted to examine the correspondences in their patterns and sequences. Consistencies were observed in the levels of consciousness and practice, but discrepancies were evident in their respective ages of attainment. Each level of practice was attained somewhat earlier than the corresponding level of consciousness. On the basis of these two sets of findings, Piaget put forth structural and developmental hypotheses: namely, that judgment is implicated in action and that children's actions are a significant source of the formation of their judgments.

Fifty years later, the contrasting views represented by Piaget and by Hartshorne and May still prevail in psychological analyses. On the one side, structural-developmental theorists (Blasi, 1980; Kohlberg, 1971; see also Chaps. 4 and 7 in this book) continued to propose interrelations in judgment and behavior. In most of the recent research the assessments of moral judgment are based on the methods and stages formulated by Kohlberg (1963, 1969, and Chaps. 3, 4, and 5 in this book). In this regard, the research is consistent with Piaget's original focus on developmental levels of the organization of moral thinking. The behavioral assessments in these studies, however, depart from Piaget's analysis of forms and levels of action in that solely behavioral products were measured (as examples, studies have been done assessing whether subjects cheat, act altruistically, engage in delinquent acts, undertake civil disobedience).

There are too many studies correlating stages of moral judgment and behavior to review them here. Fortunately, a comprehensive and cogent review by Blasi (1980) allows us to summarize the pattern of results. Two major conclusions emerge: One is that a substantial number of studies show a close relationship between moral judgment and action. The other conclusion, however, is that a fair number of studies also show moderate or low correlations between judgment and action. In other words, both consistencies and inconsistencies are evident in the research findings.

The meaning of findings of consistency and inconsistency, as well as their specific patterns, are considered later. First, however, it should be noted that contemporary socialization theorists (e.g., Aronfreed, 1968, 1976; Bandura, 1977; Grinder, 1964; Kurtines & Greif, 1974; Mischel & Mischel, 1976) still maintain the position of a duality in moral judgment and action. The Hartshorne and May data provide one source of empirical support for this contention (see especially Aronfreed, 1968, and Mischel & Mischel, 1976). Another source of claimed empirical support comes from studies that have correlated behavioral measures with Kohlberg's stages of moral judgment—and in some cases with Piaget's levels of moral judgment (e.g., Grinder, 1964). It has been asserted that assessments of the organizations and reorganizations of moral thinking made by structural-developmental theorists are no more predictive of moral behavior than are the moral knowledge tests used by Hartshorne and May.

The proposed discrepancy between judgment and behavior is associated with the socialization premise of moral development as one aspect of social learning. The individual's moral reasoning and moral behavior, it is maintained, are formed through the acquisition of modes of cultural orientations (Hogan, 1973, 1975, and Chap 13 in this book; Sampson, 1977). According to this view, social systems can be characterized by a predominant orientation of the individual to the group. Some social systems are mainly individualistic, whereas others are collectivistic. For example, North American and Western European societies are characterized by an individualistic orientation, emphasizing personal rights, egalitarianism, and autonomy. In contrast, there are cultures characterized by a collectivistic orientation, emphasizing interdependence, authority, social hierarchy, and conformity. The individual's orientation is the result of the learning of the cultural orientation. Consequently, an individualistic culture produces an individualistic psychology in its members, whereas a collectivistic culture produces a collectivistic psychology in its members.

Given the hypothesized societal or cultural source of individual social development, various combinations of reasoning, the content of specific norms held, and behaviors performed have been proposed. Some have proposed a duality between judgment and behavior that is based on a dichotomy between the structure of an individual's reasoning and the content mapped onto reasoning by cultural learning (Aronfreed, 1976; Shweder, in press; and Chap. 12 in this book). Insofar as it is proposed that there is a dichotomy between reasoning and learned content, it is also being proposed that the structure of reasoning originates from a source that is different from the source of acquired content. This position, however, carries with it ambiguities and inconsistencies. First, the source of structures of reasoning, in that it differs from the learning of cultural content, is left unspecified. Moreover, there are conceptual problems in the proposed discrepancy between the laws governing the development of reasoning and the acquisition of content. If children incorporate cultural norms through mechanisms of learning (e.g., conditioning, imitation), then why do they not also acquire "forms of reasoning" in the same way? Conversely, if children develop structures of reasoning that are not determined by the direct learning of cultural content, then why is content not governed by similar principles of development? To make matters even more complex, it is also proposed (sometimes by the same theorist) that structures of reasoning are culturally learned (the idea that the individual's moral judgments reflect the cultural orientation). In such a case, it is most plausible to suppose that if cultures have a dominant orientation (e.g., individualistic, collectivistic, liberal, authoritarian), then there would be consistency in reasoning, content of norms, and behavior. Nevertheless, the proposition that the judgments of individuals reflect their cultural orientations is made alongside the proposition that judgment is generally inconsistent with behavior.

As noted earlier, Blasi has documented that a significant number of studies have found consistencies between moral judgment and behavior. Blasi has shown, therefore, that the claim (Aronfreed, 1976; Kurtines & Greif, 1974; Mischel & Mischel, 1976) of a lack of an empirical relation between stage measures of moral judgment and behavior is exaggerated. Nevertheless, findings of low or moderate correlations between moral judgment and behavior have been obtained. As mentioned earlier, correlations obtained in different studies have ranged from low to high. The empirical findings strongly suggest that there are consistencies *and* inconsistencies between moral judgment and behavior. The task, then, is to explain both types of findings (Turiel, in press; Langer, Note 1). Findings of empirical consistency require explanation in that they do not necessarily mean that moral judgment is *the* direct cause of the behavior (though they suggest that it is significantly implicated in the behavior). In turn, findings of empirical inconsistency do not necessarily support the hypotheses of thought-action duality. Findings of inconsistencies may, instead, reflect the individual's efforts at coordinating the different types of judgments relevant to a given behavioral situation. That is, assessments need to be made of nonmoral social judgments and their coordination with moral judgments. Also, the social judgments of individuals do not solely reflect a unitary or homogeneous cultural orientation. The research findings to be considered illustrate how different types of judgments may be coordinated (in conflictful and nonconflictful ways) and provide support for the proposition that judgments and actions are multifaceted, reflecting constructed categories of social reasoning rather than stereotyped cultural orientations. In our interpretation of the findings, cultural categories are stereotypes that only partially apply to the judgments and behaviors of individuals. Aspects of what are sometimes represented as unitary cultural orientations can be seen to coexist in the judgment of individuals, stemming from their differentiated understandings of social relations and social structures.

HETEROGENEITY IN SOCIAL JUDGMENTS AND BEHAVIOR

Many readers of this volume are familiar with Milgram's (1963, 1974) experiment in which subjects were instructed to administer increasing volts, up to a very high level, of electric shocks to another person. In one experimental condition (to be referred to here as the standard condition, following Turiel, in press), it was found that 65% of the subjects followed the experimenter's instructions and continued administering shocks to the end of the scale. The remaining subjects refused to go along with the commands, terminating their participation at some point prior to the end of the experiment. (Of course, the victim did not actually receive the shocks, though he made a convincing pretense of experiencing intense pain.)

The finding that the majority of subjects obey the commands of a person in authority to inflict great harm on another person contradicts one of the assumptions regarding the cultural orientation acquired by the members of this culture. The findings belie the notion that people from this culture are mainly individualistic, autonomous, and egalitarian (note that a cross section of subjects participated in the experiments, including undergraduates from a prestigious Ivy League university). In terms of the cultural categories, behavior in the standard condition appears to reflect an orientation to conformity, authority, and hierarchy. For most subjects, their own aversion to the harm inflicted was subordinated to the perceived legitimacy of the scientific context, with its hierarchical social structure (Milgram, 1974).

The experiments conducted by Milgram, however, also do not allow for a characterization of people in this culture as having acquired a homogeneous orientation to authority, conformity, and hierarchy. Whereas it is the procedures and findings of the standard condition that are best known and most frequently cited, findings from six other experimental conditions are equally informative. Those findings are presented in Table 15.1, which shows that in all but the standard condition the majority of subjects *refused,* at some point, to go along with the experimenter's commands to continue shocking the victim. The experimental conditions listed in the table varied in the proximity or salience of either the victim or the authority, relative to the subject. In the standard condition, the victim was placed in a different room from the subject and could be heard but not seen (referred to as "voice-feedback" by Milgram). In two other conditions the victim was in closer proximity to the subject than in the standard condition: In one, the victim could be seen and heard ("proximity"); in the other, the subject was instructed actually to force the victim's hand onto a shock plate ("touch-proximity"). In four conditions the salience of the experimenter's authority varied in the following ways: The experimenter gave instructions from another room by telephone ("experimenter absent"); another subject, who was actually an accomplice of the experimenter, gave the instructions ("ordinary man gives orders"); another subject gave the instructions while the experimenter took the role of victim ("authority as victim, ordinary man gives orders"); instructions were given by two experimenters, who contradicted each other after a designated shock level ("two authorities; contradictory commands").

If we take into account the findings from all the conditions, then the behaviors of subjects in Milgram's experiments cannot be explained through anything like a unitary cultural orientation. The range of findings show that subjects from this culture cannot be characterized as individualistic or collectivistic, egalitarian or hierarchically orientated, autonomous or conformist. All of these orientations coexist in that each is reflected in the subject's actions.

The Milgram findings also relate to the question of the relations between moral judgment and behavior. Considering solely the standard condition findings, it appears that there is inconsistency between what people think and what they do. It is very likely that most subjects would have judged it wrong knowingly to inflict harm on another person. Indeed, this conclusion is documented by subjects' reactions during the experiment, as well as their responses to postexperimental debriefings (Milgram, 1974). At the same time, however, all the other experimental conditions provide evidence for consistency, for most subjects (100% in some conditions) refused to continue their participation in the experiment. Moreover, in comparing the standard condition with the others we see inconsistency in behavior from one situation to another.

The comparisons of different conditions in Milgram's experiments demonstrate that behavior is, to a fair extent, influenced by the situational context. These comparisons also suggest that subjects interpret situational contexts and that behavior is not simply controlled by environmental contingencies. The variation observed in the different conditions does *not* mean that there are no systematic relations of behavior to judgment. Rather, the findings can be interpreted to reflect a relation between the structure of social events and the different domains of social judgment brought to bear on those events (Turiel, in press). We have stated that in the standard condition there may have been inconsistencies in moral judgment and behavior because subjects

TABLE 15.1. Responses (in percentages) in Seven Experimental Conditions in Studies of Obedience to Authority

Response to Instructions to Continue	Standard Condition: Voice-Feedback	Proximity	Touch-Proximity	Experimenter Absent	Ordinary Man Instructs	Authority as Victim	Two Conflicting Authorities
			Experimental Conditions				
Stop	35	60	70	80	80	100	100
Continue	65	40	30	20	20	0	0

Source: Derived from Milgram, 1974.

would have judged it wrong to inflict harm. It is likely, however, that most subjects would also have judged it legitimate to contribute to science and respect authority. In that sense, the standard condition findings also reflect consistency between social judgments (those pertaining to authority and social systems) and behavior. A complete analysis should account for both types of judgments (those pertaining to harm and those to authority in social systems), as well as their coordination by subjects in the context of specified parameters (e.g., salience of victim, authority, etc.) of the situation.

The Milgram experiments were not designed to yield systematic data on judgments that may have been made about the moral components and the social-organizational features of the situation confronting the subjects. A series of recent studies that examined moral reasoning and concepts of convention and social organization (Nucci, 1981; Smetana, 1981a; Turiel, 1978, 1979; Weston & Turiel, 1980), however, provide a basis for investigating the coordination of social judgments in multidimensional behavioral situations. The findings of these studies indicate that the domain of moral judgment (pertaining to harm, rights, and justice) constitutes a conceptual and developmental system distinct from understandings of social conventions (uniformities serving to coordinate social interactions and forming part of social systems). The research on distinctions between domains of social reasoning also provides documentation that people in this culture are not readily characterized through unitary cultural orientations, such as individualistic, collectivistic, egalitarian, hierarchical, authoritarian, or autonomous. Most subjects display all of these orientations in their judgments, discriminating among them in accordance with domains of reasoning.

Consider a study by Nucci (1981) that illustrates some of the ways different orientations coexist in individuals' social judgments. In Nucci's study, subjects (ranging in age from 7 to 19 years) were presented with a list of descriptions of social transgressions to sort according to the criteria of rule contingency and personal jurisdiction. The transgressions presented to subjects were of three kinds, as determined by our definitional criteria (see Turiel, 1978, in press): moral (e.g., hitting, stealing), conventional (e.g., forms of address, table manners), and those referred to as personal, which in this culture are events likely to be considered out of the realm of societal regulation (e.g., choices of friendships or recreation groups). The specific events considered conventional or personal are dependent on the societal context. By definition, the content of conventions is determined by the social system. Conventions are formed by arbitrary acts that are regulated within social systems. Therefore, the specific actions forming part of the conventional system in one societal context may differ from those of another societal context. It follows that social acts judged to be independent of moral prescription or societal regulation and in the province of personal jurisdiction also vary by societal context.

A two-step categorization procedure was used. Subjects were presented with the complete list of event descriptions and first instructed to group together all the acts considered "wrong even in the absence of a rule" pertaining to the act (rule contingency). With very few exceptions, subjects at all ages classified only the moral transgressions as wrong even in the absence of a rule. Moral transgressions were evaluated as wrong whether or not there is an explicit rule governing the behavior. Subsequent to sorting the acts on the basis of rule contingency, subjects were presented with the complete list of events and instructed to group together those that "should be the person's own business" (personal jurisdiction). Again with very few exceptions, subjects classified only the personal acts as ones that should be the person's own business. The moral and conventional acts were not necessarily determined by personal choice. Therefore, the moral acts were judged to be impersonal, and their status as transgressions was independent of the existence of societal rules. The conventional acts were judged to be out of the realm of personal choice insofar as there is a relevant societal rule.

In classifying social events, subjects in the Nucci study displayed what may appear to be orientations to individualism, collectivism, and interdependence. Just as different behaviors were displayed in the Milgram experiments, different kinds of judgments were displayed in the Nucci study. For instance, subjects showed what appears to be an individualistic orientation as some acts were regarded as legitimately determined by personal choice. It also appears, however, that those subjects have a collectivistic orientation, for some acts were evaluated by the ways they are regulated within the social system. Judgments about conventional acts are nonindividualistic in that the coordination of interactions in social systems is the primary consideration. Moreover, subjects' social judgments are not encompassed by individualism or collectivism, for judgments about another set of actions were based on impersonal moral prescriptions regarding interpersonal relations.

The observation of all these judgments in the same group of subjects (also found in Davidson, Turiel, & Black, in press; Smetana, 1981a; Weston & Turiel, 1980) evidences that individuals have differentiated understandings of social interactions and cultural systems and that their social judgments do not simply correspond to a unitary cultural category.

Consequently, what might appear as opposing or contradictory orientations are all part of the individual's reasoning. These orientations are applied in noncontradictory ways insofar as they stem from conceptualizations of different types of social interactions within a cultural or social system. In other words, the meaning and functions of moral prescriptions are different from the meaning and functions of conventions in systems of social organization. Indeed, it has been found that a series of dimensions of judgment (referred to elsewhere as criterion judgments[1]) serve to define and distinguish

---

[1] Criterion judgments refer to those dimensions that are part of the identification and definition of a domain of social knowledge. Criterion judgments can be distinguished from what has been termed justification categories (Davidson et al., in press). The justification categories reflect reasons for evaluations of courses of action (e.g., fairness, welfare, social coordination, custom). It has been found that the use of criterion judgments is generally constant across ages, whereas changes in types of justifications are age related.

the two domains. The criteria for convention include rule contingency, contextualism, relativism, hierarchy, and authority jurisdiction; the criteria for morality include impersonality, generalizability, obligation, equality, and independence from authority dictates.

The research has demonstrated that all of these criteria coexist in groups of subjects from this culture. As already seen, conventions are judged to be rule contingent, whereas moral prescriptions are not. With regard to conventions individuals are relativistic: Conventions are evaluated by their social context. With regard to morality individuals are universalistic: Moral prescriptions are regarded as obligatory and generalizable (Davidson et al., in press; Dodsworth-Rugani, 1982, Turiel, in press). Conventional judgments can be based on social hierarchies, whereas moral judgments can be based on equality (Davidson et al., in press). In the use of conventions, conformity to authority is affirmed, although judgments about moral issues can be, under some circumstances, in contradiction with the dictates of authority (Weston & Turiel, 1980).

The two domains, with their respective dimensions of judgment, are associated with children's behavior in their social interactions. Observational studies of interactions in preschools (Nucci & Turiel, 1978; Nucci, Turiel, & Gawrych, Note 2), in elementary and junior high school classrooms (Nucci & Nucci, 1982), and in playgrounds (Nucci & Nucci, in press) have shown that children's interactions among themselves, as well as with adults, take on a form in the context of moral events differing from interactions in the context of conventional events.

Children's social experiences, in congruence with social judgments, are multifaceted. Within the context of each domain, there are two types of experiences that are part of children's social interactions. One type has been frequently addressed in psychological analysis: the communications and commands from adults to children (and more recently communication among children). The almost-exclusive focus on adult transmission as the source of children's social development has produced the emphasis on acquisition of cultural orientations and the presumed duality of reasoning and the content of cultural codes or norms. Children, however, also attend to the components of actions and interactions in themselves. We have found, for instance, that actions like one person causing physical harm to another constitute an important aspect of children's social experiences, influencing the formation of social inferences. Probably of equal importance to communications are the child's direct experiences (e.g., as a victim) and observations of the consequences of actions or of reactions to actions. Assessments of children's judgments about naturally occurring events have shown that children distinguish between (1) actions with intrinsic consequences, which are evaluated independently of rules and social expectations, and (2) actions considered arbitrary and evaluated in relation to rules and social expectations (Nucci & Nucci, 1982; Nucci & Turiel, 1978; Nucci, Turiel, & Gawrych, Note 2).

Moreover, communications, discussions, and dialogues are not all of one kind. The content of the dialogues observed in these studies was closely associated with the types of events involved and corresponded to forms of judgment (those measured in the studies mentioned earlier and those measured directly in the context of the observational studies). The observational studies have indicated that differentiations exist in the types of events and social communications that provide feedback on the development of social judgments. The most plausible hypothesis from our research is that social events, children's direct reactions to the events, communications, and judgments are all intertwined.

DOMAIN COMBINATIONS AND COORDINATIONS

Our research has shown that children construct concepts of social organization, along with moral concepts, that are interactive with distinct forms of social experiences in childhood. Whereas there is a fair amount of evidence supporting the proposition that morality and convention are distinct conceptual and developmental systems, and whereas in much of our research prototypical events from each domain have been used to study subjects' judgments, it is surely the case that many social situations confronting individuals are multidimensional and include moral and conventional components (as is the case in Milgram's experimental situations). Accordingly, behavioral situations often cannot be cleanly separated into moral or conventional ones.

A useful example of a situation that combines moral and organizational features has been provided by Berlin (1981) in a philosophical essay on the concept of equality. Berlin correctly pointed out that in many situations inequalities exist that are generally accepted by those who espouse the principle of equality. The example he provides is the authority wielded by the conductor of an orchestra: "Inequality in the organization of an orchestra there patently is; the reason for it is the purpose of orchestral playing—the production of certain sounds in certain ways which cannot, in fact, be achieved without a measure of discipline which itself entails some degree of inequality in the distribution of authority" (p. 91).

Berlin's example is especially interesting because in it aspects of the moral principle of equality are so readily subordinated to other ends. Similar situations in which harm is subordinated to other ends exist. For instance, an editor of a scientific journal will convey criticisms of a submitted manuscript with the knowledge that his or her comments may very well produce pain and suffering for the author. It is generally accepted, in the scientific community, that the avoidance of such harm is subordinate to aims of communication and quality of scientific work. Likewise, the applicability of the notion of just treatment ("treat all cases alike") may vary by its situational context, as has been mentioned by more than one commentator (see Hart, 1961, for examples).

Some have interpreted these types of examples as indicative of the emptiness of formal moral concepts like equality, harm, and justice. In that context, it has been maintained that the concepts take on meaning only when one looks to the content mapped onto them—content that is presumed to be, in the main, culturally determined. Hence, moral concepts, insofar as they have substance, are argued to be culturally specific.

There is another way of interpreting the examples of variability in applications of moral concepts, however. Rather than illustrating the emptiness of the concepts, the examples reflect the complexity of social life. The examples show that individuals and groups have more than one social goal and that different, and sometimes conflicting, goals are implicated in a given situational context. The variance in the application of moral concepts suggests that social situations can be multidimensional, requiring the individual to coordinate (perhaps with varying degrees of success), different social components and goals. In Berlin's example, acceptance of the goal of orchestral playing, with the perceived necessity of an authoritarian organization, generally includes acceptance of the subordination of equality to hierarchy. Similarly, the notion of justice, in Hart's sense of equal treatment, is sometimes subordinated to organizational goals.[2]

Examples of variability in the application of moral concepts are not indicative of their lack of substance (empty notions to be filled in by cultural content). In the studies mentioned earlier, it has been documented that children and adolescents do apply specifiable, substantive moral criteria in nonvariable ways to many situations. With regard to prototypical events in the domain, substantial evidence now exists in support of the proposition that children and adolescents apply distinctively moral judgments in substantive ways. The evidence comes from studies of judgment in behavioral and nonbehavioral contexts. Morality is only one component, however, in situations that include more than one goal. In weighing moral and organizational goals, individuals will sometimes subordinate one to the other. In the orchestra example, it appears that most people regard the moral aspects of equality to be readily subordinated to what is perceived as an orchestral organization necessary to accomplish its aims. In other situations, the reverse priorities, as well as conflicts, are apparent.

It is proposed, therefore, that in order to understand how decisions are made and actions taken in certain social situations, the concepts of both social organization and moral judgments should be taken into account. The separation of domains provides a methodological basis for investigation of judgments in such multidimensional situations. We have begun to research the coordination of judgments using information derived from studies of domain distinctions. The separation of domains has allowed for specification of variables in multifaceted situations and analyses of how domains of judgment are related to one another.

[2] In stating that moral concepts can be subordinated to organizational goals, it is not implied that doing so is necessarily justified from the moral viewpoint. The point is simply that when moral and organizational goals conflict, individuals may sometimes decide to give priority to the organizational factors.

In this research subjects have been presented with situations entailing potential domain conflicts (Turiel, in press; Smetana, Note 3) and with ambiguously multifaceted issues, like abortion, that lead to varying domain attributions by different people (Smetana, 1982). An example from our research (Turiel, in press) on the coordination of judgments is a situation in which conventional sex-role expectations (regarding occupational roles of males and females) conflicted with considerations of equality and reciprocity (a husband and wife taking turns at working, when only one can work at a time). Further details on this type of domain-combination inquiry are provided later through a discussion of studies on decisions about abortion—studies that included measures of behavior and reasoning. For now, suffice it to say that in both investigations one finding was that whereas most subjects were aware of and attended to different domain considerations in the situations, there were different ways of relating the domains. Three modes of domain relations emerged: (1) a predominant emphasis on one domain, with subordination of the other; (2) conflict between the two, with inconsistencies and the absence of resolution or reconciliation of the two components; and (3) coordination of the two components, such that the two are taken into account in the solution to the problem.

In another study by Smetana (Note 3), direct comparisons were made of children's judgments about within-domain and combined-domain events. Judgments on the within-domain events were consistent with the findings of other studies: Moral events were distinguished from conventional events on several dimensions of judgment. As expected, the same groups of subjects coordinated the combined-domain events either by subordinating one domain to the other or by abstracting and relating components from each. As an additional way of testing the proposition that in combined-domain events the two components are jointly considered, subjects were presented with standard countersuggestion conditions. In the countersuggestions, additions were made in the event descriptions, serving to shift the salience of the moral or conventional components (i.e., in the story one character responds to another's transgressions with statements emphasizing either a moral or a conventional issue). The countersuggestions produced no shifts in judgments about within-domain events. They did have an influence on responses to the combined-domain events, showing that in those situations subjects related the two components in their judgments.

The identification and separation of moral and organizational features in social situations (as in Berlin's example of orchestras), in conjunction with the identification of corresponding distinctions in individual judgments, *and* the notion of judgment coordinations provide a basis for interpreting the body of findings (listed in Table 15.1) from the various conditions in Milgram's (1974) experiments. Although our interpretations involve speculations regarding judgments because direct data are unavailable, they are consonant with the behavioral results.

Consider again the features of the experimental conditions—in comparison with Berlin's example of orchestral playing. Acceptance of the organization of an orchestra and the authority of the conductor is not likely to be for moral reasons, but to achieve other ends ("the production of certain sounds in certain ways"). That organization brings with it an implicit conflict with the principle of equality. The conflict is explicit and sharper in the Milgram experiments. Analogously with the orchestra example, the Milgram experiments include a social organization designed to accomplish scientific ends. The organization of the experiment includes hierarchical relations, with the experimenter in an authoritative position with regard to the implementation of the scientific procedures and goals (which are described to the subject). In addition, the conventional-organizational features revolving around scientific ends are highlighted by the experimenter's comments during the course of the experiment (i.e., statements to the effect that the experiment requires the subject's continued participation). The hypothesis is that the subject's conceptual orientation to these aspects of the experiment is social organizational. By virtue of the inclusion of actions causing substantial physical harm to another person, an explicit conflict exists. The conflict exists because in order to avoid inflicting harm the experiment would be significantly altered or terminated—thus contradicting the subject's perception of the necessity for conventional regulation and authority in that situation. Conversely, to maintain conventional authority the subject's moral prescriptions must be contradicted. The responses of subjects, it is proposed, reflect efforts at relating the two domains of judgment—efforts resulting in both coordination and conflict.

As mentioned earlier, in one experimental condition the majority of subjects continued administering electric shocks to the end of the scale. Apparently, the social-organizational considerations outweighed the moral ones. It is clear from Milgram's (1974) reports, however, that most of these subjects were highly conflicted. There is good indication that throughout the experiment subjects were concerned with the harm being inflicted and did not abandon their moral judgment (though they did not fully act on it). Furthermore, the moral considerations often did outweigh the organizational ones. In all the other experimental conditions, the majority of subjects refused to continue the experiment. As discussed earlier, the balance between the moral and organizational components in those conditions differed from that of the standard condition. Consequently, the body of findings from all seven experimental conditions can be interpreted to show that the behavioral products are a function of the coordination of different types of judgments.

SOCIAL THOUGHT AND ACTION

One way of approaching the results of the Milgram experiments is from the familiar perspective of assessing the extent of consistency between moral judgment and behavior. In this regard, the results are equivocal, for both consistency and inconsistency were found. This pattern is characteristic of research comparing stages of moral judgment with behaviors. Given the number of studies showing high levels of consistency (Blasi, 1980), it cannot simply be concluded (as was done by Aronfreed, 1976; Mischel & Mischel, 1976; and several others) that moral judgment and behavior reflect largely unrelated processes. Given that a fair number of studies showed only moderate levels of consistency, however, it cannot be concluded that moral judgment is in a direct causal relation to behavior.

The research strategy of solely estimating moral judgment–behavior consistencies or inconsistencies is limited and has produced an equivocal set of findings. The nature of the limitations is illustrated by the results of the Milgram experiments. Each experimental condition could be regarded as manifesting consistency and inconsistency—depending on the relation assessed. Insofar as a subject continued with the experiment, his or her behavior may have been consistent with conventional-organizational judgments *and* inconsistent with moral judgments. Insofar as a subject refused to continue administering the shocks, his or her behavior may have been consistent with moral judgments *and* inconsistent with conventional-organizational judgments. All these patterns were, indeed, observed. Rather than solely correlating judgment and behavior, patterns of consistencies and inconsistencies should be explained through analyses of the coordination of judgments. For instance, to understand the behavior of subjects who continued administering shocks in any given experimental condition, two interrelated factors would be considered: (1) the basis for the consistency between their behavior and their organizational concepts, in conjunction with (2) the basis for the inconsistency between their behavior and their moral judgments. This strategy would entail analyses of the coordinations (e.g., conflict, synchrony, integration, segregation) between organizational and moral concepts in the situational context.

We are proposing an analytic and empirical strategy different from one based on the question "Is moral behavior consistent with moral judgment (or do people live up to their moral standards, or does moral judgment predict behavior)?" Posing the problem in terms of inquiry into the nature of relations and coordinations among social judgments and behaviors has several implications for research strategies and methods. The methods would be closer to those used by Piaget (in his examination of correspondences in the organization of reasoning and patterns of behavior), than to the correlational methods of Hartshorne and May. Piaget, however, focused on what he regarded as a restricted range of judgments and behaviors (specifically, concepts of game rules and behavior in the context of playing the game) and thus was not concerned with criteria for identifying and separating the components of behavioral situations. Studies of multidimensional or ambiguous social situations require such criteria.

Indeed, many of the oft-used behavioral situations, including those of Hartshorne and May (Turiel, 1978), are multidimensional and from the subject's viewpoint may represent conflictful or ambiguous situations (examples are competitive games, tests of achievement in classroom contexts, situations calling for civil disobedience or contradiction of authority). Prior to the study of judgment or behavior, components of the situational contexts need to be identified. These include criteria for specifying domains involved (an example is specification of moral and organizational features in the Milgram experiments) and, if there is more than one domain, their type of relation (e.g., in the Milgram experiments they were placed in conflicting relations). In turn, the subjects' domain orientations to the situational context would be assessed. The analyses would include subjects' within-domain judgments regarding each component, as well as the coordination of domains in the situational context.

The validity of this approach is supported by the study (Smetana, 1981b, 1982) referred to earlier on decisions about abortion. The research was predicated on the assumption that abortion is a multidimensional and ambiguous issue, which would not be adequately investigated through assessments of correlations of behavior to moral judgments. One source for the hypothesis was the pervasive public debate over the fundamental nature of abortion. It was apparent that opposing positions were strongly held, and it seemed that those favoring choice regarded the antiabortion stand to entail a misattribution of moral considerations. A second source for the hypothesis was extensive pilot work indicating that judgments about abortion included life issues (e.g., that abortion is taking human life, that it is killing) and concerns with personal and reproductive choices and control over one's body and life.

An aim of the research, therefore, was to identify individuals' domain orientations and conceptual criteria regarding abortion. Three procedures were used. One was an extensive clinical interview designed to determine how individuals reason about the issue of abortion. Second, subjects were given the type of task described earlier (as used in the Nucci study) to assess criteria used in classifying abortion in relation to other social actions. As a basis of comparing subjects' domain attributions of abortion with their moral reasoning on other issues, assessments were also made of their levels of moral judgment (using Kohlberg's measures).

Another aim of the research was to examine relations between judgment and behavior. The study included a sample of single, first-pregnancy women (from 13 to 32 years of age) who were facing the decision of whether to continue the pregnancy. Furthermore, the study included a matched group of never-pregnant women, as well as a sample of adolescent women (nonpregnant) and men.

Analyses of responses to the interviews about abortion showed that, indeed, there are differences in judgments as to whether abortion falls within the moral domain. Some regarded it as a nonmoral issue to be determined by personal choices, and others regarded it as a moral issue in that it involved taking of life. The main source of variation and ambiguity was over the issue of when life begins and the status of the fetus as a person. This was the fundamental ambiguity in subjects' judgments and the basis for the different domain attributions. Therefore, differences in judgments were not over whether killing is wrong (all viewed that as wrong), but over whether abortion constitutes taking a life. Insofar as the fetus is not defined as a life, then abortion would not constitute killing. The decision to terminate a pregnancy would then be regarded as a nonmoral choice on the part of the woman regarding her own body and life. Insofar as the fetus was defined as life, then abortion would constitute killing. The decision would then be considered a moral one, requiring the subordination of personal choice to the preservation of life.

Four different modes of relating the nonmoral (personal jurisdiction) and moral aspects of the situation were evident. In one, abortion was considered a predominantly nonmoral issue of personal choice. In a second, abortion was considered predominantly an issue of life and thus viewed as a moral issue. Third, there was conflict over its moral and nonmoral attributes. Some subjects viewed abortion as an issue involving the taking of human life but also took into consideration the personal issue of the woman's control over her body and her right to self-determination. As these issues were seen as mutually exclusive, the judgments were characterized by conflict. The personal and moral aspects of abortion were taken into account and unresolved. In the fourth mode there was a coordination of the personal and moral aspects based on the time period in pregnancy. Those subjects defined life through resemblance to human form; as this was regarded to occur at some point midway during the pregnancy, abortion was considered a successively personal and moral issue. (See Smetana, 1982, for extensive discussion of each of the four modes.)

In classifying some subjects' responses as reflecting a predominantly nonmoral and personal orientation to the issue of abortion, we need to be clear about the terminology being used so as to avoid misunderstanding. In referring to subjects as using the category of "personal jurisdiction" with regard to abortion, we do not mean that they are selfish, egocentric, or self-interested. Nor does the phrase connote that those subjects fail to consider the possible moral implications of abortion. There is evidence (see Smetana, 1982) that they do consider the moral implication and that their decisions were difficult and emotionally conflictful. They considered the potential moral implications and provided justifications for its nonmoral status. The personal jurisdiction category is meant to reflect the epistemological status (using labels consistent with other research on social domains) into which the issue was placed by subjects and the associated forms of reasoning. Because the fetus is viewed as a physical and emotional extension of the mother during pregnancy, abortion is considered part of personal jurisdiction.

The expectation is that the personal and moral categories, as domains of social judgment, are used by all the subjects and that the differences are specific to an ambiguous and multifaceted issue like abortion. The results from the classification task show that this is the case. The subjects sorted a series of social events corresponding to the moral, conventional, and personal categories, as well as three items pertaining to abortion in the three trimesters of pregnancy, according to the following criteria: (1) events that are wrong in the absence of rules, (2) events whose wrongness is determined by rules, or (3) events that should be the individual's prerogative. There was strong agreement in subjects' domain categorizations of all items presented, with the exception of the three items pertaining to abortion. Respondents who considered abortion a nonmoral issue consistently placed the abortion items in the personal category, whereas respondents who considered abortion a life issue or who coordinated the two domains were more likely to place the abortion items in the moral category (wrong in the absence of rules).

All the subjects, therefore, reasoned in accordance with both the moral and personal categories, although they differed in the domain identification of abortion. Furthermore, the same modes of domain identification and relations for the issue of abortion were evident in the three groups of subjects in the study. Reasoning among the group of women facing the decision of whether to terminate the pregnancy did not differ from that of the other two groups. Therefore, the reasoning of the pregnant women was not entirely determined by the situation they faced. The decisions actually made regarding the termination or continuation of their unwanted pregnancies were closely related to the domain identification of the issue—as assessed by the interview and the classification task. Almost all the women who considered abortion a nonmoral personal issue chose to terminate their pregnancies (17 of 18 subjects). In turn, almost all the women who considered abortion an issue of life continued their unplanned pregnancies (14 of 15 subjects). Those in the conflicted or coordinated modes were more evenly divided in their decisions (6 chose to terminate and 8 to continue their pregnancies).

The results of this study support two general propositions we have put forth: that behavior is related to judgment and that such relations are associated with the coordination of social judgment. The study also demonstrated that explanations of behavior are not discernible solely through assessments of the degree of its consistency with moral judgments. It was found that the subjects' levels of moral judgment did not differ in accordance with their domain identifications or behavioral choices. Domain identification of the issue, rather than moral-judgment level, was predictive of behavior.

These results are also consistent with our interpretation of the findings from Milgram's experiments. Social behaviors can entail both consistency and inconsistency with judgments, depending on the types of judgment assessed. Consideration of different domains shows that judgments are related to individuals' interpretations of social situations in ways that influence behavior. Behavioral choices and cultural content are not dichotomous with social reasoning. An understanding of action requires study of the interrelations of different types of social judgments.

REFERENCES

Aronfreed, J. *Conduct and conscience: The socialization of internalized control over behavior.* New York: Academic Press, 1968.

Aronfreed, J. The concept of internalization. In D. A. Goslin (Ed.), *Handbook of socialization theory and research*. Skokie, Ill.: Rand McNally, 1969.

Aronfreed, J. Moral development from the standpoint of a general psychological theory. In T. Lickona (Ed.), *Moral development and behavior: Theory, research, and social issues*. New York: Holt, Rinehart and Winston, 1976.

Bandura, A. *Social learning theory*. Englewood Cliffs, N.J.: Prentice-Hall, 1977.

Berlin, I. *Concepts and categories: Philosophical essays*. New York: Penguin Books, 1981.

Blasi, A. Bridging moral cognition and moral action: A critical review of the literature. *Psychological Bulletin*, 1980, *88*, 1-45.

Davidson, P., Turiel, E., & Black, A. The effect of stimulus familiarity on the use of criteria and justifications in children's social reasoning. *British Journal of Developmental Psychology*, in press.

Dodsworth-Rugani, K. J. *The development of concepts of social structure and their relationship to school rules and authority*. Unpublished doctoral dissertation, University of California, Berkeley, 1982.

Grinder, R. E. Relations between behavioral and cognitive dimensions of conscience in middle childhood. *Child Development*, 1964, *35*, 881–891.

Hart, H. L. A. *The concept of law*. London: Oxford University Press, 1961.

Hartshorne, H., & May, M. S. *Studies in the nature of character* (3 vols.). Vol. 1, *Studies in deceit;* Vol. 2, *Studies in self-control;* Vol. 3, *Studies in the organization of character*. New York: Macmillan, 1928–1930.

Hogan, R. Moral conduct and moral character: A psychological perspective. *Psychology Bulletin*, 1973, *79*, 217–232.

Hogan, R. Theoretical egocentrism and the problem of compliance. *American Psychologist*, 1975, *30*, 533–540.

Kohlberg, L. The development of children's orientations toward a moral order: 1. Sequence in the development of moral thought. *Vita Humana*, 1963, *6*, 11–33.

Kohlberg, L. Stage and sequence: The cognitive-developmental approach to socialization. In D. A. Goslin (Ed.), *Handbook of socialization theory and research*. Skokie, Ill.: Rand McNally, 1969.

Kohlberg, L. From is to ought: How to commit the naturalistic fallacy and get away with it in the study of moral development. In T. Mischel (Ed.), *Psychology and genetic epistemology*. New York: Academic Press, 1971.

Kurtines, W., & Greif, E. The development of moral thought: Review and evaluation of Kohlberg's approach. *Psychological Bulletin*, 1974, *81*, 453–470.

Milgram, S. Behavioral study of obedience. *Journal of Abnormal and Social Psychology*, 1963, *67*, 371–378.

Milgram, S. *Obedience to authority: An experimental view*. New York: Harper & Row, 1974.

Mischel, W., & Mischel, H. N. A cognitive social-learning approach to morality and self-regulation. In T. Lickona (Ed.), *Moral development: Theory, research, and social issues*. New York: Holt, Rinehart and Winston, 1976.

Nucci, L. The development of personal concepts: A domain distinct from moral or societal concepts. *Child Development*, 1981, *52*, 114–121.

Nucci, L., & Nucci, M. Children's social interactions in the context of moral and conventional transgressions. *Child Development,* 1982, *53,* 403–412.

Nucci, L., & Nucci, M. Children's responses to moral and social conventional transgressions in free-play settings. *Child Development,* in press.

Nucci, L., & Turiel, E. Social interactions and the development of social concepts in preschool children. *Child Development,* 1978, *49,* 400–407.

Piaget, J. *The moral judgment of the child.* London: Routledge & Kegan Paul, 1932.

Sampson, E. E. Psychology and the American ideal. *Personality and Social Psychology,* 1977, *35,* 767–782.

Shweder, R. A. Beyond self-constructed knowledge: The study of culture and morality. *Merrill-Palmer Quarterly,* in press.

Smetana, J. Preschool children's conceptions of moral and social rules. *Child Development,* 1981, *52,* 1333–1336. (a)

Smetana, J. Reasoning in the personal and moral domains: Adolescent and young adult women's decision-making regarding abortion. *Journal of Applied Developmental Psychology,* 1981, *3,* 211–226. (b)

Smetana, J. *Concepts of self and morality: Women's reasoning about abortion.* New York: Praeger, 1982.

Turiel, E. The development of concepts of social structure: Social convention. In J. Glick & A. Clarke-Stewart (Eds.), *The development of social understanding.* New York: Gardener Press, 1978.

Turiel, E. Distinct conceptual and developmental domains: Social convention and morality. In H. E. Howe & C. B. Keasey (Eds.), *Nebraska Symposium on Motivation* (Vol. 25). Lincoln: University of Nebraska Press, 1979.

Turiel, E. *The development of social knowledge: Morality and convention.* New York: Cambridge University Press, in press.

Weston, D., & Turiel, E. Act-rule relations: Children's concepts of social rules. *Developmental Psychology,* 1980, *16,* 417–424.

REFERENCE NOTES

1. Langer, J. *The coordination of moral conduct.* Unpublished manuscript, University of California, Berkeley, 1975.

2. Nucci, L., Turiel, E., & Gawrych, G. E. Preschool children's social interactions and social concepts in the Virgin Islands. Unpublished manuscript, University of Illinois at Chicago Circle, 1981.

3. Smetana, J. G. *Children's reasoning about mixed domain (moral and social) issues.* Paper presented at the annual meeting of the American Educational Research Association, New York City, March 1982.

CHAPTER 16

Empathy, Its Limitations, and Its Role in a Comprehensive Moral Theory

MARTIN L. HOFFMAN

A developmental approach to moral motivation is presented. It includes a stage-developmental scheme for empathy and an information-processing type of analysis of discipline encounters that may account for a connection between empathy, guilt feeling, and the moral norm of considering others. The limitations of this approach, and of the cognitive-developmental approach, are discussed, as well as the need for both motive and principle concepts in a comprehensive moral theory.

There is no consensus among psychologists and philosophers as to what constitutes a moral issue. Most scholars would probably agree, however, that a moral issue arises whenever goals, plans, desires, and expectations of people are in conflict. It follows that one's sensitivity to the welfare and rights of others, especially when they conflict with one's own interests, is central to the moral domain. This sensitivity may be reflected in one's concerns about the consequences of one's actions for others and in one's orientation toward sharing possessions and allocating resources in general. In keeping with this implicit rough formulation, the kinds of questions usually studied in developmental research revolve around two content areas: consideration for others and distributive justice or fairness.

If resolving conflicts between one's interests and interests of others is central to morality, we expect developmental theory to focus on how children handle such conflicts and on the processes by which they eventually acquire the motive to take the interests of others into account and the tendency to feel bad when they do not do this. Indeed, the first theoretical account of moral developmental processes, the psychoanalytic, focuses on the child's coping with conflicts between impulses and social demands and tries to explain the development of moral motives along with the guilt feeling that follows transgressions. In the cognitive approach that has dominated moral development research for two decades, however, the role of conflict, motivation, and affect is minimized. The focus is on stages of moral thought, and the processes accounting for developmental progress are equilibration of discrepancies between stages, and role-taking. The only conflict, affect, and motive in the system are the discrepancy between stages, the perturbed state resulting from recognizing the discrepancy, and the need to resolve the discrepancy.[1]

I have long been working on theories that highlight moral conflict, motivation, and affect in two types of situations: (1) one is an innocent bystander who witnesses someone in pain, danger, or some other needful state and experiences conflict between the motive to help the victim and egoistic motives to continue what one was doing and avoid the cost of helping; (2) one is not innocent but has acted or contemplates acting in a harmful way or is in conflict between one's egoistic motives (sensory pleasure, material gain, approval, success) and feelings of obligation to someone. For people to act morally in either situation they must have both an egoistic, self-serving motive (without which it makes no sense to talk of moral action) and an intrinsic, internally based moral motive—a motive to consider others. (The idea that moral encounters involve conflict between egoistic and moral motives seems obvious, yet it has been overlooked in much of the moral development literature.) When the moral motive is activated, it does not ensure moral action because the egoistic motive may be more powerful, but it does ensure a moral conflict. And, if the moral motive loses out, one normally pays the price of feeling guilty. Moral action is thus not the direct expression of a moral motive but an attempt to achieve a balance between egoistic and moral motivation. Moral affect is simply the good feeling one has about oneself when one acts morally (which may coexist with feelings of deprivation over what one gave up) and the guilt or bad feeling about oneself over violating a moral norm. Whether the conscious aim of moral action is to feel good or avoid guilt and the implications of this for the definition of moral motivation are discussed later.

DEVELOPMENT OF EMPATHY-BASED MORAL MOTIVES

When moral development is cast in motivational terms, it raises these questions: What prompts people to go to the aid of someone at a cost to themselves, to refrain from doing something they want to do simply because it might hurt someone, to feel bad about themselves when they realize that their actions have been harmful to another? My answers are empathy and em-

---

[1] Personal motives are sometimes implicit in stage theory. In Kohlberg's Stage 3, for example, moral action may reflect a sympathetic concern for others. But there is no attempt to explain where the sympathetic concern comes from or how it eventually gives way to the law-and-order concerns of the following stage.

pathy-based guilt. This is not new. Philosophers have long extolled the value of empathy as a socially cohesive, moral force (see review by Hoffman, 1982a). There are also good evolutionary reasons for expecting empathy to serve as a reliable moral motive (Hoffman, 1981). And, there is considerable empirical evidence that empathy—specifically, empathic distress—and guilt function as moral motives; that is, they are dispositions to moral action (Hoffman, 1978, 1982b). I now summarize the main concepts in my developmental scheme for empathy and guilt, point up their limitations, as well as certain relevant limitations of cognitive theories, and discuss the need for both motive and principle concepts in a comprehensive moral theory.

Development of Empathy

I define empathy as a vicarious affective response that does not necessarily match another's affective state but is more appropriate to the other's situation than to one's own. Although an affect, empathy has a significant cognitive component: Older children and adults know that they are responding to something happening to someone else, and, drawing from their knowledge about others and their own experience, they have an idea of what the other is feeling; infants may be empathically aroused without these cognitions. Thus the experience of empathy depends on one's cognitive level. The research suggests four broad social-cognitive levels (Hoffman, 1975) that, when combined with empathic affect, result in the four developmental levels of empathic distress discussed in the following paragraphs.

1.   For most of the first year, witnessing another person in distress may result in a global empathic distress response. Distress cues from the dimly perceived "other" are confounded with unpleasant feelings empathically aroused in the self. Since infants cannot differentiate themselves from the other, they may at times act as though what happened to the other happened to themselves. An 11-month-old girl, on seeing a child fall and cry, looked as if she were about to cry herself and then put her thumb in her mouth and buried her head in her mother's lap, which is what she does when she herself is hurt.

2.   With the acquisition of "object permanence," including the emergence of a sense of the other as a physical entity distinct from oneself, the affective portion of the global empathic distress is transferred to the separate image-of-self and image-of-other that emerge. The child can now be aware that another person and not oneself is in distress, but the other's internal states are unknown and may be assumed to be the same as one's own. For example, an 18-month-old boy fetched his own mother to comfort a crying friend even though the friend's mother was also present—a behavior that, though confused, is not entirely egocentric because it indicates that the child is responding with appropriate empathic affect.

3.   With the beginning of role-taking, at about 2–3 years, children be-

come aware that other people's feelings may differ from theirs and are based on those persons' own needs and interpretations of events. They become more responsive to cues about what the other is feeling. And, with language, which enables children to derive meaning from symbolic cues of affect, they can empathize with an increasingly wide range of emotions including complex ones like disappointment and feelings of betrayal. Eventually, they can empathize with several, sometimes conflicting emotions. While empathizing with a victim's distress, they may also empathize with the victim's desire not to feel obligated or demeaned, hence with the victim's desire *not* to be helped.

4. By late childhood, owing to the emerging conception of oneself and others as continuing persons with separate histories and identities, one becomes aware that others feel pleasure and pain not only in the situation but also in their larger life experience. Consequently, though one may still respond empathically to another's immediate distress, one's empathic response is intensified when the other's distress is not transitory but chronic. Thus, one's empathically aroused affect is combined with a mental representation of another's general level of distress or deprivation. This representation may include vivid prototypic images of the other person in various distressful situations.

When one has advanced through these four levels and encounters someone in pain, danger, or distress, one is exposed to a network of information about the other's affective state. The network may include verbal and nonverbal expressive cues from the victim, situational cues, and the knowledge one has about the other's general affective experience beyond the immediate situation. These sources of information are processed differently: Empathy aroused by nonverbal and situational cues is usually mediated by largely involuntary, cognitively "shallow" processing modes. These include (1) the classical conditioning of empathic affect resulting from previous co-occurrences of distress cues from others and experiences of actual distress oneself, or from the similarity between the victim's current situation and one's own past distress experiences; and (2) a two-step process involving imitation of the victim's facial and postural movements (mimicry) and the resulting afferent feedback that contributes to one's understanding and feeling of the victim's affect. Empathy aroused by verbal messages from the victim, on the other hand, or by one's knowledge about the victim requires deeper levels of cognitive processing such as semantic interpretation and imagining oneself in the victim's place.

In most instances, the various cues, arousal modes, and processing levels are probably congruent and contribute to arousal of the same affect. Contradictions may occur, however, as between different expressive cues (e.g., facial expression and tone of voice) or between expressive cues and situational cues. One's knowledge of the other's life condition may also conflict with the immediate situational or expressive cues, which may consequently lose much of their force for an observer who knows they reflect only a transitory state. Imagine someone who does not know that he or she has a terminal illness having a good time playing and laughing. A mature observer is more likely to respond with sadness than with joy, or to mingle sadness and joy; a young child might simply respond with joy. In other words, the observer may respond empathically to a mental image of the other's condition. The most advanced empathic level, then, involves some distancing—responding partly to one's mental image of the other rather than totally to the other's immediate stimulus value. Indeed, once that level is reached, one may always respond at least partly to one's image of the other's condition. This response fits my definition of empathy, not as an exact match with another's feelings but as an affective response more appropriate to the other's situation than one's own.[2]

Extending the fourth level, it seems likely that with development of the ability to form social concepts one may be empathically aroused by an entire group or class of people (poor, oppressed, outcast, retarded). Although one's distress experiences may differ from theirs, all distress experiences presumably have a common affective core, and this together with the individual's high cognitive level, may allow for a generalized empathic distress capability. The combinaiton of empathic affect and the perceived plight of an unfortunate group may be the most developmentally advanced form of empathic distress. It may also provide a motive base, especially in adolescence, for the development of certain moral and political ideologies centered around alleviation of the plight of unfortunate groups (Hoffman, 1980). I will return to this point later.

Sympathetic Distress

The transition from the first to the second empathic level may involve an important qualitative shift in feeling. Once children are aware of others as distinct from themselves, their own empathic distress, which is a parallel response, a more or less exact replication of the victim's presumed feeling of distress, may be transformed at least in part into a reciprocal concern for the victim. That is, they may continue to respond in a purely empathic manner—to feel uncomfortable and highly distressed themselves—but they also experience a feeling of compassion for the victim, along with a conscious desire to help because they feel sorry for the victim and not just to relieve their own empathic distress.

What developmental processes account for this shift? First, as previously suggested, the unpleasant affect experienced as part of the child's global, undifferentiated self is transferred to the separate image-of-self and image-of-other that emerge. So, presumably, is the wish, not necessarily conscious, to terminate the unpleasant affect. There may therefore be a part of the child's

[2]But see Hoffman, 1978 and in press a, for discussions about the match between observer's and model's affect and reasons for expecting a generally high level of match.

empathic distress response that includes a wish to terminate the other's distress. I call this *sympathetic distress*. It is qualitatively different from the remaining, more "purely" empathic, component of the response that pertains to the unpleasant affect transferred to the "self."

Causal Attribution and Empathy

The partial transformation of empathic into sympathetic distress presumably occurs when the other person is truly a victim with no control over his or her fate. Other causal attributions are possible depending largely on situational cues. If the cues indicate the victim is responsible for his or her own plight, one's reaction may be incompatible with empathic or sympathetic distress because the other may no longer appear as a victim, and the observer may feel indifferent or even derogate the victim. If the cues indicate a third person is to blame, observers may feel anger at that person because they sympathize with the victim or because they empathize with the victim and therefore feel attacked themselves. If one discovered that the victim previously harmed the attacker, one might blame the victim and possibly empathize with the attacker.

When there are no clear cues indicating the source of the victim's plight, personality differences may play a role. Some observers may blame the victim to reduce the discomfort of empathic distress. There may also be a tendency to attribute the cause of another's condition to his or her own dispositions (Jones & Nisbett, 1971), perhaps to support one's assumptions about a "just world" (Lerner & Simmons, 1966). If, however, we take seriously the research showing a widespread tendency for people to respond empathically to another's distress (Hoffman, 1981), we can only assume that a derogatory attitude is not incompatible with empathy. Culture can play a role in all this: The misery of a person in an outcast group, for example, may be attributed to false cues or responded to with indifference regardless of the situation.

It appears, then, that the analysis of emphatic distress outlined earlier, including the four developmental levels and the transformation of empathic into sympathetic distress, may apply when the cause of another's plight is something over which the other has no control, such as an illness or accident, and sometimes when the cause is ambiguous.

Guilt Feeling

A special case is that in which the cues indicate the observer was the cause of the other's distress. It seems reasonable to assume that the resulting self-blame attribution will often transform one's empathic distress into a feeling of guilt. This case links the two types of moral encounters mentioned earlier, in which one's own action does or does not directly affect the other's welfare.

More attention should be given to guilt feeling, as there is substantial evidence, noted earlier, that it functions as a moral motive. It should be clear that this type of guilt differs from the early conception of guilt in the literature as a conditioned anxiety response to punishment and from the Freudian guilt that is a remnant of earlier fears of punishment that led to repression and is triggered by the return of repressed impulses to consciousness. It is rather a true interpersonal guilt—the bad feeling one has about oneself because one is aware of harming someone.

Although guilt feelings have the same cognitive components as empathy, they have other components as well, namely, awareness that one has choice over one's actions and that one's actions can affect others and the ability to contemplate an action and imagine its effect on others. These cognitive abilities are necessary for anticipatory guilt feeling and guilt over omission or inaction. The ability to engage in "social comparison processes" is necessary for another type of guilt in which people feel culpable simply because they see themselves as being in a vastly advantaged position relative to others. This "existential guilt," illustrated by survivor guilt and feelings reported by some 1960s social activists, is discussed at length elsewhere (Hoffman, 1980).

I have presented a developmental scheme for guilt (Hoffman, 1982b) in which guilt develops in parallel with development of empathy. Briefly, before children become aware of others as separate physical entities, they respond to simple expressions of pain by others with empathic distress and also at times with a rudimentary guilt feeling, even though they may lack a keen sense of being the causal agent, simply because of the contiguity of their actions and distress cues from others. Once they know that others are separate physical entities, they experience empathic distress when observing someone who is physically hurt, and the empathic distress may be transformed into guilt if they perceive their own actions as responsible for the hurt. Similarly, once one is aware that others have internal states, the empathic distress one experiences in the presence of someone having painful or unhappy feelings may be transformed into guilt if one perceives one's actions as responsible for those feelings. Finally, once aware of the identity of others beyond the immediate situation, one's empathic response to their general plight may be transformed into guilt if one feels responsible for their plight, or if one's attention shifts from their plight to the contrast between it and one's own relatively advantaged position.

Although empathic distress may be a developmental prerequisite for guilt, guilt may eventually become largely independent of empathy. Indeed, once the child is capable of guilt, guilt may become part of all subsequent responses to another's distress in situations in which one might have helped but did not. From then on, even innocent bystanders may rarely experience empathic distress without some guilt. The line between empathic distress and guilt thus becomes very fine, and being an innocent bystander is a matter of degree. If one realizes that one could have helped but did not, one may never feel totally innocent. Empathy and guilt may thus be quintessential moral motives, for they may transform another's pain into one's own discomfort and make one feel partly responsible for the other's plight whether or not one has actually done anything to cause it.

SOCIALIZATION OF EMPATHY AND GUILT FEELING

The discussion so far deals with natural processes that may ordinarily occur in most cultures because of the human tendency to respond vicariously to others. People also have egoistic needs, however, and socialization, which in part reflects society's moral norms, may build on the child's empathic or egoistic proclivities in varying degrees. I have suggested (Hoffman, 1970) that there may be little conflict between empathic and egoistic socialization in early childhood, even in individualistic societies. At some point the two may begin to clash as one learns that one's access to society's limited resources may depend partly on how well one competes. Parents know this, and it affects their child-rearing practices. For this and other reasons (the parents' personal needs and the stresses under which they operate), wide variations in these practices, and hence in children's capacity for empathy and guilt, can be expected.

I have suggested how socialization may affect empathy (Hoffman, 1982b). First, because people can empathize better with someone's emotion if they have experienced the emotion themselves, empathic capability should be fostered by socialization that permits children to experience many emotions, although the experience of certain extremely painful emotions might be repressed, rendering them unavailable for empathic response. Second, because empathy is largely involuntary if one pays attention to the victim, empathic development should be fostered by socialization experiences that direct the child's attention to the internal states of others. These experiences are exemplified by the parent's use of inductive discipline, which calls attention to the pain or injury caused by the child's action or encourages the child to imagine how it would feel to be in the victim's place. Third, we expect role-taking opportunities in positive contexts to help sharpen children's cognitive sense of others and increase the likelihood that they will pay attention to others, thus extending their empathic capability. Fourth, giving children a lot of affection should help make them open to the needs of others and empathic, rather than absorbed in their own needs. Fifth, empathic responsiveness in children should be fostered by models who not only act in a prosocial manner but also verbalize their empathic feelings. These rather benign socialization experiences may be effective because empathy develops naturally and is present in simple forms even in infancy. There may thus be a mutually supportive interaction between naturally occurring empathy and these socialization experiences.

Socialization should be even more important in development of guilt feeling because guilt is not only aversive, as is empathic distress, but also highly deprecatory and threatening to the child's emerging self-image. We may therefore expect children to be motivated to avoid guilt, and they can often succeed because many situations in which they harm others are ambiguous as to who, if anyone, is to blame, thus permitting the use of guilt-avoiding perceptual and cognitive strategies. It follows that even when children have the developmental requisites of guilt, they may not experience it unless an external agent is present to compel them to attend to the harm done and to their own role in the victim's plight. Hence there is an expectation that parental discipline plays a central role in the development of guilt feeling.

My explanation of the relation that has been found repeatedly between inductive discipline and guilt feeling (Hoffman, 1977) is an information-processing type of theory (Hoffman, 1983) and is summarized in the following paragraphs.

1.   Most discipline techniques have a power-assertive or love-withdrawal component that may be needed to get children to stop what they are doing and, more important for present purposes, pay attention to the information contained in the inductive component. The inductive component points up the harmful consequences of the child's action for someone. If there is too little of the power-assertive and love-withdrawal component, children may ignore the parent. If there is too much, the resulting fear, anxiety, or resentment may interfere with effective processing of the induction; and whether children comply or not, these feelings may direct their attention to the consequences of their action for themselves. Techniques having a salient inductive component ordinarily achieve the best balance, and if phrased in terms the child can comprehend, they draw the child's attention to the consequences for the victim. This component will often engage the child's empathic response system at whatever empathic level (see earlier discussion) the child has attained.

2.   Inductions also help make clear that the child caused the other's distress. This effect is especially important for young children who may not spontaneously see causal connections between their acts and others' states because of motivation, cognitive limitations, intense affect, or the ambiguity of the situation. The result of pointing out the connection is that children may then attribute blame to themselves. Self-blame may then combine with empathic distress, as discussed earlier, to produce a feeling of guilt. Guilt feelings aroused in this way in countless discipline encounters over time may produce a moral motive in children.

3.   Inductions also give children information about the cognitive component of the norm of considering others. Besides indicating harmful consequences of children's actions for others, inductions often communicate the parents' value on considering others, the prohibition against harming others, and reasons why certain acts are right or wrong. This information is stored and cumulatively organized by the child over time, and the resulting structure may constitute the cognitive component of the child's emerging moral norm. And, because guilt feelings accompanied the initial processing of information in discipline encounters, this moral-cognitive structure may acquire the motivational characteristics of the guilt feeling. The norm of considering others may thus become a "hot cognition" because of the synthesis of affect and cognition in discipline encounters. In the future, when the child acts or contemplates acting in a harmful manner, cues from the other person or the situation may activate the norm, which may then enter into the balance of forces

determining how the child acts, quite apart from any concerns about punishment or disapproval. The norm may then be said to be internalized.

4.   The child's mental activity in processing inductions—semantically interpreting the informational content and relating it to his or her action and to the victim's condition—makes the child's own internal processes salient. For this reason and because of the way information appears to be stored in memory (semantically processed material is cumulatively organized and integrated into one's enduring knowledge structures, whereas situational details are ordinarily processed in a more shallow manner and are relatively soon forgotten), children may over time come to perceive themselves rather than their parents as the source of the relevant information. They may also experience the guilt feelings originally generated in discipline encounters as coming from within themselves.

Although this theory stresses discipline by parents, after acquiring the early motivational base the child may be receptive to inductions from other adults Interaction with peers may also contribute under certain conditions (Hoffman, 1980), thus expanding the domain of situations in which the norm may be activated. The domain is also expanded by children's acquisition of language and social-cognitive skills that enable them to comprehend the effects of their acts on others beyond the immediate situation or to anticipate them ahead of time.

If the moral norm persists into adolescence, its domain may be expanded still further because it may render the individual receptive to certain moral, political, and economic ideologies—for example, those pertaining to changing society in order to benefit its disadvantaged members. Erikson (1970) notes that adolescents often search for moral ideologies that foster a sense of identity. Ideologies are the "guardians of identity" because they locate oneself in the world and provide coherence to one's affective and cognitive experiences. If one succeeds in finding or constructing an ideology fitting one's empathic leanings, then one's new moral viewpoint is an advancement over the simple empathy-based moral norm of childhood because it incorporates social realities previously ignored. In this way, one's ideology may become an integral part of one's moral system rather than an abstraction lacking motive force.

EMPIRICAL EVIDENCE

Support for the empathy development scheme, presented elsewhere (Hoffman, 1975, 1978, 1982b) is summarized in this section. Briefly, observations by Murphy (1937) and Zahn-Waxler, Radke-Yarrow & King (1979) suggest that when children under a year old witness someone being hurt, they may stare at the victim, appear to be agitated themselves, often cry, and seek comfort for themselves. In the second year they cry less often but their faces typically show empathic distress; they may do nothing, make tentative approaches, or actively try to comfort the victim—usually inappropriately because of cognitive limitations. By 3 or 4 years they show empathic distress but also try to help in more appropriate ways, which is true of older children and adults as well. Further, in children and adults the intensity of empathic affect and speed of overt helping responses appear to increase as the intensity of distress cues from victims increases (Gaertner & Dovidio, 1977; Murphy, 1937); and there appears to be a drop in intensity of empathic affect following acts of helping and a continuation of high levels of intensity if one does not attempt to help (Darley & Latané, 1968; Murphy, 1937). These findings fit the expected pattern if empathic distress operated as a prosocial moral motive, and they fit with the empathy development scheme presented here. The hypothesized transformation of empathic into sympathetic distress has not been tested, although there is some indirect suggestive evidence for it. The evidence comes from observational research (Murphy, 1937; Zahn-Waxler et al., 1979) and anecdotes such as those cited earlier showing that (a) children progress developmentally from first responding to someone's distress by seeking comfort for the self, and later by trying to help the victim and not the self; and (b) there appears to be an in-between stage, in which children feel sad and comfort both the victim and the self, that occurs at about the same time that children first become aware of others as distinct from themselves.

Evidence for the empathy-guilt connection is scanty. It includes the combination of findings that children usually respond empathically to others in distress and that inductive discipline, which points up the victim's distress and the child's role in causing it, contributes to guilt development. There is also experimental evidence that school children's guilt over harming others may be intensified by arousal of empathic distress (Thompson & Hoffman, 1980).

The theory about the role of induction is consistent not only with the discipline research that gave rise to it but also with the research showing that (1) optimal levels of anxiety foster semantic processing of verbal messages, whereas intense anxiety fosters attention to physical details of verbal messages, to the relative neglect of semantic processing (Kahneman, 1973; Mueller, 1979); (2) when people observe someone in distress, they typically experience empathic distress, and when they are aware of being the cause of the other's distress, they typically feel guilty (Hoffman, 1981, 1982b); and (3) semantically processed material is cumulatively organized and enduring, whereas processing of situational details is relatively short-lived (Brown, 1975; Craik, 1977; Stein & Glenn, 1979). The theory gains plausibility from its fit with these bodies of research. Hypotheses derived from the theory have yet to be tested, however. These hypotheses include that guilt is often aroused by inductions in discipline encounters, that this guilt gives a motivational dimension to the moral-cognitive structures resulting from children's cumulative integration of induction content, and that the resulting moral motive is activated in later temptation situations and contributes to the balance of forces determining how one acts.

LIMITATIONS OF EMPATHY-BASED MORALITY

I discuss in this section potentially important limitations, some of which may apply to any moral system relying on simple motive concepts.

Is Empathy a Truly Moral Motive?

One might argue, as I have implicitly, that empathy is uniquely well suited for bridging the gap between egoism and morality because it has the property of transforming another person's misfortune into one's own distress feeling, which is best alleviated by helping the victim. This very property, however, has an egoistic quality and therefore has led many writers to treat empathy as an egoistic motive (e.g., Gaertner & Dovidio, 1977). In my view, they are overlooking the distinction between the consequences of an act and its aim. Because one has a satisfied feeling afterward does not necessarily mean that one acted to have that feeling. When Eisenberg-Berg and Neal (1979) questioned preschool children about the spontaneous helping, sharing, and comforting acts observed over a two-week period, only a few said they helped because they would feel bad otherwise. Most explained their action in terms of the other's needs, their own friendly feelings or desire to help, or pragmatic considerations. Similar results were found by Darley and Latané (1968), Latané and Rodin (1969), and in my own unpublished research. These findings suggest that empathic distress is not a consciously egoistic motive, and there is no evidence as yet that people help others to reduce empathic distress unconsciously.

Even if people helped others to reduce their own empathic distress, to conclude that empathic distress is egoistic is to overlook that all motives prompt action that is potentially satisfying to actors. If a satisfied feeling afterward characterizes all motives, then it cannot serve as a defining criterion of a class of motives (egoistic motives). The satisfied feeling following actions motivated by empathic distress, then, is not a reason to define empathic distress as egoistic and disqualify it as a true moral motive. To do this would eliminate the possibility of moral motivation by definition. It would also obscure certain profound differences between empathic distress and other motives. Aside from its "egoistic" element, empathic distress has certain dimensions that clearly mark it as a moral motive. The arousal condition (another's misfortune), the aim of the ensuing action (to help another), and the basis of gratification in the actor (alleviating the other's distress) are all contingent on someone else's welfare. It therefore seems more appropriate to designate empathic distress (and empathy-based guilt) as a moral motive, perhaps with a quasi-egoistic component, than to group it with obviously self-serving motives like material gain, approval, and success.

But are there not more subtle egoistic motives that may instigate moral action? Psychoanalytic theory has long viewed people as behaving morally to avoid anxiety or to conform to an ideal, and Bandura (1977) argues that people may engage in any act, including moral acts, to gain self-reward. Although it seems plausible that people help others to gain self-reward, there is no evidence for this, and, furthermore, a reliable relation between moral action and self-reward seems unlikely because there is nothing intrinsically pro-socially motivating about self-reward, as the previous discussion indicates there is about empathy. Rather, people might reward themselves for any action depending on the cultural norms guiding their socialization. In our society people are often socialized to reward themselves for helping others but also for other actions including achieving and competing successfully against others. Some may be socialized to reward themselves primarily for moral action, some for egoistic actions, and some for both equally. Consequently, there is no more reason to expect self-reward to mediate moral behavior than there is for it to mediate egoistic behavior.

An exception may be the self-reward inherent in empathy, which brings the argument full cycle. One may feel not only a decrease in empathic distress after helping someone but also empathic relief or joy. One might then become motivated to help in order to experience these pleasurable feelings again. This view of empathic pleasure as a moral motive thus far lacks empirical support: As noted, the available evidence indicates that people do not help others primarily to make themselves feel good. If evidence does materialize, we might define empathic distress as a special type of self-reward that, unlike other types, functions as a reliable moral motive.

Empathic Overarousal as a Limiting Factor

Because empathic distress is aversive, we might expect it to be intense enough at times to direct one's attention to one's own distressed state rather than to the victim's, with the result that one does not try to help the victim. There is suggestive evidence for such an "overarousal" effect in highly empathic children (Kameya, 1976). And, student nurses have been found to experience intense conflict between the desire to help their terminally ill patients and their own empathic distress, which made it difficult for them to remain in the same room with the patients (Stotland, Mathews, Hansson, & Richardson, 1979). This empathic overarousal is probably intensified when the behavioral options for helping are limited or when one lacks the necessary skills to help. As empathic distress usually does lead to helping, the overarousal effect suggests there may be a broad, optimal range of empathic arousal—perhaps determined by one's general level of distress tolerance—within which one is most responsive to another's distress. Beyond that range, one may be too self-preoccupied to help, or one might employ perceptual or cognitive strategies to reduce the empathic distress, such as looking away from the victim and thinking distracting thoughts. This overarousal effect surely limits the effectiveness of empathic morality. The limitation should not be overdrawn in the absence of further research, however, because the overarousal effect may enable humans to preserve their energies in hopeless situations and thus be more readily available when helping may be more effective.

Limitations of Language-Mediated Empathy

Empathy is especially vulnerable to overarousal when mediated by verbal cues alone. When I asked people about their thoughts and feelings on hearing about someone's misfortune by letter, two role-taking processes emerged: (1) one simply focuses attention on the other's misfortune and imagines how the other is feeling (other-focused role-taking). This is often enough to arouse empathy. The resulting empathic feeling is heightened when one also visualizes the other's responses to his or her plight—the facial expressions, posture, tone of voice, sound of cries. One may then respond empathically to one's visual or auditory image of the other, more or less as if the other were physically present. Empathic affect may thus be mediated by transforming semantic meaning into visual and auditory images. (2) one may picture oneself in the other's place, imagining that the stimuli impinging on the other are impinging on oneself, and respond affectively to the imagined event. The resulting affect in this case may be heightened if one is reminded of similar events in one's own past when one experienced the same affect. Empathic affect is here mediated by two simultaneous transformations: Semantic meaning is transformed into imagery, as in the first process, and the stimuli impinging on someone are transformed into stimuli impinging on oneself.

The second process appears to have a built-in limitation: When one focuses on one's own affective experience, the image of the other and the other's situation that initiated the process may slip out of focus and fade away, a phenomenon I call "egoistic drift" (Hoffman, in press-a). This appears to contradict Stotland's (1969) finding that subjects instructed to imagine how someone undergoing a painful heat treatment felt (other-focused) showed less empathic distress than subjects instructed to imagine how they themselves would feel in that situation (self-focused). A possible explanation of both findings is that self-focused role-taking arouses more intense empathy because it directly connects the victim's affective state to the observer's need system, but this very connection makes self-focused role-taking vulnerable to "egoistic drift." Self-focused role-taking may thus generate more intense but less stable empathic affect. Whatever the explanation, these findings show the fragility of empathic responses that rely entirely on verbal statements of the victim's plight and raise questions about the strength of empathic moral systems. In defense of empathic morality, one need not often rely on verbal cues alone. Victims may be present and direct expressive cues of their feeling, usually visual or auditory, or situational cues may supplement verbal messages and keep empathic processes "alive" because these cues may be salient, vivid, and hold the observer's attention. Empathic morality may thus be effective in face-to-face interpersonal encounters.

Limited Scope of Empathy-Based Morality

Perhaps the most fundamental limitation of empathy-based morality is that there are aspects of moral action to which it may have little relevance. Empathy alone cannot explain how children learn to negotiate and achieve a proper balance between considering others and egoistic motives in situations. Empathy may also have little to say about a morality of justice—unless a clear victim is involved, perhaps someone treated unfairly—or about behaving morally out of a sense of duty. And although empathy may make one receptive to certain moral ideologies, as suggested earlier, it alone cannot explain how the ideologies are formulated and applied in situations.

Perhaps the most general limitation of empathic morality's scope is that although it may provide a reliable motive base for helping, caring, and considering others, it may not contribute to making appropriate moral judgments when several behaviors are to be compared or competing moral claims evaluated. Hume (1751/1957) argued over 200 years ago that empathy does contribute to moral judgment: We obviously applaud acts that further our own well-being and condemn acts that may harm us; because of empathy we therefore applaud or condemn acts that further the well-being of or harm others; and because people respond empathically to similar events in similar ways, empathy provides the common ground for impartial observers to reach consensus on moral judgments. Rawls (1971) criticized this notion because empathy lacks the situational sensitivity necessary for rational consensus. My own empathy theory, which has a heavy cognitive component, may solve part of this problem because the highest level of empathic response is based on a network of cues, including knowledge of the other's life condition beyond the immediate situation. Mature empathy thus reflects a sensitivity to subtle differences in the severity and quality of consequences that different actions might have for different people, and it may therefore contribute to informed moral judgments about behavior. A limitation remains, however: Mature empathizers may still be biased in favor of certain individuals or groups—for example, those with whom they share interests or experiences. There is evidence (reviewed by Hoffman, 1978) that people empathize more with others perceived as similar to themselves than with those perceived as dissimilar. People *do* empathize with others perceived as dissimilar, however, which suggests that they are responsive to moral claims of strangers, though less so than to those of kin. Another potential bias is that empathy may lead to moral evaluations that favor people who claim society's resources on the basis of their needs—society's victims—as opposed to people who claim resources on the basis of productivity or effort (which of course may be equally biased).

In short, to make moral judgments in complex situations may require moral principles that go beyond considering others and against which anyone's behavior can be assessed with minimal bias. Such moral principles would enable one to decide with more objectivity than empathy alone which moral claims deserve priority.

It is interesting to note that Kohlberg's theory, which deals explicitly with moral principles, may also founder on the principle issue. The problem is that Kohlberg's theory rests on the assumption that there is a universal principle of justice or fairness. Kohlberg relies heavily on Rawls (1971), who proposed an ingeniously simple analytic device, the "veil of ignorance," for generating universally valid moral principles. That is, if one does not know what one's position in society will be, then even a purely rational and egoistic perspective will lead one to prefer a just society—one that best represents everyone's interests. It seems clear, however, that any number of competing justice notions that sound like universal principles may apply in a given situation. Some may think it fair to allocate society's scarce resources according to people's needs; others may define fairness as equity and advocate allocating resources on the basis of productivity or effort; and others may think the fairest way is to give everyone the same amount. Need, equity, and equality may all be advocated from the veil-of-ignorance perspective—though by different people. People who view themselves as highly capable, for example, may equate equity with fairness and anticipate doing well in an equitable society. Furthermore, even if the veil-of-ignorance paradigm could generate acceptable principles of justice, it says nothing about what would motivate one to act morally once one knows one's position in society and one's relative competence. The principles one chooses and especially one's actual behavior may reflect one's personal interests rather than universal principles. Indeed, principles may often be chosen to justify one's expected actions, as long suggested by certain "emotive theorists" in philosophy (Brandt, 1967).[3]

If there is no universal justice principle available, there are serious questions about any theory that postulates a moral development stage sequence that is invariant and in which movement through stages brings one closer to a universal justice principle. If there is no universally accepted principle, then what are the grounds for making moral judgments comparing several behaviors, for judging one moral claim as more legitimate than another, or for assuming that one stage is higher than another?

All the shortcomings discussed in the preceding sections stem from the motive properties of an empathy-based morality: If the empathy aroused is too intense, the moral motive may be transformed into an egoistic concern for one's own distress; within the optimal range of arousal, an empathy-based morality may be biased toward people like oneself and toward people perceived as victims; if the other's distress or misfortune is communicated only through language, one's empathy-based moral motive may be fragile. Cognitive moral theories escape these criticisms because they postulate no motive.

[3] Even Supreme Court justices, who are often thought of as the most likely people in our society to render objective decisions on the basis of principle, are apparently vulnerable. Witness William O. Douglas (1980), who quotes Chief Justice Charles Evans Hughes as advising him, "You must remember . . . [that] at the constitutional level where we work, 90 percent of any decision is emotional. The rational part of us supplies the reasons for supporting our predilections."

But the absence of a motive makes it difficult for these theories to answer the kinds of questions that motivational theories are designed to answer: What prompts people to subordinate their own interests in the service of helping others, keeping promises, and telling the truth; and what makes them feel bad when they harm someone? Cognitive moral theories deal with moral principles like justice and fairness, but, lacking a motive base, these theories have difficulty explaining how these principles become activated in situations in which one's egoistic interests are involved and why people may not only advocate but also act in accord with these principles even when doing so goes against their own interests. (See recent reviews of cognitive moral theories by Hoffman, in press b and Rest, in press.)

TOWARD A COMPREHENSIVE THEORY

It follows that a comprehensive moral development theory requires both a motive and a principle component. The motive component is necessary to ensure activation of the principle and thus some connection to behavior even when one's self-interest is involved. The principle component, though perhaps inevitably lacking universality, may help clarify the objectives of moral behavior, reduce personal bias, and in general transcend many of the limitations inherent in empathy. One step toward a comprehensive theory, implicit in much of the preceding, is to recognize that moral encounters vary in complexity. I will not attempt a taxonomy of moral encounters but will only point up some examples of simple and complex ones. Perhaps the simplest is the innocent-bystander situation in which the basic elements of moral conflict are immediately present: an empathy-based motive to help someone and an egoistic motive to continue what one was doing and avoid the cost of helping. The situation becomes more complex when, in addition to an empathic motive to help, one also feels an *obligation* to do so. The source of this obligation may lie beyond the immediate situation. For example, it may be due to the activation of one's principle of care and responsibility for others, or one's principle of reciprocity (if one has been helped by the victim in the past). Situations involving mutual rights and expectations are still more complex, for example, situations in which one is caught in a conflict between fulfilling the legitimate expectations of someone with whom one is in a relationship and engaging in some other more desirable activity. In general, the introduction of moral principles becomes more essential with increasing complexity of the moral situation.

Another step toward a comprehensive theory may be to search for developmental connections between empathic distress and moral principles that have some force in our society such as consideration for others, justice, fairness, and reciprocity. Because empathic distress is a response to another's state, it may seem reasonable to expect, as I have suggested, that empathic distress will often evolve rather naturally into a motive to consider others. Although considering others may be something an empathic child does without experi-

encing it as a moral obligation, in adolescence, when one's sense of self includes how one relates to others (see Chap. 6), considering others may acquire an obligatory quality. That is, it may become a principle by which one
guides one's actions and evaluates oneself.

There may also be a link between empathy and justice or fairness principles.
For example, statements of the equity principle that people deserve what they
earn often seem to reflect an empathic sensitivity to the needs and expectations associated with people's work efforts. Consider this response by a 13-
year-old male subject to the question, Why is it wrong to steal from a store?
"Because the people who own the store work hard for their money and they
deserve to be able to spend it for their family. It's not fair, they sacrifice a lot
and they make plans and then they lose it all because somebody who didn't
work for it goes in and takes it." Responses like this suggest that empathy may
contribute to the motivation to uphold principles of equity and fairness. Another, less direct link between empathic morality and justice principles involves existential guilt, discussed earlier. If one feels bad about being in a
relatively advantaged position, this feeling should function as a limiting constraint on one's selfish action, and one should to some extent be ready to
share resources with others. My argument here is not that empathy and existential guilt explain how one acquires the justice principle but that they may
provide a motive base for being receptive to it and for guiding one's actions in
accordance with it. The link between empathy and justice is, in any case, less
direct than that between empathy and considering others, and there may be
some other as yet unknown primary motive base for acquiring justice principles.

In some cases, one's moral principles are an integral part of one's conception of what one is or ought to be as a person. People may be powerfully
motivated to act in accord with their self-conception, and if moral principles
are a significant part of it, actions that depart from the principles may produce
tension (Duval & Wicklund, 1972), a feeling of shame, or guilt. I mentioned
earlier that empathic morality is vulnerable to overarousal and more generally
to powerful egoistic motives in situations. These limitations may not be intrinsic to morality closely tied to one's self-conception. It may therefore be
exactly this type of morality that is necessary for such actions as taking a
principled stand against agencies of established moral authority.

In conclusion, I suggest three directions for future research in this area:
the search for developmental links between the simple empathy-based moral
motives discussed here and complex cognitive processes involved in choosing
moral principles, building moral ideologies, and establishing moral priorities;
the search for other motives that may provide a more direct and certain link
than does empathy to principles and ideologies involving justice, fairness, and
reciprocity; the search for processes in the development of a motivational self-
system and its possible link to moral concepts.

REFERENCES

Bandura, A. *Social learning theory*. Englewood Cliffs, N.J.: Prentice-Hall, 1977.

Brandt, R. B. Emotive theory of ethics. In P. Edwards (Ed.), *The encyclopedia of philosophy*. New York: Crowell, 1967.

Brown, A. L. The development of memory. In H. W. Reese (Ed.), *Advances in child development and behavior* (Vol. 10). New York: Academic Press, 1975.

Craik, F. I. M. Depth of processing in recall and recognition. In S. Dornic (Ed.), *Attention and performance* (Vol. 6). Hillsdale, N.J.: Lawrence Erlbaum Associates, 1977.

Darley, J. M., & Latané, B. Bystander intervention in emergencies: Diffusion of responsibility. *Journal of Personality and Social Psychology*, 1968, *8*, 377–383.

Douglas, W. O. *The court years*. New York: Random House, 1980.

Duval, S., & Wicklund, R. A. *A theory of objective self-awareness*. New York: Academic Press, 1972.

Eisenberg-Berg, N., & Neal, C. Children's moral reasoning about their own prosocial behavior. *Developmental Psychology*, 1979, *15*, 228–229.

Erikson, E. Reflections on the dissent of contemporary youth. *International Journal of Psychoanalysis*, 1970, *51*, 11–22.

Gaertner, S. L., & Dovidio, J. F. The subtlety of white racism, arousal, and helping behavior. *Journal of Personality and Social Psychology*, 1977, *35*, 691–707.

Hoffman, M. L. Conscience, personality, and socialization techniques. *Human Development*, 1970, *13*, 90–126.

Hoffman, M. L. Developmental synthesis of affect and cognition and its implications for altruistic motivation. *Developmental Psychology*, 1975, *11*, 607–622.

Hoffman, M. L. Moral internalization: Current theory and research. In L. Berkowitz (Ed.), *Advances in experimental social psychology* (Vol. 10). New York: Academic Press, 1977, pp. 86–135.

Hoffman, M. L. Empathy, its development and prosocial implications. In C. B. Keasey (Ed.), *Nebraska Symposium on Motivation* (Vol. 25). Lincoln: University of Nebraska Press, 1978.

Hoffman, M. L. Adolescent morality in development perspective. In J. Adelson (Ed.), *Handbook of adolescent psychology*, New York: Wiley, 1980.

Hoffman, M. L. Is altruism part of human nature? *Journal of Personality and Social Psychology*, 1981, *40*, 121–137.

Hoffman, M. L. Affect and moral development. In D. Cicchetti & P. Hesse (Eds.), *New directions for child development: Emotional development* (No. 16). San Francisco: Jossey-Bass, 1982. (a)

Hoffman, M. L. Development of prosocial motivation: Empathy and guilt. In N. Eisenberg (Ed.), *The development of prosocial behavior*. New York: Academic Press, 1982, 281–313. (b)

Hoffman, M. L. Affective and cognitive processes in moral internalization. In E. T. Higgins, D. Ruble, & S. W. Hartup (Eds.), *Social cognition and social development: A socio-cultural perspective*. New York: Cambridge University Press, 1983, 236–274.

Hoffman, M. L. Interaction of affect and cognition in empathy. In C. Izard, J. Kagan, & R. Zajonc (Eds.), *Emotion, cognition, and behavior*. New York: Cambridge University Press, in press. (a)

Hoffman, M. L. Moral Development. In M. Bornstein & M. Lamb (Eds.), *Developmental psychology: An advanced textbook*. Hillsdale, N.J.: Lawrence Erlbaum Associates, in press. (b)

Hume, D. *An inquiry concerning the principle of morals* (Vol. 4). New York: Liberal Arts Press, 1957. (Originally published, 1751.)

Jones, E. E., & Nisbett, R. E. The actor and the observer: Divergent perceptions of the causes of behavior. In E. E. Jones et al. (Eds.), *Attribution: Perceiving the causes of behavior*. Morristown, N.J.: General Learning Press, 1971.

Kahneman, D. *Attention and effort*. Englewood Cliffs, N.J.: Prentice-Hall, 1973.

Kameya, L. I. *The effect of empathy level and role-taking training upon prosocial behavior*. Unpublished doctoral dissertation, University of Michigan, 1976.

Latané, B., & Rodin, J. A lady in distress: Inhibiting effects of friends and strangers on bystander intervention. *Journal of Experimental Social Psychology*, 1969, *5*, 189–202.

Lerner, M. J., & Simmons, C. Observer's reaction to the innocent victim: Compassion or rejection? *Journal of Personality and Social Psychology*, 1966, *4*, 203–210.

Mueller, J. H. Anxiety and encoding processing in memory. *Personality and Social Psychology Bulletin*, 1979, *5*, 288–294.

Murphy, L. B. *Social behavior and child personality*. New York: Columbia University Press, 1937.

Rawls, J. *A theory of justice*. Cambridge, Mass.: Harvard University Press, 1971.

Rest, J. Moral development. In M. Hetherington (Ed.), *Carmichael's Handbook of Child Psychology*. New York: Wiley, in press.

Shweder, R. A. Review of Kohlberg's *The philosophy of moral development: Moral stages and the idea of justice. Contemporary Psychology*, 1982, *27*, 421–424.

Simpson, E. L. Moral development research: A case study of scientific cultural bias. *Human Development*, 1974, *17*, 81–106.

Stein, N. L., & Glenn, C. G. An analysis of story comprehension in elementary school children. In R. O. Freedle (Ed.), *Discourse processing: Multidisciplinary perspectives*. Norwood, N.J.: Ablex, 1979.

Stotland, E. Exploratory investigations of empathy. In L. Berkowitz (Ed.), *Advances in experimental social psychology* (Vol. 4). New York: Academic Press, 1969.

Stotland, E., Mathews, K. E., Sherman, S. E., Hansson, R., & Richardson, B. Z. *Empathy, Fantasy, and Helping*. Beverly Hills, Calif.: Sage, 1979.

Thompson, R., & Hoffman, M. L. Empathy and the arousal of guilt in children. *Developmental Psychology*, 1980, *15*, 155–156.

Zahn-Waxler, C., Radke-Yarrow, M., & King, R. M. Childrearing and children's prosocial initiations toward victims of distress. *Child Development*, 1979, *50*, 319–330.

CHAPTER 17

Moral Behavior as Rule-Governed Behavior: A Psychosocial Role-Theoretical Approach to Moral Behavior and Development

WILLIAM M. KURTINES

Research on moral development and behavior has traditionally emphasized person-related variables such as level or stage of moral reasoning, individual differences in moral traits and dispositions, or past reinforcement history. The effects of context on moral action and decision, in contrast, has received relatively little attention. It is therefore not surprising that little systematic effort has been made to provide a theoretically meaningful account of situation variables and that even less has been done on accounting for the conjoint effects of both types of variables. This chapter describes an approach to moral behavior and development, derived from a rule-governed perspective, intended to provide a conceptual framework for accounting for both person and situation effects on moral choices and decisions. According to this approach, moral choices and decisions are influenced by both individual differences in the use of moral rules and principles and complex contextual cues that include type and attributes of situations. Several lines of research supporting this view are described. Theoretical and metaethical implications are discussed.

The morality research literature has grown extensively over the last two decades and currently includes a diverse array of theoretical orientations. These orientations range from cognitive-developmental structuralist (e.g., Kohlberg,

The author thanks Mildred Alverez, Luis Escovar, Robert Hogan, Lawrence Kohlberg, Gary Moran, Mordecai Nisan, and Andrea Slapion for their helpful comments on an earlier version of this chapter.

1969, and Chap. 4 in this book; Piaget, 1932/1965) to individual differences–trait dispositional (e.g., Hoffman, 1975, and Chap. 16 in this book; Hogan, 1975, and Chap. 13 in this book) and learning-behavioral theory (e.g., Burton, 1976, and Chap. 11 in this book; Liebert, 1978, and Chap. 10 in this book; Mischel & Mischel, 1976; Nisan, Chap. 12 in this book). This theoretical diversity is more apparent than real, however, and a more careful examination of the literature suggests that most current research shares at least one critical feature, namely, that it is conducted within theoretical frameworks that focus primarily on person variables such as level or stage of moral reasoning, moral traits and dispositions, and past reinforcement history. One significant limitation of the current emphasis on person variables is that it oversimplifies the complex interaction that occurs between the person as moral agent, actor, and decision maker and the extensive network of socially defined rules and roles that make up social systems. Such models, this chapter will argue, have difficulty in providing a theoretically meaningful account of the effects of situation variables on moral actions and decisions because they are conceptually limited to person variables.

The social component of morality, however, need not be ignored. Theoretical alternatives to the contemporary bias toward individualistic models are clearly possible (Hogan, Johnson & Emler, 1978). One such approach is described in the following section. This approach explicitly acknowledges the psychosocial nature of moral behavior and development. According to this approach, most interesting and important forms of human behavior can be conceptualized as rule-governed behavior. Language and law, science and logic, and convention and morality all provide examples of diverse forms of human rule-governed behavior. The notion of human behavior as rule-governed behavior is, to borrow a phrase from Pepper (1972), a "root metaphor." Using this simple but powerful root metaphor as a starting point, this chapter will argue that it is possible to develop a *psychosocially integrated* framework for conceptualizing moral actions and judgments. Within this frame, moral judgments and actions will be conceptualized as *prototypical forms* of rule-governed behavior. This chapter will also illustrate how the application of such a rule-governed perspective yields some novel and interesting conclusions with respect to several issues central to the literature on morality and moral development.

The first issue is the relative influence of person and situation variables on moral actions and decisions. This chapter will argue that despite the preponderance in the current literature of models that emphasize the importance of person variables, the most empirically useful models will prove to be those that provide a theoretically meaningful account of *both* person and situation variables. The second issue the chapter will address concerns the question of ethical universalism versus relativism and the metaethical implications of a conceptual framework the root metaphor of which is "human behavior as rule-governed behavior." With respect to this issue, this chapter will argue that the metaethical implications of a rule-governed perspective are consistent with certain post-Wittgensteinian and existential developments in philosophy that suggest that moral choices and decisions are profoundly difficult not only because they involve value conflicts but also because they are decisions or judgments for which there are no absolute justifications.

PSYCHOSOCIAL ROLE THEORY

Theoretical Background

The approach to moral behavior and development described here, in contrast with that provided by current theoretical orientations, explicitly adopts a view of the individual as a moral agent whose actions and decisions take place within the context of a socially defined system of rules and roles, thereby providing a conceptual framework broad enough to account for the effects of situation as well as person variables. This approach, which will be termed psychosocial role theory, is rooted in a view of *human action* that draws on three major traditions in contemporary social theory. At a macrolevel, it draws on open systems theory (Allport, 1967; Katz & Kahn, 1978). At a more microlevel, the approach draws on traditional role theory, a heuristic whose earliest formulations can be found in the work of Charles Cooley (1902) and George Herbert Mead (1934) and more recently in theorists as diverse as Erikson, Goffman, Parsons, and Sarbin (Erikson, 1950; Goffman, 1959; Parsons, 1951; Sarbin & Allen, 1968). Finally, at the most basic level, this approach draws on an emerging view of human behavior as rule-governed behavior (Harré & Secord, 1973; Hogan, 1974; Mischel, 1969; Peters, 1958).

Psychosocial role theory is a theoretical heuristic that attempts to integrate these three perspectives on human action. Its basic units of analysis are *rules, roles,* and *systems*. Within this framework, morality is seen as performing a critical social function (system maintenance and integration), and it is conceptualized as the network of rules that govern relations between individuals within a system. From this perspective, moral dilemmas are viewed as conflicts between rules and roles within systems, and moral judgments as decisions concerning the relative priority of moral rules. Moral conduct is conceptualized as behavior consistent (or inconsistent) with those rules. Because conflict between rules within a system is inevitable and because resolutions to rule conflicts are relative to particular systems, moral judgments are, according to this view, difficult decisions whose validity is ultimately indeterminate.

Basic to the approach outlined here are four assumptions about the nature of human action, namely, that human behavior is (1) *rule governed,* in that it conforms to explicit or implicit rules and conventions applicable to particular action situations; (2) *purposive* or *intentional,* in that it takes place within action situations defined by identifiable goals, aims, outcomes, or ends; (3) *anthropomorphic,* in that human beings are self-directed agents capable of consciously employing a variety of rules, plans, or strategies in order to achieve self-selected goals, aims, or purposes; and (4) *social,* in that situation-specific behavior takes place within a larger context, network, or system of rules that provides an organizational or structural context for specific rule-governed actions.

Up to this point psychosocial role theory has been discussed as a theory of human action. The developmental component of the theory is rooted in an organicist-contextualist perspective on *human development,* of which Piagetian cognitive-structural theory (Piaget, 1932/1965) provides a classic example. Such a perspective views moral development as the outcome of an interaction between the individual rule user, follower, or maker and the network of rules that constitute the essence of morality (Piaget, 1932/1965) and focuses on the attitudes, affects, and cognitions of the individual toward those rules.

The following section of this chapter begins with a discussion of the three most basic concepts of this heuristic—rules, roles, and systems—and uses them as building blocks for developing a view of the nature of morality that is consistent with the approach described here. Subsequent sections outline a psychosocial perspective on moral development and the moral-decision-making process, respectively, and briefly summarize research that provides support for the empirical utility of the approach.

NATURE OF MORALITY

Open systems theory, applied to social behavior, emphasizes the contrived or constructed nature of social structures (Berger & Luckmann, 1967; Katz & Kahn, 1978). Social systems, unlike biological or mechanical systems, do not have a physical structure. As a consequence, social systems do not exist independent of the cognitions, attitudes, beliefs, and expectations of the individuals who comprise the systems. In systems theory, *social systems* are construed as structurally integrated recurring cycles of social events. Central to any enduring social system are specialized subsystems that fulfill critical systems functions (e.g., production, adaptation, integration, maintenance, etc.). Maintenance subsystems serve to maintain system structure. The notion of a social system (i.e., an open-ended, socially constructed, structurally integrated recurring cycle of social events) constitutes the largest operational concept used in the approach described here. Within this frame, the two basic units of social systems are conceptualized as rules and roles. A *rule* is a guide for conduct or action. A *role* is a subset of rules applicable to an individual participant in the system (see Harré & Secord, 1973). Roles consist of a constellation of rights and obligations as well as specific rules of conduct. The network of reciprocally defined rules and roles, which constitute the microelements of the basic structure of social systems, functions to preserve the fabric of interdependent behavior necessary for the accomplishment of system goals.

From such a structural systems perspective, morality can be conceptualized as the network of rules and roles that function to maintain system integration. According to this approach, morality has both a surface and an underlying or "deep" structure. The surface structure of morality is made up of its "objective" or observable features. These objective features consist of the cyclical sequence of behavioral events that structure the system. Figure 17.1 presents a schematic diagram of the structure of morality.

The cyclic sequences of actions that make up the surface structure of the moral system are the data of immediate sense experience and by themselves lack conventional meaning. The ongoing series of behavioral events are structured by a complex network of rules that provide the observable behavior with its conventional meaning. The rule system that underlies the ongoing action sequence is, in effect, the system's "deep" structure. As can be seen from the schematic diagram in Figure 17.1, the underlying structure of morality is defined by: (1) Level I, moral rules that prescribe or prohibit specific acts or activities; (2) Level II, the reciprocal moral rights that exist between occupants of roles within the system; and (3) Level III, the moral principles that underlie the rules and rights. Thus, from a systems-structural perspective, a particular act acquires its moral meaning in the context of a complex network of moral rules, rights, and principles that provide the underlying structure for the system.

The metaethical implications of the question of whether the moral principles that structure moral rule systems are universal and absolute will be addressed more fully later. For our present purposes, the following discussion of the basic principles that structure morality will be based on a modification of an ethical theory proposed by Frankena (1963). This theory recognizes the existence of at least two basic principles of morality, the principle of beneficence or utility and the principle of justice, that provide a rational organizational structure for rules and conventions normally associated with morality. The principle of utility defines an act or action as good if, all things considered, it serves to maximize the total amount of good in the world (i.e., the balance of good over evil). The principle of justice holds that the just distribution of goods (and evils) is itself a good. Frankena (1963, p. 35) terms this ethical position a *mixed deontological theory* because it recognizes the principle of utility as a valid one but insists that another principle is required as well. According to this approach, an individual's moral obligation is normally determined by the rules and conventions usually associated with morality, but in cases of conflict between the rules, the individual's moral obligation is determined by the rule that best fulfills the joint requirements of utility and justice. The principles of utility and justice are thus viewed as prima facie rather than as absolute, and the theory allows that on some occasions justice may take precedence over utility, whereas on other occasions utility may take precedence over justice. The theory further suggests that in some cases it will be difficult (if not impossible) to determine with certainty which principle should take precedence.

The systems-structural perspective used here adds the principle of pragma-

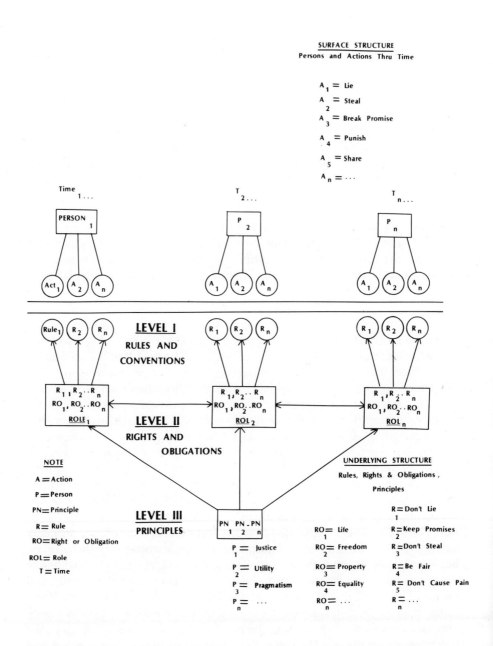

Figure 17.1. Structure of morality.

308

tism (or instrumentalism) to this basic ethical position. The pragmatism principle defines an act or activity as good if it is more useful, practical, or efficient relative to alternative acts or activities. Instrumentalism is conceptualized as a default principle applicable in those cases where the principles of utility and justice yield no clearly defined course of action.

A structural perspective on morality such as the one we have been describing requires conceptualizing moral principles as prima facie and mixed because of the sometimes mutually exclusive tasks that the maintenance subsystems perform within systems. Maintenance subsystems serve to maintain predictability and stability within systems. In order to fulfill this function successfully, maintenance subsystems must (1) regulate the interpersonal behavior of occupants of roles within the system, and (2) regulate the distribution of resources, rewards, sanctions, duties, and obligations within social systems. As the achievement of one goal is frequently incompatible with the achievement of the other, conflict is built into the social system.

Thus far we have discussed the nature of morality with an emphasis on the systems-structural properties of morality. The psychosocial nature of the approach reported here, however, is based in part on the existence of structural similarities between persons and social systems. More specifically, the approach assumes a structural *isomorphism* between the basic principles that structure the social component morality and the principles that structure the individual's thinking and reasoning about morality. Psychosocial role theory thus views each individual within a social system as having available a multi-level repertoire of cognitive rule schemata, a subset of which are roughly isomorphic with the principles that structure and organize the network of rules and rights that make up the social component of morality. The two systems (i.e., cognitive and social) are conceptualized as only roughly or partially isomorphic in the sense of existing in approximate structural congruence rather than in exact one-to-one correspondence, with individual differences and variations occurring across both systems.

At a cognitive level, very general rule schemata such as justice, utility, and instrumentalism serve as more than decision criteria; they function more broadly as cognitive structures or schemata (Bartlett, 1932; Piaget, 1936) that organize and unify the person's social knowledge or understanding. These general principles serve two basic cognitive functions: First, they provide the underlying dimensions that structure and order the person's moral rule repertoire; second, they provide the mechanism for resolving conflict within the person's rule repertoire.

MORAL DEVELOPMENT

From a psychosocial role-theoretical perspective, the development of moral reasoning involves developmental changes in the child's thinking about moral rules. These changes take place along three dimensions: the size of the moral rule repertoire, the child's consciousness of the rules, and the structure of the child's repertoire of moral rules.

In terms of size, developmental changes proceed in a linear fashion along a dimension of few and simple to many and complex. With respect to consciousness of rules, development takes place along a dimension of heteronomy to autonomy and involves three stages (Piaget, 1932/1965). The first stage is an individualistic stage, defined by the instrumental use of rules without a conscious understanding of their obligatory nature. The second stage is one of heteronomy, in which the obligatory nature of rules is recognized, but its source is perceived to be external to the child and based on unilateral respect for authority. The third stage is one of autonomy, in which rules are viewed as internally obligatory and arising from cooperation and mutual consent.

Moral development also involves structural changes in the child's moral rule repertoire that parallel the three stage changes that take place in consciousness of rules. During the individualistic stage, the basic principle that governs the child's thinking about moral rules is self-interest. As egocentricism begins to give way to a more sociocentric orientation, the child enters the heteronomous stage. At this stage the child becomes more capable of considering the viewpoint of others, and his or her thinking begins to include a rudimentary sense of justice or fairness. During the heteronomous stage, however, the child externalizes rules and regards them as properties of the external world that act on him or her and that he or she perceives as inflexible and unchanging, much as the child perceives the physical world as unchanging. At this stage, the child typically views objective consequences as more important than subjective intention and authority as more important than equality or justice. By the third stage, autonomy, the child is fully sociocentric. At the autonomous level, the child's egocentricism is moderated by an understanding of the principles of justice and reciprocity as well as a sense of cooperation and mutual consent.

MORAL DECISION MAKING

The preceding sections discuss the nature of morality and moral development from a psychosocial role-theoretical perspective; this section discusses both a typology of moral decisions and a model of the moral decision-making process.

Types of Moral Decisions

Although the current literature on moral behavior gives mixed emphasis to the role of moral judgment in moral development (see especially Kohlberg, 1969; Mischel & Mischel, 1976), moral judgment has been generally viewed as a unitary process (see Kohlberg, 1969; Mischel & Mischel, 1976; Piaget,

1932/1965). From a systems perspective, however, the two basic functions of the maintenance subsystem (i.e., behavioral regulation and resource allocation) require a distinction between two basic types or classes of moral judgments, depending on the type of decision a situation requires. According to this approach, situations involving a moral judgment require either a behavioral decision or a distributive decision. A behavioral decision involves the regulation of behavior and presents the decision maker with a choice between acting or not acting. For example, a decision involving a choice between stealing or not stealing something (or lying or not lying, or breaking a promise or not breaking a promise) requires a behavioral decision. Behavioral decisions are expressed in qualitative terms, and the judgment usually takes the form of "Should (ought) I (we) *do X* (or $\sim X$)," where X is a specific act or activity. Behavioral decisions that are nontrivial involve consequences for self or others.

A distributive decision, on the other hand, involves the allocation of resources and presents the decision maker with a choice between two or more possible distributions of some thing or activity within the system. For example, a decision involving the apportionment, allotment, or distribution of rights and obligations or resources, rewards, or punishment requires a distributive decision. Distributive decisions are expressed quantitatively, and the judgment usually takes the form of "How should (ought) I (we) *distribute X*," where X is a continuous quantity or amount of some thing or activity.

Behavioral and distributive decisions also differ in the type of criteria used in the decision-making process. Behavioral decisions are teleological in that the consequence of the act tends to serve as the decision criterion. Distributive decisions, on the other hand, are deontological in that the relative fairness (in the sense of equality or equity) of the distribution, rather than the consequences of the distribution, tends to serve as the decision criterion.

A Model of Moral Decision Making

The actual decision processes that underlie the individual's moral judgment can be described by a three-stage "successive-hurdles" model of moral decision making. The multistage model is intended to represent the minimum number of sequential stages needed to arrive at a moral decision. Briefly, the decision stages are (1) the selection and application of the appropriate Level I moral rules; (2) a test for conflict between the rule and the appropriate higher-order Level II moral right or obligation; and (3) a test for conflict between the right or obligation and the appropriate higher-order Level III moral principle. Figure 17.2 contains a more detailed flow diagram of the model.

The model assumes the existence of a multilevel repertoire of rules that function as decision criteria during the decision-making process. This multilevel rule repertoire is conceptualized as existing in the form of cognitive rule schemata, and the number and type of rule schemata available during the decision-making process is viewed as a function of the individual's socialization experiences. Persons who have had similar socialization experience can

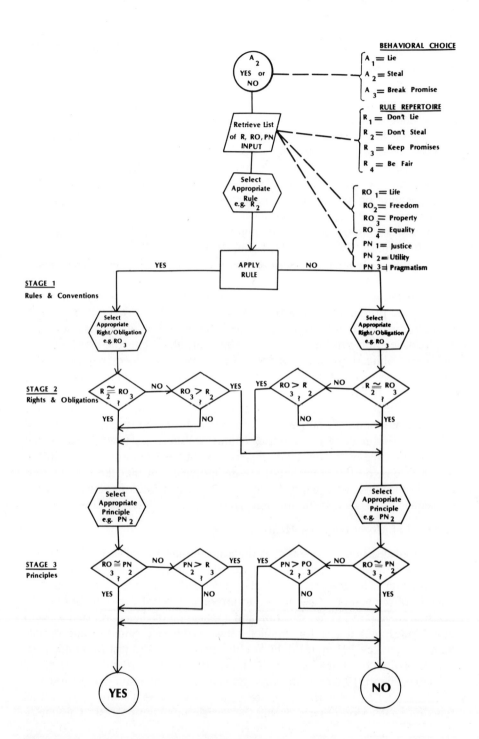

Figure 17.2. Three-stage successive-hurdles model.

be expected to have a similar (though not necessarily the same) rule repertoire. The multistage model described in this section is concerned with a rule
repertoire that consists of "moral" rules, and this particular subset of rules
is viewed as part of a larger set of rules (e.g., social, legal, grammatical, etc.)
acquired during the socialization process. As the flow diagram indicates, these
internalized moral rules are used as decision criteria during the moral-
decision-making process. It can also be seen from Figure 17.2 that for a particular act or activity to be judged morally obligatory, the rule that prescribes
or prohibits it must be consistent with at least one of the general principles
of morality, but not necessarily all of them. Further note that the moral principles that serve as final decision criteria are seen as rule-selection rules in
the sense that they are used to test the appropriateness of Level I and Level II
rules and rights. The multistage model also suggests that most moral "decisions" do not involve a moral dilemma and that those decisions that do involve a "dilemma" concern conflict between moral rules or conventions and
"higher-order" moral rights and obligations or moral principles. Further, according to the model, the moral-decision-making process involves three distinct and sequential stages, and a judgment of moral obligation must pass an
increasingly more stringent test of generalizability at each successive stage.

RESEARCH

The research outlined here, which has been reported in more detail elsewhere (Kurtines, Note 1) focuses on the interaction between individual moral-
decision-making processes and systems-structural features that characterize
situations requiring moral decisions. Data from three research studies designed to examine the effects of situation and person variables on moral decision making are presented.

Study 1: Situation Effects on Moral Decision Making

The first research study in the series of three to be briefly described here was
concerned with the effects of situational variables on the use of moral rules
and principles. Previous research has demonstrated the effects of situational
factors on dimensions of moral behavior (Mischel, Coates, & Raskoff, 1968).
More recent research has focused on the identification of mechanisms by
which situational factors affect moral decisions and behavior. A recent study
by Lynch and Cohen (1978), for example, tested a subjective expected utility
(SEU) model and examined the effect of three specific aspects of situations
(i.e., subjective probability, subjective utility, and salience of consequences)
on helping behavior. Lynch and Cohen (1978) found that a differential
weighted product-average model for combining probability and utility best
accounted for these situational factors. Building on this research, the first
study developed a method for operationalizing the effects of type of decision-

making situation and examined the effects of type of situation on moral rule preference.

From a psychosocial role-theoretical perspective, situations and persons are linked by the type of decision a situation requires (behavioral or distributive) and the type of criterion the person selects (teleological or deontological). This approach further suggests that the criterion used in a particular situation in turn influences the situational attributes evaluated during the decision-making process. More specifically, it was hypothesized that telelogical principles such as utility or pragmatism would be the preferred criterion for situations requiring a behavioral decision and deontological principles such as justice, the preferred criterion in a situation requiring a distributive decision. It was further hypothesized that in situations requiring a behavioral decision, situational factors influence moral decision making by affecting the subjective expected utility (SEU) associated with possible courses of action and that in situations requiring a distributive decision, situational factors influence moral decision making by affecting the subjective expected justness (SEJ) associated with the possible distributions. These hypotheses were tested in a study involving 58 undergraduate college students.

The research procedure for this study involved the development of a set of six simulated moral situations. To maximize the structural similarity of the situations, all six situations involved the same three fictional characters. The simulated situations were arranged in a semistructured format with a separate answer sheet. The answer sheet also contained a summary of the moral principles (i.e., justice, utility, and pragmatism) used for the study. Three of the situations involved a behavioral decision and required the respondents to make a decision about lying, breaking a promise, and stealing. For each behavioral decision, the two possible courses of action (e.g., stealing or not stealing) had potential negative consequences (e.g., getting caught or not getting caught, getting hurt or not getting hurt) for either one of the two principal characters in the story. Negative consequences were used throughout in order to make the situations parallel.

The other three situations involved a distributive decision and required the respondent to make a judgment about the distribution of responsibility, a reward, and a punishment. Each distributive decision situation involved a conflict between the two possible equity criteria, merit and need. The same equity criteria were used throughout in order to make the situations parallel. Respondents were asked which of the two distributions described in the situations they would choose if they were the main character. For all six situations, respondents were also asked which of the three moral principles (justice, utility, pragmatism) they felt best justified their choices. The order of presentation was alternated by type of decision.

The subjects in the study made a total of 328 decisions, including 161 distributive and 167 behavioral decisions. Analyses of the results revealed highly significant differences in the use of moral principles across all decision situations. The most frequently used principle was justice, and the least used was pragmatism. The results obtained when the data were analyzed by type of situation clearly support the hypothesis of the situational specificity of the use of moral principles. For the distributive decisions, the moral principle most frequently preferred was justice, whereas for the behavioral decisions, the most frequently preferred criteria were pragmatism followed by utility, both teleological principles.

Study 2: Person Effects on Moral Decision Making

The first study demonstrated that it is possible to operationally define two relatively distinct types of moral-decision-making situations and that type of situation has a significant effect on the preference for the justificatory use of moral principles. The second study was concerned with the development of a method for assessing individual differences in the use of moral principles.

As noted earier, a psychosocial role-theoretical approach views each individual within a social system as having available a multilevel repertoire of cognitive rule schemata that function as decision criteria. Previous research with young children (Kurtines & Pimm, 1983; Pimm, Kurtines, & Ruffy, 1982; Kurtines, Pimm, & Kaplan, Note 2) provides empirical support for the development sequence in moral reasoning postulated by Piaget. These data also provide evidence that during the normal course of development most individuals achieve an autonomous level of moral reasoning by the age of 12 (see especially Pimm, Kurtines, & Ruffy, 1982). Although there is evidence in the literature on developmental differences, little data currently exist on individual difference in the use of moral rule schemata such as justice and utility in individuals who are functioning effectively at the autonomous level. The second study, which involved 83 undergraduate volunteers, focused on the development of a measure of individual-differences in rule schemata preference.

There presently is a growing body of research on the role of schemata, scripts, and prototypes in the acquisition and application of social knowledge at many different levels (Schank & Abelson, 1977; Wyer, 1980). With few notable exceptions (Markus, 1977), however, individual differences in the use of social schemata have been largely ignored (Fisk & Linville, 1980).

Recent research on social knowledge processing suggests that the availability of well-rehearsed schemata facilitates the storage and retrieval of social information at various levels (Anderson & Pichert, 1978; Kendzierski, 1980; Wyler, 1980). Building on this research, a Measure of Moral Value Preference (MMVP) that uses a multimethod technique for assessing individual differences in rule usage was developed. The multiple methods include self-report, recognition, and recall, and the individual-difference measures included scales for Justice, Utility, and Pragmatism. Several analyses were conducted and indicated that the moral value preference component of the MMVP has adequate psychometric properties. First, the two main scales, Justice and Utility, appear to assess uncorrelated dimensions. Second, none of the scales appear to be subject to social desirability response set, defensiveness, sex biasis, or the effects of IQ. Finally, all of the scales display adequate reliability. The MMVP served as a measure of moral value preference for the next study.

Study 3: Person and Situation Effects on Moral Decision Making

Building on the two previous studies, the final project in this series was concerned with the conjoint effects of person and situation variables on moral decision making. This chapter has argued that because models that emphasize person variables do not provide an explicit framework capable of accounting for situational variables, the effects of such variables on moral decision making have tended to be either ignored (Piaget, 1932/1965; Kohlberg, 1976) or handled on an ad hoc basis (Mischel & Mischel, 1976). The power of a psychosocially integrated theoretical heuristic, such as the one outlined here, on the other hand, derives in part from its inclusion of a systems perspective (Katz & Kahn, 1978). Social systems are composed of recurring and inter-related sets of behavioral events. Social systems are thus rooted in interactions *between* individuals, and a systems approach shifts the conceptual focus from the individual in isolation to the individual within a social context. Situation effects, as a consequence, present no conceptual difficulty; on the contrary, from a systems perspective the effects of situational context are viewed as an integral component of the moral-decision-making process. The third study, which involved 64 undergraduate student volunteers, examined the conjoint effects of person and situation variables on moral decision making.

The dependent variable for this study was moral choice in the six simulated situations developed previously. The following person and situation variables served as independent variables. The influence of person factors on moral decision making was assessed using the individual-difference variables from the MMVP. The MMVP was scored for Justice, Utility, and Pragmatism. The influence of situation factors on moral decision making was measured by means of ratings for each of the six hypothetical situations used in Study 1. For the three behavioral decision situations, respondents were asked to make subjective ratings on a 100-point scale of the likelihood that the consequences described in the situation would occur and a subjective rating of the severity of the consequence. Similarly, for the distributive judgment situations, the respondents were asked to make a subjective rating on a 100-point scale of the relative importance of merit and the relative importance of need as equity criteria in choosing between the two distributions described in the situations. These ratings served as situation specific measures of subjective expected utility ($SEU = U \times P$) and subjective expected justness ($SEJ = M \times N$). Respondents were also asked which of the two possible courses of action or distributions they would choose if they were the main character in the situation.

The relative influence of person and situation factors on moral decision making was analyzed using multiple regression techniques. A multiple regression was conducted for each of the six situations using moral choice as the dependent variable and scores on the MMVP (Justice, Utility, and Pragmatism), SEU (Utility, Probability), and SEJ (Merit, Need) as independent variables. All regression analyses yielded significant multiple equations. More importantly, in each of the six situations, both person factors (i.e., one or more of the Justice, Utility, and Pragmatism scales) and situation factors (i.e., one or more of the SEU and SEJ ratings) contributed a significant increment of explained variance to each of the six regression equations. Thus, both person- and situation-related factors contributed significantly to the explanation of moral choice in all six situations. Multiple regression procedures, however, are asymmetrical and do not provide information regarding incremental increases that are unique to and shared by single variables and sets of variables. As the purpose of the study was to examine the conjoint effects of person and situation factors on moral decision making, the results of the multiple regressions were further analyzed using a procedure for partitioning regression variance reported by Mood (1971). This method allows for a more symmetrical analysis of the relative contribution of person and situation factors. Regression procedures are asymmetrical because of the sequential order in which the variables are entered into the regression equation. Variance associated with the variable entered first includes not only the explained variance that is unique to that variable but also the variance that it shares with other variables (Cronkite & Moos, 1978). The procedure described by Mood (1971) makes comparisons of variance more symmetric by partitioning the unique and shared variance accounted for by each variable or combination of variables in the regression equations.

Table 17.1 presents the results of the regression analyses partitioned into unique and shared variance for the person and situation variables. The most significant findings can be summarized as follows: (1) the total amount of variance that could be explained by both sets of variables varied across all six situations but was generally high; (2) the total amount of variance shared by both person and situation variables, on the other hand, also varied across all six situations but was generally low; (3) situation attributes (SEU and SEJ ratings) consistently accounted for a higher proportion of variance than did person-related factors (Justice, Utility, and Pragmatism scores); and (4) the total amount of variance that could be explained was consistently higher (more than 40%) in the distributive decision situations than in the behavioral situations.

DISCUSSION

Theoretical and Empirical Issues

The current literature on morality and moral development is distinguished by its partiality for theoretical models that focus primarily on person variables. This chapter has argued that such models tend to be unable to provide a theoretically meaningful account of the effects of situation variables on moral

TABLE 17.1. Partitioning of Explained Variance for Six Situations

	Situation					
	Behavioral			Distributive		
Variable	Lying (LY)	Breaking a Promise (BP)	Stealing (ST)	Reward (RW)	Responsibility (RE)	Punishment (PU)
Person related						
Unique variances						
Justice (JU)	.002	.000	.000	.029ᵃ	.001	.027ᵃ
Benevolence (BE)	.005	.000	.036ᵇ	.003	.004	.000
Pragmatism (PG)	.038ᵇ	.039ᵇ	.022ᵃ	.000	.041ᵇ	.000
Shared variance						
Sum of all combinationsᵈ	.015ᵃ	.000	.036ᵇ	.019ᵃ	.015ᵃ	.009
Subtotal	.060ᵇ	.039ᵇ	.094ᵇ	.051ᵇ	.061ᵇ	.036ᵃ
Proportion of R²	.431	.122	.377	.112	.149	.072
Situation related						
Unique variance						
Utility (UT) (or merit [ME])	.043ᵇ	.109ᶜ	.007	.011ᵃ	.243ᶜ	.171ᶜ
Probability (PB) (or need [NE])	.003	.017ᵃ	.033ᵇ	.203ᶜ	.004	.144ᶜ
Shared variance						
UT and PB (or ME and NE)	.021ᵇ	.015	.051ᵇ	.164ᶜ	.057ᵇ	.140ᶜ
Subtotal	.075ᵇ	.277ᶜ	.091ᵇ	.378ᶜ	.304ᶜ	.455ᶜ
Proportion of R²	.539	.868	.365	.832	.741	.915
Situation by person						
Shared variance						
Sum of all combinations	.004	.003	.064ᵇ	.025ᵃ	.045ᵇ	.006
Proportion of R²	.029	.009	.257	.055	.109	.012
Total R²	.139	.319	.249	.454	.410	.497

ᵃExplained variance greater than 1%.
ᵇExplained variance greater than 3%.
ᶜExplained variance greater than 10%.
ᵈThese combinations are (JU, BE), (JU, PG), (BE, PG), and (JU, BE, PG).
ᵉThese combinations are (JU, UT), (JU, PB), (JU, ME), (JU, NE), (BE, UT), (BE, PB), (BE, ME), (BE, NE), (PG, PB), (PG, ME), (PG, NE), (JU, BE, UT), (JU, BE, PB), (JU, BE, ME), (JU, BE, NE), (BE, PG, UT), (BE, PG, PB), (BE, PG, ME), (BE, PG, NE), (JU, PG, UT), (JU, PG, PB), (JU, PG, ME), (UT, PG, NE), (JU, BE, PG, ME), (TU, BE, PG, NE), and (JU, BE, PG, ME, NE).

decision making. One of the purposes of this chapter was to demonstrate the empirical feasibility of developing conceptual alternatives to theoretical models that emphasize person variables to the neglect of situation or context. The psychosocial role-theoretical approach outlined here, which attempts to integrate systems theory and role theory within a rule-governed framework, was explicitly designed to provide a theoretical heuristic capable of operationalizing the effects of both person and situation variables. This approach obviously represents only a first approximation of a conceptually adequate model; nonetheless, the research findings reported here suggest that such an approach has at least three significant conceptual and empirical advantages over more person-oriented approaches. First, a conceptual framework such as psychosocial role theory that allows the integration of both person and situation variables makes possible the development of explanatory models that are empirically more powerful than models that focus on either person *or* situation variables. As the data from Study 3 indicates, person and situation variables both contributed uniquely to the explanation of moral choice for all three behavioral decision situations and all three distributive decision situations. Moreover, the total amount of variance that could be explained by the conjoint effects of both sets of variables was generally quite high across all six situations.

Second, the approach provides a coherent framework for deriving procedures for operationalizing both person and situation variables. With this framework, it was possible to make theoretically meaningful distinctions between characteristics of situations (including both types and attributes of situations) as well as to derive hypotheses concerning the effects of these situation variables on moral decision making. In addition, it was also possible to derive a theoretically meaningful set of individual-difference variables and develop procedures for operationalizing them.

Third, a conceptual framework that is explicitly psychosocial reflects more accurately the full richness and complexity of the issues that define the literature. Although the approach reported here is complex in detail, such complexity is necessary in order to begin to provide an adequate conceptual framework. Moral choices are complex decisions mediated by both individual differences and situational constraints. The advantage of theoretical simplicity offered by models that are conceptually limited to person variables is gained at the expense of the capability of accounting for the effects of complex contextual cues on moral decisions. The data in Study 3 indicate that very little variance was shared by the person and situation variables and that the removal of either set of variables would substantially reduce the total amount of variance that could be explained.

Metaethical Issues

The basic thesis of this chapter has been that human behavior can be conceptualized as rule governed. Throughout, moral judgments and moral actions have been looked at as paradigmatic forms of such rule-governed behavior. The rule-governed metaphor, however, is much more powerful and pervasive. It has implications that extend beyond the development of descriptive models of moral behavior and development, which brings us to the second basic issue that this chapter addresses: namely, the metaethical implications of a rule-governed perspective. This chapter will conclude by noting that the conceptual framework described here has at least three significant metaethical implications, all of which appear to be rooted in the rule-governed nature of human behavior.

First, a conceptual framework such as psychosocial role theory that emphasizes the rule-governed nature of human behavior is also compelled to recognize the contrived and constructed nature of social organizations. Because the rule-governed nature of human action is fundamentally distinct from the "law-governed" behavior of natural phenomena, such a framework serves to restore an element of freedom and creativity to human action and existence. Using linguistic behavior as an example, Toulmin (1969) notes, "In certain crucial respects the rules to which linguistic behavior conform differ from the laws of the physical sciences. . . . The essential mark of rule-conforming behavior lies in the normative force of relevant rules. An agent who recognizes that he is deviating from a rule acknowledges (at any rate prima facie) a claim on him to correct his behavior" (pp. 86–87). Grammatical rules then, like the social and moral rules to which human behavior conforms, are normative in nature and imply standards against which behavior is evaluated. An individual's violation of a rule, consequently, in no way invalidates that rule. No such situation occurs when dealing with purely law-governed natural phenomena. Toulmin (1969) points out:

> The motion of the perihelion of the planet Mercury was observed, during the nineteenth century, to be deviating from the precise pattern astronomers had expected on the basis of Newton's dynamical theories. Yet scientists did not treat this deviation as a "failure" or "mistake" on the part of the planet. . . . It would have been laughable for them to talk of Mercury as "recognizing" that it was transgressing the "norm" set by Newtonian law so as to conform more nearly to the norm set by Mercury itself. [pp. 87–88]

This view would thus appear to suggest that human behavior is not subject to a temporally and spatially universal set of laws from which there can be no deviation. Quite the contrary, human behavior conforms to social and moral rules that, like the social organization that sustains them, are collectively created, self-imposed, and subject to change. Human beings hence not only conform to rules but also are free to change or create them in a way that physical laws cannot be created or changed.

Freedom, however, has a price. The second metaethical implication of the approach described here is that moral decisions are difficult decisions not only because they are complex but also because they are decisions for which there is no ultimate or absolute justification. If we acknowledge that we are free to create or change social and moral rules, we also must acknowledge that such rules are ultimately and profoundly arbitrary. Life is, as Kierkegaard points out, an either-or situation; choice is a fundamental fact of human existence. The dilemma of human existence, however, is that although we cannot avoid making choices, we can never be sure that we have made the right choice—we can never be *certain* that we have made the right decision. People invent universal, "objective" moral principles, Kierkegaard observes, to relieve themselves of the responsibility and the agony of choosing, but in the end even universal moral principles can be doubted. This view would thus suggest that although all social systems share certain structural similarities, and that the rules and principles that structure social systems (i.e., justice, utility, instrumentalism, etc.) will be similar across systems, in the end social systems are themselves contrived and arbitrary. Hence, although principles such as justice and utility are used to justify moral actions and decision in the day-to-day conduct of human affairs, the principles themselves have no independent, objective existence and are ultimately without justification outside their individual and collective human use. This view would thus suggest that in a profoundly Wittgensteinian sense moral principles have *no* meaning or justification apart from the human beings who use them.

We have now come to the final metaethical implication of this approach. This chapter has suggested that moral principles have no meaning or justification outside their individual and collective human use. Moreover, a case has been made that conceptual completeness requires that theoretical models recognize the social component of morality, raising the issue of individual versus collective responsibility for moral decisions. If, as Kierkegaard has argued, one cannot shift responsibility from oneself to universal moral principles, can one then shift the responsibility to one's culture or society? In other words, in the absence of an "objective" foundation for morality (see Kurtines and Gewirtz, Chap. 1), does the final responsibility for moral actions and decisions rest with the individual or society? The answer we suggest is that in the end it is the individual who bears the responsibility for moral actions and decisions. A perspective such as the one we have been developing explicitly recognizes the contrived and constructed nature of social organizations, that is, that social systems do not (indeed, cannot) exist independent of the individuals who comprise the system. Thus, although moral decisions can never be completely divorced from antecedent custom, convention, and social context that provide collective guidelines, justifications, and precedent, moral judgments are in the final analysis intentional decisions made by self-directed individuals who must bear responsibility for them.

Sartre (1949) manages to capture in drama the dialectic tension that exists between individual and collective moral responsibility as well as the conflict between abstract principles and concrete humanity that occurs in moral decision making. In Sartre's play *Dirty Hands,* which is set against the struggle for political power that took place in Nazi-occupied France, Hugo, an intellectual and assassin, has only an abstract conception of human welfare and is willing to sacrifice everything, including the lives of those who stand in his way, for the sake of his principled beliefs. His patron and intended victim, Hoederer, an immeasurably more mature person, has a conception of humanity that is more concrete and realistic. As Hoederer tells Hugo, "You can see for yourself! You don't love men, Hugo. You love only principles. . . . And I, I love them as they are. With all their saloperies and their vices. . . . For me, a man more or less in the world of counts." Thus, in Hugo's view, abstract principles are absolute and consequently more important than people. Hoederer, in contrast, places people before principles. Moreover, Hoederer recognizes that he cannot shift the responsibility for his decisions from himself to his principles or the situation in which he finds himself. On the contrary, he explicitly accepts personal responsibility for his decisions. "As for me, I have dirty hands. Up to the elbows! I have plunged them into shit and blood. And then? Do you think one can govern innocently?" (pp. 224–225).

In a world that frequently places people in situations that require complex and difficult moral decisions, we thus conclude that in the end, the responsibility for moral choices rests with the individual, not systems or principles.

REFERENCES

Allport, F. H. A theory of enestruence (event structure theory): Report of progress. *American Psychologist,* 1967, *22,* 1–24.

Anderson, R. C., & Pichert, J. W. Recall of previously unrecallable information following a shift in perspective. *Journal of Verbal Learning and Verbal Behavior,* 1978, *17,* 1–12.

Banton, M. *Roles: An introduction to the study of social relations.* New York: Basic Books, 1965.

Bartlett, F. C. *Remembering.* London: Cambridge University Press, 1932.

Berger, P. L., & Luckmann, T. *The social construction of reality.* New York: Doubleday (Anchor Books), 1967.

Brim, O. G., Jr. Socialization through the life cycle. In O. G. Brim, Jr., & Wheeler, *Socialization after childhood.* New York: Wiley, 1966.

Burton, R. V. Honesty and dishonesty. In T. Lickona (Ed.), *Moral development and behavior: Theory, research and social issues.* New York: Holt, Rinehart and Winston, 1976.

Cantor, N., & Mischel, W. Traits as prototypes: Effects on recognition memory. *Journal of Personality and Social Psychology,* 1977, *35,* 38–48.

Cooley, C. H. *Human nature and the social order.* New York: Scribner, 1902.

Cronkite, R. C., & Moos, R. H. Evaluating alcoholism treatment programs: An integrated approach. *Journal of Consulting and Clinical Psychology,* 1978, *46,* 1105–1119.

Erikson, E. H. *Childhood and society.* New York: Norton, 1950.

Fisk, S. T., & Linville, P. W. What does the schema concept buy us? *Personality and Social Psychology Bulletin*, 1980, *6*, 543–577.

Frankena, W. K. *Ethics*. Englewood Cliffs, N.J.: Prentice-Hall, 1963.

Goffman, E. *The presentation of self in everyday life*. New York: Doubleday, 1959.

Harre, H., & Secord, P. F. *The explanation of social behavior*. Totowa, N.J.: Little Field, Adams, 1973.

Hoffman, M. L. The development of altruistic motivation. In D. J. DePalma & J. M. Foley (Ed.), *Moral development and behavior: Current theory and research*. Hillsdale, N.J.: Halsted Press, 1975.

Hogan, R. Dialectical aspects of moral development. *Human Development*, 1974, *17*, 107–117.

Hogan, R., Johnson, J. A., & Emler, N. P. A socioanalytic theory of moral development. In W. Damon (Ed.), *Moral development: New Directions for Child Development* (Vol. 1). San Francisco: Jossey-Bass, 1978.

Katz, D., & Kahn, R. L. *The social psychology of organizations* (2nd ed.). New York: Wiley, 1978.

Kendzierski, D. Self-schemata and scripts: The recall of self-referent and scriptal information. *Personal and Social Psychology Bulletin*, 1980, *6*, 23–29.

Kohlberg, L. Stages and sequence: The cognitive-developmental approach to socialization. In D. A. Goslin (Ed.), *Handbook of socialization theory and research*. Skokie, Ill.: Rand McNally, 1969.

Kohlberg, L. Moral stages and moralization: The cognitive-developmental approach. In T. Lickona (Ed.), *Moral development and behavior: Theory, research, and social issues*. New York: Holt, Rinehart and Winston, 1976.

Kurtines, W., & Pimm, J. The moral development scale: A Piagetian measure of moral reasoning. *Educational and Psychological Measurement*, 1983, *43*, 89–105.

Lynch, J. G., & Cohen, J. L. The use of subjective expected utility theory as an aid to understanding variables that influence helping behavior. *Journal of Personality and Social Psychology*, 1978, *36*, 138–151.

Markus, H. Self-schemata and processing information about the self. *Journal of Personality and Social Psychology*, 1977, *35*, 63–78.

Mead, G. H. *Mind, self, and society from the standpoint of a social behaviorist*. University of Chicago Press, 1934.

Mischel, T. (Ed.). *Human action: Conceptual and empirical issues*. New York: Academic Press, 1969.

Mischel, W., Coates, B., & Raskoff, A. Effects of success and failure on self-gratification. *Journal of Personality and Social Psychology*, 1968, *10*, 381–390.

Mischel, W., & Mischel, H. N. A cognitive social-learning approach to socialization and self-regulation. In T. Lickona (Ed.), *Moral development and behavior: Theory, research, and social issues*. New York: Holt, Rinehart and Winston, 1976.

Mood, A. M. Partitioning variance in multiple regression analyses as a tool for developing learning model. *American Educational Research Journal*, 1971, *8*, 191–202.

Parsons, T. *The social system*. New York: Free Press, 1951.

Pepper, S. C. *World hypotheses: A study of evidence.* Berkeley: University of California Press, 1973.

Peters, R. S. *The idea of a social science.* London: Routledge & Kegan Paul, 1958.

Piaget, J. *The origins of intelligence in children.* New York: International Universities Press, 1936.

Piaget, J. *The moral judgment of the child* (M. Gabain, trans.). New York: Free Press, 1965. (Originally published, 1932.)

Pimm, J., Kurtines, W., & Ruffy, M. Moral reasoning in contemporary Swiss and American children. *Archives de Psychologie,* 1982, *50,* 225–235.

Sarbin, T. R., & Allen, V. L. Role theory. In G. Lindzey & E. Aronson (Eds.), *Handbook of social psychology* (Vol. 1, 2nd ed.). Reading, Mass.: Addison-Wesley, 1968.

Sartre, J. P. *Dirty hands.* New York: Random House, 1949.

Schank, R., & Abelson, R. *Scripts, plans, goals, and understanding: An Inquiry into Human Knowledge Structures.* Hillsdale, N.J.: Lawrence Erlbaum Associates, 1977.

Toulmin, S. Concepts and the explanation of human behavior. In T. Mischel (Ed.), *Human action: Conceptual and empirical issues.* New York: Academic Press, 1969.

Wyer, R. S. The acquisition and use of social knowledge: Basic postulates and representative research. *Personality and Social Psychology Bulletin,* 1980, *6,* 558–573.

REFERENCE NOTES

1. Kurtines, W. *Person and situation effects on moral decision making: A psychosocial role-theoretical perspective.* Paper presented at the annual meeting of the American Psychological Association, Washington, D.C., 1982.

2. Kurtines, W., Pimm, J., & Kaplan, A. *The juvenile justice system and the delinquent mind: A Piagetian cognitive developmental perspective.* Unpublished manuscript, 1981. (Available from William M. Kurtines, Department of Psychology, Florida International University, Miami, Florida.)

CHAPTER 18

Morality, Social Meaning, and Rhetoric: The Social Context of Moral Reasoning

HELEN WEINREICH-HASTE

This chapter examines the different assumptions of the developmental model of moral reasoning as exemplified by Kohlberg's theory and social psychological and sociological approaches to moral and social reasoning and considers the extent to which they can be reconciled. The chapter takes as basic assumptions two premises:

1. *The individual's moral reasoning and judgmental behavior depends on his or her* implicit social theory, *which is a set of implicit explanations and assumptions about how the social system works and about individual relations within the social system.*

2. *Most reasoning on moral, social, and political issues is* rhetorical, *in the sense that it is essentially an act of persuasive communication, asserting prescriptions that derive from the individual's implicit social theory.*

This chapter explores the relationship between the social origins and the individual ontogenesis of moral meaning, explanation, and rhetoric and argues that a satisfactory psychological approach must integrate the social and the individual factors, in theory and in empirical research. Hitherto there has been something of a latent conflict between the two approaches. In this chapter I describe three "territories" in which meaning, explanation, and rhetoric are generated, negotiated, and interpreted: the sociocultural, the interpersonal, and the intrapersonal. I explore ways in which these are interrelated, and I consider the implications of these interrelationships for future research.

This chapter concentrates on the expressive, the evaluative, and the linguistic forms of moral behavior. Human beings spend a great deal of their time engaging in this sort of behavior. To most of us, actual temptation and the need to make decisions about practical moral action occur relatively infrequently, but we daily engage in judging others, imposing sanctions on our fellows and dependents, and responding with censure or approval to public events. We behave as moralists, moral and social philosophers, moral apologists, and social theorists. In doing so, we are, as individuals, expressing a set of beliefs about what constitutes desirable behavior in ourselves and others. The beliefs reflect implicit theories we hold about the maintenance of social order, the necessary forms of relationship between persons, and the consequences for individuals and society of undesirable behavior. As individuals, we comment prescriptively and descriptively on the action of ourselves and others, and possibly, as a consequence of that comment, we make certain behaviors more likely or less likely to occur. As members of society, we reflect the cultural norms, values, and assumptions of the society in which we grow up and affirm and perpetuate them. We are thus engaging in both an individual and a social process.

There are two substantively different ways of explaining this behavior. Cognitive-developmental psychologists have concentrated on the processes involved in the development of individual judgment, the ontogenesis of reasoning, and the factors that affect restructuring and transformation of individual thought. Sociologists and some social psychologists offer the basis for an alternative explanatory approach that focuses on social processes. In its most extreme form, this approach explains individual moral action and expression as a response determined primarily by the demands of the social situation. The main orientation of this approach is the social situation as the crucible of specific, here-and-now meaning, and second, how the individual expression of moral ideas and moral conclusions reflects the social system and the dominant ideologies of the culture. Increasingly, those who are interested in social processes are paying attention to the role of language and symbol in the generation and transmission of social meaning and also to the role of the small group and dyad in the formulation and expression of that meaning.

Furthermore, the two approaches have different assumptions about why we are interested in morality. For the "individual" orientation, the interesting question is, How does the individual develop an autonomous ethical system and understanding of moral philosophy? For the "social" orientation, the interesting questions are about the role that moral expression and moral language play in affirming the individual in the social group, the maintaining of group identity, and the perpetuating of cultural mores.

There is at the present time a gap between the two models. The cognitive-developmental approach has been primarily concerned with *individual* processes; in this approach, social events and social experience are catalysts for the stimulation of individual thinking. Alternatively, the social event is a manifestation of individual reasoning in action. In contrast, for the theorist who is interested in social and cultural determinants and social processes, there is little space for considering the individual's own generation of meaning. In this chapter, I explore a model that may offer the possibility of synthesis. To do this, I shall, first, examine aspects of the interrelationship of the social and individual and, second, explore the idea of *rhetoric*.

I will divide the arenas of the *origin* and *operation* of moral meaning into three: the *sociocultural meaning system,* the *interpersonal meaning system,* and the *intrapersonal meaning system.* By sociocultural meaning system, I refer to the corpus of beliefs and explanations available to the individual through his or her cultural experience. The sociocultural meaning system also sets limitations and constraints on what the individual can know, on what the individual *should* know, and on the terms he or she should use in expressing and communicating that knowledge. The arena of interpersonal meaning is dyadic and small-group interaction, the most common situation of communicative experience. The many analyses of small-group discourse illustrate the great complexity of the negotiation process and the vast repertoire of rules, decoding skills, nonverbal communicative techniques, and so forth, which even very young children can use. It is the arena of intrapersonal meaning that is currently the focus of the cognitive-developmental approach. This is the area of individual cognitive organization, the individual making a coherent and meaningful personal theory out of knowledge and experience, a theory that is limited by, and reflects the limitations of, the individual's current level of cognitive complexity.

This chapter will explore the idea of *rhetoric* in three ways. First, in the field of moral reasoning, there is inevitably interfusion of fact and value. Second, any moral conclusion or act of moral reasoning, however private, has a didactic, communicative quality: If I have the conviction that I have attained the "right" solution, I have the desire to persuade others to share my meaning. Third, the knowledge and theories available in the culture, which are the sources of individual reasoning and judgments on moral, social, and political issues, are never neutral; like individual reasoning, public cultural orthodoxies confuse fact and value. They have a strong didactic purpose, and the individual learns, therefore, not only competing moral theories but also that these theories have their own built-in assertion of rectitude, truth, and universality. In this chapter, I want to show that an appreciation of the essentially rhetorical nature of moral reasoning gives us a framework for relating intrapersonal, interpersonal, and sociocultural processes.

THE CRITICAL ARENA

Much of the essence of the debate between "individual" and "social" approaches is encapsulated in the dialogues between Lawrence Kohlberg and some of his critics. Kohlberg's theory of moral development focuses mainly on the ontogenesis of individual reasoning about justice; as such, it offers an explanation of how the individual interprets moral and social events, resolves moral dilemmas, and, to some degree, acts in problematic situations (Kohlberg, 1971, 1976). Some of the objectors to Kohlberg's theory argue that he has ignored, or underestimated, the social and cultural variables that may influence or even determine the phenomena he explains in terms of a theory of the development of individual conceptions of justice. There are three main strands of such "social" objections:

1. The method of investigation is itself a social situation and, as such, has demand characteristics that make interpretation of the individual responses difficult and possibly dubious.
2. The whole exercise is culturally biased, taking as central a concept of justice that, the critics argue, is an essentially Western bourgeois concept.
3. The method and theory take no account of the social psychological work on the role of small-group interaction in the creation and negotiation of meaning and the role of language and forms of expression in maintaining the individual's membership in the group.

As a prelude to considering each of these criticisms in detail, let us look at the method by which cognitive-developmental psychologists collect data about moral reasoning. We ask our respondents to make evaluations and judgments about "moral" issues or events that conventionally are seen to be deviant or problematic. From these responses, we seek to establish the underlying reasoning and justification that the individual will give for his or her opinion. We probe, we press, and we try to take the respondent to the limits of his or her thinking (Colby, Kohlberg, Gibbs, Speicher-Dubin, Candee, Hewer, & Power, 1983).

There are certain interesting characteristics of this situation. First, it is a social situation, an interaction between the researcher and the respondent. Second, what is occurring is not a report on an action, nor is it the prediction of an action (however much the setting of the questions may seem to be in these terms). It is *reflection on* action, one's own or someone else's past or hypothetical future action. It is a commentary on the respondent's *reaction* to an action, a commentary involving explanation and evaluation. Third, it is usually the case that the situations the respondent is considering are entirely novel to him or her; the individual has no firsthand, and possibly no second-hand, experience of anything like them. To respond, the individual must draw on his or her ongoing *implicit theories* about social relationships and moral norms and functions and apply them to this novel, hypothetical situation. We are not surprised that 10-year-olds can tell us about sharing, tattling on others, the rules of games, and the logic of fair punishment; we should perhaps be more surprised that they can deal equally well with a man stealing medicine to save his wife's life, a captain's responsibilities to his company, and a doctor's decision about euthanasia. In other words, in this social situation we find that the respondent is able to react to the researcher's request to engage in a rational discourse on the proper action for a hypothetical third person. Furthermore, we find that he or she will be able to produce a set of justifications for the "properness" of the actions he or she advocates that are consistent across several diverse story dilemma situations (Weinreich-Haste, 1983).

For the cognitive-developmental psychologist, however, the interesting products of this situation are prescriptive judgments and reasons, which can be coded according to their moral and cognitive complexity. Each developmental stage of moral reasoning is a more integrated and more differentiated representation of moral thinking. The sequence of stages reflects the changing and increasing understanding of the relationship between the individual and other individuals, groups, the community, and, ultimately, society. The core moral concept that Kohlberg's moral dilemmas tap is justice, the understanding of rights, obligations, fairness, and roles. Few people familiar with the research would question that the evidence from longitudinal and cross-sectional studies does indeed demonstrate developmental change and cognitive restructuring. The objections of "social" critics concern the role of social factors in that process and the role of cultural factors in defining what is the appropriate definition of a "morally adequate" response.

The first objection is that the reasoning elicited is *situationally determined*. There are a number of versions of this. One I will call the naive positivistic; it is usually expressed as, How can we be sure that the respondent isn't just telling the researcher what he or she thinks is expected of him or her?—which means, effectively, How can we find out what he or she "really" thinks?

The naive positivist objection assumes that the individual is in some kind of negotiation with the researcher to deduce and then to produce the "right" stage or style of response. A more complex version of this objection argues that the individual is, in all social intercourse, engaged in the presentation of self fitting the cultural requirements of his or her social role in general. These requirements may be a demand for rationality, pliancy, or a display of reflective doubt, knowledge of rules, or whatever. So the individual will produce the high-flown arguments of Stage 5 if necessary, if that is what is demanded of the "rational" public self, or the instrumentalism of Stage 2, if a more Machiavellian style is required. The basis of this criticism is that "inner" individual thought processes are irrelevant to what is *really* going on in a complex social situation (Gergen, 1977; Harré, 1977, 1979).

Perhaps the most extreme form of the "social" position is expressed in the poststructuralist perspective. To quote Lodge (1981), "In the post-structuralist perspective, individual man is not to be conceived of as a unique, substantial self, existing outside language and social relations, through which he expresses himself, but as the subject who is 'produced' by the entry into language and social relations." In other words, according to such a perspective, it is never meaningful to ask such questions as, What does the respondent "really" think? The here-and-now moral discourse between the respondent and the researcher *defines* the universe of the individual's moral discourse.

The second general category of objection is that the model has *cultural biases*. Most of these objections are directed at Kohlberg's definition of justice as the central principle of morality, and *therefore* as the central issue of moral development. These criticisms are, first, anthropological: The emphasis on justice reflects a particular and specific version of Western bourgeois morality, as other cultures have moral systems based, for instance, on honor, kin-group (or other group) affiliation, or loving-kindness (Chazan, 1980; Simpson, 1974). Second, they are political: The definition of Stage 6, the telos of development, emphasizes the individual's understanding of principles of justice. It assumes that the individual is a member of a class of society that conceives of justice as a matter of civilized debate between intelligent people. It ignores that "justice" is unattainable and probably irrelevant for most people, who in reality are subject to entrenched forces of privilege and oppression (Broughton, 1978; Sullivan, 1977; Trainer, 1977).

The objection to a theory of morality that reflects only justice is not, however, confined to those who see the issues in broad cultural and political terms. There are many critics who are happy with the concept of "the child as moral philosopher" but would prefer him or her to be an ethically more eclectic creature (Locke, 1980; Peters, 1978). This position is certainly not necessarily in conflict with a cognitive-developmental model of development. Gilligan (1982), for example, has demonstrated in her work on young women's moral reasoning that there are at least two forms of morality firmly within the cognitive-developmental paradigm. One form of morality, the "original" Kohlberg model, is based on justice as defined by rights and obligations. The implicit premise of this "rights" model is that the dilemma must be conceived in terms of conflict and confrontation, and the means of resolution is to weigh the relative rights and obligations of each party. A second form of morality, which Gilligan found to be more prevalent among women, has a dominant theme of relationships and mutual responsibility. The implicit premise is that the individual is *embedded* in the social unit; individuals are bound together by mutual concern and interrelatedness. Resolution of the moral problem therefore involves the negotiating of the space between persons, not the affirmation of equity, rights, and separateness.

This sex difference in *style* of moral reasoning is an argument for taking more notice of subcultural differences in how meaning is given and utilized. The argument Gilligan proposes is that the female role emphasizes mutuality and the central role of interpersonal relations, whereas the male role emphasizes competition and laying down ground rules for establishing contractual relations to "manage" conflict.

The third category of objection concerns the role of the *small group*, dyadic interaction and peer interaction, in the development of morality. There is now an enormous amount of research in social psychology that demonstrates the importance of small-group processes in the generation of meaning and in the interpretation of social events. Traditionally, developmental psychology has looked at the peer group as a *source* of values, beliefs, and rules; the peer group is one of the channels that gives the individual access to the culture. Additionally, the peer group is a *socializing agent*, molding the individual through rewards and punishment. The relationship between the individual and the peer group is, in other words, largely a one-way channel. The work in recent social psychology has been on the *interpersonal* processes in the construction of meaning. Through group communication, a common meaning is negotiated: How does the group generate a consensual definition of the situation, and what is the individual's role in this process (Doise, 1976; Moscovici, 1976; Tajfel, 1981)?

Much moral development research has treated the small group in the traditional manner of developmental psychology. Several studies have looked at the effect of participation in "Socratic" dialogue or mixed-stage small groups on individual moral reasoning. In other words, how does the group operate as a catalyst in individual growth? (Blatt & Kohlberg, 1975; Kuhmerker, Mentkowski, & Erickson, 1980; Rest, 1979). Different from this approach is the more recent work on "moral atmosphere" and the "just community" studies. These look at the actual ongoing social processes within natural discussion groups experiencing real-life social, moral, and institutional crises and change, as well as observe the effects on individual moral reasoning (Mosher, 1980; Power, 1980).

We can summarize the fundamental differences between the "individual developmental" and the "social" approaches by considering the implicit statement "I can't accept that explanation because. . . ." For the "social" camp, the sticking point is that all forms of social reasoning, and moral reasoning in particular, serve sociological and interpersonal social functions; therefore, it is not credible to offer a model that treats the social context as virtually incidental to the developmental process and the individual as somehow an autonomous moral agent. For the cognitive-developmentalist, there is overwhelming evidence of structural-developmental changes in individual moral reasoning. This is a powerful argument against any explanation that tries to reduce moral judgment purely to socially determined reactions.

Common to both, however, is the shared assumption that what we are talking about is *meaning*. Both approaches recognize that the individual acts as commentator, imposer of sanctions, definer of group norms, presenter of self as morally acceptable, maker of moral decisions, and socializing agent of his or her dependents, all on the basis of a cognitive appreciation of what "being moral" means. The differences lie in explaining the origins and determinants of that cognitive appreciation.

MODELS OF MEANING AND RHETORIC

The common assumption is that *meaning systems* embody *theories* about the nature and function of morality and its role in the social system and in individual lives. These meaning systems are the symbolic context that makes possible expressive behaviors, communicative acts, and the interpretation of the behavior of others. They reflect explanations of cultural, or even cosmological, order.

Berger and Luckmann (1967) demonstrated that the institutions of society and the ways in which people behave normatively to one another are *legitimated* and *explained* by "theories" (expressed as "common knowledge"). These are part of the cognitive stock-in-trade of all members of society, not only those privileged to be professional theory-builders. Individual socialization is the transmission of these theories, and the "knowledge" embedded in these theories is what constitutes an enormous amount of ordinary thinking and the content of interpersonal communication. Moscovici and his associates have developed the concept of "social representation" and examined the ways in which communities and groups engage in sustaining meaning and categorizations that offer an explanatory or classificatory framework, enabling people to familiarize the unfamiliar, legitimate the status quo, and so forth (Moscovici, 1981). Therefore, "social meaning systems" are the stories people make up to explain the social and physical world. These stories have embedded in them "moral" or prescriptive assumptions and consequences. The main requirement of these stories is that they are culturally acceptable in the individual's milieu. It is, of course, highly probable that most people's stories will be culturally acceptable, because they largely derive from the culture in the first place, and "alien" stories are subject to social sanction (if only the sanction of incomprehensibility).

The two orientations I have outlined differ in assumptions about the *origins* of these meaning systems and in the way they operate in the social context. The argument I propose attempts to find a way of incorporating each orientation. Earlier, I discussed three areas of the origin and operation of meaning: sociocultural, interpersonal, and intrapersonal. I now explore how they are interrelated, rather than competing, forms of explanation. To explain the processes, I shall explore the role of rhetoric in social meaning.

When earlier in this chapter I referred to the concept of rhetoric, one of my arguments was that in most forms of reasoning on moral, social and political questions, people confuse fact and value, "is" and "ought," descriptive and prescriptive. Durkheim and Mauss (1963) identified two functions of a belief system. The first is a *speculative* function, an attempt to make the relation between things intelligible, an *explanation*. The second is a *moral* function, to regulate the conduct of human beings. In other words, a belief system embodies both descriptive and prescriptive elements, fact and value. Durkheim and Mauss were particularly interested in quasi-religious belief systems, but it is possible to generalize and consider the extent to which any system of meaning is inevitably an amalgam of explanation and prescription.

Let us look at examples of rhetoric and social theory in a standard moral judgment interview. When we ask a respondent whether Heinz should steal the medicine, we frequently receive the reply that he should not steal—a prescriptive statement. If we then probe a little, we get a justification, expressed as an explanation, such as if everyone stole, no one would be able to trust anyone else. This statement reflects the individual's understanding of the basis of social relations, his or her theory of what makes the social system work. If we ask questions that presume beliefs about "facts," such as what is necessary to maintain friendship, or what are the causes of crime, or even what X political party has achieved for the country, we will quickly find that the respondent slides into a moral conclusion: *"therefore* you shouldn't tell lies, give people too much freedom in childhood, vote for the other lot." This is the way people normally verbalize their reasoning about moral and social issues: As I have argued elsewhere, it is probably only in university seminars, with difficulty, that we can prevent people confusing fact and value.

The first element of my definition of rhetoric is that the inevitable interweaving of fact and value makes most statements about the social world into *assertions,* that is, couched implicitly in the terms "X *must* be true and Y *must* follow from X being true." The greater the pluralism of the culture, the more explicit this becomes, because where there are more explicitly conflicting "theories," there is a correspondingly greater need to justify the rightness of one's own particular point of view.

The second element of my definition of rhetoric is *communication.* Formulating moral reasons, engaging in moral judgments, or fulminating on political and social prescription is rarely an isolated, purely personal exercise. It is something to be communicated and shared. We are engaged in persuasion of one another. In order to do this, we must have a set of shared codes of communication and at least a common pool of shared theories, even if we do not necessarily agree on which is the "correct" theory. Let us consider as an example two pieces of propaganda from the First World War, recruiting posters from the United States and Great Britain. The two make quite different assumptions about what will galvanize men into action, and these assumptions reflect quite different perceptions about what the war is about and what the role of each nation is in the world (see Figures 18.1 and 18.2). The British poster appeals to a common belief (1) that the nation is directly under threat, and (2) that the individual man can do something about this. This message would in fact have been quite effective in the United States, and there was an Uncle Sam "I want you" poster (see Figure 18.3). The American serviceman poster, however, would have cut no ice in Britain. It makes two important assumptions: first, that *democracy* is a hurrah word that has a whole set of meanings and symbols associated with it, and second, that it is America's responsibility to preserve democracy in the world at large. Britons did not and do not feel that way either about democracy or about their world role; other British posters at that time appealed to the *honorable* man's duty to stop the imperialistic goals of the frightful and inhumane Hun, words that stirred the British breast quite well because they reflected British theories about their world roles and British rhetoric about "honor" (Haste, 1977).

Let us look at another example, in the domain of interpersonal persuasion. If you are about to engage on a course of action that I think is likely to be disastrous, I am likely to urge you to "be rational." This concern assumes that you and I *share* a common assumption that rationality matters. In developing my theme, I will exhort you to preserve your image of being a rational person, to behave in such a way as to preserve, by your example, a general rational mode of behavior, which we both believe is beneficial to wider society, and so forth.

In doing this, in this way, I am doing two things. I am assuming a shared *theory,* and I am also assuming a shared *level of complexity.* You are my peer; intuitively I will address you at the same moral stage as myself. If, however, you are my child, I will naturally wish to foster in you this rhetoric of rationality, this particular theory about social relations. I will therefore stress the issue of rationality to you in various ways; I will try to behave in a rational way, and I will try to elicit from you rational styles of talking and deter you from using other rhetorics, such as a rhetoric of anger, revenge, or pride. But additionally, I shall attune my level of discourse for your benefit; I shall intuitively use a Stage 2 or Stage 3 level of complexity. In doing this I am simultaneously transmitting a meaning system that both explains and admonishes and also engaging in a Socratic dialogue that I hope will stimulate you, as my child, to a more complex stage of understanding and conceptualization.

In these examples, I have illustrated the way that a public body, the recruiting office propagandists, can assume that the general public will respond to a few key words and symbols that evoke a whole symbolic meaning system. In the case of the "democracy" poster, that public body can make that assumption, because they know that American schools attempt to inculcate in children a theory about the conduct of relations among small groups and

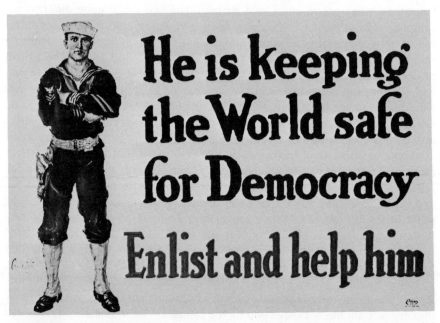

Figure 18.1.   World War I American recruiting poster (reproduced with permission of the National Archives, Washington, D.C.).

Figure 18.2. World War I British recruiting poster (reproduced with permission of the Imperial War Museum).

Figure 18.3. Uncle Sam recruiting poster (reproduced with permission of the Imperial War Museum).

communities based on a central idea of democracy. No American child can escape knowledge of that theory, any more than he or she can escape knowledge of other theories that define stealing, lying, and breaking promises as undesirable. In the second example, I illustrated one kind of interpersonal interaction. In the example of two adults talking, two people of the same level of cognitive complexity are engaging in a debate. In this debate, a meaning system, rationality, is shared, is understood by both, but is not necessarily endorsed by both. In the example of adult versus child, the advantage of superiority of age and greater cognitive complexity gives the adult access to a larger range of theories about social relations and greater familiarity with the usual counterarguments. Nevertheless, the child is quite capable of an impassioned defense of a theory that honorable existence as a member of the third grade depends on taking revenge on the child who deliberately sabotaged her bike. The adult could, if she chose, offer the child a good Stage 5/level defense of her theory of honor; she chooses, however, to give the child a Stage 3 rundown on rationality.

In the preceding, I have demonstrated two separate dimensions: first, the variation in the rhetorical and theoretical meaning systems available within a culture, and second, the way in which any rhetoric or theory can operate at different levels of complexity. My examples show the way in which institutions and individuals intuitively adjust both the *content* and *structure* of their message to make effective communication possible.

TERRITORIES OF MEANING: THE RELATIONSHIP BETWEEN THE INDIVIDUAL AND THE SOCIAL

Sociocultural and Intrapersonal

Let us now consider the ways in which the concept of rhetoric can provide a link between sociocultural, interpersonal, and intrapersonal meaning systems. In the earlier recruiting example, I described a relationship between sociocultural and intrapersonal meaning. The sociocultural meaning system offers a range of available theories, explanations, rhetorical positions, and language. The rhetorical effectiveness of any theory, explanation, or linguistic form of communication depends on its being shared by the sender and the receiver. "Shared" means mutually comprehensible. The individual will be familiar with many different theories and explanations; hence everyone within the shared cultural milieu is able to show at least a moderate competence when asked to engage in discourse couched in a common rhetoric—for example, a rhetoric of justice. The characteristics of the individual's *intrapersonal* meaning system, however, will moderate the communication process. First, the individual's level of complexity will moderate his or her interpretation of sociocultural meaning. The volunteers who rushed to save the world for democracy would have expressed their common cause in very different terms, depending on their level of cognitive complexity. In a recent study, we asked young people to explain the basis of social order; following are three different examples of their answers, which reflect different levels of complexity of reasoning (the figures in parentheses are the stages of moral reasoning as coded overall for these respondents on the Kohlberg measure of moral judgment), (Weinreich-Haste, Duff, & Cotgrove, Note 1):

> "If they break the rules they are put in jail. A lot of people think it's not worth it. Once you have a record, you have no chance of getting a job." (3A).
> "I think everyone is trying to conform, because if you didn't you would have people doing their own thing. But it's the law nowadays to conform, to work to earn money, have a family. So I think everyone's trying to conform to a law." (3/4).
> "Disorder, unemployment, lack of education, ignorance, bad housing, bad standard of living, poverty—tends to lead to breakdown of social order." (4/5).

Second, the individual's own experiences will cause him or her to give different weight to different theories and rhetorics. In the example of the discussion between the adult and the child, one of the differences was that the adult was invoking rationality, the child, honor. Gilligan's women respondents were invoking responsibility and mutuality, in contrast with many of the male subjects in Kohlberg's longitudinal sample, who more frequently talked in terms of rights. Even within the longitudinal sample of males, however, there were variations in their preferred "dominant theory," which remained consistent over time. Let us consider two contrasting individuals from Kohlberg's longitudinal study, Cases 23 and 42 (Figures 18.4 and 18.5). These two young men had a similar pattern of *stage* development throughout the period, yet they differed considerably in their basic values and implicit social theories. Case 23 as a teenager was politically and socially conservative. He swung to an extreme radicalism while in Britain as a graduate student, and this mellowed into a liberal humanism in his late 20s. But throughout he remained preoccupied with the relationship between legal and moral *rules;* his personal theory expressed a search for a rational system based on law. At several ages he reiterated, not a means by which justice can be attained, but a means by which decisions about moral and legal rules can be made—this kind of reasoning remained consistent despite the extreme changes in his social and political assumptions. Case 42, in contrast, concentrated on relationships and responsibility through the whole period of his teens and young adult years. For him, assuming personal responsibility for one's actions was the key issue in maintaining a good social system. His personal theory of morality and of social relations depended throughout on the responsible and concerned enactment of roles and the maintenance of mutual trust and respect.

Stage 4 (3)   (age 16) What's legally right is accepted, well it's written law actually, and morally right, . . . it's been accepted in a general way but morals aren't defined rigidly. . . . It's a worse offense if you break the law instead of a moral or mores, or a folkway.

Well a promise is something . . . while it isn't written, it helps more or less to keep the peace and keep ties between factions. Without it, nobody would be able to trust anyone; without this sort of agreement we wouldn't be able to live very long without warring factions.

Stage 4 (3)   (age 20) He's [Heinz] right, but I don't know really how you can express the type of right he's doing when he does it. I don't think it's moral or legal because I definitely think that's wrong, but I don't know, self-conscious right. I think it's right that most people would do in this particular case.

[Stealing versus obtaining money by lying] I think they both did equally poorly. In one case he's robbing a store and breaking the law, and that's wrong, and in the other he's defrauding a sick old man and he has if not a legal obligation, a moral obligation to pay him back later.

Stage 4 (5)   (age 24) [Heinz] is violating property rights in the light of a higher law . . . human passion.

The whole idea of a promise, and the whole idea of consent is something that is based on the whole idea of private property and the liberal norm. Because you have to in some way establish a right to property and the only way you can do this is through some kind of contract.

[Should Bob tell on his brother?] I don't think he necessarily has a moral obligation to his brother not to tell his father. At the same time, I don't necessarily think he has a moral obligation to his brother not to tell his father. I think the obligation he'd have is simply in terms of what he could resolve, his own conscience.

The father had made a commitment and because of that he had assumed a sense of responsibility.

Stage 5 (4)   (age 28) It is important that there is a proper means of punishment so there is effective rehabilitation so that people recognise that there are certain limits to freedom, certain responsibilities that one has to have in society, as being a member of society . . . allowing him to see somehow the relationship between freedom and security and the trade-off in terms of existing in society.

What we have done is to turn any moral situation into a verdict of whatever the nine judges of the Supreme Court decide the issue is going to be . . . a concept of being born equal going extremely wild so you are very pragmatic in a very rational situation, in which men no longer control what is going to be the limitation, but in effect it is a law that people are going by. . . . I think that the law really lies in the core of philosophy in the moral situation in America and that has to do with the fact that America has very little moral tradition.

Figure 18.4   Kohlberg's longitudinal study, Case 23.

Stage 3 (2)   (age 13) [Should the brother tell the father that Joe lied?] I think that would be the right thing to do because he knows he's doing wrong and since he's an older brother he should feel some responsibility to try to help him and make him grow up right.

I would tell what he had done to try to straighten things out, because the father was wrong in the first place.

Don't think it's right to steal—definitely wrong—could have pleaded with the doctor or some high person in the state to get the druggist to lower the price.

Stage 3 (4)   (age 16) His father was definitely breaking a promise and refusing the boy to do as he wished, and treating the boy more as an infant than as a young teenager. . . . If I was in his position I'd talk it over with my dad and try to explain it to him.

[Should brother tell?] I think he probably should tell his father, but he should also tell him why Joe did what he did. Try to make their father understand the reasons for it and look at it from their point ofview. If he makes his father realise this so that they could reach some kind of understanding.

[What would the judge think?] It depends on the judge's feelings and attitudes. If he is a strict observer of laws and everything he would feel that [Heinz shouldn't steal], but if he is a man who has a good education and a fairly responsible person who could be counted on to make wise decisions. I think he might be able to put himself in the man's place, or at least see his position.

Stage 4   (age 23) [Stealing the medicine] I'm not sure whether I'd have the nerve to do it, but in a situation where your wife is dying, I think I'd feel more personal emotional and logical responsibility to my wife than to this guy whose behaviour is rather anti-social in the sense that he is trying to make a lot of money on it.

[Has Joe a duty to his father?] I don't think being a good son involves that kind of duty. I know his father is supporting him, but I think that is a responsibility his father took on the moment he was conceived.

[What should the judge do in Heinz's case?] I think the judge could suspend the sentence and work out or act as a sort of intermediary and work out a financial settlement between [the druggist and Heinz], I think this would probably be the more responsible solution.

Stage 4 (5)   (age 28) [Father's authority over son] I think it is a limited kind of authority. It doesn't include the right to treat the son as a nonperson, someone without feeling. I think the son owes the father some sense of obedience, but I think the father at the same time owes the son a great deal of responsibility or commitment to responsible action.

I am unwilling to condone a situation where the value of the druggist's profit gets in the way of someone's life.

I think all of us ought to be concerned with everyone else's behaviour and improving it, but this goes deeper because they are brothers.

Figure 18.5   Kohlberg's longitudinal study, Case 42.

In terms of level of moral reasoning, these two young men scored similarly. They differed in their implicit theories and the rhetoric they invoked to deal with the hypothetical dilemmas presented to them and with the real-life dilemmas they personally encountered. Cases 23 and 42 can only utilize the implicit theory and the rhetorical system that they do because they are products of a culture in which these are available—for example, Case 23 describes vividly how he was exposed in another country to an alternative radical system quite outside the experience of his Republican upbringing. Yet he incorporated that radicalism at a level consistent with his current level of cognitive complexity, and, as we have noted, this experience of radicalism modified his way of thinking but did not alter his fundamental legalistic preoccupation.

Interpersonal and Intrapersonal

Earlier I described imaginary discussions between two adults and between an adult and a child on the desirability of rationality. These imaginary situations can be seen as an example of the relationship between intrapersonal and interpersonal areas of meaning. The individual brings to the interaction in dyad and group his or her own limited capacity for conceptualization and his or her own preferred theories. In the group situation, however, what he or she uses of this is regulated by the normative context, and he or she moderates, verbally and nonverbally, his or her behavior. Some flavor of this process can be gleaned from some quotations from Damon's (1977) study of the negotiations of sharing.

The setting is three 10-year-olds who are deciding how to allocate candy bars among a group of themselves plus one other, Dennis, who have been making bracelets.

E [Experimenter]:   We talked with you all and couldn't decide, so *we thought you should decide together.* (1) What do you think is the *best way to give it out?* (2)

CRAIG: Would Dennis get some?

E: *If you think so.* (3)

NORMAN: He has to be here too.

E: *Well, you all decide among you.* (4)

BONNIE: I was thinking, we could give it out one a bracelet, because Dennis did one and we all did three. Or give two and a half to everybody. *That way everybody gets the same thing.* (5)

CRAIG: Maybe Dennis should get one and we get three.

NORMAN: No, *it isn't fair.* (6)

BONNIE: Also, *Dennis is younger* (7) and he left earlier.

E: Well, what do you think? Is that the best way? (8)

NORMAN: No.

E: Why not, Norman?

NORMAN: Because if he were here too, *and he's a child too* (9), so *he should get even* (10) [material omitted].

E: *So far you've got one for Dennis, three for you Craig, three for Norman and three for you Bonnie.* (11)

BONNIE: (mumbles something) That's what Dennis should get.

NORMAN: No. He's not, that's what I'm getting at. *That's what I'm putting in your mind, in your mind, in his mind* (pointing to each member in group). (12)

BONNIE: Well, let's split these in half. Everybody gets two and a half.

NORMAN: *Right. . . . It's the best way, everyone gets the same amount.* (13)

BONNIE: *Craig's is the prettiest, Norman's is the neatest, and I did the most.* (14)

NORMAN: *I was the most well behaved* (15) [material omitted].

NORMAN: *You're not putting Dennis' mind into your little mind. . . . I know how he would feel. . . . Well, you're not reasoning about him. If we did that he would* say (whiny voice) *"Come, you guys got this and I only got that," and he'd start bawling.* (16) (Damon, 1977, pp. 128–130, italics added throughout)

This extract shows decision making that relies on various forms of justice and fairness. But also it reveals several different theories about relationships, and it demonstrates the assertion of various rhetorics for the purpose of persuasion, which reflect the way each child is trying to define the social situation. The experimenter, for instance, in pieces 1, 2, 3, 4, and 8, sets the scene not only for negotiation but also for negotiation based on rational discourse and decision making. The language he uses, and the nonverbal cues (inflection, use of query) indicate this. Additionally, it is clear that he is setting some concept of "best" way, which the children pick up in different ways. For Norman, "best" means equal shares (6, 10, 13). For Bonnie, "best" has connotations of performance, and she constantly refers to the criteria that for her denote excellence or worth (14). She is, however, willing to waver under the pressure of Norman's egalitarianism (5 and later). Norman, however, also makes an explicit statement of his theory of the negotiation process (12) and the way people should be reacting to one another in the situation (16).

The extract is also very illuminating for what it reveals of the appropriate criteria for making "best" and "fair" judgments, such as "prettiest," "neatest," and "well behaved." This is obviously a rhetoric that is not specific to the justice-fairness task at hand. The kind of language a child uses as a *generic* "good" label reflects underlying theories about the conduct of human relationships. "Fair" is obviously a widespread term, because justice is a common rhetoric. "Nice," which implies concern with style, traits, and manner, is frequently used by Damon's respondents.

As Breakwell (1983) has argued, another role of rhetorical language is to define and maintain group identity. The individual acquires a culturally appropriate set of terms of abuse and approval that he or she learns, through experience of interpersonal situations, to use to establish his or her own membership of the group and the identity of his or her group vis-à-vis others. In that extract, Norman made reference to Dennis's status as a child (9), affirming therefore that he is a member of the group, despite his absence. The acquisition of this language also provides the individual with the wherewithal to demonstrate his or her own worth and legitimacy as a person—in general and in specific contexts. Terms such as *nice, fair, polite,* and *well behaved* are reflections of the individual's personal theory of "proper" self-presentation (Harré, 1979).

Berger and Luckmann (1967) illustrate this process:

It is language that must be internalised above all. With language, and by means of it, various motivations and interpretative schemes are internalised as institutionally defined—wanting to act like a brave little boy, for instance, and assuming little boys to be naturally divided into the brave and the cowardly. These schemes provide the child with institutionalised programmes for everyday life, some immediately applicable to him, others anticipating conduct socially defined for later biographical stages. . . . These programmes, both the immediately applicable and the anticipatory, differentiate one's identity from that of others, such as girls, slave boys, or boys from another clan. Finally, there is internalisation of at least the rudiments of the legitimating apparatus; the child learns "why" the programmes are what they are. One must be brave because one wants to become a real man, one must perform the rituals because otherwise the gods will be angry; one must be loyal to the chief because only if one does will the gods support one in times of danger; and so on. [p. 155]

Berger and Luckmann were looking at how the child learns the language and the implicit explanatory justifications of appropriate roles and virtues. The work on sex-role development in particular has shown how important the peer group and play interaction are for the child's learning of the language of sex-roles and the explanations to support them. Even if parents may wish to offer an alternative rhetoric of sex roles, they find themselves in conflict with the powerful rhetoric of the peer group, learned in a social situation where the child is acquiring the skills of social negotiation and consensual meaning and simultaneously learning how to be effective in self-definition and self-presentation as a "proper" boy or girl.

The relationship between interpersonal and intrapersonal is two-way. There is constant interaction between individual and social construction of meaning, between the *individual's* intrapersonal cognitive organization, the *group's* generation of meaning and frames of reference and negotiation, and the individual's *interpretation* of group meaning.

Habermas (1979) has offered a model of the relationship between intrapersonal and interpersonal that focuses on the development of individual competence and its relationship to social experience. In the course of development, the child increases his or her competence in what Habermas terms "communicative action." The child's *interaction* with others is the source of his or her own symbolic universe. Competence in communicative action expands, through the development of reciprocity with single others, the group, and the community, and finally with the expansion of competence the individual's symbolic universe expands. Habermas argues that moral reasoning stages reflect the changes in the symbolic universe and in the levels of communicative action. In his model, the relationship is of action *upon* and *within* the social world; it is not simply a matter of change in capacity to conceptualize the social world.

Sociocultural and Interpersonal

The final relationship I want to consider is between sociocultural and the interpersonal. The group exists within a culture that provides categories of meaning; each group is constrained and limited by the options the culture makes available. In addition, as we have noted, each group is constrained and limited by the intrapersonal characteristics, the cognitive limitations, of its members. But as well, each group generates its own interpersonally negotiated meaning. In the example quoted earlier, the children in Damon's study acquiesced happily enough to the definition by one group member, the adult, that (1) the group task was about sharing, and (2) the exercise would be conducted according to culturally defined "rational discourse." On another occasion, it is quite possible that the group may have chosen to decide the issue of fairness by a show of physical strength or of abuse—behaviors that would have probably redefined the group into "winners" and "losers" and thus redefined the boundary of who was entitled to the candy bars. Some of the differences between the groups might be attributable to the moral stage of the individual group members. In the discussions of moral dilemmas and moral issues in the school community situations studied by Higgins, Power, and Kohlberg (Chap. 5) and the kibbutzim studied by Reimer and Power (1980), it was clear that the general level of moral reasoning of the individuals in the group does affect the negotiated consensus; these are examples of the intrapersonal constraints operating within the group.

There are several options of moral theory and moral rhetoric, however, that are equally acceptable to the culture. The research in the field of intergroup relations demonstrates the vast range of possible rhetorics available for groups within the culture, any one of which can be used to affirm the "in-group" or "out-group" status of individuals; for example, compare the entirely acceptable rhetoric of justice and fairness, which is used for dealing with friends, and the equally acceptable rhetoric of honor, which is used for dealing with foes.

The sociocultural meaning system therefore defines the universe of possibilities for interpersonal meaning, as it does for intrapersonal meaning. But it is not solely a one-way process. It is not uncommon for powerful or influential groups to generate new rhetorics, explanations, and definitions that eventually become incorporated into the broader cultural meaning system. Over the last decade there has been intensive interpersonal discourse on the issue of sexism, much of it in the form of consciousness-raising groups. This has had a noticeable impact on concepts and use of language. In periods of rapid social change, new ideas, new explanations, and new rhetoric are frequently generated among a small group of people, and these become incorporated and disseminated quickly within the culture. This process is an integral part of social change.

CONCLUSION

In this discussion I have tried to depart from the dichotomous representation of individualistic structuralism, which focuses on the processes of individual construction and the development of individual understanding, and social structuralism, which sees individual meaning solely as a functional reflection of public language, cultural determinants, or the requirements of public self-presentation. I have tried to take a fresh look at the social context of moral reasoning, to look aslant at what have been, effectively, two opposing models of determinism. In this, I have looked at both the "what" and the "how" of moral reasoning and tried to see the ways in which these two are interwoven. My main argument has been that moral reasoning and social explanation are constructed *through* the social interaction processes by which they are communicated to others. The explanations, and associated rhetoric, which are elicited through the hypothetical dilemma resolution, are also the basic discourse of ordinary, real situations, the ordinary thinking of individuals about their personal life, about their relationships with significant others and with the institutions of society. They are part of the individual's "theory" about wider social and moral issues. These explanations and rhetorics are available to the individual through cultural and interpersonal experience; people do not, usually, think and theorize in isolation. The process of negotiating one's definition of oneself and one's world takes place in small groups and dyads, where one learns to negotiate meaning *with* others and *for* oneself; the two processses are integrally related. The one cannot exist without the other.

REFERENCES

Berger, R., & Luckmann, T. *The social construction of reality*. London: Allen Lane, 1967.

Blatt, M., & Kohlberg, L. Effects of classroom moral discussion upon children's level of moral judgement. *Journal of Moral Education,* 1975, *4,* 129–162.

Breakwell, G. M. Moralities and conflict. In H. E. Weinreich-Haste & D. Locke (Eds.), *Morality in the making.* New York: Wiley, 1983.

Broughton, J. M. Dialectics and moral development ideology. In P. Scharf, *Readings in moral education.* Minneapolis, Minn.: Winston Press, 1978.

Chazan, B. Jewish education and moral development. In B. Munsey (Ed.), *Moral development, moral education and Kohlberg.* Birmingham, Alabama: Religious Education Press, 1980.

Colby, A., Kohlberg, L., Gibbs, J., Speicher-Dubin, B., Candee, D., Hewer, A., & Power, C. *The measurement of moral judgement: Standard issue scoring manual.* New York: Cambridge University Press, 1983.

Damon, W. *The social world of the child.* San Francisco: Jossey-Bass, 1977.

Doise, W. *Groups and individuals.* Cambridge: Cambridge University Press, 1976.

Durkheim, E., & Mauss, M. *Primitive classification.* Chicago: University of Chicago Press, 1963.

Gergen, K. The social construction of self-knowledge. In T. Mischel (Ed.), *The self.* Oxford: Basil Blackwell, 1977.

Gilligan, C. *In a different voice.* Cambridge, Mass.: Harvard University Press, 1982.

Habermas, J. *Communication and the evolution of society.* London: Heinemann, 1979.

Harré, R. The self in monodrama. In T. Mischel (Ed.), *The self.* Oxford: Basil Blackwell, 1977.

Harré, R. *Social being.* Oxford: Basil Blackwell, 1979.

Haste, C. *Keep the home fires burning.* London: Allen Lane, 1977.

Kohlberg, L. From is to ought: How to commit the naturalistic fallacy and get away with it in the study of moral development. In T. Mischel (Ed.), *Cognitive development and epistemology*. London: Academic Press, 1971.

Kohlberg, L. Moralization. In T. Lickona (Ed.), *Moral development and behavior*. New York: Holt, Rinehart and Winston, 1976.

Kuhmerker, L., Mentkowski, M., & Erickson, V. L. *Evaluating moral development*. Schenectady, N.Y.: Character Research Press, 1980.

Locke, D. The illusion of stage six. *Journal of Moral Education*, 1980, 9, 103–110.

Lodge, D. Saving their subject. *Times higher education supplement*, November 20, 1981.

Moscovici, S. *Social influence and social change*. New York: Academic Press, 1976.

Moscovici, S. Social representations. In J. Forgas (Ed.), *Social cognition*. London: Academic Press, 1981.

Mosher, R. *Moral education: A first generation of research and development*. New York: Praeger, 1980.

Peters, R. S. The place of Kohlberg's theory in moral education. *Journal of Moral Education*, 1978, 7, 27–31.

Power, C. Evaluating just communities: Towards a method for assessing the moral atmosphere of the school. In L. Kuhmerker et al. (Eds.), *Evaluating moral development*. Schenectady, N.Y.: Character Research Press, 1980.

Reimer, J., & Power, C. Educating for democratic community: Some unresolved dilemmas. In R. Mosher, *Moral education: A first generation of research and development*. New York: Praeger, 1980.

Rest, J. *Development in judging moral issues*. Minneapolis: University of Minnesota Press, 1979.

Simpson, E. L. Moral development research: A case of scientific cultural bias. *Human Development*, 1974, 17, 81–106.

Sullivan, E. V. A study of Kohlberg's structural theory of moral development: A critique of liberal science ideology. *Human Development*, 1977, 20, 352–376.

Tajfel, H. (Ed.). *Differentiation between social groups*. London: Academic Press, 1978.

Tajfel, H. *Human groups and social categories*. Cambridge: Cambridge University Press, 1981.

Trainer, F. E. A critical analysis of Kohlberg's contributions to the study of moral thought. *Journal for the Theory of Social Behaviour*, 1977, 7, 41–63.

Weinreich-Haste, H. E. Social and moral cognition. In H. E. Weinreich-Haste & D. Locke (Eds.), *Morality in the making: Thought, action and social context*. New York: Wiley, 1983.

REFERENCE NOTE

1. Weinreich-Haste, H. E., Duff, A., & Cotgrove, S. F. *The inter-relationship between social, political and moral reasoning*. Paper presented at the International Symposium on Moral Education, University of Fribourg, Switzerland, September 1982.

CHAPTER 19

Two Moralities? A Critical Discussion of an Ethic of Care and Responsibility versus an Ethic of Rights and Justice

GERTRUD NUNNER-WINKLER

This chapter reinterprets Gilligan's assumption of two moralities. It attempts to show the following: First, some of the sex-specific differences noted are not differences in moral orientation but concern conceptions of the good life. Second, morally relevant differences are differences not in ethical positions but in emphasis of one against the other of two types of moral duties (positive versus negative duties), which both belong to morality. Third, the consideration of situational particularities does not discriminate between the two moral approaches. Finally, some data that do not support the assumption of sex-specific moral judgments are presented.

Gilligan (1977, Note 1; see also Murphy & Gilligan, 1980; Langdale & Gilligan, Note 2) has recently claimed that there are two contrasting approaches to morality: an ethic of care and responsibility and an ethic of justice and rights. The first approach, more typical for females, corresponds to the experience of the self as part of relationships, as "connected self"; moral judgments consider specific details of concrete situations and are guided by an interest in minimizing the overall harm done. The justice orientation, more characteristic of males, on the other hand, is an expression of an autonomous, independent, "individuated" self; moral judgments follow principles defining rights and duties without "due" consideration of specific circumstances and costs implied. Gilligan accuses Lawrence Kohlberg of stating the justice orientation as the only valid moral orientation, thus neglecting the contribution of the other approach to morality.

In this chapter I shall try to reinterpret Gilligan's position. First, differences noted between the "male" and the "female" approach, as far as they are

I am indebted to E. Tugendhat for valuable suggestions and criticisms.

moral, I take to be differences not in ethical position but in emphasis of one against the other of two types of moral duties. Second, the consideration of situational particularities does not discriminate between the two moral orientations. Third, a considerable part of the sex-specific differences are not moral differences: Gilligan's description of an ethic of care and responsibility includes questions concerning the conception of the good life that do not belong to morality proper. In the last part of the chapter I shall attempt to derive several hypotheses about sex-specific moral preferences formulated in terms of theoretical distinctions introduced in the first part and shall test them against empirical data collected in a study on adolescent development.

THE DISTINCTION BETWEEN PERFECT AND IMPERFECT DUTIES

For theoretical clarification I consider a distinction that was introduced by Kant in his *Metaphysik der Sitten* (1977) and later elaborated especially by B. Gert in his *The Moral Rules* (1973), namely, the distinction between perfect and imperfect duties. Perfect duties are *negative* duties, that is, duties of omission (e.g., do not kill, do not cheat, etc.); imperfect duties are *positive* duties, duties of commission, which, however, do not prescribe specific acts but only formulate a maxim to guide action (e.g., practice charity). This maxim thus delineates a broad set of recommendable courses of action some of which the actor realizes by, at the same time, applying pragmatic rules and taking into account concrete conditions, such as individual preferences, contingencies of location in space and time, and so on.

Perfect duties, because they require only *not* to act, can, at least in non-conflictual cases, be followed strictly by everybody at any time and location and with regard to everybody (Gert, 1973). Imperfect duties, on the other hand, can never be observed completely: It is impossible to practice charity all the time and with regard to everybody. Positive maxims do not define limits of their application, do not specify which and how many good deeds have to be performed and whom they are to benefit so that the maxim can be said to have been followed. Due to this latitude, the following of maxims requires what Kant calls power of judgment (*Urteilskraft*). The asymmetry between perfect and imperfect duties is also reflected in the differential reactions to transgression. The failure to meet perfect duties is considered a vice (*Laster*), the failure to meet imperfect duties is lack of virtue (*Untugend*).

THE ETHIC OF CARE AND RESPONSIBILITY AS AN ETHIC OF IMPERFECT DUTIES; THE ETHIC OF RIGHTS AND JUSTICE AS AN ETHIC OF PERFECT DUTIES

The characteristics Gilligan (1977) enumerates show the ethic of care and responsibility to be primarily an orientation to imperfect duties, the ethic of rights and justice to be primarily an orientation to perfect duties. Thus, the most eminent goals of the ethic of care are the wish to care for and help others, to meet obligations and responsibilities, a concern for others and feelings of compassion, a responsibility to discern and alleviate trouble in this world (p. 511). This orientation to imperfect duties finds its most concise expression in one woman's statement in the interview: "Is it right to spend money on a pair of shoes, when I have a pair of shoes and other people are shoeless?" (p. 510). The very form this reflection takes, the interrogative, is proof of its being derived from an imperfect duty, namely, the principle of charity, which does not define its own form of application, its own limits, and the degree to which it is binding.

The ethic of rights and justice, on the other hand, is depicted as being mainly concerned with rights of individuals and their protection, that is, ways of ensuring that rights of individuals will not be interfered with by others. Such rights, it seems, are conceived to be invulnerable, absolute rights valid at all times and places and for all persons; they are conceived as rights corresponding to perfect duties. No one would deny that both kinds of duties are considered part of one morality, the unity of which is constituted through adherence to some universalizing procedure. How, then, is Gilligan's claim that it is still a question of contrasting moral approaches to be understood. I think it can be interpreted to mean that females (1) feel more obliged to fulfill imperfect duties than males, and (2) in cases of conflict will more likely opt for the fulfillment of imperfect duties, whereas males will insist more rigidly on having the perfect duties respected. The first part of the statement, I think, is more adequately construed as a difference in moral action and moral character and not as a difference in ethical position, for the latitude of imperfect duties per definition requires that individuals make use of their moral understanding to derive concrete action decisions. This kind of difference in interpersonal orientation parallels the distinction between diffuse and specific role relationships that Talcott Parsons (1964, pp. 65f., pp. 153ff.) notes: In diffuse relationships, that is, relations between relatives, friends, neighbors, it is assumed that one may ask for any kind of support, and the burden of proof rests with the role partner who withholds help. In specific relationships, on the contrary, the kind of help that may legitimately be asked for is clearly specified and limited, and the burden of proof rests with the partner demanding support. The hypothesized sex-difference in orientation might thus be a consequence of the fact that traditionally females are much more exclusively involved in diffuse relationships than are men and therefore feel bound to meet any need arising, whereas men are much more used to specific relationships and tend first to question the other person's "right to demand help." This hypothesis I shall take up in the last part of the chapter.

The interpretation that in cases of conflict females opt for fulfilling imperfect duties, and males perfect duties, implies a difference in ethical positions insofar as females might be assumed to reverse the male order of priority of perfect over imperfect duties. Yet this interpretation is implausible, for Gilligan

(1977) ascribes to the ethic of care an orientation to contextual particularities— "It is the reconstruction of a moral dilemma in its contextual particularity which allows an understanding . . . and thus engages the compassion and tolerance considered previously to qualify the feminine sense of justice" (p. 511)— which is incompatible with an a priori strict ordering of one set of rules over the other. In fact, it is precisely this consideration of contextual particularities that Gilligan (Note 1) sees as lacking in the ethic of rights and justice—"Kohlberg retains his conception that principles of justice are context free" (p. 83). This differential awareness of situational specifics marks one of the main differences between the two ethics.

The plausibility of this implied equation between an orientation to imperfect duties and contextual particularity, respectively, to perfect duties and their contextual independence will be discussed in the following passages. I want to show that this equation holds true only for a very specific aspect of Kant's moral position that is shared by scarcely anyone, namely, that perfect duties allow no exceptions. It does not hold true for Kohlberg, even though he presents his construction of rights in such a misleading way that it does provoke the kind of criticism Gilligan voices.

THE ROLE OF SITUATION-SPECIFIC KNOWLEDGE IN MORAL JUDGMENT

In the nonconflictual case, the following of perfect duties presupposes scarcely any knowledge of situational specifics. As all that is required is *not* to act in a specified way at any time or location and with regard to everybody, all one needs to know are some general empirical facts valid for *all* situations (e.g., what substances are poisonous, giving strong enough poisons to a human being will kill him or her, etc.) or at best some narrowly limited specific facts (e.g., if that person does not receive a specific medicine now, he or she will die) or truth values for specific statements (e.g., it is true that X happened). Yet the range of concrete facts one might need to know is clearly confinable and can deductively be determined: only those facts are relevant that pertain immediately to the rule in question; that is, for the rule do not kill, relevant facts are all potential risks to life; for the rule do not lie, only the empirical truth of statements asked is relevant.

Imperfect duties, on the other hand, require situation-specific knowledge, for they demand contextually situated decisions in regard to when and where to act and in regard to whom. Thus, Gilligan's proposition that the ethic of care takes situational details into account, whereas the ethic of rights does not, seems plausible: Imperfect duties require by their logical characteristics a concrete specification that perfect duties do not. Yet the picture gets more complicated as soon as one considers cases where duties collide. Only if one assumes that there are rules without exceptions can there be any moral judgments that can be made without taking note of situational specifics. This actually is Kant's position. Kant (1959) maintains that perfect duties enjoy absolute priority over imperfect duties, that is, allow for no exceptions. Thus, he explicitly states that even if lying to a murderer might save a friend's life, it cannot be justified, for "truthfulness . . . is a *perfect duty valid under all circumstances* (p. 205).[1]

This position is extreme, however, and is shared by scarcely anyone. In the modern discussion the justifiability of exceptions to rules is widely accepted. It finds a clear expression in the differentiation between actual duties and prima facie duties that W. D. Ross (1930, pp. 8–31, 61f.) introduced: Rules are valid only prima facie, that is, under normal circumstances, when there are no other moral considerations that bear on the decision. In Gert's (1973) exposition, the "except" clause plays the same role. Thus Gilligan's claim that the ethic of care is oriented to situational particularities that the ethic of rights will neglect is valid only at first sight. For even to observe perfect duties requires—if exceptions are deemed justifiable—that the question of consequences of different courses of action in a specific situation has to be examined: For it might well be that the imperfect duty to prevent harm may in a concrete case legitimately override obligations following from a perfect duty. Therefore I think one cannot very well hold context orientation to be a feature that constitutes contrasting approaches to morality. Context orientation is a prerequisite for *all actual moral judgments*.

One problem still remains open: how moral decision is to be reached in such cases of conflicting duties. Moral choice in dilemmas is based on a process of reflection on the potential universalizability of the specific solution, found by taking all particulars of the concrete situation into account. It is this compatibility of universalism with an orientation to situational particularities that has often been overlooked. Hare (1963) makes this point very lucidly in his distinction between universality and generality: "The thesis of universalizability does not require moral judgments to be made on the basis of highly general moral principles. . . . Moral development . . . consists in the main in making our moral principles more and more specific by writing into them exceptions and qualifications to cover kinds of cases of which we have had experience" (p. 40).

It may very well be true that people will come up with different solutions: People will differ in the weight they will give to various considerations. As Gert (1973) puts it: "One man might publicly advocate killing one man in order to save ten others. . . . Another man might not publicly advocate violation in this situation. He might feel that a significant decrease in the protection from violations of the rule plus general anxiety due to added uncertainty more than offsets the possible benefit" (p. 99). This is true because

---

[1]Cf. "It cannot be that opposing rules are simultaneously obliging: if it is [strict] duty to act according to one rule, then it is not only not duty to act according to a contrary one, but it is even undutiful. Thus a collision of duties and obligations is unthinkable. It can be, though, that two reasons of obligations collide. . . . [In that case] it is not the stronger obligation but the stronger reason of obligation that dominates" (1977, p. 330).

"evils are ranked in too many diverse ways" (p. 126). It might also be true that sex-specific differences in the ranking of evils might show up; thus, for instance, I would assume, in accordance with the hypothesis put forward earlier, that females might weigh consequences on the level of the social system as less grave than consequences on the level of interpersonal relations. Yet this could be taken to be a sex-specific filling in of a latitude that is conceded within the limits of morality, whereby morality is understood as constituted through an obligation to some universalizing procedure, that is, to impartiality.

One minor point may still be noted pertaining to the question of methodology. Gilligan (Note 1) tends to see Kohlberg's use of hypothetical dilemma as another indication of the abstraction of moral problems from the "contingencies of human social existence" she criticizes in him:

> While the analytic logic of justice is consonant with rational social and ethical theories and can be traced through the resolution of hypothetical dilemmas, the ethic of care depends on the contextual understanding of relationships. . . . While the analytic logic of justice can be traced through the deductive resolution of *hypothetical* dilemmas and the understanding of systems of rules, the ethic of care is manifested through the understanding of *actual* situations of moral conflict and choice. [pp. 9–10]

I think this is a misunderstanding. If exceptions are allowed, concrete circumstances have to be taken into account in solving a moral conflict—be it a hypothetical or an actual conflict. There is a difference, namely, that in actual dilemmas one can never be sure whether facts are correctly perceived. Yet this difference lies on the level of empirical truth of descriptive statements, not on the level of normative judgment.

KOHLBERG'S POSITION

The main criticism Gilligan (Note 1) directs against Kohlberg is that he neglects situational particularities in making moral judgments: "Kohlberg built a theory of moral development on a unitary moral conception of fairness and justice. . . . Thus the social concept of moral decision was replaced by the structures of formal thought which provided a rational system for decision that was autonomous and *independent of time and place*" (p. 7). Kohlberg's "principles of justice [are] *context-free* and [can] generate *objectively right* solutions to moral problems" (Murphy & Gilligan 1980, p. 83). Yet by the logic of his own moral convictions Kohlberg by necessity must orient his moral judgments to concrete situational circumstances. This is because in a conflict between perfect and imperfect duties he not only maintains—unlike Kant—that the perfect duty *may* be violated but almost requires that it *must* be violated; that is, Kohlberg adopts a radical female position, however ironic this may sound. Thus, for instance, in the Heinz dilemma the issue is whether

Heinz may break into the druggist's store to steal a drug to save his wife's life. In terms of the distinctions introduced earlier, the Heinz dilemma depicts a conflict between a perfect duty (not to steal) and an imperfect duty (to prevent evil, namely, the death of the sick woman). Kant would have denied that Heinz may break into the store: If one may not lie in order to save a life, one may not steal either. Kant (1959) gives another example that proves the same point: A man has been entrusted with a large sum of money. The owner dies without the heirs knowing anything of the deposit. The man, a charitable and philanthropic person, lost all his fortune without any fault of his own; his wife and children are starving. The heirs, however, are unkind, rich, and wasteful, and "it were just as well that the additional wealth were to be thrown into the ocean" (p. 82). Even in this extreme situation the man may not keep the money to feed his wife and children, for "it is wrong, it contradicts duty" (ibid.)—that is, it is wrong under all circumstances, context free.

Kohlberg, quite on the contrary, demands that Heinz steal the drug "because the right to life supercedes or transcends the right to property" (Colby, Gibbs, Kohlberg, Speicher-Dubin, & Candee, Note 3, p. 80). This justification rests on the assumption of a clear hierarchy of differentially binding duties and obligations. Yet whereas in Kant the hierarchical ordering of duties is based on their formal characteristics (perfect duties, as they are negative duties, which can be followed and are to be followed under all circumstances and with regard to everybody, are superordinate to imperfect duties, which only formulate maxims that can never be completely followed), Kohlberg seems to posit the hierarchy of rights by content: "There is a hierarchy of rights and values. Stealing is justified as serving a universal right to or value of life which is prior to laws" (ibid.). Because of its utmost priority, this universal right to life is henceforth treated as if it were a perfect right corresponding to a perfect duty in Kant's sense: It is a right that must be granted universally; that is, it implies seemingly perfect duties regardless of concrete circumstances or of personal ties. Thus, for Kohlberg it is as much a duty to steal for a stranger as it is to steal for one's own wife: "It would be right to steal for a stranger because the right to life should be accorded universally to all men whose lives can be saved regardless of personal ties" (ibid., p. 82). The problem with this position is that "saving life" by its structural characteristics is an imperfect duty, which does not specify its own limits: A universally accorded right to life implies the universal duty to save "all men whose lives can be saved regardless of personal ties," even if that would require violation of property rights. Thus we all are not only required to give away all the money we own but also justified—in fact, maybe even obliged—to rob all banks as well as all members of our society who own more than they need to feed themselves so as to be able to save the starving children in the third world, whose sad fate is well known to all of us.[2]

I assume Kohlberg would not support such a revolutionary Robin Hood

---

[2] Langdale and Gilligan (Note 2, pp. 52–53) also point out this difficulty in Kohlberg.

strategy. If this were correct, it follows that, for Kohlberg as well, decisions in moral dilemma hinge on concrete circumstances: Thus, it may be justifiable to rob for one's own wife or even a stranger one has met, but it may be less justifiable to rob with the intent to send the money to India. Yet in Kohlberg's own justifications, the factual dependency of moral judgments on a consideration of concrete circumstances is veiled; thus Gilligan rightly denounces the neglect of situational contingencies on Kohlberg's part. This neglect, though, I take—in contrast to Gilligan—not to be characteristic of a certain type of morality, the morality of rights and justice; rather, it is because Kohlberg has not clearly recognized the logical structure of imperfect duties. This can be seen from the misleading formulation he uses. He speaks of a universal right to life, which seems to imply a universal, hence perfect, duty to save life. Perfect duties, however, can be formulated only in the negative: All one can say is that every human being has a right *not* to be killed, disabled, deprived of freedom by others.

MORALITY VERSUS QUESTIONS OF THE GOOD LIFE

Thus far only part of Gilligan's position has been discussed: the assumption that an orientation to care can be juxtaposed to an orientation to rights, whereby only the former takes situational particularities into account, whereas the latter denies their relevance. The second half of this assumption has been refuted: Consideration of concrete situational details is indispensable for *all* moral judgments (if exceptions are allowed). The first part has been reformulated: Females feel more obliged to fulfill imperfect duties of charity, whereas males adhere more strictly to the perfect duties of noninterference, although both types of duty belong to morality.

Yet Gilligan's conceptualization of the two approaches to morality is more encompassing than has hitherto been stated. Gilligan sees them as emanating from different experiences of the self in the world: "The principle of nonviolence and an ethic of care . . . informs the world of the connected self, the principle of fairness and an ethic of justice . . . informs the world of the separate self" (Langdale & Gilligan, Note 2, pp. 42–43). The experience of the self in the world is itself a process of development, described for the ethic of care as the unfolding of the concept of responsibility. I think that in this conceptualization of the "connected self" and of stages of responsibility, moral orientation and development is mixed with aspects of ego development and with questions of the good life. To substantiate this claim I will analyze two examples. In the first, concerning ways of conflict resolution in child play, "social connectedness" is interpreted by Langdale and Gilligan as the basis of a specific moral orientation, although it might well be simply an expression of specific ego interests. The second example concerns reflections about life plans at pregnancy; in the decision of this issue questions of the good life are confounded with moral problems.

In the first example, two 6-year-olds respond to the dilemma "created when, in playing with a friend, they discover that they and their friend want to play a different game." Characteristic of the little girl are the following statements: *"We don't have a real fight"* and "we agree what we should do" and "we should play one . . . , then the other"; while the little boy starts out by stating: "I wanted to stay outside—he wanted to go in" and ends with the statement *"I would do what I want—he would do what he wants."* The italicized statements are pointed out by the authors as especially good exemplifications of the contrasting principles of care versus fairness. As long as it is so described, however, this dilemma is not a moral dilemma, but the inner conflict of an individual choosing among his or her own conflicting needs. Each child has two desires: the desire to play a specific game and the desire to play with a specific friend. The little girl forgoes the chance to play the preferred game (at least for some time) yet in return maintains the chance to play with the friend. The little boy, on the other hand, proves to be more interested in playing the preferred game, and be it alone, than in playing with his friend. Thus far each child may have chosen among different needs that proved not to be simultaneously satisfiable. There is nothing moral about this choice: It is well known that females are more interested in relationships and males more in things (objects).[3] Neither one or the other of these preferences is morally more recommendable. Gilligan might consider this very construction of the dilemma to be a male version while she sees it as a moral dilemma, that is, not as an intraindividual choice among one's own conflicting needs but as an interindividual choice between satisfying one's own needs or the needs of others. Yet I do not think that it really is a moral question. Adequately satisfying each other's needs is what a good relationship means. If a relationship is not good, that is, if both partners cannot find satisfaction and enrichment in sharing alter's interests, separating and searching for a more congenial partner might—so long as no other considerations must be considered, such as marriage and children—be better than a permanent pseudo-moral adoption to alien interests.

Once the friendship dilemma comes to be seen as a moral dilemma of conflicting needs of ego and alter, however, the central issue of imperfect duties arises immediately: how far to go in fulfilling the needs of alter. It is this issue around which Gilligan presents the female moral development as revolving. Different levels of the conceptualization of responsibility formulate different answers: On the first level, responsibility centers on the self and on relationships that are self-serving; on the second level, responsibility orients to the needs of others such that the satisfaction of one's own needs is considered selfish and self-sacrifice is deemed as "good"; on the last level, the focus of responsibility

---

[3]This difference in interests also is reflected in career choices. In our study, for example, 27% of the girls but only 5% of the boys mentioned "contact with other people" as one of the most important criteria in selecting among different careers. On the other hand, 25% of the boys and only 12% of the girls report specific factual interests that they want to follow up in a career, such as interest in cars and in natural sciences.

is shifted to the relationship itself, the stability of which is comprehended as depending on the fulfillment of the needs of self *and* other. This developmental sequence, although it answers a central problem of imperfect duties, is too narrowly conceived as moral development: It is a more encompassing learning process; it is a process of the development of self as an autonomous person, as a competent actor. Thus on the third level the insight is developed that the second-level understanding of goodness as self-sacrifice is a welcome device to avoid taking upon oneself the responsibility for one's own actions. And it is only on the third level that the individual can clearly recognize his or her own needs and interests and separate them from externally obtruded ones and becomes willing to assume the responsibility for the consequences that the following of one's own needs may entail. This competence is a prerequisite for all life choices (career, partner, world view, political conviction, etc.), of which moral decisions make up only one part.

Gilligan, I think, unduly treats this general process of ego development as moral development and treats as moral choices what in reality are decisions about ways of life. This can be seen very clearly in the way Gilligan (1977) presents her interviews on abortion. The women questioned answer not the issue of whether an abortion is morally justifiable but rather questions of the "good life": namely, What kind of person do I want to be? What kind of life do I want to lead? This claim may seem unjustified, for most of the women do start off the discussion with formulating moral considerations, such as, "I don't believe in abortion. Who can say when life begins" (p. 497), or even "It is taking a life" (p. 499). Yet in fact these considerations do not enter the decision process; the question of abortion is dealt with as a choice between different ways of life. This can be seen if one examines the kind of reasons that are put forward by the same woman who considers abortion as taking life. Among the reasons she lists for having an abortion are the fear of losing a good job, losing independence, difficulties in handling the relationship with the father of the child; among the reasons against having an abortion she mentions enjoying more home life, being admired by others for bringing up a child alone; having less feelings of guilt. Another woman is quoted as comprehending through pregnancy her own "inner conflict between the wish to be a college president and to be making pottery and flowers, having kids and staying home" (p. 508).

I do not want to deny that morally relevant considerations do sometimes enter into the question of life choice. Thus, for instance, the woman quoted earlier hesitates about a professional career for fear of losing her compassion on the way up. Yet most considerations mentioned concern for morally neutral ego goals, such as a desire for a fulfilling occupation or the desire to avoid internal conflicts of priority between family and job, and the decision seems mainly to involve a morally neutral balancing out of different ego interests.

To summarize, I tend to think that not all the differences Gilligan sees as constitutive for two contrasting approaches to morality are really differences in moral orientation. Social connectedness is largely a result of greater social-than task-oriented interests; stages of responsibility describe a process of disentangling self from conformity expectations, which is a general process of ego development in as much as conformity expectations extend to many non-moral issues. It may still be true that females feel more obliged than males to fulfill imperfect duties, to answer to concrete needs of others, even at their own costs. It also seems plausible that this characteristic is, as Gilligan suggests, a consequence of women's greater social involvement. It might also be, however, merely a consequence of an inability to recognize and stand up to one's own needs, that is, a consequence of lack of ego strength, of an inability to say no. If this is true, the status of a "female" approach to morality would be very ambiguous, indeed.

SOME DATA CONCERNING SEX DIFFERENCES IN MORAL JUDGMENT

In this last section I employ the data Rainer Döbert and I have collected. We interviewed 112 male and female adolescents in the age range of 16–22 years and of different socioeconomic backgrounds. The interview covered intensity of adolescent crisis, moral judgment, coping and defense styles, parental patterns of conflict resolution and child rearing, political socialization, and so on. It was not designed specifically to test sex-specific morality, yet some of the results may serve to test the following hypotheses derived from the assumptions of an ethic of care and responsibility:

1. Females feel more bound by imperfect duties than do males; that is, in a conflict between a perfect and an imperfect duty females will more likely opt for transgression of the perfect duty.
2. In moral decisions females will take more situational details into account.

To test these hypotheses, a subsample of 98 subjects was drawn from the original study, that matched male and female subjects on educational background and, as far as possible, on age as well. The subjects are distributed as shown in Table 19.1.

TABLE 19.1.   Distribution of the sample over the variables age, education, and sex

Variable	Male			Female		
Education	High	Medium	Low	High	Medium	Low
Number of subjects	15	17	17	15	17	17
Average age	18.5	17.1	16.2	19	16.8	16.5

To test the first hypothesis, three different morally relevant decisions will be used. The first concerns the decision in Kohlberg's mercy-killing dilemma: A woman who is incurably ill and suffers unbearable pain asks the doctor for an extra dose of morphine to make her die. Should the doctor give it to her or refuse it? This story depicts a conflict between a perfect duty, do not kill, and an imperfect duty, relieve pain. The action decision was classified into four categories:

The doctor should give the drug, notwithstanding the law, because the woman suffers so much and should be allowed to decide for herself (active mercy killing).

The doctor should not give the drug, because the law is legitimate; at most he may stop excessive medical support (passive mercy killing).

The doctor should not give the drug so as not to risk punishment.

Undecided: the doctor should, because of pain, yet should not, because of punishment.

The subjects responses are distributed over these four categories as is shown in Table 19.2.

The data show that in this dilemma females do not feel more bound by the imperfect duty to relieve pain. If anything at all, females more eagerly seek to avoid punishment. This finding might be taken as proof of the female tendency to consider consequences in making moral decisions, yet the moral ambiguity of this tendency is that it is not specified how consequences for the different persons involved are to be balanced. Any procedure balancing costs to ego versus benefits to alter would, I assume, have to make use of some universalizing procedure.

In the second morally relevant decision, subjects were asked to pass a moral judgment on the following action: A person talks an old-age pensioner into ordering a useless journal. The judgment could take the following form: I find this action very bad (3), pretty bad (2), not particularly bad (1). From the "female" point of view, this action might be interpreted as exploitation of a weak or poor elderly person by a skillful salesperson who simply tries to maximize his or her own profits at all costs. From the "male" point of view,

TABLE 19.2.   Distribution of Answers to the Mercy-Killing Dilemma

Response	Male	Female
Doctor should—pain	30	24
Doctor should not—law	7	8
Doctor should not—punishment	11	14
Undecided	1	3

one might defend this action as a legitimate pursuit of business interests, based on the assumption that all market partners can take care of themselves and look out for their own interests. Thus, one might expect females to condemn this action more than males. This is not the case, however: The average evaluation of this action by males and females is identical; both find it pretty bad (2.0).

For the third morally relevant decision, the same format was used for an evaluation of the following action: A person does not want to lend some money to a friend and therefore pretends not to have any money. Again, females might be expected to deny help less readily when asked for it, and therefore to condemn this action more strongly. Again, the data do not bear out this expectation: Males and females alike judge this action as not particularly bad (males 1.4, females 1.3).

To test the hypothesis that in moral decisions females will take more situational details into account, responses to the following dilemma (taken from Gleser Ihilevich, 1969) depicting an interpersonal conflict were analyzed. "You live with your aunt and uncle, who have taken care of you since your parents were killed in an accident when you were only five years old. One stormy night you have a date with a friend, but your aunt and uncle will not let you go out because it is late and the weather is bad. You are about to leave anyhow when your uncle issues the order: 'You stay at home because I said so.' " No situational details were considered to have been taken into account in responses such as these: "I'd go anyhow"; "That's none of his business"; I'd be furious and leave." Situational details were considered to have been taken into account in these: "I would go, if the date was very important to me, if not, I'd stay"; "If I'd accepted them as parents, I would stay, because I respect them"; "It depends how they handle conflicts in other situations—if they forbid everything, I'd go"; "If we were meeting in a group and it was only 8 o'clock, I'd go, if we were meeting alone and it was 10 o'clock I'd stay at home."

Of the subjects, 14 of the males and 12 of the females considered concrete situational particularities when making their decisions on how to act in this interpersonal conflict. Those taking situational details into account are slightly older (.35 years) and of higher socioeconomic background (of the lowest educational level, only 16%, of the two higher levels, 42% consider concrete circumstances).

Certainly one could not hold the analysis of these few data to be an adequate test of sex differences in moral judgment. Still, it should be noted that the data presented do not lend support to the assumption that females (at least in the age range tested) observe imperfect duties more closely than do males or give more consideration to contextual particularities.

REFERENCES

Gert, B. *The moral rules.* New York: Harper & Row, 1973.

Gilligan, C. In a different voice: Women's conceptions of the self and of morality. *Harvard Educational Review,* 1977, *47*(4), 481–517.

Gleser, G. C., & Ihilevich, D. An objective instrument for measuring defense mechanisms. Journal of Consulting and Clinical Psychology, 1969, 33(1), 51–60.

Hare, R. M. *Freedom and reason*. New York: Oxford University Press, 1963.

Kant, I. Über den Gemeinspruch: Das mag in der Theorie richtig sein, taugt aber nicht für die Praxis (1793). In *Kleinere Schriften zu Geschichtsphilosophie, Ethik and Politik*. Hamburg: Felix Meiner Verlag, 1959.

Kant, I. *Die Metaphysik der Sitten*. Frankfurt: Suhrkamp, 1977. (originally 1797)

Kant, I. Über ein vermeintliches Recht, aus Menschenliebe zu lügen. ibid. pp. 199–206.

Murphy, J. M., & Gilligan, C. Moral development in late adolescence and adulthood: A critique and reconstruction of Kohlberg's theory. *Human Development*, 1980, *23*, 77–104.

Parsons, T. The social system. New York: Free Press, 1964.

Ross, W. D. The right and the good. Oxford: The Clarendon Press, 1930.

REFERENCE NOTES

1. Gilligan, C. *Do the social sciences have an adequate theory of moral development?* Unpublished manuscript, Harvard University, 1980.

2. Langdale, S., & Gilligan, C. *The contribution of women's thought to developmental theory: The elimination of sex bias in moral development research and education*. Interim Report submitted to: National Institute of Education.

3. Colby, A., Gibbs, J., Kohlberg, L., Speicher-Dubin, B., & Candee, D. *Standard form scoring manual*. Unpublished manuscript, Center for Moral Education, Harvard University, 1979.

PART SIX

Philosophical and Historical Perspectives

CHAPTER 20

The Principle of Principles

DWIGHT R. BOYD

Two popular views of the nature of morality are identified as in opposition to each other. The contest between them is seen as a threat to the notion of principles in morality and as generating contentious conclusions about correct moral judgments. Each side, however, expresses a sound insight into morality, as grounded by our experience of moral judgment situations: one view concentrating on objectivity, the other on autonomy. An attempt is made to shift attention away from the issue apparently contested, namely, a belief concerning the existence of fundamental moral principles. This is done first by showing how both views share a common but questionable assumption that appeals to principles must be thought of deductively and then, more positively, by outlining an alternative, constructivist view that accommodates both objectivity and autonomy.

As a philosopher, and one who is interested in examining philosophical problems in an educational context, I think that we can often find our issues writ large by looking at what is happening in our schools. If we look at the contemporary state of morality in our society through the lens of what is happening in education, a very disturbing picture emerges. There seems to be a tug-of-war going on for the minds and hearts of children—and the battleground is the moral arena. On one side are those who insist that kids learn to toe the line—and they are intent on doing this even if it means indoctrination. On the other side are those who insist that defining the moral line is entirely up to the kids—and they are intent on doing this even if it means lapsing into an insidious relativism. Each side seems equally certain that it is right and the other side is being wrongheaded, if not just downright evil, in trying to "educate" kids to join its side. Each side is more than willing to pull the other through some mud to persuade us that it is right. And both sides have sufficient political clout to ensure that their views show up in educational policy statements, never mind that, of course, the policy is thus riddled with incoherence!

This is not *just* an educational problem, although I do think we have very good reasons for wanting to avoid either indoctrination or laissez-faire as our educational stance in the moral realm. Rather, I believe the sides drawn represent general forces within contemporary society, and the battle threatens to pull society apart at the seams. I believe that as professionals speaking to issues of morality and moral development in the decade of the 1980s, we must address such problems. It is part of our responsibility to be attuned to the existence of such broad movements or forces in society and to try to understand the conflict between them. Moreover, we should be especially careful that our theoretical models for studying morality do not simply reflect these conflicts at a more abstract level.

In this chapter I shall focus on one dimension of the moral arena within which the tug-of-war is being waged. Other chapters in this volume address a variety of different dimensions, and, as is suggested repeatedly in these chapters, some general integration of different theoretical perspectives is clearly needed for an adequate understanding of the moral arena. My aim here is not to seek this synthesis directly but rather to explore one cognitive dimension of moral experience, a dimension that, although receiving a lot of attention by name, I believe is unsatisfactorily understood. Moreover, I think that the misunderstanding of this dimension by the opposing sides in the tug-of-war is a common one, one which constitutes not only the core issue in this particular conflict but also one of the theoretical barriers to a more comprehensive account of morality that would be psychologically sound. The tug-of-war in our schools, then, provides a highly visible and real entry point into a more abstract philosophical problem that has implications for how we conceive and study moral development.

My approach in this chapter will take the following form. First, I sketch the conflict in a way that metaphorically illustrates my concern about how the notion of moral principles is being treated and reveals my aim to clarify how moral principles function in contributing to correct moral judgments—to explore the principle of principles, as it were. In the face of an objection prevalent in the psychological study of morality, I will try to legitimate my sense that this is worth doing by anchoring it in what I think is our common, shared experience within real moral judgment situations. After grounding my concern in this way, I return for a closer look at the two sides in the contest, attempting to draw out a simple but accurate schematic of each side's pulling stance. Then I argue that although they look like opposites and have some legitimate complaints about each other, both depend on an implicit assumption that appeals to moral principles in moral judgment must be thought of in terms of a deductive model. I want, then, to question this assumption, to show how it can be seen as figuring into the contentious claims of both sides. More positively, I will suggest that we need to look for a more constructivist model of the working of moral principles. To provide some substance to this suggestion, I will utilize some central notions from John Rawls's theory of justice in order to indicate how a model of this sort might incorporate the valid insights of each side but avoid the errors that generate the legitimate complaints.

THE PROBLEM

What exactly is this tug-of-war I have alluded to? And why should we focus our attention on it? For our first approach to the problem, I want you to engage in a little anthropomorphic fantasy with me. Now you, as a moral agent, probably feel quite comfortable in thinking solely in terms of *using* moral principles (or, at least, I *hope* you do). But have you ever imagined this from the point of view of the principles themselves? If you did, then I think it probable that you would be concerned about *how* you were being used. And you might not restrict your attention to just a given instance of one person using you, but rather, take a wider view and wonder how your kind was being treated as a class. And if you did *this,* then I suggest you would focus on the tug-of-war I have mentioned because the way in which each side talks about using you has a rather harsh ring to it. Moreover, you might especially wonder what kids would think about you if you found yourself in an educational context.

To continue this fantasy just a bit, let us look at the protagonists in this tug-of-war from the point of view of how their claims might sound to principles. On one end of the rope we have a group I call the "Fundamentalists." This label is meant not to pick out any one real group and the entirety of its beliefs, but rather to draw together as one force a variety of real groups, based on how they talk about moral principles. Forming this side are those who quite often stop moral discussions by emphatically asserting something like this: "But it's just the principle of the matter! That's just wrong, period. And that's all there is to say." Other times they seem to describe morality as being constituted by acting "on principle," where the important thing seems to be the "sticking to" the principle, rather than the quality of the principle being followed. From the point of view of principles, this way of using you begins to sound a little oppressive when you realize that what this side really wants to say is that one must always *"stand on"* principles. As the leader of the Moral Majority, the Reverend Jerry Falwell (1981) says, "People who take a weak stand on morality inevitably have weak morals" (p. 221). You are useful only to the extent that somebody can *stand* on you—and if you are not dependable enough to be stood on firmly, without any flinching from the weight of society, you are no good.

On the other end of the rope are those who seem to have decided that if you were ever any good, it was in the long-lost days when things were a lot simpler than they are today. Those on this end I call the "Free-thinkers," again wanting not to identify any real groups, but to collect together those who think about principles in a similar way. It is not as easy to identify those on this end in terms of how they use the term *principles,* because they would rather not waste their breath talking about something that is essentially an object of historical wishful thinking. Principles are, for this side, those drab and dreary verities, those outmoded relics of simplistic thinking, those inauthentic escapes from personal existential choice, that we should avoid mentioning when we are in good company. And if we are in the company of kids, you as a principle might again feel oppressed when you realize that, at best, you are to be locked up in a museum, an interesting oddity of simple people and simple lives.

Just once more keep your identification with principles and imagine what you would worry about when your attention is drawn to these sides and how they are using you. At best, it seems that your function in society is being severely limited. The choice between being rigidified and "stood on" and being fossilized as a museum piece is really not much of a choice. Neither, as I will try to show later, allows you to do all of your real work. And I think you would quite legitimately feel even more threatened in an educational context, when you begin to notice what kids seem to think of you when they are the spectators to this tug-of-war.

Some real examples of what kids actually say about that arena within which you function would only confirm your fears that you are simply not part of their world. For instance, consider what some local 11th-graders said in letters to the *Toronto Star* about the question of values education in the schools (Harpur, 1978). One student said: "Moral values cannot be taught and people must learn to use what works for them. In other words, 'whatever gets you through the night, it's alright.' The essence of civilization is not moral codes but individualism. . . . The only way to know when your values are getting sounder is when they please you more." Another put it more bluntly: "What one person thinks is bad or wrong, another person might think that it is good or right. I don't think morals should be taught because it will cause more conflicts and mess up the student's mind." The danger that is illustrated in these comments from students is not just that principles no longer have much use but rather that they cease to exist! It is not simply that moral principles get dragged through a little mud in this tug-of-war, but rather that from the point of view of the kids, the contest is not even worth watching. Or, to switch metaphors, in yet another variation of the baby-and-bathwater theme, principles get thrown out with the protagonists, in this case, ironically, *by the* baby!

JUSTIFICATION OF THE CONCERN

At this point a substantive objection to this whole project must be acknowledged, and dealt with in a way that legitimates the concern just expressed. If Augusto Blasi (1980) is correct in his recent review of the literature, this objection would be quite at home in the "most prevalent view" in the psychological study of morality. Perhaps the most straightforward way of putting the objection is this: If we can transcend our fantastical identification with moral principles, why *not* just let them get thrown out? From a sound psychological perspective they are just, at best, interesting epiphenomena anyway. Thus, what we should focus on is what *causes* people to behave in certain ways, not how they understand their choices and use moral principles in deciding how to act.

Of course, there is a competing perspective within the psychological study of morality. In this view then, "without judgment, an action, no matter how beneficial, would not be moral" (Blasi, 1980, p. 4), and moral principles are commonly seen as the grounds for such judgment. Although my concern in this chapter would thus clearly be shared by this tradition within psychology, I do not want to rest my case by simply identifying myself with one side of a theoretical division within psychology. Nor do I want to get into a discussion of the theoretical issues around which this division resolves, other than to suggest that until we are clearer on how to conceptualize the nature of principled moral judgment, we might not make much headway on some of the other issues. Instead of trying to answer the objection directly at the theoretical level, I want to answer it through a brief appeal to shared experience as the appropriate testing ground for such a claim. That is, I want to ground my concern first by referring to examples of a kind of experience I think we all have had, and then by drawing your attention to the assumption that, in my opinion, must be made to be congruent with that experience.

In short, I think we all know what it is like to be in a moral judgment situation, and I want to draw your attention to two aspects of such situations *as experienced from within them.* For this purpose you can think of any example you want, as long as it bears on the welfare of persons in some way and in a context that picks out deontic concepts such as duty, obligation, rights, justice, and fairness. Although there are many different situations that meet these criteria from which your imagination or memory could draw, let me point to three that we can take as concrete examples:

1. A situation in which your relationship with a lover has resulted in an unwanted pregnancy. Together you are trying to decide whether to have a doctor perform an abortion.

2. A situation in which you have observed a colleague, perhaps a friend as well, repeatedly making claims on the time, performance, and attention of a student of the opposite sex in ways not directly tied to the student's academic interests. The student appeals to you for help, and you are wondering what you ought to do.

3. A situation in which you are on an academic admissions committee faced with the task of admitting a limited number of applicants to study in your department and dividing a limited amount of scholarship money among them. You have filled all the openings except one, given out all the money except for one scholarship, and narrowed the final

applicants down to two of almost equal promise, one white and one
from a minority group. Then you are trying to decide whom to admit
and how to speak to that choice in front of the committee.

Of course, it is not necessary that you have been in all of these situations;
any one of them, or your own example brought to mind by them, will suffice
for my purpose here. But I do think it is indisputable that we have all been
in situations similar to these in the relevant ways and that we recognize some
sort of appeal to moral principles as characteristic of how we seek to deal
with them. Moreover, I believe that, however else we might *also* try to handle
them or whatever else might be relevant factors of our experience, we all
know that such situations are experienced as calling for our choice of the right
course of action, as justified by the best reasons we can think of. If this description is true, I think we have revealed at the level of our real experience
two different aspects of morality, with which any theoretical account must be
congruent and neither of which can be entirely reduced to a chimera of chemistry or conditioning.

The first of these aspects is identified in our experience of *choice*. As
Chazan (1973) has put it, "The heart of the moral dilemma and situation is,
in fact, the confrontation and wrestling with alternative options" (p. 46). All
of the moral judgment situations I described put *you* in the position to *choose,*
to *decide,* to *make up your mind* what to do. It is this experience of the necessity of personal choice that is often picked out at the theoretical level by referring to the mature moral agent as having some degree of "autonomy" in
moral action (Baier, 1973). This autonomy, however, can be properly understood only within the context of the second aspect of our experience in real
moral judgment situations, identified in our looking for the "best reasons" indicating how we ought to act. Again, in the examples I gave, you were not in a
position of simply opting for some decision in a manner reflecting the orientation that any decision is as good as another as long as it is *yours.* Rather, you
were in a position of recognizing the need to act in such a way that could be
justified from some more general perspective. It is this experience of the requirement to choose a course of action that can be rationally supported as right
that is usually picked out at the theoretical level by making a search for "objectivity" a criterion of mature moral judgment.

To summarize my response to the objection raised, I have tried to ground
my concern motivating this project by focusing attention on your experience
when you face the sort of real moral judgment situations that normally generate talk of moral principles. I believe that when we reflect on this experience,
we must recognize at least two unavoidable and irreducible aspects, identifiable as choice and justification. On the basis of this acknowledgment, I assert
that attempts to understand morality without accommodating to these givens
of experience must in the end fail to satisfy; in short, when you are in a moral
judgment situation, regardless of how complex and reliably predictive your
cherished explanatory framework is, it will not and cannot make the choice

for you or justify it. Or more positively, I am proceeding on the assumption that to be congruent with our experience of morality we must be able to talk in terms of both autonomy and objectivity—and that is what we are after when we are concerned with moral principles.

A CLOSER LOOK AT THE CONFLICT

Assuming that I have illustrated how we share a sufficient stake in the principle of principles, we need to return for a closer look at the tug-of-war that contextualizes my concern. I want to show how this tug-of-war seems to result from a disagreement about the existence of fundamental principles but in fact is rooted in a shared, but limited, view of how principles can work. I will proceed by articulating the direction each side is pulling, and I will do so by offering a simplified and abstracted schematic of the relevant claims made by each. In both cases I will articulate the schematic in terms of three claims, the first of which is thought to be the starting point, and the other two, roughly to follow in sequence in kinds of conclusions. Note that in only a very loose sense does the second claim follow from the first, or the third from the second, in either position. I do think, however, that it is true that the arguments are elliptical in pretty much this form, as they function for each side as a psychological stance toward and reaction to the other.

If we look first at the Fundamentalists, I think the stance of this side can be accurately captured in the following three claims:

1. There *are* fundamental moral principles. Therefore,
2. Morality is an objective matter. Therefore,
3. Correct moral judgments express absolute truths.

In contrast to these, the stance of the Free-thinkers can be captured in a different set of three claims, namely:

1. There *are no* fundamental moral principles. Therefore,
2. Morality is a matter of individual autonomy. Therefore,
3. Correct moral judgments are simply expressions of strongly held personal preferences.

As opposing sides in our tug-of-war, it is the direction of these sequences of claims as manifested in the arrival at the third claim that identifies the opposition. The Free-thinkers, then, put up resistance to and pull against the Fundamentalists' third claim, that correct moral judgments express absolute truths. Thus, they complain that the stance of the Fundamentalists leads to dogmatism, rigidity, overconformity, closed-mindedness, inauthenticity, and so on, and the educational danger of these is expressed in our worry about indoctrination. On the other side, the Fundamentalists put up resistance to and pull against the Free-thinkers' third claim, that correct moral judgments are simply expressions of strongly held personal preferences. Thus, they complain that the stance of the Free-thinkers leads to relativism, situational ethics, uncontrolled egoism, the "mess" the world is in today, and so on, and the educational danger of these is expressed by the worry about schools turning out "moral morons."

In the end I will suggest that we should not start pulling for either of these two sides because what they are both pulling on can be dropped safely. But before I get to that, I will point out sound insights of both positions. First, I take the *complaints* of both sides to be legitimate. Although I cannot support it here, I think that the Free-thinkers are correct when they worry about dogmatism, rigidity, closed-mindedness, and so on, and the corresponding educational evil of indoctrination, *if correct moral judgments are understood to be absolute truths,* as they are by the Fundamentalists. Similarly, I think that the Fundamentalists are correct when they worry about relativism, situational ethics, egoism, and so on, and the corresponding evil of "educated" people not knowing how to act morally, *if correct moral judgments are merely personal preferences,* as they are for the Free-thinkers. In other words, I think both sides' complaints about the implications of their opponents' third claim properly identify those conclusions as extremes, ends of the rope, so to speak. And I see no compelling philosophical reason to hang on to either. In short, I reject both sides' third claim.

On the other hand, I do not see how these legitimate complaints threaten the second claim of either side. I think both sides have sound insights into the nature of morality as expressed loosely in their second claims. As we have already seen in our description of moral judgment situations, morality *is,* as claimed by the Free-thinkers, a matter of individual choice or autonomy. When *I* am facing a moral problem, it is *I* who must choose or decide how to act. Thus, I believe the Free-thinkers are quite right to pick out this aspect. But that is not *all* morality is, as they mistakenly go on to suggest. Rather, as claimed by the Fundamentalists, morality is also a matter of objectivity. When I am faced with a moral situation, I fail to treat it as such if I just act on the strongest inclination that occurs to me simply because it is mine. On the contrary, I must face it as calling for my *judgment,* that is, as requiring my attempt to find the best reasons for acting in this situation, reasons whose cogency does not depend solely on their source. Thus, I believe the Fundamentalists are quite right to pick out this aspect of morality, though this does not entail seeking absolute certainty, as they mistakenly go on to suggest.

So far I have suggested that we should reject the third claim of both sides; correct moral judgments are neither absolute truths nor merely personal preferences. But I have also suggested that both sides are correct when one says that morality is a matter of objectivity, and the other, that it is a matter of individual autonomy. So what are we supposed to do—the good liberal thing and pull equally for both sides, as long as they do not make us go too far? On the contrary, I think we can and must avoid this vacuous conclusion. What we really need to do is to examine the starting points of both sides, or, more precisely, what underlies them. And when we do that, I think we can see a way of dropping the rope before we get to the unacceptable ends, but yet not before we have pulled adequately for both autonomy and objectivity.

THE COMMONALITY

The question we must address is, Why, in both cases, does the first claim lead to the third? It is true that a complete answer to this question might need to address a host of psychological questions about the people who are inclined in these directions. But, as far as possible, I want to avoid these kinds of issues and suggest instead that we can uncover quite a bit simply by filling in an assumption that seems to fit the logic of the jumps. To anticipate, it seems apparent that a view about how principles function in moral judgment is shared by both sides. They are both pulling on the same rope, but in opposite directions, because they both are assuming that the only model we have for using principles is a *deductive* model. That they have opposite beliefs about the existence of fundamental moral principles is not the real issue, but more like the red flag tied to the rope in the middle.

In order to make the case that both sides are joined by the common assumption of a deductive model of how principles do their work, we need first a clear identification of this form of argument. Then we will be able to see why the belief about the existence of fundamental moral principles functions so prominently for both sides and also how the characteristics of deductive argument lead them in the opposite directions of their (arguably) illegitimate conclusions about moral judgment.

First, there are, of course, different forms of valid deduction. An example of a common and simple form is the following:

Major premise:	Every mammal has a heart.
Minor premise:	All horses are mammals.
Conclusion:	(Therefore) Every horse has a heart.
	(Salmon, 1963, p. 14)

Although some forms are more complex than this, when valid, they all share with this example at least two primary characteristics:

1. If all the premises are true, the conclusion *must* be true.
2. All of the information or factual content in the conclusion was already contained, at least implicitly, in the premises. (ibid.)

If we take this as our understanding of deductive thinking, I think it can be seen as figuring into both sides in roughly the following way.

First, both sides clearly agree that whether fundamental principles exist is a crucial question. I think that the assumption of a deductive model is what makes this question so crucial. It is in the realm of deductive argument that the specter of infinite regress in moral justification rears its ugly head. It goes something like this: If we think of a particular moral judgment as a conclusion for which we must have rational support, then it is our task to find a set of premises that, combined in proper form, will clearly show that judgment to be warranted. Some of these premises will be factual or quasi-factual in nature, and they will serve as minor premises. But the crucial element in this chain will be the moral principle that serves as the major premise. It is here that the justification buck stops, so to speak. But the problem is that, on this model, it is hard to avoid noticing that the buck could still get passed. That is, if we can look for deductively valid covering reasons for our particular moral judgments, why can we not ask what are the even more primary covering reasons for *these* reasons? And once this process gets a hold on one's thinking, there is no clear place to stop. In fact, one *cannot* stop until one has arrived at *the* rock-bottom, granddaddy (or grandmother) principle. And if it cannot be found, the game is up: All effort to justify our moral judgments is no more than whistling in the dark.

Each of the sides in the tug-of-war we have been examining can then be seen as a different response to the infinite-regress problem. It is in this context that the belief about the existence of fundamental principles becomes so crucial. On the one hand, assuming the deductive model of moral thinking, the Fundamentalists attempt to close off the regress by the firmness of their *stand on* some principle or set of principles. By fiat, some principle is given a privileged epistemological status in the anticipated chain of premises, thus making the regress finite instead of viciously infinite. On the other hand, also assuming the deductive model, the Free-thinkers see no way of stopping the regress in a nonarbitrary authentic way, so they simply refuse to start it. They attempt to finesse the problem by circumventing the whole notion of rational justification in morality.

Then, in addition, the suggestion that a deductive model is being assumed by both sides also reveals why they are inclined toward their respective conclusions, with respect to which, as we have seen, each side can lodge legitimate complaints against the other. Or, more precisely, a differential emphasis on the two primary characteristics of deductive argument can be seen as behind the jumps to the unwarranted conclusions in each case. On the one hand, the Fundamentalists may be focusing on the first characteristic of a deductive mode, namely, that if all the premises are true (and the argument valid), then the conclusion *must* be true. Then, following from their firm stand on (some) principles, or from their granting these a privileged epistemological status as major premises, the Fundamentalists have a way of giving substance to our sense that morality is an objective matter—that we can in principle determine what is the right thing to do. But from exactly the same source comes the problematic additional move that correct moral judgments are absolute truths.

That is, on the first characteristic of deductive argument, *certainty* becomes not only possible but also *necessary!* If the premises are true, and they are simply assumed to be, then the conclusions, particularly moral judgments, are mistakenly seen as absolute truths.

On the other hand, the Free-thinkers may be focusing on the second characteristic of a deductive mode, namely, that all of the information or content in the conclusion is already contained, at least implicitly, in the premises. Then following from their belief that there are no fundamental moral principles that *can* serve as the anchoring major premise supplying the moral content of the argument, the Free-thinkers have a way of giving substance to our sense that morality is a matter of individual autonomy—that the agent is always in a position of *choice*. But, again, from exactly the same source comes the problematic move that correct moral judgments are strongly held personal preferences. That is, on the second characteristic of deductive argument, if the moral content in the conclusion cannot be got out of the major premise, because there *is no* fundamental principle to serve as a major premise, then *all* of it must be provided by the agent. In short, correct moral judgments are then mistakenly seen simply as expressions of strongly held personal preferences.

AN ALTERNATIVE

As already implied in my analysis of what the real issue is, I want to question the commonality that joins the two sides. That is, I do not think we should hang on to the deductive rope, at least when we are in a moral judgment situation of the sort I have been considering. My case against doing this has been mainly circumstantial: I have tried to show that doing so seems to lead to opposite conclusions about the nature of correct moral judgments, both of which we have good reasons to want to reject. On the other hand, in outlining this case, I have also indicated that each side apparently has something going for it insofar as it does have a way of accounting for *one* of the two aspects of morality that I have assumed are revealed in our experience of real moral judgment situations. That is, the Fundamentalists can make some sense of the aspect of objectivity, and the Free-thinkers can make some sense of the aspect of autonomy. But I have not really argued why we must let go of the deductive rope if we want our conception of principled moral judgment to accommodate both of these.

Although I think there are good arguments that can be made, the problem at this point is that if these arguments were successful, we would then be left in a somewhat negative position. I would have shown the inadequacy of deduction as the principle of principles, but I would not have given any indication of how we *can* think of principles in a way that saves both autonomy and objectivity without buying into the problematic conclusions of either the Fundamentalists or the Free-thinkers. Therefore, instead of trying to develop these arguments, I want to suggest a more positive alternative. All I can do here, however, is suggest the direction in which I think we should be looking for this alternative and why it is a plausible direction.

A clue to what we need can be inferred from what has already been said about deductive argument, that is, by noting how the force of deduction is always one-directional, or, as is often said, how it goes from the general to the particular. Principles determine the relevance of some facts, and then principles and relevant facts together justify particular moral judgments. On this model it is hard to see how our perception of the relevancy of some new or previously unnoticed facts can contribute to a reformulation of principles, or how any firmly believed particular judgment could make us question our principles (*or* provide any further support to what they already have). But it seems clear to me that both of these things *do* happen. As Crittenden (1979) has put it: "It is a characteristic of moral standards and principles that they often define the existence of a problem rather than provide an answer" (p. 257).

The general problem, I must remind you, is how to think of moral principles—or the principle of principles—in a way that is congruent with our experience of moral judgment situations in terms of both autonomy and objectivity. The answer to this problem, I believe, is to start thinking in much more complex and "constructivist" terms about moral reasoning. And for our problem here, I think the essential step is to conceive moral reflection and justification as requiring a two-way street between principles and moral judgments. The best example I can think of to make this concrete is in the work of Rawls (1971), in particular, his notion of our seeking "reflective equilibrium" through a decision procedure such as the "original position." I cannot go into Rawls's complex theory of justice in anything more than a superficial level here, but I want at least to point to how his notions are related to our problem in this chapter.

A brief explication of the relevant aspects of Rawls's two notions is needed. First, Rawls intends his now-familiar notion of the original position to be seen not as descriptive of some actual state of affairs but rather as a hypothetical construct showing a way of entering moral argument by persons of a certain sort (1971, p. 19). The original position is a position of equality, one in which persons are conceived of primarily in terms of having two powers, "the capacity for an effective sense of justice" and "the capacity to form, to revise, and rationally to pursue a conception of the good," and in terms of being "moved by two highest-order interests to realize and exercise these powers" (1980, p. 525). Then these persons are required to evaluate different conceptions of justice, as expressed through various principles or sets of principles, which they would want to adopt for characterizing the basic structure of their society. But the catch is that they must do this from behind what Rawls calls the "veil of ignorance." That is, in Rawls's (1980) words:

> They do not know their place in society, their class position, or social status,
> nor do they know their fortune in the distribution of natural talents and

abilities. It is assumed also that they do not know their conception of the good, that is, their particular final ends; nor finally, their own distinctive psychological dispositions and propensities, and the like. Excluding this information is required if no one is to be advantaged or disadvantaged by natural contingencies or social change in the adoption of principles. [pp. 522–523]

Then Rawls (1980) understands this situation as defining a task of "pure procedural justice." That is, "there exists no independent criterion of justice; what is just is defined by the outcome of the procedure itself"; or in other words, "the principles of justice themselves are to be constructed by a process of deliberation, a process visualized as being carried out by the parties in the original position" (p. 523).

As I have already suggested, this whole device can be seen as a way of entering moral argument—as the structure of a response to moral judgment situations of a certain kind, if you will. As such, it is a way of seeking what Rawls calls "reflective equilibrium" between considered moral judgments and moral principles. That is, it is a way of moving back and forth between our considered moral judgments and our provisionally formed moral principles so that they fit together in one coherent scheme, sometimes allowing our firm judgments the overriding force, and sometimes modifying our judgments to match our principles. By carefully defining the conditions of the parties in the original position and the constraints under which they are to deliberate and then by examining how well these conditions and constraints are congruent with our considered moral judgments and would yield our general moral principles, we have a constructivist vehicle for driving the two-way street between judgments and principles.

For my purpose in this chapter we need not follow Rawls's subsequent refinement and use of these notions to argue for a particular conception of justice, as expressed in his two lexically ordered principles of social justice. In fact, we would probably have to redefine the original position in some ways when dealing with more general questions of justice, and *especially* when dealing with other principles of the right. But the general idea is what I am after here: at least for one clear case we can get a picture of an alternative model for describing the relationship between principles and judgments that affords us the possibility of making sense of our assumptions of both autonomy and objectivity without necessarily leading to a view of correct moral judgments as either absolute truths or mere personal preferences.

First, a constructivist view such as Rawls's is congruent with what we want to say about autonomy. As Rawls (1980) points out:

The parties as rational agents of construction are described in the original position as autonomous in two respects: first, in their deliberations they are not required to apply, or to be guided by, any prior and antecedent principles of right and justice. . . . Second, they are said to be moved solely by the highest-order interests in their moral powers and by their concern to advance their determinate but unknown final ends. [p. 528]

Then our experience of autonomous choice within the moral judgment situation can now be accounted for. In short, it is captured by our readiness to enter something like the original position, to affirm the principles that would be supported by such a procedure, and to publicly acknowledge this approach as appropriate for anyone in a relevantly similar situation. If this is true, it also clarifies why we need not follow the Free-thinkers into identifying correct moral judgments with personal preferences: Their extrapolation of autonomy into subjectivism is blocked by the recognition of the original position as necessarily open to anyone meeting its conditions and as constructive through our mutual participation.

Then in addition, this constructivist view also accommodates what I think is essential about objectivity. The notion of objectivity in moral judgment is often misunderstood and, as a result, much maligned. Although it is a complicated question that I cannot go into here in any depth, I think there is a fairly straightforward and uncontroversial way of stating what a belief in objectivity in morality amounts to. When we are in the moral judgment situation, we are, as I noted earlier, faced with the need to identify the best reasons we can for how we think we ought to act. Then when we are concerned with objectivity in this situation, we are concerned with a criterion for assessing our choices and reasons for those choices. And in the context of the moral, this criterion of objectivity amounts to an identification of the various ways in which we can err in the direction of favoring ourselves in reaching our judgments. It is, in short, an essential consideration that others, *especially* those whose interests are affected by our act, would be able to agree with our choice and reasons for it. Given this view of objectivity, it is clear that Rawls's notions provide a substantive picture of just exactly this concern. As Rawls (1980) puts it,

> We have arrived at the idea that objectivity is not given 'by the point of view of the universe,' to use Sidgwick's phrase. Objectivity is to be understood by reference to a suitably constructed social point of view, an example of which is the framework provided by the procedure of the original position. [p. 570]

It is the way we go about constructing this point of view and how it affords the possibility of reflective equilibrium between judgments and principles that constitutes objectivity in moral judgment. Again, as in the case for autonomy, if that is true it also clarifies why we need not follow the Fundamentalists into seeking the certainty of absolute moral judgments. On this model we can see how our concern for objectivity cannot be reduced to a search for unquestionable conclusions. Instead, this move is blocked by the recognition that objectivity is constituted by our construction of a shared perspective from which we can all participate in the continual task of both affirming and questioning the judgments we are inclined to make.

CONCLUDING COMMENTS

By way of conclusion I want to return briefly to my metaphor of the tug-of-war. I have tried to describe the sides in this contest in a way that illuminated both their strengths and their weaknesses, their sound insights and their unwarranted conclusions. And then after locating the source of the problematic claims of both sides in the common assumption of a deductive view of moral principles, I tried to sketch an alternative view that I labeled constructivist, and which might accommodate the sound insights of both sides. There are, of course, problems with this constructivist alternative that need further work if it is to function successfully as our model of the principle of principles. One problem is how such a theory of justification can avoid collapsing at some point into a circularity that is perhaps vicious; on this I think we might take a valuable lead from Daniels's (1979) discussion of "wide reflective equilibrium," a move that sets the search for equilibrium between principles and judgments within a broad context of an independent "set of relevant background theories." Another problem is how to account for the commonsense belief that moral judgments are matters of truth and falsity, the notion of truth being seen as picking out something more than the results of a social construction. In this area one of the more promising solutions has been suggested by Perry (1976) in his distinction between different levels of moral judgment, one at which truth claims are appropriate, and a more basic level at which one *can* only claim reasonable justification. I do not, however, have space here to elaborate on either of these problems. Rather, my final point is that I think this constructivist model, if successfully developed, will have implications regarding the tug-of-war beyond that of affording a view of principles that accommodates both autonomy and objectivity. In order to show this, I need to back up and question one of my implicit starting assumptions; that is, I think we might legitimately question whether either side in this contest has in front of it a full sense of the interests of the children in whose name the contest is engaged. Both believe that what the other side is doing amounts to miseducation, but as I have suggested, there is very little to say in favor of either side's stance within which the complaints are anchored. The further point then is that from a constructivist point of view, we can see that both sides are failing to respect as equals the persons of the next generation. In short, in neither case is the person who is being educated allowed to decide whether a view of the world that includes a belief in the existence of fundamental moral principles is one he or she wants to adopt. That is the issue over which the tug-of-war is being waged by adults who have already decided for the next generation. The children are prizes, but not really participants. By contrast, in a constructivist view the principle of principles is necessarily intergenerational. Its aim is not to decide that question for the next generation, but rather to invite them into a conception of morality within which we can express our respect for one another as free and equal persons despite such differences that might separate us.

REFERENCES

Baier, K. Moral autonomy as the aim of moral education. In G. Langford & D. J. O'Connor (Eds.), *New essays in the philosophy of education*. London: Routledge & Kegan Paul, 1973.

Blasi, A. Bridging moral cognition and moral action: A critical review of the literature. *Psychological Bulletin*, 1980, *88*(1), 1–45.

Chazan, B. I. The moral situation: A prolegomenon to moral education. In B. I. Chazan & J. F. Soltis (Eds.), *Moral education*. New York: Teachers College Press, 1973.

Crittenden, B. The limitations of morality as justice in Kohlberg's theory. In D. B. Cochrane, et al. (Eds.), *The domain of moral education*. Toronto: Ontario Institute for Studies in Education, 1979.

Daniels, N. Wide reflective equilibrium and theory acceptance in ethics. *The Journal of Philosophy*, 1979, *76*, 256–282.

Falwell, J. *Listen, America!* New York: Bantam Books, 1980.

Harpur, T. If it gets you through the night it's alright, grade 11 student says. *Toronto Star*, Sat., March 18, 1978.

Perry, T. D. *Moral reasoning and truth: An essay in philosophy and jurisprudence*. Oxford: Oxford University Press, 1976.

Rawls, J. *A theory of justice*. Cambridge, Mass.: Belknap Press of Harvard University Press, 1971.

Rawls, J. Kantian constructivism in moral theory. *The Journal of Philosophy*, 1980, *77*(9), 515–572.

Salmon, W. C. *Logic*. Englewood Cliffs, N.J.: Prentice-Hall, 1963.

Sumner, W. *Abortion and moral theory*. Princeton, N.J.: Princeton University Press, 1981.

CHAPTER 21

On Avoiding "Single Vision and Newton's Sleep": Sketches From an Unorthodox Moral-Education History

HENRY C. JOHNSON, JR.

The growingly problematic nature of moral education has its origin in the generation bracketing the opening of our present century, when most of the fundamental choices governing our educational thought and practice came to be made. A perceived social and educational agenda called for a particular sort of methodological solution. The source of this solution (essentially reductive behaviorism) and its concomitant content, stemmed largely from a particular reading of Darwin, coupled with a messianic notion of practical science. These developments are chiefly sketched as embodied in one figure, Edward Lee Thorndike, whose work became at least puzzling, if not contradictory, even to him. The issues raised by his approach to moral education (and that of others) remain significant.

> Now I a fourfold vision see,
> And a fourfold vision is given to me;
> 'Tis fourfold in my supreme delight
> And threefold in soft Beulah's night
> And twofold Always. May God us keep
> from Single vision & Newton's sleep.
> WILLIAM BLAKE, VERSE LETTER TO THOMAS BUTTS (1802)

The recently renewed emphasis on the moral function of education and schooling is both obvious and significant. It is also fraught with difficulties and dangers. The purpose of this chapter is to suggest, from a historical perspective, something of the potential mischief that can arise from overly facile and narrow resolutions of the "moral education question." More specifically, my purpose is to make plain the dangers inherent in reducing moral development to purely psychological terms, attractive though that is in our current intellectual and cultural milieu. To be blunt, we tried that before, roughly at the turn of our present century, and it succeeded only in emptying the enterprise of most of its vital meaning and content. Our attempt was understandable, in the context of a largely moribund philosophical climate and a brash, omnicompetent, and technocratic psychology—but it was hardly acceptable. Our efforts were part of a vain project to create a "science of education" that would solve all of our problems quickly and efficiently, a mistake we need not repeat.

Laying an adequate foundation for this essay would require an extensive review of the development of education and schooling in the West. I have done this elsewhere (Johnson, 1980, 1982) and here I can only lay down certain presuppositions of my perspective without providing either flesh or justification for these bare bones: Education has always been an implicitly moral-ethical enterprise and usually explicitly so. Education, as a normative developmental process, rests necessarily on justifications of value. Furthermore, as it presupposes the development of acting beings, the quality of their action is always paramount, and hence the concern of educators has always had a central ethical focus. This tradition carried itself uninterruptedly into the American context. When, just prior to the middle of the nineteenth century, Americans chose to institutionalize the educational process in a single and ostensibly compulsory system, as a deliberate social policy—a process we are most familiar with in the form advocated by Horace Mann—a further social and political factor was added. But that was, of course, only to anchor it even more firmly in moral and ethical concerns.

Within 50 years, however, by the turn of the century, that whole new educational enterprise with its new form of systematic and universal schooling was already being called into question. It was not fulfilling its promise, though admittedly it had come to face social and cultural problems that none would have anticipated at its birth. The generation from 1890 to 1915 was an era of drastic, rapid, and fundamental educational and pedagogical change, and the question of what to do with the moral-ethical aspects of education and schooling became highly problematic. The analysis that I offer thus begins, as any drama, *in medias res,* in the thick of things. Major efforts to reform and to make more efficient both elementary and secondary education had been made by the mid-1890s. But, particularly in respect of secondary education, these efforts were deemed insufficiently radical and new proposals were made over several years, culminating in the famous *Cardinal Principles of Secondary Education* of 1918 (National Education Association [NEA], 1918). By this point, the question of the proper nature and method of moral education was enormously important, and a vast array of projects and proposals for dealing with it were already underway, both here and abroad.

The framers of the *Principles* pointed to dramatic social change "profoundly affecting the activities of the individual" as the precipitating cause of their efforts (pp. 7–8). Life had become far more complex for everyone, as citizen, as worker, and as the beneficiary of a radically increased "leisure." Industrialization and technology, entailing a crucial new division of labor, had fundamentally altered the worker's function and status. The home was becoming increasingly less effective at nurturing satisfactory and satisfied persons. It was beginning to lose (perhaps abandon) its traditional responsibility. Under the impact of urbanization, "less unified family life" and the breakdown of community were widely manifest, even in rural areas. Despite their traditional role, neither the family nor the community appeared able to provide for adequate moral development. The churches, once the pivotal institutional influence, carried less weight as formative agencies, with their relevance and their influence eroded by the sweeping tide of secularization.

The Commission believed that a "new" notion of democracy was urgently needed, one with a heavy emphasis on the quality of personal conduct. "The purpose of democracy," it argued "is so to organize society that each member may develop his personality primarily through activities designed for the well-being of his fellow members and of society as a whole." The new democratic "ideal" is, consequently, "that the individual and society may find fulfillment in each other." Similarly, the goal of the new secondary education must be to "develop in each individual the knowledge, interests, ideals, habits, and powers whereby he will find his place and use that place to shape both himself and society toward ever nobler ends" (p. 9). The only guarantee that the "new" democracy, which "sanctions neither the exploitation of the individual by society, nor the disregard of the interests of society by the individual" (p. 10), can realize its objectives depends on the schools' conscious developing of the individual's "ethical character." Hence, the seventh cardinal principle, "Ethical Character," was declared "paramount among the objectives of the secondary school" (p. 15).

The Commission's subcommittee on "Moral Values in Secondary Education" attributed the need for more intensive moral education to the prevalence of a crude individualism and a concomitant moral egoism abundantly manifested in "political corruption" and social insensitivity and focused with particular clarity by the war (NEA, 1917, p. 12). Although deprecating the attachment of a "moral" to every unit of study, the committee viewed individual courses in the curriculum as opportunities for ethical *thinking* in the sense of moral analysis and judgment, citing "social studies" as an obvious example (pp. 20–24). The vocational studies were to emphasize the necessity of viewing commerce and industry not as self-justifying activities but as activities to be judged by the criteria of social benefit and the development of persons as individuals. "Work," for example, was to be understood not just as "making a living" but as an activity that "should help not hinder the making of lives" (p. 31). It is also interesting to note that in regard to the natural sciences, the committee focused on biology and singled out the "mischief" that "results from regarding men too exclusively as the kinsman of the lower orders." "It is," said the committee, "quite possible to interpret man in terms of his likeness to his inferiors; but this is only half the story" (p. 29).

As one examines this critical, formative period in the career of moral education in the public schools, certain tendencies of great significance for our discussions gradually become visible. Because the Commission on the Reorganization of Secondary Education had a palpably practical aim, the question of instructional method is always present. (Indeed, the whole project closely parallels that impulse to rationalization and efficiency most egregiously visible in the "Taylorism" then sweeping the country. The notion that "practical science," defined largely in terms of measurement and record keeping, when joined to business organization, would transform everything and everyone was hard to resist, and its methods and categories were being eagerly adopted everywhere, not least in the schools.)

As to method, the *Cardinal Principles* simply decree that the new (and very practical) science of psychology will determine method (NEA, 1918, pp. 8–9). Perhaps more surprising, the Commission's moral education subcommittee had already reached the conclusion that the collapse of the "formal discipline" school of psychological and pedagogical opinion—largely the consequence of the famous Thorndike-Woodworth experiments, of course—meant that the school could not achieve moral development by cultivating general habits or dispositions (NEA, 1917, p. 18n). Learning is concrete and particular. Hence the school's objectives must be equally concrete and particular. Less obviously, but still closely related, the notion of a "new" democracy espoused in the report of the full Commission, despite its vocal appeal for a *balance* between the individual and society as a whole, appears under careful examination to describe a society that exists essentially *for* the individual. As we shall see, subsequent developments in the progress of moral education increasingly favor the very individualism the 1918 report so loudly repudiates. The triumph of an individualistic psychology, seen as determinative of method, and joined to a curiously self-centered "democracy," might have suggested the trouble that lay ahead. The hand was the hand of John Dewey, Felix Adler, and the great moralists, but the voice was the voice of Thorndike. The relation between reason and conduct and the possibility of any genuine moral principles would be obviously problematic.

What in fact came to pass, however, as so frequently in American schooling, was a practical middle course. The "trait" approach paid lip service to both sides but, like most hybrids, turned out to be sterile. On the one hand, "traits" could be seen as only new names for old "virtues." On the other hand, these new traits or virtues were clearly cut off from their philosophical-anthropological roots and were generated by ostensibly scientific observation of concrete cases. What was important was that these essentially behavioristic "traits" were teachable and measurable—characteristics very important in the real world of schooling where an unprepared army of teachers was struggling with a dramatically expanding school population. Hence, the flood of practical programs and "scientific investigation," which flowed into the 1920s and often claimed to be the result of the Commission's recommendations, were largely cast in terms of atomistic traits, defined in the aggregate as composing general moral behavior.

The problematic quality of such an approach to moral education was made dramatically obvious with the appearance, at the end of the decade, of the work of Hugh Hartshorne and Mark May and their colleagues in the "Character Education Inquiry" (Hartshorne & May, 1928–1930). According to their study, not only was there no empirically verifiable relation between the acquisition of the traditional "traits" and practical moral behavior, but there was little correlation between the influence of any of the traditional agencies of moral development, family, church, and school, and any individual's general moral character—whatever, indeed, the latter would be.

The problem, as Hartshorne and May see it, is that learning is situation specific (1930b, pp. 754–755). Character is not a "summation of virtues and vices" as a result of which any "transfer" can be anticipated. Rather, it is correlated with individual reactions within social groups and concrete situations. Thus, if a particular person appears to manifest truth telling, courage, or concern for others in one particular situation or context, that fact will of itself say little about whether the same individual will do likewise in other situations or on other occasions, except as these different social contexts may resemble one another. A child who does not lie or cheat in his Sunday school class, for example, may not cheat in other similar settings, or with his Sunday school mates in other settings. What he will do at home or at his neighborhood school has, however, little if any relation to his conduct in the former situation or group.

Hartshorne and May (1930b) and their fellow investigators did not resist the rigorously nominalistic tendencies of their empirical research: "Honesty," they insist, "is simply a name used to describe conduct as observed in specific situations" (p. 755). There *can* be no character trait or quality toward which we can aim in educating, nor is there any effective general moral principle that is grasped by the mind in some general form and then regulates conduct in the various areas of one's life. As a consequence of exhaustive observation, they can find "very little evidence of unified character traits." Furthermore, they can find "no specific relations between moral knowledge and conduct, but only general relations," because any "correlation between knowledge and conduct is not due to a fundamental and organic relation existing in the minds of children but is a group phenomenon and is due probably to the relationship between the group code or standards and group conduct" (756–757).

The practical consequences of all this for the school are, Hartshorne and May (1930b) believe, plain to see. Not only are "abstract ideals" ineffective to "control behavior," they are likely to be counterproductive and even unhealthy. They disrupt or block the individual's adjustment to the various groups and situations in which he or she participates, inasmuch as each of these has its own code or set of norms. It is participation in such groups, including the sharing of these norms, that brings about a healthy, unified personality. They insist that the "quality of any act is . . . found from its contribution to the life of the group." The real aim of character development is in fact the formation of a "consistent self" through a process of "social idealization." This process needs to begin early, if possible before the fifth grade—

one notes the strain of romantic maturationalism—and, all in all, leads to a striking conclusion: To be effective we must have, they propose, either 24-hour schooling or the total reconstruction of society. The latter, the "building of a functional ideal for society" in general would make possible harmonious social adjustment for all and thus bring the possibility of a unified moral development for the individual (p. 762; see also p. 757).

If the matter was to be settled in the manner exemplified by Hartshorne and May—and most seemed to agree in theory that it was—their studies should have proved decisive. Nothing else of similar scope or depth has in fact ever been done. In a certain sense, their influence lingers still. But the question of moral education in schools has never been the product of theory-building or empirical research alone. In the midst of the publication of their findings, the stock market crashed and the Great Depression began, and these events seemed, with good reason, to point a moral of their own. They also added an enormous sense of urgency.

In 1932 the NEA was ready with another report, entitled *Character Education* (1932) and produced by its Department of Superintendence as its *Tenth Yearbook*. The underlying analytical framework was straightforwardly sociological: Our confusion stemmed from a continuing period of "profound" social change and its attendant "unrest, discord, and maladjustment." Only as these irresistible social dynamics ran their "course," could they "produce the necessary modifications in both the material and the spiritual culture" that would bring about "equilibrium." Yet, if it was inevitably clear that our "mores" would have to "undergo fundamental revision," how could anyone speak in the midst of such a darkling plain? Obviously, only with difficulty and rather considerable tentativeness. Hence, it is not surprising that although the "Commission on Character Education," which had brought forth the report, decreed (1932) that "new conceptions of right and wrong must be forged; and human character itself must assume unwonted forms" (p. 9), Denver Superintendent A. L. Threlkeld (1932) was perforce modest in its presentation: "This Yearbook presents no specific plan of character education as such, . . . Who are we, that we should attempt to tell what you should do in order to be good?" (p. 546). Rather, as the Commission (NEA, 1932) itself maintained, "the position taken in the *Yearbook* is that character education consists of constructive reactions to life situations without thought on the part of the individual as to whether his reaction in a particular situation is one calculated to bring about his own self-improvement" (p. 5). Keeping its promise, the *Yearbook* exhaustively analyzed "several hundred" courses of study, books, and articles and found at least 17 major notions of what character and character education might be.

The reader may find this dreary catalogue of research and practice open to the point of vacuousness in respect to what character education should be. But there is strong—nay, rigid—agreement, almost paradoxically, both on what it should not be and on what its foundations are. A later commentator (McKown, 1935) found the volume's title instructive. The term *character* had been adopted *in lieu* of such "academic" and "goody-goody" terms as *morality* or *ethics* and the theological baggage they carried (pp. 1–12). (He preferred the even more bloodless term *good citizenship,* in fact, and correctly predicted that it would subsequently become the term of choice.) The Commission (NEA, 1932) itself was afraid that the individual's moral development could not be a critical rational process, or even "self-conscious," without the danger of "poisoning" him or her (p. 75)—a caveat not only present in Hartshorne and May, as we have seen, but also traceable to prestigious Harvard moral philosopher G. H. Palmer (1909). Furthermore, about one thing more there is no dispute possible: Any "adequate program of character education," the Commission insisted, "must rest" on "the foundations of scientific study" (NEA, 1932, p. 79).

One is tempted to summarize this period—only a little unfairly—as a period of uninterrupted progress. American public schoolmen came to know less and less *what* to do, but more and more about *how* to do, or not to do, it. A profusion of projects, experiments, and proposals came and went, muted somewhat by the renewed sense of fervor engendered by a new war that was, almost all agreed, safely moral. *Citizenship* did replace *character,* which had replaced *ethics.* A slim and tenuous apprehension of social responsibility, largely defined by some sort of group feeling, provided most of what little content there was. The teachable-trait approach outlasted its critics, reinforced—and perhaps that is not a bad pun—by the growing practical dominance of an atomistic behaviorism in the circles of instructional theorists and curriculum developers. Few philosophers bestirred themselves to address the issue of moral education—the view from the Vienna Circle was, after all, not promising for such projects. Ryle's sixth chapter, emotivism, and analysis, carried the day. All were psychologized; everything was sociologized; and little could be philosophized.

A fitting terminus to our exploration might be the 1973 report of the *new* "National Commission for the Reform of Secondary Education" sponsored by the Charles F. Kettering Foundation. Its recommendations were specifically drafted to replace those of 1918. Needless to say, "ethical character" was no longer "paramount" among the schools objectives. Instead, at the tail end, we encounter something called "responsibility for citizenship," a vague "respect for personal property," and an "acceptance of social duties," the precise nature of which are never made clear (pp. 28–34). But the 1973 report was already an anachronism. By this time, thanks to more adequate psychological trends and a more receptive philosophical climate, a much more adequate approach to moral development and its relation to education and schooling was already strongly in evidence—the movement of which this book is a part.

I have tried to trace, all too briefly, some phases of the curious career of moral education in the American public school, ending in a kind of vague and stultifying puzzlement about what to do, if not how to do it. Certain themes are obvious. Moral instruction had been a perennial and unselfconscious element in Western education. It was manifest, however, not just in philosophy but principally in literature, history, religion, and a body of folk wisdom. In this content were conveyed *images* of human action that were intelligible but not the product of abstract deductions and rule making. Suddenly, at the turn of the last century, moral development became highly self-conscious and at the same time obviously problematic. Why? As America entered the last decade of the nineteenth century, its social and cultural situation was chaotic and frightening. Change and reform were in demand on every side, our nostalgic accounts of the "Gay Nineties" or the placid "Edwardian Age" notwithstanding.

Two institutions then enjoyed widespread popular trust, though with qualification: schooling and business (commerce and industry). That faith was in some ways paradoxical, however, as the effectiveness of schooling was already being severely questioned and the competence of the "professional" classroom teaching force put in grave doubt—for example, by the empirical studies of Joseph Mayer Rice (1893, 1914). Likewise, business was the source of many of the socio-political and economic problems that touched everyone and called for moral reform. But business was also producing palpable miracles that were transforming the lives of ordinary folk.

How? Business organization, ostensibly through its hierarchy of talent and vision that freed the "great man" to subdue nature and transform human life, appeared to many to be primarily responsible, however its power might be corrupted in *individual* cases by ignorance or moral failure. The key to its success was the controlled allocation of resources and the specification of tasks through strict accounting and the measurement of results. Furthermore, there lay behind the "captains of industry," as Thorstein Veblen called them, the unquestioned and unquestionable authority of applied science, messianic in its claims and Baconian in its principles.

The logic, then, was simple: If schooling could be recast in the same image, it would produce similar palpable miracles, transforming persons in parallel with the new world in which it would be their privilege to live. The schools would need, in short, a corresponding new organization and authority. The new organization was rapidly achieved by a new kind of administration, hierarchical, efficient, allocating resources and specifying tasks through measurement—both the large-scale measurement of the rapidly proliferating "surveys" and the corresponding "tests" that measured individual teachers and students against time and native talent.

In regard to authority, educational thinkers and practitioners quickly abandoned the old theological and philosophical grounds as bankrupt and unpersuasive—indeed divisive. A new warrant was needed for the transformation of schooling, the new secular missionary campaign. Viewing education's prospects on the eve of the new century, William T. Harris (1900) put the matter clearly in language still redolent with religious rhetoric: The new missionary agency is the school. The "Anglo-Saxon race" has, he argued, pushed forward the borders of civilization by "the industrial results of science and the application of the powers of nature to the subjugation of elemental forces." Consequently, "the people of every race and tongue must go to school to this highest ideal of education, learn to command nature by means of science and learn to convert it to human uses." What will they learn? Harris singles out one of the "lessons" of civilization to be mastered in this educational process as "how to conquer nature by means of machinery" (pp. 201–202).

The problem was, What could provide the new foundations, what could restructure education and schooling as a practical science along productive lines? The specific answer would come from the new science of behavior, which would both furnish a new form to shape educational activity and carry the new authority necessary to bring about the revolution in content and practice. Furthermore, by fastening on discrete "behaviors," a comparable "unit" that could be inserted in the widely demanded cost-benefit equations was available. No one, I believe, more completely embodied this logic than Edward Lee Thorndike, and he knew it.

Thorndike had mastered the new field, traced it to what he took to be its evolutionary roots, digested its lessons, written and published his thesis on *Animal Intelligence* (1911), and translated it all into a practical regimen for teachers (and the teachers of teachers), just in time to answer the new demand. During a career spanning some 50 years, and through the medium of nearly 500 published works (including 78 books), he became midwife to the issue that resulted, the new technopedagogy that complemented the new technoscientific society and culture.

The principal element was the reform—*regeneration* would perhaps not be an inappropriate term—of man and his institutions through the agency of science, and particularly by a science of education, which Thorndike now thought possible. His argument is frequently repeated (see, for example, 1906, pp. v, 1–9). What we want is the improvement of man and his world. Because, Thorndike thinks it is fair to say, that is what life is about, it is also what education is about, in its character as the deliberate "production" of such changes. The key to this development was that we had discovered what he liked to call man's "original bodily nature" and the laws that governed both its structure and, in psychology, its behavior. Eschewing the old literary and "philosophical" psychology of James and Hall—the examples are his—Thorndike found in favor of the new sort of behavioral science done by men who were, he pointed out, more frequently "first trained in physics or engineering" (1936, pp. 263, 270). Because, he believed, "in the long run, the only cure for national ills and the only foundation for progress is science, sure and verifiable knowledge, directing a good will toward men," the crucial activity is the quantitative analysis of psychological data, not the speculations of the sort produced by James or Royce or Dewey (1910, p. 80). Such performances filled him with some "admiration," but it was "tinged with irritation and amusement" (1936, p. 263). What is important to note, however, is that such speculations are, for Thorndike, unnecessary, because the truth is at last in our grasp. We need only follow it out. Late in his career, Thorndike could argue that "the best work of all" in psychology had perhaps been done "by men such as Galton, who gave little or no thought to what it [psychology] is or should be" (1936, p. 270).

The task, then, is to bring humanity itself under control, and that control is the kind of "rational" control characteristic of the messianic technoscience then manifest in industrialism. It was possible because "psychology does apply in detail to the work of the classroom" (1936, p. 266). The new science can, so to speak, offer exact guidance for practice in education, just as physics can determine directly what constitutes good procedure in engineering. It will work because we have discovered the true nature of the learning *process,* and that furnishes the principle of manipulation and control. Having discovered the "original bodily nature" of man and the "law of original behavior" or "the law of instinct" (1911, p. 243) that accompanies it, we know that all subsequent change in *any* organism is the consequence of an associative mechanism and is definable in terms of stimulus and response. All else flows from these principles and laws, including the so-called higher faculties on which educators have wasted their efforts for some 2500 years. The "higher" faculties are nothing but "those aspects of behavior which the term [*learning*] has come historically to signify, that is, . . . intellect, skill, *morals,* and the like" (p. 243, italics added).

Although it cannot be fully dealt with in this chapter, it is easy to show that this process is essentially atomistic, mechanistic, and radically reductivist. "No animal," says Thorndike (1911), "*can* have an original nature that does not *absolutely prescribe* just what the responses shall be to every stimulus" (p. 242, italics in original). Thus, "a baby twiddles his thumbs or waves his legs for exactly the same sort of reason that a chick pecks at a worm or preens its wing" (p. 243). The "reason" is that "neurone" satisfaction occurs, and that process is fundamentally and continuously the same through every living organism (pp. 246–249). "The bodies and minds of men are a part of nature," and "their history is as natural as the history of the stars" (1910, p. 79).

The new science, as Thorndike understands it, thus opens up a "Nature" that is a tightly woven casual web. Now that we have its laws in respect to behavioral change (i.e., learning) we can fashion what we like. Education and schooling can become productive processes. The world of natural science is a world of parts and laws in which every event, "each successive act in the world drama," is but "the outcome of all that have gone before and the cause of all that are to come" (1910, p. 79). Correspondingly, "the first law of behavior, one fraction of the general law of the uniformity of nature, is that with life and mind, as with mass and motion, the same cause will produce the same effect—*that the same situation will, in the same animal, produce the same response*" (1911, p. 241, italics in original). The climax of the doctrine, in terms reverberating clearly with the notions (and even the words) of Francis Bacon, Auguste Comte, Hippolyte Taine, and Thorndike's own master, Galton, is crucial:

Thus, at last, man may become ruler of himself as well as of the rest of nature. For, strange as it may sound, man is free only in a world whose every event he can understand and foresee. Only so can he guide it. We are captains of our own souls only in so far as they act in perfect law so that we can understand and foresee every response which we will make to every situation. Only so can we control our own selves. *It is only because our intellects and morals— the mind and the spirit of man—are a part of nature, that we can be in any significant sense responsible for them, proud of their progress, or trustful of their future.* [1910, p. 78, italics added]

It took Thorndike (and those who shared his vision) but a few short years to accomplish their task. By 1912, the prestigious Harvard Schoolmasters Club assembled to celebrate the manifest victory of the new approach to education and schooling and to chart a course for the future. Representatives of every level of schooling from the elementary school to the university were brought together, and they spoke to the nation through the pages of the influential *School Review*. The sense of destiny that pervaded the meeting was clearly articulated by Leonard P. Ayres (1912), statistician, surveyor of the educational efficiency of schools, and (especially later) adviser to the federal government and the banking trade. Ayres focused on the fact that the hue and cry had initially been raised by Joseph Mayer Rice. The education profession had at first been unable to accept Rice's criticisms and proposals. But the prophet, once dishonored, was now vindicated. Ayres pointed out that administrators were now almost totally preoccupied with putting to work in the schools Rice's proposals for a scientifically based, industrially defined, efficiency (pp. 300–301).

In his paper "Measuring Educational Processes through Educational Results" (1912), Ayres points out that "the basal proposition underlying this entire mass of discussion was that the effectiveness of the school, the methods, and the teachers must be measured in terms of the results secured." At long last, "we have awakened to a startled realization that in education, as in other forms of organized activity, applied science may avail." The movement in educational thought away from a regimen born in "the slow process of philosophy" and stemming from "the cloister" is, Ayres proclaims, "no passing fad or temporary whim." It is, rather, a "transformation" in "what we think as well as what we do in education," and one that is "permanent, significant, and fundamental" (p. 301).

Thorndike then gave his testimony, with customary élan, in a paper significantly entitled "The Measurement of Educational Products" (1912). The thrust of his argument is clear. The crucial nexus between educational theory and practice, and between it and the new efficiency movement in industry, is the field of scientific measurement. Although the field is not yet quite ready to accept the task, Thorndike's purpose is to assure his audience that its achievement is but a few days (a few experiments) away.

Thorndike begins his paper by noting that the "business of man" is reform

(p. 289). Education is "the name of the process," and "science is about to become its method." It is only "about to" because, for the realization of that goal ("the production and prevention of changes in human beings"), it "must measure them" (p. 290). Educational processes are "extraordinarily complex," he admits, but we must persist until we have reduced them to what he calls "component ability atoms." More precisely, we must meet the requirements of "a valid scale of measurement in general" (pp. 290–291). These are, first, "a series of perfectly definable facts"; second, the identification of differing amounts of "the same kind of thing"; third (and most difficult), we must arrive as a "perfectly defined" interval or "unit of difference." (For example, the interval between 4 and 5 grams is precisely the same as the interval between 47 and 48.) Finally, we must have an absolute zero point.

After some illustrations of how these developments are even now being realized, Thorndike stakes the claim with his customary clarity and certainty:

> If we get scale points defined, and their distances defined, and establish an absolute zero, *there is no further difficulty in constructing a scale for achievements of human nature. Such scales have every logical qualification that any of the scales for physical measurement have.*
>
> *There is no limit, theoretically, to the kind of thing for which scales are practicable.* I have chosen for convenience the simpler and easier cases. But the arguments apply *equally* to the sense of evidence in history, excellence of judgment in affairs, devotion to the common good, or *any* quality, *no matter how complex,* that one may take. [pp. 298–299, italics added]

In closing, Thorndike brushes aside such objections as the notion that "the personal, spiritual work of education" is "not in the domain of exact science" in a manner that illustrates, I think, his superb ability to meet practical opposition at the level whence it actually arose: "Mothers," he assured his audience, "do not love their babies less who weigh them" (p. 299).

Given such a conception of education and teaching, as Thorndike had said as early as 1906, it is easy to see what the task of educational research is to be: the development of a perfect science of education along very precise lines. And Thorndike, again, did not fail to make what he meant as clear in print as he did in the lives of his thousands of colleagues and students, whose efforts he inspired and directed. Warning his readers that psychology was still but an imperfect science, he nonetheless was confident of what it should and could become because he already knew what it was in principle (1906). Were it perfect, it would comprise "a perfect and complete knowledge of human nature." As a consequence,

> it would tell the effect of every possible stimulus and the cause of every possible response in every possible human being. A teacher could then know just what the result of any act of his would be, could prophecy [!] just what the effect of such and such a page read or punishment given or dress worn would be—just how to get any particular response, or attention to this object, memory of this fact or comprehension of that principle. [p. 9]

By 1929, Thorndike put it even more simply (Thorndike & Gates, 1929). "It is," he said, "the task of the science of education to know the effect of everything that any teacher can do upon every person to whom anything can be done." The resultant "total possible facts" will furnish the unshakable foundation for educational progress (p. 236).

What was the basis for all this, the real source of its authoritative demeanor and its widespread acceptance? The possibility of the triumphal role for applied science as manifested in education was grounded, as Thorndike and most others saw it, in one source: the work of Charles Darwin. Invited to participate in the widely observed fiftieth anniversary of the publication of the *Origin of Species* in 1909, Thorndike formulated "Darwin's Contribution to Psychology" (1910) in clear terms to which he adhered faithfully throughout the balance of his career. It was Darwin who had liberated us from our unsatisfactory and unproductive intellectual and educational past. There were four "important direct contributions to psychology": First, that the "instincts and the moral and aesthetic capacities of man are subject to variation and natural selection"—that is, that "intellect and character have a natural, not a miraculous, history"—second, his doctrine of sexual selection; third, his "account of the bodily expression of the emotions"; and fourth, his study of mental development in infancy, through observations of his own son, "to ascertain the resemblances of the mental life of infancy to the mental life of the lower animals (pp. 67–68).

This was "the evolutionary point of view" as applied to psychology. Unlike the old psychology, which "had studied the human mind by itself alone and had taught that our minds were all made after one pattern mind, which worked as it did for no intelligible reason, but just because it did," the new evolutionary psychology was to be historical—that is, "comparative and genetic." That meant "careful observations and experiments" that are "made with reference to animal learning, to the mental powers of primitive man" and finally to "the mental evolution of the human species" (p. 70).

"No 'ideas' or 'thinking' of the human sort are necessary to account for" this sort of learning, says Thorndike. Amphibians and reptiles, "next in the line of descent, show the same sort of intellect," the only "difference" being that they are more "sensitive" to a greater number of "kinds of situations," can make more "kinds of responses," and, finally, that they can connect the latter with the former in more ways. Still further along the scale, "the mammals other than the primates" demonstrate "this same learning by the direct selection of one response for association with a situation as the main component of the animal's intelligence." But there are "obscure traces of the life of ideas"—"ideas" being "thoughts of things past and to come, of things bound to the actual present situation only by connections made in the animal itself." Yet all this is no more than the ability "to learn more and different habits, not by learning them in a more human way" (pp. 72–73). Thus he can conclude that "by extending the animal learning far enough, it of itself produces ideas, and ideas produce all the rest" (p. 74).

In discussing Darwin's role in "making psychology a natural science,"

Thorndike sketches a history of human culture culminating in the triumph of science. "Primitive thinking explains events of every sort by supposing that someone wishes the event to take place." When mankind was a child, trying to "control events by wheedling or bribing someone," it was "a fool." Gradually seeing, at first in "certain very easy cases," that such explanations do not work, mankind at length came, in the person of its "men of science," to be "converted to natural causation." Yet progress had stalled over the question of explaining "living matter" until Darwin "showed a natural way," thus "depriving theological or supernatural causes from their last remnant of power in the minds of men." We had brought "the behavior of bodies in motion, the action of heat and light, the affinities of chemical substances" (which we also once thought reflected the "caprices of persons—of gods, goddesses, fairies and elves") to be explicable inside "nature" through the sciences of astronomy, physics, chemistry, and geology. Just so we could now finally explain not only life in general (through biology) but (in the new psychology) also the "present nature" of man—that is, his present character and abilities (pp. 76–77). Thus, Darwin had at last shown that human behavior is "as natural as the behavior of an atom of hydrogen" (p. 79). In such a world, persons in the traditional sense are an anomaly—in fact, an impossibility—because the notion of any free, sovereign agency is simply incompatible with the system as a whole. Nor does Thorndike shrink from such a judgment. "Darwin's work," he tells us, "did not suffer the caprice of persons to be considered a cause of mental events, of human psychology, of the history of men and nations" (p. 78).

Two questions arise at this point. The first is whether the account of Darwin's "theory" that Thorndike gives is a correct one. The second question is whether the general sort of account given by Thorndike was *thought* to be correct, and, if so, what the educational effect of that acceptance might be. In answer to the first question, I do not think it was, although a thorough examination of that crucial problem cannot be undertaken here. In answer to the second question, I believe that the kind of cartoon of Darwin's position Thorndike offers, and (perhaps even more importantly) the sort of practical implication Thorndike saw, in general terms, to flow from it, was accepted with little substantial alteration by a majority of educational thinkers and leaders, especially in the fields of educational psychology and the closely allied enterprises of methodology and research.

There were, of course, philosophers and psychologists who disagreed with much of this. My point is, however, that they were not the ones who were effective in shaping educational thought or practice. In fact, it is fair to say that there were at least two "Darwinisms." The first, accepted by folk like Thorndike, James Cattell, and Galton, was founded on the notion that Darwin had *answered* all the problems—and in a particular way. He was the "Second Newton"—that is to say, the figure who had brought human individual *and* social phenomena under the same simple mechanistic structure as that which governed the natural phenomena as created by Newton. For others—for example, Charles Sanders Peirce, James, Dewey, and J. M. Baldwin—Darwin *raised* new problems, calling into question the whole mechanistic structure (including a mechanistic science) that had provided comfort in the past. If Thorndike's perspective is accepted, the explanation of education is reduced to a search for units, variables, and processes isomorphically corresponding to those of the reigning "hard" sciences and corresponding to the reigning forms of life that have already made such a transformation—that is, the new technological society. In the context of our discussions here, we are warranted, I believe, in interpreting the subsequent history of moral education as a substantially parallel attempt at self-transformation.

The wages of the Thorndikean perspective are deadly, however, especially when extended to the question of moral development. Persons, institutions, forms of life, become at best epiphenomenal if they do not pass out of existence all together. Human life becomes itself problematic, necessarily denied by the rigidly reductivist, monistic methodology that (after Thorndike) saw teachers-to-be studying nerve ends rather than children. Morals likewise fade from view in the deepening Thorndikean twilight, lost either in an atomistic singularity of "behaviors" or a vague generality of "attitude." Ideas and reasons as potential springs of human action lose substance in the search for the behaviors needed to make the system work. He had early decreed that the "ideo-motor theory" of human action appeared to be "contrary to fact" (1913–1914, vol. 1, p. 174; see also pp. 176–185, 289–293). Hence, it is not, says Thorndike, by moral thinking that one learns to do "the right thing." If a person "learns to do the right thing [for Thorndike, this was a social given, it should be noted] in a thousand particular situations, he will, so far as he has the capacity, gain the power to see what act a new situation demands. If he is made to obey a thousand particular 'This is right's' and 'That is right's, he will, so far as he has the capacity, come to connect respect and obedience with the abstractly right and true" (1916, p. 294; see also 1906, 179–197).

All of this mirrored doubt about the general role of reason in conduct. As Thorndike's colleague, Goodwin Watson (1927) put it, "Modern clinical psychology has demonstrated the deep and devious roots of much human behavior." For example: "Mary may tell lies, not so much because of inadequate training in truthfulness as because of an unrecognized need to escape from some intolerable situation or because of identification with some admired and adept liar or because of satisfactions of phantasy" (pp. 288–289). Dennis Clayton Troth (1930), reviewing the field of moral education, could insist that "a learned psychologist has described the intellect as a mere speck floating in a sea of feelings and emotions. The intellect, though it be educated to the n'th degree, is dominated by the feelings and emotions" (p. 360; also Chassell, 1935).

It is thus not surprising that Thorndike's discussions of moral development are mere routine. In his 1929 *Elementary Principles of Education* (written with Arthur Gates), the methodological canon is clearly specified: "The primary requirement is that the child be given exercise in making the approved reaction and that it yield a satisfying result, and, conversely, that, to the extent possible without too much artifice, the child be prevented from making the disapproved reactions and that, when one is made, it results in annoyance" (p. 146). There are problems and subtleties, of course—for example, in respect of "novel situations"—but because all learning is identical and all methodology is one, the problems of moral education *cannot* be significantly different, especially when "the right thing" is nothing more than a social given. Primary emphasis will be on school activities and the opportunities that arise in the course of the "fundamental subjects" (p. 152). Specific moral instruction can help "in some measure," provided it is conducted from "materials in history, literature, science, and other subjects which describe in concrete, vivid, and intelligible form the characteristics of noble conduct and the satisfactions which it may bring" (p. 153).

We must, however, bring this analysis to an end. What it comes down to is that the strategy many educators chose, for whatever reasons, in the crucial generation at the turn of the century, has proved not only unproductive but inherently unworkable, a reverse image of the very educational process it was their intent to save. In a curious way, Thorndike himself seems to have arrived at such a conclusion—though without recognizing it, however odd that might sound. Having come to the end of his incredibly productive career, he was honored with the James Lectureship at Harvard. Published in 1943 as *Man and His Works,* the lectures repay careful study. In all but some details, and the advent of a few new problems with the changed times, his mind has not altered. He lays out essentially the same analytical and substantive structure that he first began to formulate with his chickens in James's Cambridge basement. He entertains his audience with the same participatory demonstrations of the effectiveness (and, hence, presumably the validity) of his psychology as those he had used to delight and persuade his listeners and readers over five decades. He cites again his numerically massive studies of the late 1920s, the results of which he finds as convincing as ever—enhanced, he in fact believes, by recent progress in physiology and genetics.

Thorndike then settles in to answer the important question of what this now fully qualified science of behavior can contribute to man, in terms of his institutions. He looks at our legal institutions, among others. Here, Thorndike believes, behavioral science can contribute a great deal, explaining as it does why men do what they do. The difficulty is that this explanation, as he believes the psychologist must develop it, is in fact straight-out deterministic. But, the logic of courts, of trials, laws, and punishment, and of guilt and innocence is, unfortunately, a logic of freedom, entailing the notion of responsibility. In theory, then, psychology has moved beyond (or behind) all that sort of thing, and, hence, it might be suggested that we should sweep away the whole moralistic legal-judicial enterprise. But, at the level of common sense, Thorndike concludes, we ought not do so, if only because people are not quite ready for such a thoroughly rationalized reform. Besides, he thinks, perhaps some great psychologist of the future, such as Bentham, may come along and change it all for us.

Thorndike appears not to notice the irony. Psychology of the sort to which he has devoted his life, and which he believes has now reached maturity, has come to portray human behavior in such a way that human institutions of the most fundamental character are now contradictions. If psychology, the science of human behavior, is right, then the principal presuppositions of law and jurisprudence are wrong, mere anomalies left over from a dark past.

Quoting extensively from Sir James Fitzjames Stephen, under the heading "voluntary actions by a person free from compulsion," Thorndike characterizes Stephen's discussion of free human action as "an antiquated and indefensible faculty psychology" and insists that "no psychologist of today would accept this as sound and adequate science." Why, he asks, have we retained such "archaic definitions of action, voluntary, involuntary, intention, the will, motive, choice, etc.," when they contradict what "lawyers and judges [now] learn in even elementary courses in psychology"? "Propositions" concerning such things "are not, and never were, essential to the law, but are, and were, mainly decorative." What *was* essential? "The psychology which the law really used and uses is a simple behaviorism" (1943, pp. 133–135).

Furthermore, and most important for our purposes, Thorndike does not see that precisely the same is true for education and schooling, including most obviously moral education. If Thorndike's presuppositions are true, and if his presuppositions (or others of substantially similar bent) are directly applied and thought sufficiently (let alone exhaustively) descriptive of the object of the educator's interest, then schooling and educating also turn out to be anomalies, contradictions, denials of our "real knowledge."

All in all, one is reminded of the story of the rabbi who was visited by two women of his congregation. One is the owner of a large cat; the other has accused the cat of consuming her five-pound tub of fresh butter. The rabbi, searching for that Solomon-like wisdom his role demands, asks for the cat to be produced, whereupon he weighs him. The cat tips the scales at exactly five pounds. Well, says the rabbi, we have found the butter; the question now is, Where is the cat?

It is easy to be amused, or appalled, at a Thorndike, who appears to have lost the very phenomenon he was seeking to save in the maze imposed by his metaphysical and methodological monism. As Alfred North Whitehead once wisely remarked, when our doctrines reach the point that life as we know it appears to be false, it is time to give up the doctrines, not life. It is part of the utility of history to remind us that our pure systems of thought are in fact incarnate and life-bound at every moment and most dangerous precisely when we regard them (or ourselves) as pure. Our task, particularly when dealing with education, is to avoid that "single vision" of which Blake speaks in the passage at the head of this chapter. Alas, that applies to philosophers, psychologists, and educators in our day quite as much as in Thorndike's—and possibly even to historians.

REFERENCES

Ayres, L. S. Measuring educational processes through educational results. *School Review*, 1912, *20*, 300–309.

Chassell, C. F. *The relation between morality and intellect.* New York: Teachers College, Columbia University, 1935.

Harris, W. T. Response to Nicholas Murray Butler. In National Education Association, *Journal of addresses and proceedings of the 39th annual meeting.* Chicago: National Education Association, 1900, pp. 199–203.

Hartshorne, H., & May, M. A. *Studies in the organization of character* (3 vols.). Vol. 1, *Studies in deceit;* Vol. 2 (with J. B. Maller), *Studies in service and self-control;* Vol. 3 (with F. Shuttleworth), *Studies in the nature of character.* New York: Macmillan, 1928–1930. (a)

Hartshorne, H., & May, M. A. A summary of the work of the character education inquiry. *Religious Education,* 1930, *25,* 607–619, 754–762. (b)

Johnson, H. C., Jr. *The public school and moral education.* New York: Pilgrim Press, 1980.

Johnson, H. C., Jr. Moral education. In *Encyclopedia of educational research* (5th ed.). New York: Free Press, 1982.

McKown, H. C. *Character education.* New York: McGraw-Hill, 1935.

National Commission on the Reform of Secondary Education (sponsored by the Charles F. Kettering Foundation). *The reform of secondary education: Report to the public and the profession.* New York: McGraw-Hill, 1973.

National Education Association. *Moral values in secondary education* (H. Neumann, Ed.). Published as [United States] Bureau of Education Bulletin, No. 51. Washington, D.C.: Government Printing Office, 1917. (Actual printing date, 1918.)

National Education Association. *Cardinal principles of secondary education: A report of the commission on the reorganization of secondary education.* Published as [United States] Bureau of Education Bulletin, No. 35. Washington, D.C.: Government Printing Office, 1918.

National Education Association. *Character education (10th yearbook of the Department of Superintendence).* Washington, D.C.: National Education Association, 1932.

Palmer, G. H. *Ethical and moral instruction in schools.* Boston: Houghton Mifflin, 1909.

Rice, J. M. *The public school system of the United States.* Englewood Cliffs, N.J.: Prentice-Hall, 1893.

Rice, J. M. *Scientific management in education.* New York: Hinds, 1914.

Thorndike, E. L. *Principles of teaching.* New York: A. G. Seiler, 1906.

Thorndike, E. L. Darwin's contribution to psychology. *University of California Chronicle,* 1910, *12,* 65–80.

Thorndike, E. L. *Animal intelligence.* New York: Macmillan, 1911.

Thorndike, E. L. The measurement of educational products. *School Review,* 1912, *20,* 289–299.

Thorndike, E. L. *Educational psychology* (3 vols.). New York: Teachers College, Columbia University, 1913–1914.

Thorndike, E. L. *The elements of psychology* (2nd ed.). New York: A. G. Seiler, 1916.

Thorndike, E. L. Edward Lee Thorndike. In C. Murchinson (Ed.), *A History of Psychology in Autobiography* (Vol. 3). Worcester, Mass.: Clark University Press, 1936.

Thorndike, E. L. *Man and his works.* Cambridge, Mass.: Harvard University Press, 1943.

Thorndike, E. L., & Gates, A. I. *Elementary principles of education.* New York: Macmillan, 1929.

Threlkeld, A. L. Introducing the report of the character education commission. In National Education Association, *Journal of addresses and proceedings of the 70th annual meeting.* Washington, D.C.: National Education Association, 1932, pp. 545–547.

Troth, D. C. *Selected readings in character education.* Boston: Beacon Press, 1930.

Watson, G. B. Virtues versus virtue. *School and Society,* 1927, *26,* 286–290.

CHAPTER 22

Moral Development in a Historical Perspective

HOWARD KAMINSKY

The modern science of moral development seems to a historian to be oriented toward the understanding and eventual manipulation of modern man, in particular the mass man of contemporary Western society. It seems taken for granted that cooperation, altruism, and sharing are "prosocial" and that egoism, aggression, domination, and the competitive drive for achievement are the reverse. History, however, knows no periods in which dominating elites are absent or not essential to the life of the society, and no historian would consider modern society an exception. Here and elsewhere many scientists of moral development seem to take over popular modes of thought without realizing that they are culture bound. A historian's experience points him or her in the opposite direction, and one is apt to think in terms of differential moralities within and among societies, of morality as essentially a dependent variable of culture and mentality. A historian who considers the long-term development of ideas and social forms is forced to realize that the price of the new is the loss of the old, and he or she cannot imagine any objective reason to judge the one better than the other. It is, however, possible to imagine a directional history in the sense outlined by Freud, namely, toward increasing repression and alienation. The prevalent ideas of modern moral development would fit into this scheme.

A historian invited to travel in the field of moral development can only feel flattered on behalf of his or her own discipline, especially if, like the present author, he is a medievalist and therefore unused to attention from the outside. Euphoria quickly turns into dismay, however, as one reads the literature and realizes how remote one's own study of the public action of defunct elites is from one's hosts' concern with the development of children and the day-to-day behavior of individuals in general. At the same time one begins to per-

400

ceive the gulf between one's professional effort to submit to the more or less alien mentalities of one's subjects and the psychologists' professional assumption that their cognitive enterprise is destined to provide guides to action. For if the psychologists of moral development begin with a theoretical recognition of "the need for understanding the origins and nature of moral reasoning and behavior," they quickly go on to ask more practical questions:

[1] How does a person become moral? [2] What is a conscience? [3] What does it mean to be "a person of principle"? [4] What factors influence the way people really behave in moral situations, not simply how they think? [5] What can parents and society do to help children grow into morally mature adults? [Lickona, 1976a, p. x]

If the first four of these questions are more or less purely cognitive, implying neither one particular definition of the content of morality nor a belief that a single definition is possible, the last one not only is manipulative per se but also in its context implies a manipulative motive behind the others as well. Thomas Lickona, the author of the passage, says as much further on: The scientist cannot study moral development from a value-neutral standpoint because the idea of development itself implies movement toward something higher, *and also* because "to be able to construct a moral hierarchy is required for any kind of social intervention" (pp. 7–9). Lawrence Kohlberg (1971) had once argued in the opposite sense "that no psychologist would engage in moral research with the notion that the use of such research is the creation of instrumentalities of manipulation and control to be made available to adult 'socializing agents'" (p. 153), but he has more recently (1978) joined the overwhelming majority of his colleagues in advocating intervention: "The educator must be a socializer, teaching value content and behavior," and "in becoming a socializer and advocate, the teacher moves into 'indoctrination'" (p. 84). In the Western tradition, at any rate, knowledge has always meant power, and the more scientific the knowledge, the more effective the power.

One does not have to be a historian to see these things, but a historian may perhaps claim that his or her perspective can reveal implications of the psychological enterprise that its practitioners are apt to miss. For one thing, a historian can appreciate the significance of the psychologists' evident belief that our own society cannot properly form its human material without their help, for help of this sort was not used in the past. This historian, who has never in the course of his studies encountered a single man or woman whom a moral developer would call "morally mature," will naturally wonder why it is necessary today to create such people in large numbers. In a less ironic mood he will wonder just what specifically modern function the morally mature masses are destined to play, and in considering this question he will not, as a historian, attach undue importance to the hopes and ideals of the psychologists, for if history teaches any lesson at all, it teaches that what people think they are doing is quite different from what they turn out to have done. When this historian sees how pervasively the literature of moral development is dominated by an idealism oriented to what is called "prosocial" behavior, and when he realizes how meaningless this term is within his context of historical experience, he can hardly avoid asking what it may turn out to mean when its present-day context is viewed, however speculatively, as itself a stage of history.

Prosocial behavior has been defined as positive social behavior, "behavior that benefits other people" (Staub, 1978, p. 2). It is striking that the author of a whole book on the subject sees the problematic aspect of this definition only in the calculus of intended benevolence—as, for example, when giving food to hungry nations allows their population to grow to the point that still greater suffering results (ibid.). To a historian the problem appears quite differently, for if he or she can accept the notion of a prosocial *intention* according to the preceding definition, he or she can hardly see prosocial *action* otherwise than as action that either promotes the integration of a given society or causes it to change in ways that resolve its contradictions. To the moral developer, prosocial behavior manifests an ethic of sharing and cooperation, being constructive, altruistic, helpful, and considerate. An egoist ethic of aggression, domination, competition, and achievement is "morally despicable" and presumably antisocial (Mischel & Mischel, 1976. pp. 88–91). This historian, however, knows no societies whose very existence has not depended on domination of the many by the few, and whose health has not been the beneficent result of egoistic drives for excellence and achievement; he cannot see such drives as antisocial in an objective sense. He also suspects that our own society is no exception. Taking his people as he finds them, moreover, this historian must regard the allegedly antisocial traits as fundamental potentialities of the human spirit, hence not to be excluded from the concept of morality, and he will note both the Greco-Roman and Christian views that moral character is developed precisely through the conflict within the soul in which divergent drives are variously harmonized, sublimated, or repressed. Eliminate selfishness, aggression, and the like, and what is left? Can one even imagine an ego composed only of prosocial traits? Hardly. One can, however, imagine a prosocial ego formed by repressive deformation, and Friedrich Nietzsche in *The Will to Power* (1966) pointed out its function for the subordinate classes in a society dominated by elites:

> A doctrine and religion of "love," of *keeping down* self-affirmation, of patience, resignation, helpfulness, and cooperation in word and deed may be of the highest value within the confines of such classes, even in the eyes of their rulers: for it keeps down the feelings of rivalry, of resentment, and of envy,—feelings which are only too natural in those who have been short-changed [*die Schlechtweggekommenen*],—and, even under the ideal of humility and obedience, it deifies for them the condition of the slave, of the dominated, of the poor, the sick, the lowly. This explains why the ruling classes (or races) and individuals have always upheld the cult of unselfishness, the gospel of the lowly, the "God on the Cross." [p 78]

Although a contemporary moralist cannot be oblivious of the evil uses to which Nietzschean ideas have been put in our century, neither can he or she afford, as psychologist or as historian, to suppose that a genius's insight into the human condition may be dismissed as merely evil or perverse. The ideal of humanity cultivated by the thinkers of the eighteenth-century Enlightenment may well represent the loftiest ideal our civilization has ever achieved, and Kohlberg may well be right when he takes the ethical teachings of Immanuel Kant as the substance of his Stage 6—the highest stage attainable in the moral development of "the individual"—but that was 200 years ago. In the interval we have been taught—by Karl Marx as well as by Nietzsche—that the transcendental sublimities of the Enlightenment were bought at the price of ignoring the actual conditions under which the great mass of people live in Western society (to say nothing of others), conditions of exploitation and domination that are no less decisive even when mitigated by social reforms and concealed by civil liberty and democratic ideas of equality. Although it is true today that the image of a class-divided society which appeared more or less clearly a hundred years ago has been obscured by structural changes that have made the very concept of class a subject of controversy (Birnbaum, 1969; Dahrendorf, 1959), even those sociologists who talk of a postcapitalist mass society still think in terms of integration through a division of labor that includes managerial, directive, and other elites (ibid.; Giddens, 1971; Ortega, 1957). Such elites must be formed by educative processes that foster self-assertion, competitiveness, ambition, and other expressions of egoism. However this is done, it will not be the work of psychologists of moral development whose aim is to find how to make people "prosocial" and then make them so. In historical perspective, then, the psychology of moral development would seem to be our society's most self-conscious technique for fulfilling the mission adumbrated by Nietzsche, namely, socializing the masses into the good behavior required not only by the elites but also by the interests of the whole, including the masses themselves.

If these statements seem rather critical of the discipline, it is partly because phrases like "socializing the masses" carry a negative charge, partly because any essay in defining the ulterior historical import of an enterprise is apt to challenge the self-image of those engaged in it. As a token of good faith I can remark that I have more than once been outraged by what psychologist friends have told me I was really up to in my devotion to medieval history. Such considerations must not be allowed to prejudice the inquiry. Socializing the masses in a mass society means in effect promoting their moral development, and if we follow the "socioanalytic" theory of the discipline propounded by Robert Hogan and others (1978), we will regard morality itself as hardly more than playing "the social game" according to the rules—it is a "general principle for regulating interaction with others, a principle variously called reciprocity, fairness, turn taking, and justice." Moral development, then, is the formation of a character structure based first on "rule attunement," then "social sensitivity," with a third stage of "autonomy"—

the ability to choose freely what is best—identified as a moral ideal that is traditionally supreme but practically unattainable for all but a very few. This view has the strength of a comprehensive sociocultural perspective, in which moral development "is properly considered within the context of personality development as a whole," so that due attention can be given, at least theoretically, to such realities as "aggressive self-expression, . . . competitive tendencies, status seeking, self-aggrandizement, and dominance behavior" (pp. 1–16). Although these tendencies are recognized as positive, inasmuch as they "reinforce hierarchical order and ensure a steady supply of effective leadership," they seem to be dealt with in practice, however, as sources of delinquency and rule violation (ibid.; cf. pp. 7, 12). That is, the psychologists' insistence on empirical investigation by means of testing and scoring seems to require the "prosocial" ideology that the sociological theory had overcome. A sympathetic amateur can only ask if tests have been or could be developed that would discriminate between genuine delinquency and potential for "effective leadership," so that the psychologist could not only socialize the masses but also help our society identify and form its future elites.

It is indeed striking, to a historian at any rate, that the reports of empirical research which constitute the overwhelming bulk of the literature of the discipline are so uniformly concerned with undifferentiated subjects like "the child" or "the individual." One can understand why a scientific enterprise oriented so largely to the development of children should draw much of its information from children's responses to questionnaires and little stories posing moral dilemmas, and it seems clear also that a scientific methodology adopted from the natural sciences necessarily tends to departicularize its individual subjects, so that what is true for them will be true in general. A similar result proceeds from the scientific insistence on experiments that will yield hard, measurable, scorable data and that can be verified by others, for these criteria can most easily be satisfied by studying deliberate behavior, conscious decisions, and explicit opinions. The inner depths of the individual psyche remain out of reach, and the psyche is treated as a sort of black box— one works around it. When we read programmatic statements like "This work examines the effectiveness of punishment learning in producing internalized suppression of the child's punished behavior" (Aronfreed, 1976, p. 57), we first shudder as we visualize the Dickensian possibilities of "punishment learning," then shudder again at the thought that the child might as well be a dog. Similarly the generalization "Each individual acquires the capacity to construct a great range of potential behaviors, . . . and different individuals acquire different behavior construction capabilities in different degrees" (Mischel & Mischel, 1976, p. 86) introduces a line of experiment intended "to *assess* an individual's potential for the construction of a particular behavior," not to figure out what that potential really consists of in the way of inner structures and forces at work in the soul. Discourse of this sort pervading the literature of moral development evokes the impression of a weird population of phantoms whose essence is totally contained in their be-

haviors and who move in a hypothesized demimonde of volition and ratiocination. The individuals we read about are in fact fictively individualized
universals, Hegel's "species-beings" come down to earth, and attempts to
relate them to real social beings necessarily remain locked in the levels of abstraction where alone the phantoms can exist. It is, for example, most unlikely that "a strong and stable relationship has been found between delinquency and the deprived environment of the lower class in our society"
(Burton, 1976, p. 196) if these terms are taken at face value and in their
concrete reference, because there have been many lower-class groups in our
society whose poverty has not in general led them into crime. But a few lines
further down all is set right when we learn that the terms in fact refer to
blacks. It is no accident that the author deals with black criminality by means
of concepts that have little to do with the realities of race, racism, and the
cultural deformations due to these, for his method requires that the particular
case of blacks must be represented by differentials moving down from the
universal ("deprived," "lower-class")—otherwise, the particular case would
have to be studied by methods adapted to its peculiar essence, and a Pan-
dora's box of exotic factors would be opened.

Historians are not of one mind about such matters, as the desire for certainty according to the model of the natural sciences has led some of them
into a similar methodology of quantification, measurement, and statistics.
Many of us today, however, and virtually all of us in the past have seen our
subjects as individual, particular people or phenomena, and insofar as we
necessarily resort to general theories about motivation or processes, we do
so *ad hoc,* amateurishly, and without much principle. One tells a story or
draws a picture and relies on its artistic unity to carry conviction; the pro-
fundity of the story or picture depends on the quality of the historian's mind,
not on the theories he or she may use. That is why Thucydides is still the
best. It is from this point of view that the pseudoindividuals appearing in the
discourse of moral development seem so irrelevant to any effort to understand how real individuals think and act. History is one such effort, and the
men and women whose actions it studies are driven by inner forces they do
not understand and pursue culturally valued goals whose ethical quality or
practical utility are always encoded in symbolic forms. Rational choice implies a discrimination among utilities perceived as such, but the need to participate in the meaningfulness of culture's symbolic forms proceeds from a
total engagement of the psyche—its reason, but also its desires, emotions,
fantasies, and whatever else lies inside the black box.[1] Understanding this
sort of behavior would require a theoretical apparatus designed to penetrate

---

[1] Much of the extensive modern literature on symbolism and metaphor relates to this point;
one does not find it well reflected in writings on moral development. The distinction between rational thought, which purports to separate the subject from the object, and symbolic thought, which unites them, is discussed most thoroughly by Ernst Cassirer (1953–
1957). For a brief but inspired treatise, see D. H. Lawrence, 1931/1966, pp. 45, 80–83, and
passim.

the depths of the black box—something like Freudian theory, which is un-popular among developmental psychologists because it seems intractable to experimental methods of measurement, or a theory of the physiology of the brain, which is not yet available.[2]

The psychology of moral development, however, has one theory that concerns itself with structures of the mind. It is based on the work of the Swiss psychologist Jean Piaget, who found a fundamental "cognitive-structural" development in children's mentalities, with the turning point coming at about age 10. Before that age, children do not distinguish clearly between the self and the outside world and therefore do not subject the latter to critical judgment. Rules and prohibitions are taken as given; infractions are deemed to deserve punishment as such; acts are judged in terms of their consequences without regard to circumstances or motives. This morality of constraint then gives way to a morality of cooperation under the influence of social interaction. The child becomes aware of the interests and viewpoints of others, begins to take a rational and critical attitude to rules, comes to think of punishments in terms of purpose, assigns blame on the basis of intention (Lickona, 1976b; Phillips, 1969; Radding, 1978). Kohlberg (1976) developed these ideas into a more comprehensive theory of a six-stage development of the moral faculties, still within the framework of cognitive structures. His data drawn from elaborate longitudinal and cross-cultural studies have convinced him that the stages are universal, with variations only in the rate of progress and the height an individual may reach and with both of these variables arising from differences in the intensity of social interaction. Moral development thus appears as an absolute in respect to both its cognitive structures and its sequential content, for both of these are viewed as inherent in the nature of the human mind, rather than as the specific products of a given sociocultural order or as the projections of the psychologist's own idealism (Kohlberg, 1971).

The implications of this theory for ethical philosophy are obvious, and so is its potential relevance to the humanities and social sciences. That it has been the target of much criticism, including indeed Kohlberg's own revisions, is not necessarily significant in our context, for one can imagine any number of modifications in stage constructs and assessment methodology that would not affect the basic concept of an inherent, structured succession of cognitive and moral faculties. (Conclusive disconfirmation of the basic concept would,

---

[2] The September 1979 issue of *Scientific American* is devoted to laying out the extent and limits of our current knowledge of the physiology of the brain. In a concluding summary, "Thinking about the Brain," F. H. C. Crick observes that "pure psychology is, by the standards of hard science, rather unsuccessful," chiefly because "psychology attempts to treat the brain as a black box," studying only inputs and outputs. But with such a method "a stage is soon reached where several rival theories all explain the observed results equally well." This is evidently the current stage of psychology. He goes on to note that there is an urgent need for "a general theory of the brain" that would go into the black box and that "we have a long way to go" (pp. 221f., 232).

of course, be something else, but the present author is not qualified to judge whether claims to this effect [e.g., Schweder, 1982] are valid.) Thus, for example, Kohlberg's current elimination of Stage 6—identical to Kant's categorical imperative in all its implications—as a distinct stage is relatively unimportant for the very reasons that have persuaded him to give it up: One does not find it among "individuals" in general (Kohlberg, 1978). Another revision, Anne Colby's (1978) "differentiation of stage structure from normative content in moral judgment" (p. 101), is in fact a "purification" of the stage construct that makes it, if anything, more useful to students in other disciplines. Jürgen Habermas (1976a) has indeed called for such a differentiation, on more general grounds than Colby's, while at the same time taking over Kohlberg's basic theory for his own wide-ranging historical, sociological, and philosophical work, and has even added a Stage 7 (Habermas, 1976b, 1976c).[3]

It is significant that Habermas's engagement with the cognitive-structural theory of moral development is set forth in essays grouped under the title "Towards the Reconstruction of Historical Materialism." The Hegelian-Marxian concept of the historical process as progress toward the realization of ever higher human potentialities embodies much of the best that the nineteenth century has to offer us, and it is still popular today even though the experiences of our own century have caused many intellectuals to reject the concept of progress or to revalue it in various unpleasant ways. Those who define the successor to bourgeois-liberal capitalist society as the mass society, rather than as socialism or communism in Marx's terms, are apt to be more impressed by that society's horrors than by its opportunities for emancipation of the human spirit. Thus Hannah Arendt (1951) has explained totalitarianism in both Nazi Germany and Soviet Russia as a phenomenon of modern society in which great masses of people in fact and consciousness stand outside any class organization and must therefore create by violence the meaningfulness that their social superfluity denies them within the traditional sociocultural order. Leading figures of the Frankfurt sociological school— Max Horkheimer, Theodor Adorno, Herbert Marcuse—have reacted to the same modern experience by projecting an image of our society that includes mass democracy as well as totalitarianism in a vision of total rationalization, total integration, total alienation—hence the liquidation of individuality and of its characteristic ego structures (e.g., Marcuse, 1964; cf. Habermas, 1976b, p. 114, 1976c, pp. 64–66). In this view the progress of Western civili-

---

[3] Characterizing Kohlberg's Stage 6 as one of "universalistic obligations," "moral freedom," and a "formalistic obligation ethic," Habermas (1976a) distinguishes his Stage 7 as "universalistic interpretation of one's needs," "moral and political freedom," and "a universal speech-ethic" (p. 83). The last term, *universale Sprachethik,* defines a movement beyond the preformed cultural-traditional conception of needs (*Bedürfnisse*) by means of intersubjective rational discourse that desolidifies objectively defined values so that they can be freely analyzed and variously appropriated by individuals. Moralization of needs is seen as resulting from the rationality of discourse.

zation is seen as involving an ever greater division of labor and consequent impoverishment of the individual, an ever greater degree of repressive sublimation and consequent alienation of the individual self, and, paradoxically, a development to ever greater freedom that consists of an ever greater internalization of repression. Habermas's rejection of the whole pessimistic orientation of such visions is carried through precisely by resort to the unambiguous idea of progress inherent in the cognitive-structural theory of the development of the ego. For in this theory, as we have seen, the individual is not created by his or her society but rather is developed by its stimuli, so that our mass society appears not as a nightmare but as a festival of opportunities. In the same way the process of history becomes a sort of ego development writ large, for each stage in the evolution of the productive forces is accompanied and conditioned by a development of "moral insight, practical knowledge, communicative action, and the consensual regulation of transactional conflicts," which that evolution also makes possible (Habermas, 1976a, pp. 11–12). In other words, the possibility of each stage in the modern individual's cognitive development has been created by a corresponding stage in the historical process that has produced the present.

The historian's interest in these perspectives lies in their power to explain not only change in general but also the particular realities that add up to this or that moment of change. Thus a recent essay by Charles Radding, "Evolution of Medieval Mentalities: A Cognitive-Structural Approach" (1978), uses the stage theories of Piaget and Kohlberg to explain the revolutionary changes of the twelfth century in every sphere of life and thought. The changes themselves have long been appreciated in positive terms. There was an eruption of individuality and subjectivity that produced fine lyric poetry, the new romances, movements of religious pietism, and an ethos of love that transformed both courtly and monastic culture. At the same time there was a similarly explosive activity of reason; all of a sudden, from the end of the eleventh century on, western Europe produced intellectuals whose minds could not only master the fixed and limited contents of the traditional learning but also go on, insistently, to subject the tradition to rational analysis, to pose new questions in logic and metaphysics, and to acquire new material by obtaining Latin translations of the Aristotelian corpus. Radding notes the profound changes of this sort, recognizes that many historians have studied the trends they manifest, but complains that no adequate comprehensive account of them has been given; general explanations have usually referred, more or less vaguely, to "social and economic change."

Radding's own contribution consists in a definition of the new in contrast with the old. Thus, a monastic ethos among the Cistercians based on the erotic fervor of personal devotion can be contrasted with the traditional Benedictine ethos of liturgical performance, unquestioning obedience, routinized duties, and strict punishments. An interest in intention on the part of both legal and ethical thinkers can be contrasted with earlier views—in the Germanic law codes, in early medieval penitentials—that considered only the immoral or illegal act and assessed penalties on a fixed schedule. The acceptance of the tradition in theology and other areas, in the earlier period, implied an attitude of mind that regarded doctrine as something exterior; the twelfth-century intellectual who penetrated doctrine by his own reason, took it apart, and then systematized it into a logical structure, obviously had a different kind of mentality. So too in the political and social spheres, theological and other conceptualizations of authority that represented it as absolute and given gave way to ideas and institutions based on a sense of the rights of the community. Radding suggests that all these and, indeed, other twelfth-century transformations can be understood comprehensively as manifestations of a fundamental change in cognitive structures. Summarizing the work of Piaget and Kohlberg in this area, he points out how closely the changes in question correspond to those Piaget observed in children before and after age 10; in Kohlberg's terms, the changes would consist of a movement into Stage 3, with an opening into Stage 4. We thus glimpse the possibility of a new way of understanding not only the twelfth-century Renaissance but also the earlier medieval centuries, the later ones, and the whole subject of the individual's relationship to society and the changes in this relationship that constitute much of history.

Toward the end of his essay Radding notes the "disturbing" or even "creepy" aspect of his hypothesis, namely, "the evident parallel between the evolution of medieval culture as a whole and the ontogeny of thought in modern children" (p. 595). His own responses to this alleged problem are not decisive, and we can do better by referring to Habermas's discussion, noted earlier, of the reasons why changes in the socioeconomic infrastructure are dialectically coordinate with changes in cognitive faculties. It is not at all surprising that a century in which a still predominantly rural society was penetrated by new towns, local markets, simple commodity production, and the use of money at all levels should have been the century that saw a cognitive-structural transformation due, in the light of Piaget's and Kohlberg's theories, to a much greater quantity and intensity of social interaction. Assuming the nature of the human mind as posited by these theories, and the consequent universality of the developmental stages, we would have no reason to doubt their relevance to history. We need not, and for that matter cannot, consider here whether the theories are fully established or whether their use in history can become more than a sort of translation of one set of categories into another. The big problem lies elsewhere, in what such a historical projection implies about the respective values inherent in the successive moral and cognitive stages. Kohlberg's claim (1971) is that each stage is higher than the preceding one in respect to cognitive power, as rated according to criteria of difficulty and inclusiveness, and also in respect to moral adequacy; that is, it preserves the logical features of earlier stages, adds new ones, and succeeds in handling problems unrecognized by or unresolved by lower stages. Both Kohlberg and Piaget refer generally to maturity as the goal of such development. One can readily accept this sort of evaluation in studies of children, who must after all grow up, but even here one can point to the values lost in the process—the child's disconcertingly clear vision of truth, uncluttered certainty of judgment, ability to create powerful statements in works of art. To see our history in such a perspective is to come close to what historians often call, contemptuously, the "Whig theory" of historical progress popular in the last century; it took satisfaction in history's advances but did not attend to the corresponding losses. If, in Kohlberg's view (1971), a higher stage of morality is "radically different" from a lower one (despite preservation of its logical features), then the virtues of the lower one are lost (pp. 225–226). But, as R. G. Collingwood (1946) has argued, unless progress means gain of the new without any loss of the old, it has no genuine meaning at all: "If there is any loss, the problem of setting loss against gain is insoluble" (p. 329).

If, for example, we join Piaget in regarding "absolutism of moral perspective" as immature, "awareness of different viewpoints" as mature (in Lickona, 1976b, pp. 220–221), so that a modern liberal intellectual comes out better than a blue-collar red-neck (although even here the record of performance is not always convincing), is he or she also more mature than Charlemagne or St. Bernard of Clairvaux? If so, is he or she *better?* Is a Stage 6 refusal to support a friend who is in the wrong superior to a Stage 3 loyalty to that friend? A medieval nobleman would say no, and history suggests to us that if we repudiate that nobleman's sense of right, we are also repudiating the civilization created in resonance with his mentality, as well as those elements of the aristocratic ideal that have formed the modern sense of individuality. The issues here come down to more than just a few paradoxes. For one thing, personal loyalty has obvious virtues that are lost when friendship or affection is made conditional on abstract rightness. For another, it is the essence of history, in our modern age, to recover the past that has been lost by "progress"—not for reasons of antiquarian devotion but from a well-founded sense that we need it all, the values of dominance along with those of submission, those of tradition as well as those of freedom, mystery as well as rationality, the work of the creative will along with the fruits of calculation. It was not an accident that the systematic enterprise of historical scholarship in this sense should have been created in the same nineteenth century that cut us loose from our past by its revolutions in science and technology. In an odd sort of way, this line of thought is confirmed when we consider Habermas's (1976b) positive answer to his own question, "Can complex societies develop a rational identity?" For the kind of ego he has in mind, his Stage 7, as noted earlier, forms itself by free selection and combination of the elements of the traditional culture. Such an ego has no *fixed* content, but it does have content, and although it constructs that content through a continual process of intercommunicative learning, the subject matter of communication would be "the critical remembrance of the tradition" (p. 121). When Stage 7 says goodbye to Stage 6, it lets back in, however critically, the immature past that Stage 6 abolished: One sees the difficulties faced by a historically oriented mind when it tries to make use of the cognitive-developmental model.

A historical perspective on moral development, as explored rather discursively in these pages, yields ambiguous but stimulating visions. It can make contact with the prosocial enterprise of the experimenters only by pointing to that enterprise's peculiarity as a work of modern mass society, with perhaps a consoling afterthought that a society without crime or delinquency might indeed be more pleasant than the world we see around us. On the other hand, it can take a lively interest in the cognitive-structural theory as providing history with a potentially valuable heuristic instrument. Only future work will show how useful it may be. At the same time, a historian cannot help recognizing the contradiction between his or her own intention of redintegrating the past into the present consciousness and the psychologists' intention of moving from the alleged immaturities of the past into a society of purely rational beings. The moment of recognition can be instructive for the historian. Can it also be so for the psychologist? Yes, if—and only if—the psychologist is prepared to learn what history has to teach, namely, that both society and the individuals who constitute it are still mysteries whose nature cannot be represented by models postulating universal ratiocination as the context of behavior. One can study behavior by measuring it; one can understand individuals only by submitting to their intractable particularities in an effort to imagine what lies inside the psyche. The effort would involve an appreciative acceptance of all the residues of the past that we call tradition, and these include much that is "antisocial." In any case, an orientation to understanding would exclude a manipulative intention, at least for the moment, and this historian must unhappily suppose that most psychologists would regard the prospect as regressive.

REFERENCES

Arendt, H. *The origins of totalitarianism.* New York: Harcourt Brace, 1951.

Aronfreed, J. Moral development from the standpoint of a general psychological theory. In T. Lickona (Ed.), *Moral development and behavior: Theory, research and social issues.* New York: Holt, Rinehart and Winston, 1976.

Birnbaum, N. *The crisis of industrial society.* New York: Oxford University Press, 1969.

Burton, R. V. Honesty and dishonesty. In T. Lickona (Ed.), *Moral development and behavior: Theory, research and social issues.* New York: Holt, Rinehart and Winston, 1976.

Cassirer, E. *The philosophy of symbolic forms* (3 vols.; R. Manheim, trans.). New Haven, Conn.: Yale University Press, 1953–1957. (Originally published in German, 1923–1929.)

Colby, A. Evolution of a moral-developmental theory. In W. Damon (Ed.), *Moral development: New directions for child development* (Vol. 1). San Francisco: Jossey-Bass, 1978.

Collingwood, R. G. *The idea of history.* Oxford: Oxford University Press, 1946.

Crick, F. H. C. Thinking about the brain. *Scientific American,* 1979, *241*(3), 219–232.

Dahrendorf, R. *Class and class conflict in industrial society.* Stanford, Calif.: Stanford University Press, 1959. (Originally published in German, 1957.)

Damon, W. (Ed.). *Moral development: New directions for child development* (Vol. 1). San Francisco: Jossey-Bass, 1978.

Giddens, A. *Capitalism and modern social theory.* Cambridge: Cambridge University Press, 1971.

Hogan, R., Johnson, J. A., & Emler, N. P. A socioanalytic theory of moral development. In W. Damon (Ed.), *Moral development: New directions for child development* (Vol. 1). San Francisco: Jossey-Bass, 1978.

Habermas, J. Historischer materialismus und die Entwicklung normativer Strukturen. In *Zur Rekonstruktion des Historischen Materialismus* (Trans. in Habermas, 1979, pp. 95–129). Frankfurt: Suhrkamp Verlag, 1976.

Habermas, J. Können komplexe Gesellschaften eine vernünftige Identität ausbilden? In *Zur Rekonstruktion des Historischen Materialismus.* Frankfurt: Suhrkamp Verlag, 1976. (b)

Habermas, J. Moralentwicklung und Ich-Identität. In *Zur Rekonstruktion des Historischen Materialismus* (Trans. in Habermas, 1979, pp. 69–94). Frankfurt: Suhrkamp Verlag, 1976. (c)

Habermas, J. *Communication and the evolution of society* (T. McCarthy, Trans.). Boston: Beacon Press, 1979.

Kohlberg, L. From is to ought: How to commit the naturalistic fallacy and get away with it in the study of moral development. In T. Mischel (Ed.), *Cognitive development and epistemology.* New York: Academic Press, 1971.

Kohlberg, L. Moral stages and moralization. In T. Lickona (Ed.), *Moral development and behavior: Theory, research, and social issues.* New York: Holt, Rinehart and Winston, 1976.

Kohlberg, L. Revisions in the theory and practice of moral development. In W. Damon (Ed.), *Moral development: New directions for child development* (Vol. 1). San Francisco: Jossey-Bass, 1978.

Lawrence, D. H. *Apocalypse.* New York: Viking, 1966. (Originally published, 1931.)

Lickona, T. (Ed.). *Moral development and behavior: Theory, research, and social issues.* New York: Holt, Rinehart and Winston, 1976. (a)

Lickona, T. Research on Piaget's theory of moral development. In T. Lickona (Ed.), *Moral development and behavior: Theory, research, and social issues.* New York: Holt, Rinehart and Winston, 1976. (b)

Marcuse, H. *One-dimensional man.* Boston: Beacon Press, 1964.

Mischel, W., & Mischel, H. N. A cognitive social-learning approach to morality and self-regulation. In T. Lickona (Ed.), *Moral development and behavior: Theory, research, and social issues.* New York: Holt, Rinehart and Winston, 1976.

Nietzsche, F. Aus den Nachlass der Achtzigerjahre. In *Werke in drei Bänden* (Vol. 3). Munich: Carl Hanser Verlag, 1966.

Ortega y Gasset, J. *The revolt of the masses.* New York: Norton, 1957. (Originally published in Spanish, 1930.)

Phillips, J. L., Jr. *The origins of intellect: Piaget's theory.* New York: Freeman, 1969.

Radding, C. Evolution of medieval mentalities: A cognitive-structural approach. *American Historical Review,* 1978, *83,* 577–597.

Schweder, R. A. Liberalism as destiny. *Contemporary Psychology,* 1982, *27,* 421–424.

Staub, E. *Positive social behavior and morality. Social and personal influences* (Vol. 1). New York: Academic Press, 1978.

Author Index

Note: Page numbers in **boldface** type are primary references.

415

Subject Index

Abortion, 278
Absolutist, 177, 178, 185, 188
Activating conditions, 177, 178, 185, 188
Aggression, 241, 246, 250
Alienation, 407
Altruism, 186, 187
Antisocial behavior, 241, 246, 250
Antisocial traits, 400, 404, 411
Authority, 135, 212, 255, 265, 267
Autointerpretation, 230, 238, 277
Autonomy, 28, 132, 155, 228, 231, 232, 233, 265, 365, 370, 377

Behaviorism, 227
Behavioral, 193
Behavioral orientation, 194, 196
Behavioral situations, multifaceted aspects of, 261, 277

Cheating, 55, 187, 197, 204, 217, 218, 263
Cognitive-affective relations, 29
Cognitive behavioral approach, 183, 185, 205
Cognitive developmental, 220
Cognitive developmental model, 411
Cognitive developmental research, 31
Cognitive developmental theory, 24, 39, 41, 50, 74, 128, 205, 283
Cognitive level (stage) of moral interaction, 159, 168, 172. *See also* Levels of interaction; Moral Discourse, cognitive stages of
Cognitive structural theory, 220, 406
Cognitive structures, 161, 168, 200
Collective norms, 74, 98
Communication:
 Child-child, 272
 Child-adult, 272
Communication Coordinating Complexity, 162
Communicative action:
 competence in, 344
 moral reasoning, 344

Communicative compactness, 159, 163, 172
Communicative speech acts, 160
Community valuing, 89, 90, 91, 98
Components of moral content, 211
 cognitive, 215
 evaluative, 213
Components of morality, *see* Morality, components of
Components of moral orientation, 144
Conditioning, 208
Conflict resolution strategies, 154
Conformity, 228, 232, 265, 267
Consequence(s), 140, 150, 151, 177, 179, 180, 202, 203, 241, 244
Convention:
 criteria, 271
 definition of, 270
Cooperative orientation, 264
Counternorm, 96, 97, 100
Cruelty, 241, 242, 248, 258

Darwinism and education, 393
Darwinism and pragmatists, 384
Darwinism and psychology, 393
Decision, moral, *see* Moral decision; Moral decision making
Delinquent, 252
Democracy as rhetoric, 333
Deprivation, 405
Developmental stage, 329, 334, 338
Distributive justice, 113, 117, 169, 283
Domain combinations, 273, 283
Domain coordinations, 261, 273, 275, 278
Duties, perfect and imperfect, 349
Duty, 177, 348

Ego controls, 71
Ego development, 355
Ego strength, 24, 33
Elites, 400, 402

421